Sports AND THE American Jew

Sports and Entertainment
Steven A. Riess, *Series Editor*

Sports AND THE
American Jew

EDITED BY Steven A. Riess

 Syracuse University Press

First Edition 1998
98 99 00 01 02 03   6 5 4 3 2 1

Permission to reprint from the following essays is gratefully acknowledged: Steven A. Riess, "A Fighting Chance: The Jewish-American Boxing Experience, 1890–1940," *American Jewish History* 74 (March 1985), 238–54. Reprinted by permission of the American Jewish Historical Society. Gerald R. Gems, "Sport and the Forging of a Jewish-American Culture: The Chicago Hebrew Institute," *American Jewish History* 83 (March 1995), 15–26. Reprinted by permission of the Johns Hopkins University Press. Peter Levine, "The *American Hebrew* Looks at 'Our Crowd': The Jewish Country Club in the 1920s," *American Jewish History* 83 (March 1995), 27–49. Reprinted by permission of the Johns Hopkins University Press. William M. Simons, "The Athlete as Jewish Standard Bearer: Media Images of Hank Greenberg," *Jewish Social Studies* 44 (Spring 1982), 95–112. Reprinted by permission of the Indiana University Press. Donald J. Fisher, "The Rochester Royals and the Transformation of Professional Basketball, 1945–57," *International Journal of the History of Sport* 10 (April 1993), 20–48. Reprinted by permission of Frank Cass Publishers. Allen Guttmann, "Out of the Ghetto and on to the Field: Jewish Writers and the Theme of Sport," *American Jewish History* 74 (March 1985), 274–86. Reprinted by permission of the American Jewish Historical Society. Eric Solomon, " 'Memories of Days Past' of Why Eric Rolfe Greenberg's *The Celebrant* is the Greatest (Jewish) American Baseball Novel," *American Jewish History* 83 (March 1995), 83–107. Reprinted by permission of the Johns Hopkins University Press. Edward Shapiro, The World Labor Carnival of 1936: An American Anti-Nazi Protest," *American Jewish History* 74 (Mar. 1985): 255–73. Stephen R. Wenn, "A Tale of Two Diplomats: George S. Messemsith and Charles H. Sherill on Proposed American Participation in the Berlin Olympics," *Journal of Sport History* 16 (Spring 1989): 27–43.

The paper used in this publication meets the minimum requirements of American National Standard for Information Sciences—Permanence of Paper for Printed Library Materials, ANSI Z39.48-1984. ∞™

Library of Congress Cataloging-in-Publication Data

Sports and the American Jew / edited by Steven A. Riess. — 1st ed.
    p. cm. — (Sports and entertainment)
  Includes bibliographical references and index.
  ISBN 0-8156-2754-8 (cloth : alk. paper). — ISBN 0-8156-2761-0
(pbk. : alk. paper)
    1. Jewish athletes—United States—History. 2. Jews—United
States—Social life and customs. 3. Sports—United States—
Sociological aspects. I. Riess, Steven A. II. Series.
GV709.6.S76 1997
796'.089'924073—dc21   97-20930

Manufactured in the United States of America

In memory of Herman Riess (1913–1989)

Hakoah fan, survivor of Dachau,
and the best father in the world,
who kindled my interest in sport by taking me
to my first baseball and soccer games.

Contents

Illustrations

Tables

Acknowledgments

I have had a great deal of help in preparing this book for publication. I wish to thank Marc Raphael, the editor of *American Jewish History,* who first approached me to edit a special volume of his journal devoted to sport history and then came back ten years later to have me work on a second. This provided the impetus for what years later emerged in this collection of essays. I also want to acknowledge the suggestions of those historians I schmoozed with about this endeavor, particularly Melvin Adelman and George Kirsch. Eli Liebow helped with the Yiddish translation, and Allen Bodner, author of *When Boxing Was a Jewish Sport* (1997), which appeared after this book was completed, generously provided me with a copy of Ray Arcel's interview from the Weiner Library. I want to thank all the contributors for their support, and the anonymous critics who helped sharpen the selection of essays and my own arguments. The staff at Syracuse University Press has, as usual, been outstanding in their support, from Director Robert Mandel, who first expressed interest in this project, on down. In particular I want to thank acquisitions editor Nicole Catgenova. Linda Borish, Pamela Cooper, and the photographic departments of the Chicago Historical Society and the National Baseball Hall of Fame helped with photographic research. Finally, I want to thank my wife, Tobi, for her forbearance when I escaped all household responsibilities to lock myself in my office to work on this project; I also want to recognize her editorial assistance in this work. I want to thank

Jamie and Jennie, too, for allowing me to share their computer with them, and for generally just being terrific kids who let Daddy do "his thing."

Steven A. Riess

Skokie, Illinois
April 1997

Contributors

Linda Borish is Associate Professor of History at Western Michigan University. She received her Ph.D. from the University of Maryland, where she studied with Hasia Diner. Book review editor (with Gerald Gems) of the *Journal of Sport History,* she has published extensively in women's history, rural history, and sport history, and is the author of a forthcoming book on New England rural women's well-being and health reform.

Pamela Cooper received her Ph.D. in History at the University of Maine. Currently a researcher and historical advisor for *Runner's World,* she has taught American history at Texas A&M University, Corpus Christi. Her book, *The American Marathon* (1998), is published by Syracuse University Press.

Donald M. Fisher completed his Ph.D. in history in 1997 at the State University of New York, Buffalo. His dissertation is entitled "Contested Ground: North American Cultures and the History of Lacrosse." He is on the faculty of Niagara County Community College.

Gerald R. Gems is Chairperson of the Department of Physical Education, North Central College, Naperville, Illinois. Book review editor (with Linda Borish) of the *Journal of Sport History,* and editor of volume 5 of *Sports in North America; A Documentary History,* he has also authored *Windy City Wars: Labor, Leisure, and Sport in the Making of Chicago* (1997).

Allen Guttmann is Professor of American Studies at Amherst College. His books include *The Jewish Writer in America, From Ritual to Record: The Nature of Modern Sports,* and *The Games Must Go On: Avery Brundage and the Olympic Movement.*

Peter Levine is Director of American Studies, Michigan State University, and the author of several books, including *Albert G. Spalding and the Promise of American Sport* and *Ellis Island to Ebbets Field: Sport and the American Jewish Experience.*

Steven A. Riess is Professor of History at Northeastern Illinois University in Chicago. The former editor of the *Journal of Sport History,* his books include *Touching Base: Professional Baseball and American Culture in the Progressive Era* and *City Games: The Evolution of American Urban Society and the Rise of Sports.*

William M. Simons is Professor of History at the State University of New York, Oneonta, and has published several articles and interviews on American Jewish sport. His essay "Athletics, Society, and History" was published in the spring 1995 issue of *Teaching History: A Journal of Methods.*

Eric Solomon is Professor of English at San Francisco State University. A specialist in British and American fiction, and the author of two books on Stephen Crane, he has written extensively on the literary fascination of American Jews with baseball. He is completing a book entitled *Jews, Baseball, and American Fiction.*

Abbreviations

AB	Avery Brundage Collection. Special Collections. University of Illinois, Champaign.
AH	August Herrmann Papers. National Baseball Library. Cooperstown, New York.
AJA	American Jewish Archives. Hebrew Union College. Cincinnati, Ohio.
AJC	Weiner Oral History Library. American Jewish Committee. New York Public Library.
AJH	*American Jewish History.*
BBHFL	National Baseball Library. Baseball Hall of Fame. Cooperstown, New York.
BDAS	Porter, David L. 1987–89. *Biographical Dictionary of American Sports.* Westport, Connecticut.
BHF	Naismith Basketball Hall of Fame. Springfield, Massachusetts.
Box. Scrap.	Boxing Scrapbooks. 24 volumes. Chicago Historical Society. Chicago.
BV	Baruch Charney Vladeck Papers. Tamiment Collection. New York University.
CFLPS	Works Projects Administration. Chicago Foreign Language Press Survey. Special Collections. University of Chicago Library.
D&C	*Rochester Democrat and Chronicle.*
DFP	*Detroit Free Press.*

EA   Educational Alliance.

EA Archives   Educational Alliance Records. YIVO Archives. YIVO
                Institute for Jewish Research. New York.

EJS   Postal, Bernard, Jess Silver, and Roy Silver. 1965. *Encyclo-
                pedia of Jews in Sports.* New York: Bloch.

JSH   *Journal of Sport History.*

NPG   *National Police Gazette.*

NYHT   *New York Herald Tribune.*

NYT   *New York Times.*

92d St.   Young Women's Hebrew Association Records,
YM-YWHA   92d Street. Young Men's–Women's Hebrew
Archives   Association Archives. New York.

PJAC   Young Women's Union, Neighborhood Center Records.
                Philadelphia Jewish Archives Center at the Balch Insti-
                tute. Philadelphia.

TSN   *The Sporting News.*

T-U   *Rochester Times-Union.*

YIVO   YIVO Archives. YIVO Institute for Jewish Research. New
                York.

YWHA   Young Women's Hebrew Association.

W.S.A.   Women's Swimming Association Archives. The Henning
Archives   Library, International Swimming Hall of Fame, Ft. Lau-
                derdale, Florida.

Sports AND THE American Jew

1

Sports and the American Jew

An Introduction

Steven A. Riess

Few ethnic groups in the United States have been as intensively, and extensively, studied as Jewish Americans. An enormous literature exists on nearly all aspects of their lives in the United States, ranging from their neighborhoods and religious communities to education, assimilation, and social mobility. We know probably more about Jewish businessmen, entertainers, radicals, gangsters, and women than probably any other ethnic group (A. Fried 1980; Joselit 1983; Howe 1976; Lipson 1965; Gabler 1988; Desser and Friedman 1993; Erens 1984; S. Cohen 1983; Schreier 1994; Glenn 1990; Baum, Hyman, and Michel 1976). However, until recently, little attention has been given to the Jewish American athletic experience.[1]

One reason for this lack of interest was that Jews were historically stereotyped as physically weak, unfit, and intellectual, rather

1. Sport history remains a minor theme in Jewish American historiography and has yet to be integrated with the general discourse, as indicated by its almost complete neglect in the five-volume series Jewish People in America. See, for example, Sorin 1992, which has no citations on "sport," and the cursory coverage by Feingold 1992, 19, 20–21, 60, 61.

than athletic and brawny. They were considered the people of the book, rather than men and women of the bat (Howe 1976, 182–83). The conventional wisdom was that Jews were not very much involved in sports, and thus wiseacres would list a volume on Jewish sports heroes among the "shortest books in the world." Furthermore, there have been very few prominent Jewish athletes over the past few years, and there were several years in the 1980s when there seemed to be not more than a dozen Jews playing in the National Football League, National Basketball Association, National Hockey League, and major league baseball combined. Yet contemporary Jews are making notable contributions to sport, which has long been a significant institution in Jewish American life. Jews were among the very first professional baseball players and among the most outstanding early American track stars. They dominated inner city sports such as basketball and boxing during the 1920s and 1930s, and produced star performers in virtually all sports. Since World War II, as Jews became relatively prosperous, they were particularly successful in such upper-middle-class sports as tennis, swimming, and gymnastics. Jews completely dominated Ping-Pong—Gentile men won the U.S. singles titles just twice between 1945 and 1964, and non-Jewish women only twice between 1947 and 1957 (EJS, 440–41). Furthermore, throughout the twentieth century, American Jews have fulfilled major roles in the business, communications, and literary aspects of sport.[2]

A second major factor militating against research into Jewish American sport history is that sport has only recently been considered an appropriate subject for scholarly inquiry. Until the 1970s, historians did not give more than passing attention to sport as a topic for research. In the late 1960s and early 1970s a younger generation of historians—influenced by contemporary social events,

2. Since the 1970s, prominent Jewish American athletes in the so-called minor sports would include Mark Spitz (swimming), Brian Gottfried, Harold Solomon, Brian Teacher, Eliot Teltscher, and Pete Sampress (tennis), Marshall Holman and Mark Roth (bowling), Mitch Gaylord (gymnastics), and Amy Alcott and Corey Pavin (golf). Pavin recently converted to Christianity.
The first studies of Jewish American sport sought to demonstrate that Jews had made important contributions to American sport (Frank 1936; Ribalow 1948; and EJS). For an introduction to ethnic sports, see Eisen and Wiggins 1994; Riess 1989, chap. 4; 1980, 35–38, 184–98; Sorrell 1972, 117–26; and Mormino 1982, 5–19.

left-wing scholarship, and a desire to make history more "relevant"—
became very interested in social history, particularly the history and
culture of common people. This concern included such mundane
subjects as sport. The interest in sport history became formally
institutionalized by the establishment of the North American Society for Sport History in 1973 and its scholarly periodical, the
Journal of Sport History the following year, which helped foster serious investigations into the study of sport.

Historians study sport to understand its internal history and to
comprehend how it influenced and reflected the broader society.
One of the major concerns of sport historians has been the analysis
of ethnic groups. They have analyzed how such groups employed
athletics as a vehicle for assimilation and acculturation, a means to
gain acceptance from the broader society, and as a way to support
a sense of shared peoplehood.

Much of the early attention to Jews and sport focused on the 1936
Berlin Olympics. Indeed, the first major scholarly book to deal with
a topic related to American Jewish athletes was Richard Mandell's
The Nazi Olympics (1971), a study of the 1936 Olympics held in
Germany where the Nazis tried to use the games to demonstrate the
superiority of the Aryan race, the German culture, and the Nazi
social system. One year later Moshe Gottlieb published his innovative essay "American Controversy over the Olympic Games" in
American Jewish History, examining the debate over American participation in the 1936 games. Gottlieb demonstrated that there had
been considerable opposition to sending a team to the Olympics
because of the German government's discriminatory policies. He
reported widespread resistance from the American Federation of Labor, various Jewish and Catholic organizations, several governors and
congressmen, and even President Jeremiah Mahoney of the Amateur
Athletic Union (AAU). However, President Avery Brundage of the
American Olympic Committee (AOC) convinced his board that
German Jewish athletes were not treated unfairly, and that the United
States should participate (Gottlieb 1972, 181–213. See also Mandell
1971, 68–82; Kruger 1978, 42–57; Kidd 1978, 20–40; Kidd 1980,
1–18; Marvin 1982, 81–106; Eisen 1984, 56–77; Shapiro 1985,
255–73; Levine 1989, 399–424; Wenn 1989, 27–43; Wenn 1991,
319–35; Guttmann 1984, esp. 68–73; Levine 1992, chap. 11).

The growing interest in Jewish American sports was reflected by
the publication in 1985 of a special issue of *American Jewish History*

entitled "Sports and the American Jew." The issue included mono-graphs on boxing, the radical response to the 1936 games, an analysis of Jewish writers on sport, and an interview with Adolph Schayes, the outstanding Jewish player in the early NBA. Ten years later *AJH* published a second special issue that included essays on country clubs, a Jewish settlement house, sports at Brandeis University, the editorial reception to Roger Kahn's *Boys of Summer,* a critique of Eric Rolfe Greenberg's novel *The Celebrant,* and an interview with Cal Abrams, a journeyman ballplayer with the Brooklyn Dodgers during the early 1950s. In the interim, two important scholarly books were com-pleted, Peter Levine's *Ellis Island to Ebbets Field: Sport and the American Jewish Experience* (1992), an analysis of the eastern European Jewish sporting experience, primarily in New York City from the early 1900s to the 1940s, and Gerald Sorin's *The Nurturing Neighborhood: The Brownsville Boys Club and Jewish Community in Urban America, 1940–1990* (1990), a study of the Brownsville Boys Club (BBC). Levine argues that sport was a middle ground between the Jewish commu-nity and the core culture, Jews and other ethnic groups, and immi-grants and second-generation Jews. It offered "ethnic experiences that served Jewish community ends while inadvertently encouraging in-tegration into the American mainstream" (271). Sorin examines a club organized by teenagers in one of New York's poorest neighbor-hoods after they were closed out of an after-school center. The club used sports to take local youths off the street and portrayed athletes as positive role models instead of the neighborhood hoodlums. The BBC formed a democratic federation of some fifty boys clubs, which six years later attracted adult interest and philanthropic support. In 1953 the BBC opened a $1.25 million center that was soon taken over by the city (2–4, 25).[3]

3. For an overview of American sport history, see Rader 1995. One of the essays in "Sports and the American Jew," Edward Shapiro's "The World Labor Athletic Carnival of 1936," won an award as the best article in the journal that year.

Recent valuable popular studies of the Jewish American pugilistic experience include Blady 1988, Fried 1991, and Anderson 1991. For a more scholarly account, see Riess 1985, 223–54. On basketball, see Peterson 1990. On Jewish owners, see Halberstram 1981, a journalistic account of the Portland Trailblaz-ers, and Fisher 1990, 20–48. On Jewish owners of NFL franchises, see Klein and Fisher 1987; Dickey 1991; and Ribowsky 1991. On Jewish baseball owners in Cleveland and Baltimore, see Miller 1990 and Torry 1995. See also Greenberg 1989, an excellent autobiography of a Jewish American icon who became a prominent baseball executive.

The essays in this book examine the contributions of Jewish men and women to the American sporting scene and the social functions that sport has played in the Jewish American community. The essays illuminate such central themes in American Jewish history as acculturation, structural assimilation, intergenerational conflicts, entrepreneurship, social mobility, gender roles, and anti-Semitism. The primary focus is on second-generation Jewish males who used sport to become acculturated and seek structural assimilation. They employed sport to gain self-esteem and public recognition from their community as well as the broader society, fight stereotypes and anti-Semitism, and escape inner city poverty. Sport was largely a male bastion among ethnic groups but we also point out the unrecognized extent of female Jewish participation in athletics. Finally, we demonstrate not only how sport encouraged assimilation but also how sport promoted Jewish identity through ethnic sports organizations (Conzen 1992, 3–6).

Anglo-Jews, German Jews, and Sport in America

Little was inherently anti-athletic in Jewish culture and theology so long as physical culture did not take one away from study and piety. The sporting experience Jewish immigrants brought to America was more a product of their regional cultures than of their religious beliefs. The Jews of the Bible admired physical strength, speed, and stamina, and the Bible mentions long-distance runners (who carried information between communities), ball playing, belt wrestling, weight lifting, and such martial skills as archery, horseback riding, fencing, and javelin throwing. In the Hellenic era there was much interest in Greek sports, but opposition emerged because the philo-Greeks participated in the nude, often avoided religious duties, and their games were identified with pagan rites. After the destruction of the temple, the rabbis opposed sports because they were identified with pagan Greek and Roman culture. However, in the talmudic era, useful sports such as swimming were encouraged, and several positive references to ball playing and other nonviolent sports are in the Talmud. Yet physical violence was considered "un-Jewish" in a community that placed spiritual values over sensual and physical values. There was also, though, a recognition that mind and body were indivisible and affected each other. Maimonides, the great eleventh-century philosopher and physician, promoted ball playing, calisthenics, and moderate exercise to promote good health. In the Middle Ages rabbis often permitted ball playing, even on the Sabbath, although they were opposed to gambling sports and hunting for pleasure. Jews inside the ghetto walls raced pigeons, ice-skated, and enjoyed other sports. The major canonical edict on sport in the *Shulchan Aruch,* the definitive sixteenth-century rabbinical code, banned Sabbath sports (*EJS,* 3–9; Poliakoff 1984, 48–65; Alouf 1973, 39; Eisen 1991, 105; Zborowski and Herzog 1952, 340–41; Baskhi 1973, 50; Hoberman 1989).[4]

A number of nineteenth-century Jewish newcomers from western Europe arrived with some familiarity with athletics that they sustained in the New World. They came from modern countries where physical culture was already an important recreational activity. Athletically inclined English and German newcomers used their prowess to gain the respect of the gentile community and organized ethnic sporting clubs to maintain and promote their collective identity. These voluntary associations preserved Old World pastimes and would provide facilities for American athletic contests.

The first major Jewish sportsmen in the United States were English immigrants and their sons. In the early nineteenth century, England was the primary locus of sport in the Western world. A proud Anglo-Jewish pugilistic heritage had already been established, dating to Daniel Mendoza, the late-eighteenth-century English boxing champion. London's impoverished Jewish West End was renowned then as a breeding ground for professional fighters, and at least twenty major Jewish fighters grew up there (Endelman 1979, 219–33; *EJS,* 297).

Far more important than the small English migration were German Jewish newcomers, a segment of the largest immigrant group to the United States. Emancipated German Jews were not very distinguishable from their Protestant countrymen in their leisure pursuits. As Patricia Vertinsky points out, "German Jews began to embrace the sport and physicality deemed necessary for 'Germanness'" (Vertinsky 1995, 49–50). Just five years after Friedrich Jahn had started the turner movement in 1811 in response to the roman-

---

4. Andrew R. Heinze (1990, 118) emphasizes that for devout Jews, their traditional culture discouraged entertainment that was not tied to religious observation.

tic nationalism that swept the German states, there were Jewish members in the Hamburg turnverein.

Jahn believed that through gymnastics the moral and physical might of the German people would be restored. He set up an outdoor *Turnplatz* near Berlin with various apparatus including towers, platforms, ropes, and rings. The turners were considered too democratic for the reactionary regimes that dominated the German states after the Congress of Vienna, and were banned in Prussia in 1819. Antiturner restrictions were lifted in 1842, and the movement attracted many young revolutionaries who advocated constitutional government (Leonard and Affleck 1947, chap. 11; Barney 1982, 282 n.7).[5]

After the failure of the 1848 democratic revolutions in Germany, many turners fled to America and founded turner societies, beginning that year in Louisville, Cincinnati, and New York. These athletic clubs were open to all men of German backgrounds, regardless of their social class, and, like many other secular German institutions re-created in the United States, often had Jewish members. The turner societies promoted not only gymnastics but also German culture, political activism (republicanism or socialism), respect for working-class concerns, and physical education. The prominence of Jews in turner societies was reflected by the election of Jews to the presidencies of the major Chicago and Milwaukee turner units shortly after the Civil War (Metzner 1924; Wagner 1988, 221–40; Ueberhorst 1979; Wittke 1952, 147–48; Riess 1989, 23, 96–99; Louis and Gartner 1963, 114; Meites 1924, 470; Kramer and Stern 1984, 227–29).

The gymnastic exercises of the turners had limited appeal to second-generation German Jews who fully participated in the sporting culture of post–Civil War America. Philo Jacoby, an immigrant Prussian printer who arrived in San Francisco in 1859 at

5. In 1860 German turners formed the *Deutsche Turnerschaft*, which became fervidly nationalistic, conservative, and eventually, highly anti-Semitic. They also became ardent opponents of modern sport with its characteristics of instrumental rationality. The turners felt that sport promoted self-pride, the development of an asymmetrical and unhealthy physique (soccer was decried as barbaric), and undue concern with record keeping and specialization. Sport was also castigated for hindering moral improvement and the building of nationalism. They preferred noncompetitive mass displays of exercises (Guttmann 1994, 143–45). Despite anti-Semitism, 5 percent of German turners in 1880 were Jewish, five times their proportion of the national population (*EJS*, 10, 297).

age twenty-two, was one of the first athletes of German ancestry to achieve renown in competitive sport. He was an outstanding rifleman who won the Berlin Shooting Championships in 1868, making him perhaps the first individual American to win an international sports championship.

German Jewish athletes made notable contributions in mainstream American sports, including track and football. Daniel Stern, the fourth member of the New York Athletic Club (NYAC), which later became an anti-Semitic organization, won the first American amateur walking championship in 1876, while Lon Meyers of Richmond was the preeminent nineteenth-century American runner, holding every national record from fifty yards to the mile. Lipman Pike, a Brooklynite of Dutch descent, became one of the first professional baseball players in 1866 when he was compensated to play second baseman for the Philadelphia Athletics. He later starred with the New York Mutuals and the Brooklyn Atlantics, and in 1871 played and managed the Troy franchise in the first professional league, the National Association of Professional Base Ball Players. Five years later Pike played in the National League's inaugural season of 1876, and led it in homers the following season when he briefly managed the Cincinnati club. There were even German Jewish football players, including Lucius Littauer, the first Jewish coach, who played (1875, 1877) and coached (1881) at Harvard, and Princeton quarterback Phil King, who made second-team all-American in 1890 (*EJS*, 32–35, 212–13, 215–16; Willis and Wettan 1975, 93–111).[6]

6. On an early Jewish ballplayer in California, see Franks 1991, 174–91, 234–36. Littauer was the future "Glove King of America," a five-time congressman, and an outstanding philanthropist. King later converted to Christianity (*EJS*, 216, 214).
    In 1875 a Jewish periodical, *The New Era,* came out opposing the growing intercollegiate sports program. Although the editors considered rowing a good form of exercise, they urged limitations on rowing at colleges, probably in response to Cornell president Andrew White's gushing praise of his school's eight: "Like every other pleasure, its pursuit may be carried to excess, and to excess it will be carried, if it be permitted to occupy, either in thought or in practice, the hours that properly belong to other occupations. . . . If the students of a college be told by their president, that the victorious crew have done more to make their college known than all the men of worth and learning that have emerged from its halls, what wonder can it be, if these students attach more importance to the exercise of rowing than to the furnishing of the chambers of the mind?" (Oren 1985, 35).

Well-to-do second-generation German Jews organized Jewish-oriented sports associations, particularly after the rise of overt anti-Semitism in the late 1870s when metropolitan men's clubs instituted restrictive admission policies. The first important Jewish sports organization was the Young Men's Hebrew Association (YMHA). The YMHA's origin dated to 1854 when a club was formed in Baltimore primarily to encourage moral recreation, sociability, and literature for young German Jewish men. The club also supported physical fitness and spirituality on the model of the YMCA. By the mid-1870s there were more than twenty YMHAs, including New York's preeminent 92d Street YMHA, established in 1874. Two years later the Philadelphia YMHA introduced the first women's program, which New York did not copy until 1890. The YMHAs were generally in German Jewish neighborhoods and were equipped with gymnasiums and other athletic facilities. By 1900 there were a hundred Y's, with twenty thousand members. Beginning in 1880, the Y's hired experienced turners to supervise their fitness programs that became one of their cornerstones. Later in that decade the YMHAs began focusing on the problems of immigrant assimilation. Night classes were organized to teach English (Emma Lazarus was an English instructor), civics, and home economics. YMHA leaders became ardent advocates of what would be considered muscular Judaism well before Dr. Max Nordau invented the expression in 1901. After the turn of the century, competitive sports, particularly basketball, were added to their programs, and they also provided meeting space for various athletic clubs (Rabinowitz 1948, 11–12, 53, 62, 75, 78, 85).[7]

Prosperous German (and Sephardic) Jews also formed status-oriented sports clubs that had no religious connection because they were unwelcomed in prestigious WASP athletic and country clubs. The 1893 blackballing of businessman Herman Freund by the Detroit Athletic League attracted such notoriety that it led to an

7. The YMHAs were at first closed on the Sabbath, but the New York Y decided to open up on Saturday for "lighter exercises" (EJS, 14). A particularly attractive feature were the outdoor camps that Y's sponsored (Kraft 1954; Langfeld 1928; Hertzberg 1978, 118, 123; Sachar 1992, 157). For candid assessments of the New York YMHA program, see "YMHA Yearbook and 31st Annual Report of the Physical Division" 1905, esp. 73–74.

On Max Nordau, see Baldwin 1980, 99–1920, and on his "muscular Judaism," see Gilman 1991, 53–54.

intense debate in the *Detroit Evening News* on anti-Semitism (Dinnerstein 1994, 51). Even when the renowned attorney Louis Brandeis was admitted to the Dedham Polo Club, which his partner, club president Sam Warren, had helped found, most members would not associate with him (Dinnerstein 1994, 52; Baltzell 1959; Hardy 1982). For example, in 1906 a group of prosperous young New York Jews, including Bernard Baruch, formed the City Athletic Club because they could not get into any high-status athletic club, such as the NYAC, that discriminated against Jews. Initiation fees were $100 and dues were $75 ($25 for juniors). Within a few years the thousand members included names such as Guggenheim, Morganthau, Seligman, Warburg, and Gimbel. Similarly, when wealthy Jews could not get into suburban country clubs that provided a sporting environment modeled after English gentry life, they established their own ("The City Athletic Club" 1908, 74; "City Athletic Club Constitution, By-Laws and House Rules"; Wirth 1928, 170; *EJS*, 11). In Chicago, for instance, the three-hundred-acre Lake Shore Country Club was established to help distinguish German Jews from even the richest parvenus of eastern European origins. Its members included Leonard Florsheim, Modie Spiegel, and Julius Rosenwald (Ebner 1988, 233). Their club emphasized expensive sports, such as golf and tennis, and social affairs to help their sons and daughters meet appropriate potential spouses.

In " 'Our Crowd' at Play: The Elite Jewish Country Club in the 1920s," historian Peter Levine analyzes the German Jewish country club. Levine examines the development of the Jewish country clubs as a haven for "Our Crowd," who were restricted from the high-status WASP clubs but desired a place where they could be separated from lesser sorts. These facilities proved especially important for Jewish women, who had the opportunity to participate in prestigious sports and socialize with the right people. Levine concludes his study by focusing on Los Angeles's Hillcrest Country Club, which became less a bastion of German Jews than of the Hollywood elite, largely self-made new immigrants who wanted to be accepted and respected by the broader gentile society. They were often on their second wives (blonde *shiksas*), and yet felt most comfortable amid the tumult of *Yiddishkeit* and *landsman* at their (eastern European) country club.

Although German American Jews rarely took part in the most elite sports of polo or yachting, they did make inroads into thoroughbred racing. Participation as an owner, breeder, or member of a jockey club provided considerable social prestige. The most important Jew in nineteenth-century racing was financier August Belmont, an immigrant from Alzey, Germany. He was the first president of New York's prestigious American Jockey Club, founded in 1865, which established Jerome Park one year later to revive northern horse racing. Other early members included an Einstein, Isaacs, Kohn, Levine, and an Oppenheim. Belmont was a successful owner and breeder, and his Nursery Stud was one of the finest breeding farms in the world. He won many major races, including the Belmont Stakes (which had been named in his honor) in 1869, and he led the nation in earnings in 1889 and 1890. Belmont encountered discrimination and anti-Semitism, but mixed in elite society, and became the first Jew admitted to the New York Yacht Club. Belmont married Caroline Slidell Perry, and the two raised their children Episcopalian, but he never converted. He exhibited no interest in Jewish affairs, and was disowned by the Jewish community. Other notable Jewish racing men in the late nineteenth century included yeast manufacturer Charles Fleischmann, who spent about $800,000 on his turf interests between 1891 and his death in 1897, and Julius Cahn, whose Typhoon II won the 1897 Kentucky Derby. However, no Jew was ever admitted to the prestigious Jockey Club, a voluntary association established in 1894 to supervise the turf, until 1951 when Harry F. Guggenheim was voted in, followed by John M. Schiff and Jack L. Dreyfus Jr. Journalists credited Guggenheim with the major role in establishing the New York Racing Association and the rebuilding of Aqueduct Racetrack.[8]

Although many German Jews sought status through sport, some used sport for business purposes. The first notable Jewish businessman

8. Jews were successful on the turf earlier in Canada. In the 1830s Ben Cohen was treasurer of the Maryland Jockey Club, and lawyer Philip Hart of Montreal won the first King's Plate in Three Rivers, Canada (*EJS,* 305–33). For a detailed biography of Belmont's personal life and his racing interests, see Black 1977 and *DAB* under "Belmont, August." In Atlanta, Aaron Haas was a founding member of the Gentlemen's Driving Club in 1887 (renamed the Piedmont Driving Club in 1895), the city's leading association for harness racing. However, no other Jew was ever invited to join (Hertzberg 1978, 171). August Belmont II was the first president of the Jockey Club. On Jews and the Jockey Club, see Livingston 1973, 30, 261–67. Guggenheim's Cain Hoy Stable led the nation in money winnings in 1959, and Dreyfus shared the "Best Breeder of the Year" award in 1962 (*EJS,* 310, 312, 327).

in sport was John M. Brunswick, a Swiss immigrant who came to the United State at fifteen in 1834, and eleven years later designed a billiard table that became the standard in the industry. After his death in 1886, the John M. Brunswick Billiard Manufacturing Company was taken over by his son-in-law, Moses Bensinger, who two years later moved the firm into the bowling business (*EJS*, 131–32).

During the late nineteenth century, German Jewish businessmen were also very much involved in professional baseball to make money and demonstrate their civic pride. German Jewish baseball club owners were especially common in southern cities such as Atlanta, Augusta, Birmingham, Houston, Macon, Mobile, and New Orleans where they wanted to gain recognition as public-spirited citizens. There were also several German Jewish major league team owners, whose numbers nearly exceeded the Jews on the diamond. Cincinnati, a city with an important Jewish community, had several Jewish baseball executives, including Nathan Menderson, Cincinnati president in 1880; clothier Aaron Stern, who owned the team from 1882 to 1890; and Louis Kramer, a founder and later president (1891) of the American Association (then one of two major leagues). One of the chief stockholders in the Reds in the early 1900s was Julius Fleischmann, the mayor of Cincinnati.

The two most influential Jewish magnates at the turn of the century were Barney Dreyfuss, an immigrant who owned major league franchises in Louisville and Pittsburgh from 1889 until his death in 1932, and Andrew Freedman, a New York Tammanyite who owned the New York Giants (1895–1902). Freedman made a fortune in real estate and other businesses in cooperation with Tammany boss Richard Croker, and used his political connections to push around other owners. Freedman became one of the most hated owners of all time. He encouraged rowdyism on the field, fought with fans, ballplayers, umpires, and sportswriters, was miserly with his employees, and went through sixteen managers in eight years (Riess 1980, 67–69, 90–91; *DAB* under "Freedman, Andrew"; *BDAS: Baseball* under "Freedman, Andrew"). Freedman was involved in one of the first notable instances of anti-Semitism in baseball history. In the summer of 1898, during a game at the Polo Grounds against the Baltimore Orioles, former Giant Ducky Holmes responded to derision from his old teammates by retorting,

1.1. Andrew Freedman, owner of the New York Giants, 1895–1902. *Courtesy of the Andrew Freedman Home for the Aged.*

"Well, I'm glad I'm not working for a sheeny any more." Freedman demanded that umpire Tom Lynch kick Holmes out for his vulgar language, but Lynch demurred, claiming he had heard nothing. Freedman then took the Giants off the field, forfeited the game, and returned the fans' money (Voigt 1966, 184).

Over the next several decades Jews remained prominent in the National League, although the only Jewish magnates in the rival American League were the Frank brothers, who ran the short-lived Baltimore Orioles club (1901–2). The National League had several Jewish owners, including Pittsburgh's Dreyfuss, Judge Emil Fuchs in Boston (1923–36), Sydney Weil in Cincinnati (1929–33), and advertising executive Albert D. Lasker, who was a major stockholder in the Cubs in the World War I era, and was largely responsible for creating the commissioner system. When Dreyfuss died in 1932 he was succeeded by his son-in-law, Bill Benswanger, who from 1936 until the team was sold in 1946 was the only Jewish owner in major league baseball (*EJS*, 28–29, 39–40, 56; Riess 1980, 57–58; *DAB* under "Lasker, Albert D."; Gunther 1960, 98–125; Frank 1936, 75–91).

Sport and the Eastern European Jew

The cultural experience of the two million eastern European Jewish immigrants who arrived in the United States between 1882 and 1914 was different from that of their modernized German counterparts. They came from the static premodern world of the *shtetl,* and had no familiarity with sport, which was largely unknown in eastern Europe. These newcomers looked and dressed differently from American Jews, spoke Yiddish, and were strictly Orthodox. Their arrival played a notable role in the new wave of nativism and anti-Semitism of the late nineteenth century, and many German Jews blamed the newcomers for the discrimination they suddenly encountered (Dinnerstein 1994, 53–54; Sachar 1992, 98–102, 125–26; Higham 1963). Yet although German Jews were uncomfortable with the arrival of hundreds of thousands of strangely garbed and impoverished Orthodox Russian Jews, they felt an obligation to aid their coreligionists adjust to life in urban America and sustain their Judaic heritage. The established German Jews organized a wide variety of social institutions, such as the Hebrew Immigrant Aid Society, and settlement houses, such as New York's Educational Alliance, founded in 1892 by philanthropists Jacob Shiff, Isaac Guggenheim, and Isidor Straus, that became a model for other Jewish social settlements.

Russian Jews were stereotyped as weak, unhealthy, physically unfit, and unaccustomed to "manly" labor, traits many Americans believed fit all Jews. In a 1907 speech to Harvard's Menorah Society, President Charles Eliot unfavorably compared contemporary Jews to the fighting qualities of the ancient Maccabees, and noted that his Jewish students were less active in outdoor sports than their peers ("Jewish Physique" 1909, 200). In response, *The American Hebrew* recommended that Jews moderate their emphasis on academics through athletics, even though "the world was now governed by brains not brawn." The periodical further pointed out the prominence of Jews in prizefighting, and that Jewish record holders in weight lifting and the running jump demonstrate that "Jews are capable of developing their muscular system equally as well as other folk and that there is no inherent difficulty in acquiring athletic qualifications if these be desired" ("Dr Eliot on Jewish Physique" 1909, 207). Even more critical than Eliot was the noted sociologist E. A. Ross, who in 1914 described the Jewish immigrants as "the polar opposite of our pioneer breed. Not only are they undersized and weak-muscled, but they shun bodily activity and are extremely sensitive to pain" (Ross 1914, 289–90).

The familiarity of *shtetl* immigrants with physical culture was at best limited to ice-skating, sledding, and ball playing, except for members of the Haskalah movement, who supported acculturation and modernization and had engaged in exercise and even contact sports back in Europe. The newcomers identified athletic contests as strange "Yankee" institutions that were inappropriate for themselves and their children. They took sports to task on moral grounds (horse racing for its gambling and boxing and football for their violence) or as foolish wastes of time. Baseball was particularly considered a ridiculous amusement in which adults wearing short pants tried to hit a ball with a stick and ran around in circles. Immigrants made fun of other newcomers, such as Jake (Yekl) the Tailor, protagonist of an Abraham Cahan novelette, who was a baseball and boxing fan (Cahan 1896, 6). Even if American sports were enticing, poor Orthodox newcomers had little free time or discretionary income to devote to hobbies. They worked hard and long, and their precious leisure moments largely consisted of socializing with family or friends. If they spent money for entertainment, it would likely be within their own community, such as at the Yiddish theater. As Philadelphia social worker Charles S. Bernheimer pointed out in 1905 (35), "The money which another workman perhaps might spend on drink and sport he devotes to the improvement of his home and the education of his children" (Riess 1980, 36–37).

Parents exerted pressure on sons against playing sports that were dangerous, distracted them from study or work or both, or encouraged behavior that drew them away from a traditionally strict Orthodox upbringing. As Eddie Cantor remembered, the worst thing a parent or grandparent could call a child was "you baseball player, you" (Howe 1976, 182). The Russian Jews saw sports as a threat to their sons' ethnic identity, but could not prevent them from becoming big sports fans (Smith 1939, 111–16). Boys identified sport with American society and wanted to become acculturated. The second generation avidly participated in sports and followed sports heroes in the press, although they rarely could attend professional contests because of the cost. Playing and following sports provided a means to become Americanized and gave youths of all backgrounds a topic for conversation. Jewish athletes who were especially proficient gained recognition and status among their peers in the neighborhood. They considered sport a meritocratic and democratic institution and expected that their achievements would gain them personal acceptance and respect for the ethnic group from the broader society. Furthermore, participation provided a means to display manliness. In the Old Country, a *mensch* took care of his familial, community, and religious responsibilities (ideally a talmudic scholar), but in America, working-class manliness was less a matter of character than of strength, courage, and virility (Gorn 1986, esp. 140–47).

Second-generation eastern European Jews were historically most successful in the sports that did not require much space, provided fame and recognition, and held out the promise of a better life. They took advantage of whatever opportunities were available to take part in athletics, often under the auspices of settlement houses or Jewish organizations that catered to their interests. The best athletes envisioned sport as a means to escape the slums through professional athletics, a college scholarship, or a good job achieved because of their renown. Inner city Jews, along with other impoverished ethnic groups, did less well in expensive amateur sports that provided no tangible rewards.

Besides parental opposition, opportunities for the second generation to enjoy sport were curtailed by religious obligations (that were frequently circumvented), high dropout rates among students, and especially economic and spatial factors. As long as Jewish youth lived in crowded inner city neighborhoods, their athletic options were curtailed by spatial variables. There were not many baseball or football fields on the Lower East Side of New York, and large suburban parks were often inaccessible or a costly streetcar ride away. Playing a recreational game such as stickball in a crowded alley or street was just not the same thing as playing baseball in a uniform on a well-manicured field.[9]

Some spatial problems were alleviated by the small-park movement at the turn of the century, whose advocates included Lillian Wald, Samuel Gompers, and Nathan Straus. These reformers encouraged philanthropists and municipalities to secure land and construct modest-size parks, recreational piers, and swimming pools in and around inner city neighborhoods, where they would be accessible to local residents. The reformers expected that youthful park goers would become Americanized and improve their health by breathing fresh air. Ironically, playground advocates sometimes encountered community resistance from people who felt that housing demands overrode the need for parks and playgrounds (Riess 1989, 132-40; Gurock 1979, 35, 42, 161; Goodman 1979, 56). An unexpected result of the park movement was that these public spaces became contested space between rival ethnic groups. Instead of becoming sites for structural assimilation, urban parks, or at least certain sections, developed a strong ethnic character if one group dominated them. Parks between opposing ethnic groups were likely to become the scene of violence as they contested for control of scarce public space (Riess 1989, 145–46; Rosenzweig 1983, chap. 5; Haller 1971–72, 221–27; Suttles 1968, 54–56). After World War I, for instance, Chicago's Douglas Park was a no-man's-land

9. Inner city youth did have opportunities to enjoy organized recreational sports such as handball. One popular version was "Chinese" handball in which players would line up on the sidewalk along a flat wall and position themselves in separate boxes marked off by the sidewalk cement. Players used either a soft rubber ball ("spaldeen") or a regulation black handball, which was smaller and very hard. The ball was hit on a bounce to the wall and returned off a bounce. Good players would make returns difficult by applying a slice and keeping the ball low and close to the wall (Kazin 1951, 84). The better known variant was "American" handball, which was mainly played outdoors in city parks on a wall and court. In this game, all returns, off a bounce or "on the fly," had to hit the wall without bouncing. The world's greatest player was Vic Hershkowitz, who dominated the sport after World War II, with thiry victories in 1952, more than double the previous record (*EJS*, 301–2). His successor as the world's leading player was Jimmy Jacobs, who also achieved renown by amassing the world's outstanding collection of boxing fight films and then by becoming Mike Tyson's manager.

between Jewish North Lawndale and the mainly Polish Lower West Side. When Polish youths playing in the park saw Jewish toughs coming, they would leave, and vice versa. Relations between the groups were particularly sensitive in the summer of 1921 when there were pogroms in Poland. Chaos broke out in the park on a Saturday when Jewish baseball players were attacked by about thirty Poles. When word of the fighting reached the poolrooms on nearby Roosevelt Road, tough teenagers and young men, amateur boxers, and roughnecks from the Miller brothers gang rushed into the fray, eager to "wallop the Polack[s]" (Thrasher 1963, 134–35).

Jewish youths were often introduced and trained in sports at nonsectarian settlement houses, such as New York's Henry Street Settlement, or at German–Jewish sponsored facilities, such as New York's Educational Alliance (1892), financed by philanthropists Jacob Schiff, Isaac Guggenheim, and Isidor Straus, or Chicago's Hebrew Institute (1903), supported by Sears, Roebuck president Julius Rosenwald, who donated $75,000.

By 1910 at least seventy-five Jewish settlements and community centers and another fifty mainly catered to a Jewish clientele. They usually had an assembly hall, gymnasium, library, and synagogue, and offered a comprehensive program that included classes in English, civics, American customs, music, art, Yiddish, and Hebrew. The Educational Alliance even had summer camps in the Catskills (Rabinowitz 1948, 75; Wald 1915; Davis 1967; Lissak 1989; Carson 1990).

German Jewish sponsors believed that adult-directed sport and play Americanized their second-generation Russian Jewish clients, raised their moral standards, improved their health, and eliminated the canard that Jews lacked physical courage (Goodman 1979, chap. 3, esp. 37–40; Eisen 1991, 113, 116). An 1897 report of the Educational Alliance asserted

> The Educational Alliance will not merit its name unless it comprises the education of the body as well as the mind. The importance of physical training for our down-town brethren cannot be over estimated. Our co-religionists are often charged with lack of physical courage and repugnance to physical work. Nothing will more effectively remove this than athletic training. Let a young man develop his body and he will neither shrink from imaginary danger nor shirk manly work. (*Fifth Annual Report,* 28)

Another report eight years later applauded the work of the athletic department.

> The gym in its relation to the people of our neighborhood occupies a unique position. Many of the immigrants arrive at our shores are not only ignorant of the prime concepts and meaning of physical culture and bodily improvement, but even take an antagonistic attitude to any advance therein. Physical Culture is associated in the minds of many with worldliness and frivolity. This idea the gym sternly and successfully combats in its work not only with men, but even with the girls, to whom this activity has been also foreign. The people have been given to understand that a sound body is . . . the very first essential in correct and sound living as well as in sound thinking. Especially the young people have taken hold of athletics in the most surprising manner. For example, runners, ballplayers and experts in almost every branch of athletic activity, both indoor and outdoor, have been elevated, and now the gold colors are often victorious in the varied meets. Indeed, a tend toward professionalism has been noticed in some individual cases, especially in the indoor work, of course, all such ideas have been suppressed, because our aim is not to educate tumblers and acrobats. (*Thirteenth Annual Report,* 43)

Settlement workers and their patrons identified adult-supervised physical culture as a panacea. Inner city Jewish boys could learn self-defense, dribbling, and patriotism, all in a Jewish environment. Jewish juvenile delinquency would be prevented by keeping youths gainfully occupied and off the streets where their favorite activities were lighting fires and getting into fights. Clients could exercise, play games, and participate in individual sports that taught discipline and in team sports that taught such important values as cooperation and respect for authority.

Settlement workers particularly hoped that their recreational programs would provide an alternative to neighborhood poolrooms that were considered hangouts for loafers and criminals who debauched local youths. A 1911 recreational survey of a Lower East Side neighborhood located ten poolrooms, which exceeded the neighboorhood's dancing academies or movie theaters (Davis 1911, 7–8; Riess 1989, 73–74). In the impoverished Brownsville section of Brooklyn, where as late as the depression there were three times as many poolrooms as playgrounds, one of the most famous hangouts in the 1910s and for many years thereafter was Label's Pool Hall. There you could play pocket billiards, meet your pals, and find "someone to break a head, beat up a guy, break a strike, buy junk, set a fire, plan a robbery or muscle a peddlar" (Hirschberg 1957, 37). As Sammy Aaronson, an orphan who virtually lived there, remembered, "The place was always alive with junkies and firebugs and shylocks and killers and pimps and rag-pickers and bookies and pickpockets, and one or another always had some errand to be run or some chore to be handled" (Hirschberg 1957, 43, 27, 30–32, 34–35, 42–43, 47–50). Several "one-way rides" involving gangsters such as the Amboy Dukes or the Shapiros would start out from Label's. However, the gangsters "wouldn't ask a kid they knew was all right to do something wrong" (Sorin 1990, 25).[10]

Brownsville in the 1930s and early 1940s was still one of the roughest neighborhoods in the United States. For example, one day Jacob Baroff was playing punchball when he and his pals found a car parked at what was normally first base. They asked the driver to move, but found he had been shot in the head. As historian Gerald Sorin recounts, "These Brownsville boys, apparently not *too* terribly surprised, and certainly undeterrable, released the brake, pushed the car and played ball." There was much interaction in the area between hoodlums and local youths. For example, when the Sackonians, a BBC team, were invited to play at the Sing Sing penitentiary, their uniforms were provided by Murder, Inc. (Sorin 1990, 26).

Brownsville boys in the 1930s and 1940s played punchball, stickball, and two-hand touch football in the street. When they could not afford a real football, they used a rolled newspaper. Max Zaslofsky, a future NBA star, remembered how they played basket-ball: "We just got those peach baskets and hooked them on to a pole or something like that. And if we were lucky we found a beat-up rubber ball until maybe we could afford fifty-cents to go out and buy one." There was virtually no park space that could be used for play as the city and the WPA both neglected Brownsville, and there was little indoor space during the winter compared with more prosperous Brooklyn communities, such as Flatbush, which had a JCC, and Borough Park, which had a YMHA (Sorin 1990, 31, 34).

10. For a more benign view of a 1920s Bronx poolhall when that borough was just becoming developed, see Greenberg 1989, 9.

Gerald Gems, an expert on Chicago working-class sport, explores the rise of sport at a Jewish settlement in his essay "The Rise of Sport at a Jewish Settlement House: The Chicago Hebrew Institute, 1908–1921." The CHI provided a place for boys and girls to become Americanized in a controlled ethnic setting in which sport was both a carrot to attract their interest and a vehicle to transmit socially desirable traits. By the 1930s the institute had become so successful and Jewish youths were so fully acculturated that they found its appeal less attractive. Furthermore, Jewish families were moving out of the first and second areas of settlement into better neighborhoods. Settlement houses responded by broadening their appeal outside the Jewish community or by physically moving with the community. They became Jewish Community Centers, offering the social, athletic, cultural, and even political services desired by acculturated and increasingly middle-class Jews within a Jewish American environment.

The major settlement sports were basketball, boxing, wrestling, and track for young men and basketball for young women. These activities required little space or equipment, and fit in well with an inner city environment. Settlement house coaches taught boxing, not to prepare future prizefighters but to build self-confidence and promote fitness among their charges. As pointed out in my essay "Tough Jews: The Jewish American Boxing Experience, 1890–1950," boxing fit in well with poor urban neighborhoods that were the principal breeding ground for future prizefighters. Boxing was a useful skill to master because these young men lived in dangerous communities. Unless one was resilient, tough, and courageous, or at least had a friend with such qualities, it was hard surviving in impoverished Jewish areas surrounded by hostile groups. The "tough Jew," like Chicago's "Nails" Morton, who stood up for his coreligionists and defended them against Polish, Italian, or Irish thugs, became neighborhood heroes. Young Jews often got into fights with youths of rival ethnic groups who lived nearby and interfered with them when they went to school, *chedar*, or the neighborhood swimming pool. Jackie Fields, a future welterweight champion, grew up on Chicago's Maxwell Street during the late second decade, where he and his friends often had to fight their way at the local swimming pool to get into the water. They were invariably greeted by comments such as "What are you doin' here you Jew bastard?" (Berkow 1977, 142) and a fight would follow. No sissies allowed! Street fighting prepared Jews such as the Miller brothers for careers as policemen, hoodlums, or prizefighters (Haller 1971–72, 221–27; Bell 1960, 127–50; Riess 1980, 188–89; Landesco 1968, 231–32).

Boxing was abhorred by parents and by the ethnic press, but was popular with the American-born generation for whom it was a means to prove their manhood and the courage of the race. Amateurs fought at stags or local boxing gyms for prizes or badges that they turned into cash, and top amateurs might go on to become professionals. Leading fighters were neighborhood heroes who proudly represented the community against its enemies, sought fame and fortune, and aspired to the championship. Boxing provided a means of legally using street-fighting skills to make much fast money and thereby escape the slums. Jews were among the most successful fighters in America in the first half of the century, especially in the interwar era, and built on their fistic success to gain prominence in the business aspects of pugilism.

The crowded character of inner city neighborhoods also fostered interest in basketball, a game invented by James Naismith in 1891 as a winter diversion for football players. Basketball rapidly became a popular indoor sport in congested cities because it did not require much space or expensive equipment. Inner city youth played basketball in school yards, settlement houses, and churches, although it could even be played in the street. As Maclyn Baker, the NYU captain in 1921, remembered, "We played in the streets with a rag ball and used ashcans for baskets. We stressed team play rather than shooting because rag balls didn't bounce" (EJS, 79).

The game was originally a violent sport—players wore knee pads and hip pads—and the courts were surrounded by a wire-mesh cage to keep the ball in play so competitors would not make madcap dashes into the stands or up to running tracks to retrieve balls. Nonetheless, opinion makers in the Jewish community favored the game as a clean moral sport that "requires a lot of quick thinking, lightning like rapidity of movement and endurance, and does not call for brutality and brute strength" (Frank 1908, 477).

Second-generation Jewish Americans were among the most renowned basketball players. In the early 1900s many New York intersettlement championships were won by teams representing such Lower East Side institutions as Clark House and the University

Settlement. These squads became the breeding grounds for future interscholastic, collegiate, and professional stars. Jewish girls also played basketball at settlements such as Chicago's Hull House, whose largely Jewish basketball side was one of its most successful teams. They played under rules adapted for women by Lithuanian immigrant Senda Berenson (sister of art historian Bernard Berenson), the director of physical education at Smith College (*EJS,* 77–78; Vincent 1991, 236).

Jewish young men frequently organized basketball clubs that met at local settlement houses. One of the most successful neighborhood teams was the Atlas Club of New Haven, formed by high school boys in 1906. Members felt it was their mission to demonstrate the athleticism and vigor of Jewish youths to the gentile world. They played on Friday nights in violation of the Sabbath so they could draw the largest crowds (Oren 1985, 78–80). Joseph Weiner, an Atlas alumnus who in 1914 was the first Jew on the Yale varsity, remembered that the team played in cities where there had never before been Jewish athletes: "We looked upon ourselves not simply as another team of players but also as a group of goodwill representatives on behalf of the Jewish community. We were shattering the stereotype of the *nebbich* [*sic*] Jew" (*EJS,* 97–98; Levine 1992, 26–51).

The success of Jews in basketball at settlement houses and high schools led to their being recruited to play for college teams at a time when prestigious institutions had quotas for Jewish students. Athletic skills made a Jewish applicant more palatable for schools such as Yale, which was among the most prejudiced. After a 1922 charity game attended by three thousand spectators (then the largest crowd in New Haven history) in which the Atlas Club beat the all-gentile Yale quintet, 42–22, an alumni committee investigated the college's basketball program and blamed anti-Semitic coaching as a major factor. Thereafter, Jews were recruited to play basketball, and in 1923 Yale went from the cellar to the championship. Nonetheless, a study eight years later by Heywood Broun and George Britt found that at Yale, Harvard, and Princeton, "discrimination is somewhat subtle and under cover . . . yet real and punishing" (Oren 1985, 80).

Urban basketball maintained a strong Jewish flavor in the 1920s and 1930s. Eastern high school competition was dominated by teams with predominantly Jewish rosters. During the 1930s, fraternal groups such as B'nai B'rith organized basketball leagues, as well as men and women's bowling and softball leagues. B'nai B'rith basketball teams had national competitions and played non-Jewish fives. In Chicago, for instance, one of the biggest annual games was the B'nai B'rith All-Stars against the CYO (Catholic Youth Organization) All-Stars. Chicago-area championship games of ethnic organizations drew more than ten thousand spectators (Vincent 1991, 246–47).

From the 1930s and 1940s when New York City basketball was at its zenith, and Madison Square Garden was the mecca of college basketball with its intersectional doubleheaders, through the 1950s, Jews dominated the local intercollegiate scene, and were major players at the national level. CCNY had the highest proportion of Jews on its roster, usually about 80 percent, reaching 90 percent during the depression. Eight CCNY Jewish players made all-American. Under long-term coach Nat Holman, CCNY was a national power, and in 1950 became the only school to win both the NIT and NCAA championships in the same season. Jews were nearly as prominent on the rosters of New York's private and Catholic universities. NYU had eight all-Americans and Long Island University and St. John's University had seven. From 1929, when the first all-American poll was taken, through 1964, there was at least one Jewish all-American except for 1935, 1951, and 1952. But by the mid-1960s, their presence became less visible, and they were completely supplanted by African Americans (EJS, 81, 90, 103, 105, 126, 127; Vincent 1991, 266–70).

The public identification of basketball as a heavily "Jewish" sport was negatively reinforced by the basketball scandal of 1951. Jews had been very much involved in basketball gambling since the 1930s when point spreads became popular. In the 1940s Leo Hirschfield, who had reputedly invented the "point spread," established the betting lines for college games. Rumors of bribed college players dated to at least 1931 when Max Posnack of St. John's Wonder Five was reputedly offered $3,000 to fix a game. Another source of corruption were the Catskill hotel summer leagues established in the early 1920s. Hundreds of college players worked in the resorts over the summer and played basketball to entertain the guests. Many were later presumed to have taken bribes from gamblers who bet on the total points scored. The first confirmed case of fixing games came at the start of the 1944–45 season when a

CCNY player was secretly removed from the squad for offering a teammate a bribe, and then in January 1945 five Brooklyn College players admitted receiving bribes to fix a game with the University of Akron. In the 1951 betting scandal, many of the gamblers involved were Jewish as were eight of the fifteen New York City collegians convicted of taking bribes. New York City intercollegiate basketball was badly hurt when Madison Square Garden discontinued its college basketball doubleheaders and local schools such as CCNY de-emphasized the sport. Peter Levine argues that the scandal was not overly identified as a Jewish failing because of its national dimensions. However, the widespread presumption was that the corruption *was* a "New York" phenomenon involving several Jewish gamblers and players, particularly collegians from CCNY, a "Jewish" college. Only after the scandal hit the University of Kentucky was the bribery problem considered a national dilemma (Rosen 1978; Cohen 1978; Figone 1989, 44–61; Levine 1992, 85).[11]

Successful amateur Jewish basketball players frequently moved on to professional basketball. In the early days of professional basketball, many of the first players were settlement alumni. Two of the best were Barney Sedran, a future CCNY star, and Max Friedman, who played on the "busy Izzies" of the University Settlement House that won the Metropolitan Amateur Athletic Union championship. Despite their short stature, they played professionally for fifteen and seventeen years respectively on independent clubs and on teams in long-forgotten leagues. Sedran eventually made as much as $12,000 in one season, making him the highest paid player of an era when most made just $15 to $75 a game. Most early pros were semiprofessionals who used basketball to supplement their primary livelihood. In 1921 Sedran, Friedman, and Nat Holman, another local Jewish star, played together on the New York Whirlwinds, a weekend team organized by sports promoter Tex Rickard, who was trying to bring pro basketball to Madison Square Garden (*EJS,* 77–83, 92; Vincent 1991, 246–47; Peterson 1990, 70–72).

11. In 1961 another major betting scandal erupted that was orchestrated by lawyer Jack Molinas, a former Columbia basketball star, who had shaved points while in college and got away with it. Molinas was kicked out of the NBA in his rookie season in 1954 for gambling on his team, the Fort Wayne Pistons. He was later murdered in a gangland killing (Wolf 1972, 80–84, 97–100, 103).

Early in 1922 Holman joined the (New York) Original Celtics, a predominantly Irish barnstorming team that was the premier professional team of its day. The Celtics went 193-11-1 in the 1922–23 season, emphasizing constant movement, short passes, high-percentage shots, and aggressive man-to-man defense. A second Jew, Davey Banks, joined the club in 1925. The Celtics entered the American Basketball League in 1926–27, an eastern association that, according to Levine, was about 20 percent Jewish. The Original Celtics won ABL championships in 1926–27 and 1927–28, but then were broken up when the owner went to prison for embezzlement. Banks and Holman, who was making nearly $10,000, then joined the New York Hakoahs, considered the "Jewish" team in the ABL (Peterson 1990, 69–94; Levine 1992, 56–62, 85–86). The club was named for the Viennese Jewish sports club whose soccer team won the European championship in 1926 and then toured the United States. A New York exhibition game drew forty-six thousand fans, a national soccer record that stood for decades (Horowitz 1977, 375–82; *Jewish Daily Forward* 1928, May 5). Chicagoans were so energized by the tour that a Jewish Junior Soccer League was formed (*Sunday Jewish Courier* 1927). Holman made many important contributions to the sport, including authoring *Scientific Basketball* (1922) and coaching the CCNY basketball team for thirty-eight years (Levine 1992, 56–59).

The early Jewish professionals encountered considerable discrimination. John "Honey" Russell, an outstanding pro of the 1920s, recounted in his autobiography that Sedran and Friedman would find coffins and hangmen's nooses painted on gym floors to mark their spots. "In one hall the team was greeted with signs around the balconies saying, 'Kill the Christ-Killers.'" Furthermore, in their travels, teams played at sites where "the Jew-baiters got there early— they'd have stones inside the snowballs and it was hell getting inside the hall, much less playing the game" (Peterson 1990, 119). In 1938, when author Paul Gallico in *Farewell to Sport* recognized the Jewish success in basketball, a game "they flock to . . . by the thousands" and could play as roughly as any other group, he concluded his left-handed praise by explaining: "The reason . . . that it appeals to the Hebrew with his Oriental background, is that the game places a premium on an alert, scheming mind and flashy trickiness, artful dodging and general smartaleckness" (325).

The Original Celtics had only two major rivals, the Harlem Renaissance Five, a pioneering African American quintet, and the SPHAs (South Philadelphia Hebrew All-Stars). The SPHAs date to the Combine Club, a group of elementary school boys organized in 1910 who later played at the South Philadelphia High School. The club won several settlement house and Jewish junior league championships, and then in 1917 reorganized under the leadership of Eddie Gottlieb, sponsored by the South Philadelphia Hebrew Association. The team, now known as the SPHAs, played professionally as an independent club and in the early 1920s won three championships in the minor Philadelphia League. They vividly proclaimed their ethnicity by wearing a Star of David on their uniforms, and adorned their jerseys with the Hebrew letters *samech, pey, hey,* and *aleph.* The SPHAs added their first gentile players for the 1925–26 season. Then known as the Philadelphia Hebrews, they defeated the Original Celtics in a two-out-of-three series and won a two-game series with the Harlem Rens. Gottlieb's team, renamed the Philadelphia Warriors, joined the ABL in 1929, and after its demise in 1931, joined the less prestigious Eastern League. In 1933 Gottlieb's all-Jewish club, again known as the SPHAs, joined a revived ABL, and won six championships in thirteen seasons.

The SPHAs was a prominent South Philadelphia institution that instilled ethnic pride and gained respect from other ethnic groups. Local young men and women often attended games at the Broadwood Hotel as couples—tickets cost sixty-five cents for men and thirty-five cents for women—and then stayed for the postgame dance. In 1946 when the Basketball Association of America was organized (the BAA was the forerunner of the NBA), Gottlieb's club, renamed the Warriors, joined the new league with three Jewish players, and won its first championship (Levine 1992, 59, 61, 62–65, 298 n.42; Peterson 1990, 119–23, 197–99).

As Levine has pointed out, the ABL was a very Jewish league with two "Jewish" teams, the SPHAs and the Brooklyn Jewels. One-half of its players in 1937–38 were Jewish, and in 1945–46, the ABL's last season as a prominent organization, the league was still nearly 45 percent Jewish. Thereafter, the Jewish prominence in pro basketball declined sharply, although in 1948 Max Zaslofsky won the BAA scoring championship. The best Jewish player in the NBA was Adolph Schayes, a 6'8" alumnus of NYU who played from 1949 to 1964. He was an all-star for twelve straight years and established records for most points (19,249), free throws, field goals, rebound, games played (1,059), and consecutive games (764) (Simons 1985, 287–307). From 1949 when the NBA was founded until 1965, there were about forty-two Jewish players. But thereafter, they have been few and far between. This decline reflected the migration of Jewish families out of inner cities, the locus of great playground competition necessary to develop the skill required for the NBA. The drop also reflected the relatively short stature of Jewish males, and the enormous competition for basketball jobs. Even when Jews dominated the eastern ABL, they were less visible in the midwestern National Basketball League (1937–49), which reflected their smaller midwestern presence. Furthermore, postwar Jews had many alternative routes to success, unlike inner city African Americans, who now dominate the NBA and see the sport as one of their few viable vehicles for social mobility.[12]

The Jewish prominence in basketball extended beyond the court to include referees (Mendy Rudolph, Norm Drucker), coaches (Red Auerbach, Red Holzman, Larry Brown), and especially management. Jews have had far more success in the business of professional basketball than any other team sport. Frank Basloe, who began in the basketball business in 1903 at age sixteen when he organized a team in Herkimer, New York, was one of the pioneer basketball promoters. Eleven years later Basloe's Globetrotters was the first team to make a national tour. In 1926 Chicagoan Abe Saperstein organized the Harlem Globetrotters, a traveling team of outstand-

---

12. The ABL continued as a minor league until 1953. By 1951 it was only 9 percent Jewish (Levine 1992, 66, 70, 71).

Not much is known about the subsequent careers of early professional basketball players. However, Jewish basketball players of the interwar period probably achieved considerable social mobility, because basketball scholarships provided poor youth with the opportunity to go to college. College athletes usually graduated, unlike today when most Division I basketball players do not. In 1988 the graduation rate for Division I players was 27 percent (Lapchick Interview 1989).

A sample of forty-four early professional basketball players (pre-1940) who were mainly Jewish, German, or Irish found that the great preponderance (74.4 percent) of men who played professionally had attended college (five times the national rate), and nearly all (95.1 percent) ended up in white-collar occupations (Riess 1990, 92–93).

ing African Americans, which eventually became a multimillion-dollar business. When the BAA was organized in 1946, its president was Maurice Podoloff, and he subsequently served as the first NBA commissioner (1949–63). Early NBA owners included Ben Kerner (St. Louis Hawks), Max Winter (Minneapolis Lakers), Eddie Gottlieb (Philadelphia Warriors), and Walter Harrison (Rochester Royals). The tradition of Jewish leadership in the NBA has been maintained into the 1990s with league president David Stern and such owners as Larry Weinberg (Portland Trail Blazers) and Jerry Reinsdorf (Chicago Bulls). Overall, four-fifths of NBA teams in operation in 1994 had Jewish owners at one time or another (*EJS*, 80, 118, 124; Quirk and Fort 1992, 446–59).

Donald M. Fisher's essay "Lester Harrison and the Rochester Royals, 1945–57: A Jewish Entrepreneur in the NBA" analyzes the career of Lester Harrison, a former professional basketball player, who became a sports entrepreneur in his hometown of Rochester. Harrison organized an independent touring team in the early 1940s that joined the midwestern National Basketball League in 1945. Three years later his club entered the BAA, which had by far the biggest cities and the largest arenas. Fisher examines the business problems Harrison encountered and how he tried to profitably resolve them. These dilemmas included his need to recruit star players with box office appeal, the competition from rivals who were virtually all in larger markets, and the competition from other entertainments, particularly TV. Harrison ultimately had to move to the larger Cincinnati market after the 1957 season (Fisher 1993, 20–48).

Besides boxing and basketball, the third major inner city sport in which Jews excelled was track, a sport that did not require much space for training, sophisticated equipment, or highly technical coaching. Jewish youths at the turn of the century participated in running contests at settlement houses, YMHAs, and public schools. Particularly important was New York's Public Schools' Athletic League, established in 1903, which became a model for youth sports programs throughout the United States. The PSAL promoted fitness for all city youths to improve their health and character. It encompassed both interscholastic competition and "sports for all" through class athletics and athletic badge tests. The Yiddish press supported the PSAL for giving Jewish lads a chance to improve their health and gain the respect of the broader community. From 1910 to 1919 Manhattan championships were dominated by students from Lower East Side elementary schools (Riess 1989, 109, 160–64; Jable 1984, 219–38).

Youngsters who competed in track had important role models, most notably Myer Prinstein, a Russian American Jew, who set the world record in the long jump in 1900. He won four gold medals and one silver medal in the long jump and triple jump in the 1900, 1904, and 1906 Olympic Games, and would have probably won another gold medal in 1900, but Syracuse University forbade its star from competing on the gentile Sabbath at the Paris Olympics. Yet despite Prinstein's brilliant achievements, he and other Jewish track stars were barred from the most prestigious athletic clubs. Prinstein and other world-class Jewish athletes, such Abel Kiviat, 1500-meter world record holder and silver medalist at the 1912 Stockholm Olympics, and Alvah Meyer, who came in second in the 100-meter event at the same games, competed for lower-status athletic clubs, such as the Irish American A.C. (*EJS*, 469–70, 474, 480–82; Frank 1908, 477; "The Jewish Athlete" 1908a, 544; 1908b, 171). The dearth of track clubs for Jewish athletes was the subject of an address by YMHA superintendent Mitchell at a meeting in recognition of the formation of the Atlas (track) Club in 1907. He pointed out the need for such clubs because of "the many Jewish athletes who at present are barred from other clubs, partly on account of their religion and partly because they find themselves in an environment which is not congenial" (*Y Bulletin* 1907).

Jewish athletes also achieved considerable proficiency in long-distance running. Historian Pamela Cooper examines the Jewish participation in long-distance running in her essay "Jews and the Making of American Marathoning, 1896–1960." Cooper argues that the dominant American marathon culture was originally ethnic, working class, and New York based. The marathon was at first a low-status event. The top runners were mainly from blue-collar ethnic backgrounds that precluded membership in high-status athletic clubs. Today long-distance running is a very reputable activity, indulged in by upper-middle-class professionals and business people to improve their health and self-awareness, and to gain status (Cooper 1992, 244–56; Rader 1991, 255–67; Roberts and Olson 1989, 220–34).

During the first third of the century, American Jews on the international sporting scene mainly excelled in boxing or track.

Five of the first eight gold medals won by Jewish Americans between 1900 and 1928 were in track and the other three were in boxing, which, unlike track, offered the added attraction of a professional career. American Jews competing in the first eleven summer Olympics (1896–1936), won twenty-six medals compared with ninety-seven for European Jews. Unlike the early American Jewish Olympians, who were predominantly second generation and of working-class backgrounds, European Jewish medalists, primarily fencers and gymnasts, were well assimilated middle- and upper-middle-class citizens of western and central European countries. In 1896, for example, Germany's Flatow brothers won five gold medals in gymnastics at the first modern Olympics. Then in the 1908 and 1912 games, Jews from Hungary, Belgium, and France won seventeen gold medals in fencing.[13]

From the perspective of American Jews the most important Olympics were the 1936 Berlin games and the 1972 Munich games. The 1972 games were highlighted by Mark Spitz's seven gold medals in swimming and the Palestinian terrorist attack on the Israeli athletes. Before the 1936 games, a broad-based movement had developed in the United States and several other countries to boycott the event unless the discriminatory German government's actions against Jews, other minorities, and political dissenters were redressed. The American protest was led by Jewish, Catholic, and labor organizations, the AAU, and such magazines and newspapers as the *Christian Century* and the *New York Times.* A Gallup Poll reported that 43 percent of the American people supported the proposed ban. However, the boycott movement was defeated by Avery Brundage (Gottlieb 1972, 181–213; Kruger 1978, 42–57; Guttmann 1984, 68–73; Marvin 1982, 81–106; Eisen 1984, 56–77; Wenn 1989, 27–43; Mandell 1971, 68–82; Levine 1992, chap. 11).

Brundage chastised American Jews for trying to use the Olympics as a weapon in the boycott against Germany and its products.

13. American Jews won gold medals in 1900, 1904, 1906, 1920, and 1924 (*EJS,* 391–92). Irving Jaffee of the Bronx won two gold medals in speed skating in 1932. On his problems with anti-Semitism, see *EJS,* 338–40. The first (half)–Jew to win a winter medal was Fritzie Burger of Austria, silver medalist in figure skating in 1928 and 1932. The father of figure skating in North America was Canadian Louis Rubenstein, a Polish Jew, who won the world championship in 1890 before the Olympic movement (*EJS,* 341–42; Rosenberg, Morrow, and Young 1982; Morrow and Keyes 1989, 23–31).

He wrote A. D. Lasker, a member of the American Jewish Committee, suggesting a donation of more than $50,000 from Jewish sources to the AOC to make up for the adverse publicity from certain "misguided Jews" who were against the Olympics, which had led to "great and growing resentment in athletic circles . . . against the Jews" (Brundage to Lasker Mar. 3, 1936, AB, box 234; Lasker to Brundage Apr. 14, 1936, AB, box 234). Evidence from the Brundage Papers strongly suggests he was anti-Semitic, and at the very least, highly receptive to the correspondence of overt anti-Semites (AB, box 153). For instance, Brundage wrote early in 1936,

> So far as our campaign . . . is concerned, rest assured that we are not depending on any Jews or Communists. As a matter of fact, a letter is being sent this week to all members of the AOC and its subcommittees calling upon them to reaffirm their loyalty. We intend to clean house. If the traitors, the lukewarm and the indifferent do not resign, they will be thrown out. (Brundage to Edward James Smythe Jan. 6, 1936, AB, box 153)

Several Jewish athletes from around the world boycotted the games, although one American Jew participated in the winter games at Garmisch-Partenkirchen, and six at the summer games in Berlin, including a participant in the baseball exhibitions (Jacobson 1990, 71–72). Only two Jews were on the track squad, collegians Marty Glickman and Sam Stoller, who were scheduled to run in the 400-meter relay. Glickman naively believed in living with bigotry and anti-Semitism: "I qualified my desire . . . to be on the Olympic team in Nazi Germany by rationalizing that if a Jew could make the Olympic team and run in Germany and win, then he would help disprove this myth of Nazi Aryan supremacy" (Glickman interview; Levine 1989, 399–424).[14]

14. For a full discussion of Glickman's views, see also his autobiography (1996).

The Weiner Library collection of more than two thousand memoirs was established in 1969 under the auspices of the American Jewish Committee to record aspects of modern Jewish American history. Among the dozens of sports figures for whom interviews have been completed, mainly by journalist Elli Wohlgelernter, are Marv Albert, Ray Arcel, Howard Cosell, and Hank Greenberg. The interviews range in length from about thirty pages for Greenberg to nearly four hundred pages for Glickman. A few years ago the materials were transferred to the Jewish Division of the New York Public Library, where they are available for examination by appointment.

Both runners had seemingly been guaranteed places on the relay team by qualifying as one of seven finalists at the U.S. tryouts. However, one day before the preliminary qualifying races they were dropped from the squad. Head track coach Lawson Robertson reported that the Germans were holding back their best sprinters from the 100-meter to concentrate on the relay, and consequently added Ralph Metcalfe and Jesse Owens to assure victory. Glickman believed that victory was certain regardless of which Americans competed, and blamed anti-Semitism and the influence of Brundage, a friend of assistant track coach Dean Cromwell. Although anti-Semitism was certainly involved, the added runners were African Americans and not WASPS. Furthermore, Cromwell was the USC head coach, and certainly wanted his old college runners, Foy Draper and Fred Wykoff, who had bested Glickman and Stoller at the Olympic trials, to participate in the race (Levine 1992, 224–29; Glickman interview; Glickman 1996, 8–35).

While the Olympics were being celebrated in Berlin, a left-wing counterfestival was held in Barcelona. An American team was sponsored by the Committee on Fair Play, a left-wing ad hoc group that had been formed to fight for the Olympic boycott. Alternate games were also organized for New York under the lead of Charles Ornstein of the 92d Street Y and the Jewish Welfare Board. Ornstein was a former AAU vice president who had been recently dropped from the AOC board of directors. The Alternate Games were staged at New York's Randall's Island by anti-Brundage athletic leaders in cooperation with the Jewish Labor Committee. The event received considerable attention in the left-wing papers and the Jewish press, particularly the *Forward*, but limited coverage from the mainstream press. The Alternate Games got little significant support from abroad, and the attendance of twenty-five thousand spectators at the two-day affair was well below expectations. Historian Edward Shapiro has argued that the Labor Athletic Carnival was an important part of the American anti-Nazi campaign, but was less successful at encouraging the growth of an American workers' sport movement ("Alternate Games Files"; *NYT* 1936, Aug. 5, Aug. 17; Sachar 1992, 470; Shapiro 1985, 255–73). A second Labor Athletic Carnival was staged in 1937 with the support of unions such as the ILGWU and the Amalgamated Clothing Workers, and was attended by Gov. Herbert Lehman. The meet highlight was Elroy Robinson's

1:49.3 in the 800-meters, a new world's record ("Alternate Games Files"; *NYT* 1937, July 10, July 11).

The workers' sport movement was never very strong in America, especially compared with Europe, because assimilated working-class Americans in the 1920s had many opportunities to participate in mainline sports (Wheeler 1978, 191–210; Steinberg 1978, 233–51). A left-wing Jewish sporting culture was established in that decade by the Workman's Circle as part of their social service program. The circle's primary focus was on helping immigrant workers adjust to America, but in 1926, the executive secretary, P. Geliebter, recommended that the circle extend its programs to attract the interest of the American-born children of radicals, which meant giving due attention to competitive sport (Shapiro 1970, 26–46, 86–88; Hurwitz 1936, 218–19, 224, 226). As Peter Levine points out (1992, 22–24), the Young Circle League made sports an important part of its social program. However, it never had more than four-thousand members (of whom only about 42 percent paid dues), and they were more interested in sports than in socialism.[15]

The Randall's Island Games did encourage the workers' sports movement that was particularly strong among left-wing Jewish needle-trades unionists. A Labor Athletic Council of Greater New York was established to stimulate regular training. Mark Starr, educational director of the International Ladies Garment Workers Union, argued that "labor ought to encompass the whole life of the workers, give them an outlet for their love of sport and entertain and drama instead of leaving such things to the bosses" (Starr 1937, 2; *Sport Call* 1937, Oct. 26, Nov. 27; 1938, Mar. 19, Apr. 23, May 28).

The ILGWU and the Amalgamated Clothing Workers Union pioneered in the development of educational, social, and athletic programs for their members, including summer camps in the

---

15. The Communist Party's Labor Sports Union, organized in 1927, mainly attracted members from foreign workers' clubs who preferred European sports such as soccer. To appeal to the American-born, the *Young Worker* from 1928 to 1935 gave more attention to American sports than any cultural activity. Beginning in 1936, one-eighth of the *Daily Worker* consisted of a sports page. At first, coverage was very ideological, but by 1933 historian Mark Naison argues, its reportage was very much like, albeit more critical than, the bourgeois daily press (Naison 1985, 130–32, 135–36, 138).

Catskills. Y leaders were also important participants in the Jewish Labor Committee that helped organize the Alternate Olympics. The ILGWU in the mid-1930s sponsored various sports competitions among its members, including soccer, basketball, baseball, volleyball, and swimming, including women's events. The weekend evening basketball games were often followed by a dance (*Justice* 1934, July 1; 1935, Jan. 2, Jan. 15, Feb. 1, May 1, June 15, July 15).[16]

Jews in Baseball and Football

The participation of second-generation Russian Jews in sports that did not fit in well with the inner city environment was more limited than in boxing, basketball, or track. They were unlikely to achieve renown in football or baseball, not to mention golf or tennis, unless their families had moved to better neighborhoods in less densely populated localities or in communities where Jews were highly assimilated.

Football fit in poorly with the social conditions of poor second-generation eastern European Jewish youth at the turn of the century. Parents were frightened by this rough and violent sport and it required considerable space and costly equipment. Football was primarily played by high school and college students, but impoverished inner city youths were already working by then. However, by the early 1920s, when Jews moved out of the slums (to the Bronx, for example), and as growing numbers of second-generation youths attended high school, significant numbers of Jewish boys appeared on high school football teams. Historian Paula Fass found (1989, 240–41) that in the 1930s and 1940s, 37.8 percent of a selected sample of New York City high school students playing football were Jewish, which was significantly less than their representation (44.9 percent) in the entire cohort. The star player in New York in the mid-1930s was quarterback Sid Luckman of Erasmus Hall, who went on to become all-American at Columbia

16. A fund of at least $75,000 was amassed by the ILGWU to promote cultural development (*Detroit Jewish Chronicle* 1936, July 19; BV scrapbooks), while the AAU announced that the ILGWU had amassed a $150,000 fund (*NYHT* 1937, June 30; BV scrapbooks).

(Glickman 1996, 39–43). Jews did somewhat better in track (41.3 percent), and far better in basketball (51.5 percent). The proportion of Jews in other sports was 45.3 percent. Among a similar sample of female students (44.8 percent of whom were Jewish), only one-third (33.7 percent) of the basketball players were Jewish, but nearly half in all other sports were Jewish.

Jewish participants in college athletics, especially football, the most important college sport, generated community pride, demonstrated they were not too scholarly or unfit, and provided them with an opportunity to gain greater acceptance in the broader society. Periodicals such as *American Hebrew* looked to sports to remove prejudice at college campuses. Sport was probably among the least discriminatory of collegiate extracurricular activities.[17]

Despite the hurdles Jewish football players had to surmount, they were far more common and widespread in the interwar period than generally recognized. In 1929, for instance, more than five hundred Jews played college football. Jewish names appeared on the rosters of all colleges, including Protestant and Catholic schools. Notre Dame, for example, had a half-Jewish all-American in Marchmont Schwartz. There were only a few eastern European football players in the early 1900s, most notably Sig Harris, son of a Polish immigrant, who grew up in Minneapolis, and was an all-American quarterback at the University of Minnesota in 1903 and 1904. During the 1920s many second-generation eastern European football players achieved considerable recognition, including the Horween brothers. After naval ser-

17. Daniel Oren (1985, 36) has argued that the first Jewish athletes at the most selective colleges, such as Yale, were most visible in individualistic sports, citing as his evidence the case of Robert Moses, the future urban builder who swam for Yale in the early 1900s, and that Yale's boxing and wrestling coaches then were "Mosey" King and "Izzy" Winters. However, athletes in these minor sports had minimal visibility, and Jews were not found in such individual sports as golf or tennis. Besides, already renowned Jewish football players were already at Harvard and Princeton in the nineteenth century. On college football in the interwar period, see Levine 1992, 190–215, esp. 200, 205. In 1936 journalist Stanley Frank authored *The Jew in Sport* to promote ethnic pride in Jewish athletic accomplishments. By then many Jewish community weekly newspapers carried substantial coverage of Jewish sports. Among the journalists who covered this beat was a young Irv Kupcinet, who had starred at football at North Dakota State, and then briefly played in the NFL. He has been a fixture in the Chicago media, with sixty years at the *Chicago Sun-Times,* along with many years as a popular TV talk show host and radio color man for the Chicago Bears.

vice in World War I, Ralph and Arnold Horween were respectively honorable mention and first team all-American fullbacks for Harvard. Arnold led Harvard to consecutive undefeated seasons (1919–20) and a Rose Bowl victory, and served as the Crimson's first Jewish captain. The brothers played professionally in the early 1920s for their hometown Chicago Cardinals under the surname McMahon, and then Arnold returned to Cambridge as football coach from 1926 to 1930 (*EJS*, 208–10, 231–33, 245–48; Levine 1992, 203). However, the preeminent Jewish football player in the 1920s was Benny Friedman, son of a Russian immigrant tailor, who was an all-American quarterback at Michigan in 1925 and 1926, and became a great star in the NFL. In 1928 Tim Mara of the New York Giants bought the Detroit Wolverines team just to get Friedman, who he thought would be a big draw in New York (EJS, 244–48; Simons 1995, 65–81; Quirk and Fort 1992, 35).

In the 1930s, when Jews were becoming fairly visible in major league baseball, they were more successful in professional football. Tough Jewish alumni from colleges across the country, including USC, Minnesota, Tulsa, Georgetown, Baylor, Texas Christian, and Alabama, played in the NFL. In 1939, for example, two of the NFL's most heralded rookies were halfback Marshall Goldberg of the Chicago Cardinals and quarterback Sid Luckman of the Chicago Bears. Luckman came from Brooklyn, but Goldberg was from Elkins, West Virginia, hardly a major center of Jewish American life. A recent tabulation of Jewish pro football players by encyclopedist Jesse Silver identified 151 Jews who played in the NFL before 1993. More than 73 percent of them (111) played before 1950, including 25 in 1936 alone (*EJS*, 207–90; Wallman 1993, 16).[18]

18. Samuel Jacobson organized a football team in the late 1880s called the Syracuse Athletic Association, and played for them in 1890. The squad was not paid salaries, but the SAA's share of gate proceeds was turned over to them. This predates the first recognized professional football player, Pudge Heffelfinger, who in 1892 was paid $500 to play for the Allegheny A.A. against the Pittsburgh A.C. (*EJS*, 211).

It would be interesting to examine the geographic origins of Jewish football players. The first professional football players mainly came from the Midwest and Pennsylvania. Such cities as Chicago, Pittsburgh, and Cleveland were historically very good producers of NFL players. New York, on the other hand, was always underrepresented (merely 13 percent of its proportionate share of pro football players in 1960), which hindered Jewish participation. It is likely that Jewish players were likewise from outside metropolitan New York (Riess 1991, 227).

Despite the Jewish American fascination with the national pastime (Solomon 1994, 75–102; 1984, 43–46; Levine 1992, 87–143), they were consistently underrepresented on major league rosters.[19] Baseball, like football, was not a viable inner city participatory sport because of the lack of space, inadequate opportunities to develop expertise, and parental opposition. In 1903 an immigrant father wrote to the *Forward* about his opposition to baseball.

> It makes sense to teach a child to play dominoes or chess. But what is the point of a crazy game like baseball? The children can get crippled. When I was a boy we played rabbit, chasing each other, hide and seek. Later we stopped. If a grown boy played rabbit in Russia they would think he had lost his mind. Here in educated America adults play baseball. They run after a leather ball like children. I want my boy to grow up to be a *mensch*, not a wild American runner.

Baseball to him, and many immigrants like him, lacked *takhlis,* or purpose. The *Forward*'s editor, Abraham Cahan, agreed that this was a common problem for parents, but recommended "let your boys play baseball and play it well, as long as it does not interfere with their education or get them into bad company. . . . Let us not so raise the children that they should grow up foreigners in their own birthplace" (Howe and Libo 1979, 51–52). Four years later the *Forward* printed an article entitled "Der iker fun di base-ball game, erklert far nit keyn sports layt" (The fundamentals of baseball explained to those unfamiliar with sports) accompanied by a diagram of the Polo Grounds (Manners 1972, 278; Barth 1980, 150f.).

Settlement house workers, teachers, and other youth workers encouraged Jewish boys to participate in baseball, which they believed was one of the best means of acculturation. Inner city boys

---

19. Solomon (1994, 77–78) asserts that Jews "could find America *in* baseball yet hold on to . . . a Jewish identity *through* baseball." He argues that Jews loved baseball because (a) it provided a great means for acculturation and assimilation; (b) its historical and statistical orientation appealed to "the argumentative dialectical Jewish intellect . . . trained in Hebrew school in the . . . close reading of religious texts"; (c) parents opposed playing, so they sought vicarious participation as fans, writers, artists; (d) the urbanization of the game; and (e) its folklore and mythology.

were enthusiastic baseball fans, who carefully followed the progress of their favorite players and teams in the daily press, but seldom attended games because of the expense of tickets and transportation. In the 1890s young Morris Raphael Cohen of Brownsville walked to the Brooklyn Dodgers field (Eastern Park) where he watched games through knotholes in the fence (Cohen 1949, 80–81). Years later the world-renowned philosopher considered baseball a moral equivalent of war (Cohen 1919, 57–58). Harry Golden, who grew up in the Lower East Side in the early 1900s, was one of the few boys in his crowd who regularly attended Giants ball games because he delivered pretzels to the Polo Grounds during the summer, and afterward ran errands for the ballplayers (Golden 1969, 54).

Besides rarely attending games, Jewish youths growing up in crowded neighborhoods in Manhattan, Boston, or Chicago rarely had access to baseball diamonds or large parks where they could gain proficiency as players. They were more likely to play street ball games such as punchball, stickball, or stoopball. Where free of adult supervision, they used rules based on oral tradition and the peculiarities of their playing field (Riess 1980, 25–26, 37). Comedian George Burns (1980, 9–10) remembered how his pals adapted baseball to their limited space on the Lower East Side.

> Our playground was the middle of Rivington Street. We only played games that needed very little equipment, games like kick-the-can, hopscotch, hide and go seek, follow the leader. When we played baseball we used a broom handle and a rubber ball. A manhole cover was homeplate, a fire hydrant was first base, second base was a lamp post, and Mr. Gitletz, who used to bring a kitchen chair down to sit and watch us play, was third base. One time I slid into Mr. Gitletz; he caught the ball and tagged me out.

Jews who lived outside of such neighborhoods as the Lower East Side or Chicago's Near West Side had far more opportunities to play ball. For example, when the family of Al Schacht, a future major leaguer, moved to the Bronx in the early 1900s, he could play ball in school yards, city streets, and empty lots that made "the Bronx much like a wilderness." However, Al could not afford tickets to see his favorite New York Giants play, so he would climb up Coogan's Bluff overlooking the field to watch free and bring two cents for a frankfurter (Marazzi 1986, 34–35).

Largely because of spatial and cultural factors, few Jewish ballplayers achieved sufficient proficiency in baseball to make the major leagues. David Spaner, in his definitive listing of ethnically Jewish ballplayers who played in the major leagues (1871–1996), identified 134 individuals, or about 1 percent of the number of ballplayers. He found only five Jewish big leaguers in the period 1900–1909, and thirteen between 1910 and 1919 (Levine 1992, 100; Riess 1980, 186, 189–90; Lynn 1987; Bjarkman 1990, 343; Spaner 1997, 181–82).[20]

Contemporary sportswriters were puzzled by the dearth of Jews in professional baseball when they were so visible in boxing. In 1903 Barry McCormick noted in the *St. Louis Republic*, "He [the Jew] is athletic enough and the great number of Jewish boxers show that he is adept at one kind of sport at least" (*Cincinnati Enquirer* 1903, Nov. 17). However, McCormick could identify only two Jewish major leaguers. A 1910 book of sports humor noted, "In looking over the list of names comprising the American and National Leagues we fail to discover any of those well worn Semitic cognomens, such as Moses, Abraham, Ikey, Solomon, Aaron, etc., or the tribe of numerous Skys. Something wrong. Is the work too arduous?" (Leitner 1972, 205).

The rare Jewish ballplayer who made the major leagues encountered much discrimination from teammates, owners, fans, and even the media. Even the revered Branch Rickey has been accused of anti-Semitism by Bob Berman, a Bronx native, who briefly played for the Washington Senators. Berman told an interviewer many years later that in 1918 while attending DeWitt Clinton High School, he was scouted by Rickey, then with the St. Louis Cardinals. Berman recounted that Rickey gave him a contract, but asked

20. Determining the Jewish ethnicity of ballplayers is an inexact science, especially for players whose names were not Jewish sounding, or had a gentile father and a Jewish mother. Although there are individual player files and extensive records on ethnicity at the National Baseball Library in Cooperstown (Allen files), the data are incomplete for the earlier players. Spaner emphasizes Jewish ethnicity rather than religion, and thus includes athletes who had a single Jewish parent.

for it back when he found out that the prospect was Jewish (Sanders 1985, 36–45). To protect themselves against anti-Semitism, talented Jewish ballplayers often altered their identity to hide their ethnicity. The first seven major leaguers whose surname was Cohen all played under pseudonyms, such as Bohne, Ewing, and Kane, to avoid harassment and anti-Semitism (Gerstein 1952, 21–22; *TSN* 1897, June 13).

The anti-Semitism in baseball was not limited to the baseball field, but reared its head in the sporting press as well. In 1908 *The Sporting News* thusly reported the public reaction in New York to Giants rookie Buck Herzog (a gentile player): "The long-nosed rooters are crazy whenever young Herzog does anything noteworthy. Cries of 'Herzog! Herzog! Goot poy Herzog! go up regularly, and there would be no let-up even if a million ham sandwiches suddenly fell among these believers in percentages and bargains" (White 1996, 250).

Between 1920 and 1960 there were only about seventy-six Jewish major leaguers, most of whom played after 1935 (Allen notebooks; Lane 1926, 341). They included fifteen in the 1920s, twenty-four in the 1930s, and peaked at twenty-six in the 1940s (computed from *Baseball Encyclopedia* 1969; Bjarkman 1990, 343; Spaner 1997, 179–80).[21] By this time Jewish youths had become well assimilated, were staying longer in school, and were moving out of the slums into less densely populated, more prosperous areas where there was more space to play baseball. Well-assimilated Jewish ballplayers were recruited from cities and towns throughout the country, even Hamburg, Arkansas. Just one-third came from New York City even though about one-half the Jewish population lived there. Jewish ballplayers such as Andy Cohen and Hank Greenberg were popular attractions for Jewish baseball fans, but were hardly children of the ghetto, Cohen having grown up in Waco, Texas, and Greenberg in the Bronx. Cohen's father, an immigrant cigar maker, was himself a good enough ballplayer to have had a tryout with the Baltimore Orioles. Peter Levine suggests that many successful Jewish athletes were sons of sports fans,

21. Bjarkman (1990, 343) found twenty-one Jews in the 1950s, twenty-two in the 1960s, fifteen in the 1970s, and ten in the 1980s. However, his cohort for the 1970s and 1980s include Rod Carew, who has a Jewish wife, but never converted.

which gave them a leg up compared with Jews whose parents discouraged their interest (Levine 1992, 91–92, 101).

The Dodgers and Giants, but not the Yankees, sought Jewish players to draw Jewish fans. In 1923 Moses Solomon, an outstanding all-around athlete who hit forty-two homers and batted .429 to lead the Southwestern League, was bought by the Giants. However, the "Rabbi of Swat" played only two late-season games, making three hits, and was sent back to the minors (Raphael 1979, 333). His short tenure may have been related to manager John McGraw's anti-Semitism. Three years later, in 1926, Andy Cohen was brought up to the Giants as "the Great Jewish Hope." After a brief stay he was sent to Buffalo of the International League where he was the all-star shortstop. Cohen started the 1928 season at the Polo Grounds, replacing superstar second baseman Rogers Hornsby, who had been traded to the Boston Braves because of his unpopularity with teammates and his gambling problems. Cohen immediately became a big hero to the city's Jewish population. He attracted numerous Jewish fans, including many who had never been to a game. In the opening-day game against the Braves, attended by thirty-thousand spectators, many of whom were Jews, Cohen drove in three runs and scored two more in a 5–2 victory. After the final putout, he was carried off the field by his supporters (Alexander 1995, 141–45). Cohen performed capably, batting .274 (albeit 100 points less than Hornsby) and earned a 53 percent raise to $11,500, probably more than his statistics merited. He hit .294 the following season, but was dropped back to the minors. Some observers felt he was under too much pressure, carrying the aspirations of the Jewish people in major league baseball, though Cohen himself relished that challenge (Baseball files, AJA; Cohen interview; Levine 1992, 113–14; Edelstein 1983, 53–56).[22]

During the interwar years baseball dominated the summers of Jewish youths as it did all other young people. Baseball diamonds in the parks were in constant use from morning to night. By then Jewish fans could afford to attend games, especially in Brooklyn on Thursdays, which was Ladies' Day, when women got into Ebbets Field for just ten cents. May Abrams, wife of Dodgers outfielder

22. Jonah Goldman joined the Cleveland Indians in 1928 when he also "was the victim of considerable ballyhooing" (Sports Files, AJA).

Cal Abrams, remembered that in the late 1930s, when she was growing up in Brooklyn, "the radios. . . . In the summer . . . everybody had their windows open; you could hear the ball game coming out of every apartment. . . . You sat on the stoop and, whether you wanted to know about baseball or not, you had no choice" (Abrams interview, 113).

Roger Kahn captured his own youthful fascination with baseball in *The Boys of Summer,* which is as much about him growing up as about the Brooklyn Dodgers of the early 1950s. Much of Roger's bonding with his father came when they talked about baseball, played catch, and attended games at Ebbets Field. Like many New York boys who were baseball fans, Roger mainly played stickball, which did not need a lot of space. They used a rubber ball ("spaldeen"), and created unique ground rules depending on each street's spatial patterns. There was also a gender division between boys and girls playing in the city streets; boys played stickball and punchball, while girls played slapball (Kahn 1972, 37).

Jewish major leaguers were idolized by Jewish fans, who read about them in the mainstream and ethnic press, held special days honoring them, and invited them to synagogue groups. They were expected to refrain from participating on High Holy Days and speak out against overt anti-Semitism, which was probably a bigger problem for minor leaguers who played in less cosmopolitan communities. When Cal Abrams in the late 1940s played in the South, fans asked him if he was a Baptist Jew or a Methodist Jew.[23] Several major leaguers, notably Buddy Myers, Hank Greenberg, and Al Rosen, were considered "tough Jews" who beat up malicious anti-Semitic players. Jews were also very proud that their athletic heroes stood up for the underdog, as when Greenberg provided encouragement to rookie Jackie Robinson in 1947 (Levine 1992, 123, 126–29, 131; Greenberg 1989, 52–53, 82–84, 102–4, 106–7, 190–91; Torry 1995, 2, 5–6).

Hank Greenberg was the preeminent Jewish athlete in the first half century. Hank was a huge, powerful man at nearly 6'4", 215

23. For an insightful interview of a Jewish player's struggle in the minors in the 1940s and his time with the Dodgers in the early 1950s, see Wohlgelernter 1995, 109–22, which includes discussions of anti-Semitism, or the appearance of it. The published interview was drawn from the Abrams interview (AJC).

pounds, the precise opposite of the stereotyped effete Jew. He batted .313 during his career and had the fifth highest slugging average of all time. Hank hit 58 homers in 1938 (then second only to Babe Ruth's 60), set an American League record for RBIs with 183 in his MVP season in 1937, and led the Detroit Tigers to four pennants. Hank grew up in the Bronx to an observant middle-class family that owned a textile business. He preferred sports to school, so neighborhood women considered him a loafer and a bum. The only one of four siblings not to graduate from college, he remembered, "I was Mrs. Greenberg's disgrace" (Levine 1992, 133).

William Simons in "Hank Greenberg: The Jewish American Sports Hero" considers the symbolic importance of Hank's decision to play baseball during the High Holy Days in the 1934 pennant race. Greenberg went to synagogue the day before Rosh Hashanah, but played on the Jewish New Year, stroking two home runs to win the game 2–1. However, he went to synagogue on Yom Kippur, for which he was widely praised in the daily and Jewish presses (Greenberg 1989, 57–62; Levine 1992, 132–43). Greenberg also stood up against any anti-Semitism hurled in his direction and served longer in the military during World War II than any other major leaguer, having been drafted early in 1941. This all made Hank a leading role model for American Jews. Yet Greenberg was not an observant Jew, and his Jewish identification was apparently so tenuous that a son attending in prep school identified himself as Episcopalian even though his mother, a Gimbel, was also Jewish. Later in his life Greenberg did strongly identify with Jewish causes, and wanted to be remembered as a Jewish ballplayer. He became a successful baseball executive after retiring from the diamond, serving as the Cleveland Indians general manager in the early 1950s, and built their great 1954 team, which won 110 games.[24]

Although the presence of Jewish players on the field contested anti-Semitism and negative stereotyping, the apparent Jewish in-

24. Greenberg owned 20 percent of the stock in the Indians when he left the club. Rosen also fared very well after leaving the diamond, becoming a stockbroker and eventually president of the San Francisco Giants. I strongly suspect that former Jewish ballplayers did markedly better after retirement than their peers, because of their education, entrepreneurial tradition, and family support, which reflected the overall Jewish occupational success in the United States (Torry 1995, 23, 25, 29).

volvement in the 1919 World Series fix strengthened anti-Semitism. The public believed that Jews were prominent in baseball gambling, an idea crudely expressed in *The Sporting News* on October 9, 1919, which referred to rumors questioning the integrity of the series: "There are no lengths to which the crop of lean-faced and long-nosed gamblers of these degenerate days will go" (4). One week later, after sportswriter Hugh Fullerton's questioning of the play of certain Black Sox, *The Sporting News* (Oct. 16, 4) argued that rumors of foul play were undoubtedly false even though "a lot of dirty, long-nosed, thick-lipped, and strong smelling gamblers butted into the World Series."

One notable Jewish person who was directly involved in the fix was former featherweight champion Abe Attell, a known associate of Arnold Rothstein, the prominent New York gambler. Attell met with the ring leaders of the crooked White Sox players and then presented Rothstein with a plan to fix the series. Rothstein turned the proposal down, but Attell went ahead anyhow, negotiating with the players on his own, giving them the impression that Rothstein was backing him. In the meantime, Rothstein may well have financed a portion of the fix through Sport Sullivan, a Boston bookmaker. He reputedly won $350,000 betting on the series (Katcher 1958, 148). The Chicago grand jury in late 1920 indicted Attell, who was later found innocent, but Rothstein was never charged with a crime. The conventional wisdom that Rothstein had debauched baseball was reflected by the character Meyer Wolfsheim in F. Scott Fitzgerald's *The Great Gatsby* (1925).

Anti-Semites such as Henry Ford blamed underworld Jews for the Black Sox scandal, which helped fuel the growing anti-Semitism of the 1920s. The *Dearborn Independent* published two articles in September 1921, entitled "Jewish Gamblers Corrupt American Baseball" and "The Jewish Degradation of American Baseball." According to Ford, "If fans wish to know the trouble with American baseball, they have it in three words—too much Jew" (Nathan 1995, 97). Furthermore, "[T]he Jews are not sportsmen. . . . The Jew saw money where the sportsmen saw fun and skill. The Jews set out to capitalize rivalry and to commercialize contestant zeal. . . . If it [baseball] is to be saved, it must be taken out of their hands until they have shown themselves capable of promoting sports for sports sake" (Kruger 1978, 55). The scandal exemplified to bigots how Jews were insidiously destroying the inner fabric of American society by ruining the national pastime (not to mention motion pictures and Wall Street), and thereby subvert American institutions and undermine American morality (Nash 1970, 130–32; Levine 1992, 116–18; Nathan 1995, 94–100).

White Sox owner Charles Comiskey's efforts to cover up the fix were abetted by his Jewish associates, attorney Alfred Austrian and secretary Harry Grabiner, who kept a diary that recorded Comiskey's machinations (Veeck 1965, 252–99). Austrian arranged for Al Cicotte, "Shoeless" Joe Jackson, and Lefty Williams to confess to the grand jury in an effort to divorce Comiskey from the bad publicity, but then just before the trial arranged for the outgoing state's attorney, MacClay Hoyne, to divert the documents from his office before trial. If the players were found innocent, Comiskey hoped they would return to his club, but Commissioner Kenesaw M. Landis banned them from baseball despite the jury verdict. In 1924 Jackson sued for back pay, but the confessions were conveniently discovered by the White Sox, and Jackson lost his case (Gropman 1992, 218–23).[25]

American Jews and the Turf in the Twentieth Century

Since the turn of the century, high-status upper-class Jews and not-so-respectable Jews have played a significant role in turf sports. Jewish thoroughbred owners at the turn of the century were still exclusively German Jews, but by the 1920s newly rich eastern European Jews were entering the racing game. The most notable was Chicagoan John D. Hertz, a former newsboy and boxing manager, who established the Yellow Cab Company in 1915 and later the famous car rental agency. He began racing thoroughbreds in 1921, and seven years later Reigh Count won the Kentucky Derby. However, Hertz's greatest stallion was Count Fleet, who won the Triple Crown in 1943. His Sonter Creek Stud won 2,955 races and earned more than $9 million (Hertz and Shipman, 1954; *EJS,* 313–14). Motion picture mogul Louis B. Mayer was another important Russian Jewish owner. Mayer helped lead the rebirth of California racing in the 1930s. His horses won more than $2 million, and

---

25. On the baseball scandal, especially useful are Asinof 1963 and Seymour 1971, chaps. 14–15. On sports gambling, see Katcher 1958, 117–18, chap. 11; Haller 1979, 98–108; Kefauver 1951, chap. 3; and Devereux 1980, 469–78c.

horses he had bred another $8 million. Yet neither one was ever elected to the Jockey Club (*EJS*, 313–14, 331).

Turf historian Bernard Livingston argues (1973, 260–79) that the post–World War II "New Crowd" in racing was largely Jewish despite the continuing discrimination in the sport. These horsemen included Julie Fink, who brazenly sued the Jockey Club, challenging its power to license participants in the sport. More recently there have been noted Jewish owners such as entrepreneur Louis Wolfson, whose Harbor View Stable was the nation's leading money winner in 1963.

Wealthy Jews were also very active in establishing and managing racetracks. Jews were particularly active in metropolitan Chicago where lawyer Albert Sabath, nephew of the city's first Jewish congressman, used his legal expertise to help revive the local turf in the 1920s and served as president of Hawthorne Park. He also became a noted breeder and owner, best known for the $700 purchase of Alsab, who won the 1942 Preakness (*EJS*, 325). In 1929 Hertz helped keep Arlington Park out of the hands of the underworld by organizing a syndicate that included Leonard Florsheim to buy the track. As chairperson of its executive committee, Hertz promoted steeplechase races, raised purses, and reinvested profits back into the facility (*EJS*, 314). Benjamin Lindheimer, the politically well-connected realtor, was another major Chicago racing magnate. His syndicate bought Washington Park in 1935, and supported Mayor Edward Kelly's campaign that year to legalize bookmaking in Chicago. However, the proposal was courageously blocked by Illinois's Jewish governor, Henry Horner, at the risk of his political career. Lindheimer expanded his racetrack holdings by buying Arlington in 1940 and later Balmoral. He maintained Chicago as the center of midwestern racing and was honored in 1955 by the Jockey Guild as Horseman of the Year (Livingston 1973, 267–79; Biles 1984, 50; Littlewood 1969, 151–54; *Chicago Tribune* 1950, Oct. 6; Messick 1978, 20–21).[26]

26. Lindheimer's adopted daughter, Marje Everett, ran Arlington Race Track after Lindheimer's retirement. She was involved in the bribery of Gov. Otto Kerner, who was later impeached for this crime while serving on the federal bench. Everett moved to California where she operated racetracks. Despite her responsibility in the Kerner malfeasance, Marje received a license to operate in California because she had never been convicted of any crime (Messick 1978, 224–25).

Elsewhere, Jake Isaacson, a former boxing promoter and sports editor, established Omaha's Ak-Sar-Ben Race Track in 1935, and ran it for twenty-eight years. Herman and Ben Cohen took over Maryland's Pimlico Racetrack in 1952 and six years later added the Charles Town Racetrack. Immigrant Morris Shapiro, who made a fortune in scrap metal, operated Laurel Racetrack in the 1940s, and turned it over to his son in 1950. On the West Coast the Hollywood crowd was very active in track operations. Movie mogul Harry M. Warner was a major stockholder in Hollywood Park, and Oscar winner Mervyn LeRoy, son of the president of the old Emeryville Racetrack in Oakland, was president of Hollywood Park from 1952 into the 1960s. During the 1930s southern Florida became an important racing center with a significant Jewish presence. Investors in Tropical Park, and probably Gulfstream Park, included the notorious Meyer Lansky, who also controlled racing in Havana (*EJS,* 316, 318–20, 326–27; Riess 1989, 191–94). Jews were also very much involved in the less prestigious sport of harness racing. In 1940 lawyer George M. Levy founded Roosevelt Raceway on Long Island, the first successful night-trotting facility in the United States (Littleton 1957; Akers 1947, 347–54; *NYT* 1954, Mar. 15). Levy was described by *The Sporting News* as "the Jewish Brigham Young . . . who led the sport out of the wilderness into the Zion of milk and pari-mutuel honey" (*EJS,* 319).

The Jewish involvement in racing was not limited to the rich who raced horses and operated racetracks. Jews also made notable contributions as jockeys, trainers, and especially gamblers. Jacob Pincus of Charleston, the leading American jockey in the 1850s, was the first of several outstanding Jewish trainers. Pincus trained horses for August and Pierre Lorillard, including Iroquois, the first American-bred horse to win the Epsom Derby. In the twentieth century two of the most outstanding trainers were Max Hirsch (1880–1969), of Fredericksburg, Texas, who started out as a teenage jockey, and Hirsch Jacobs (1904–70) from New York City. Max Hirsch's horses won over $15 million in purses, including three Kentucky Derbies. His best horse was Triple Crown winner Assault (1946). Hirsch Jacobs had an unusual background for a trainer, because he did not get into the turf until he was twenty-two, using his winnings from pigeon racing. Hirsch won more than $11 million in purses and won more races than any other trainer. He established a family tradition, bringing two younger brothers and nephew Buddy Jacobson into the business. Jacobson was the nation's lead-ing trainer in 1963 and 1964, with 140 and 169 victories, respec-tively (*EJS*, 314–18; *BDAS, Outdoor Sports* under "Jacobs, Hirsch"; "Hirsch, Max").

Jews even achieved distinction as jockeys, although few occupa-tions would seem as inappropriate to the Jewish American experi-ence. The most outstanding were Jacob Pincus, Walter Miller, and Walter Blum, the national champion in 1963 and 1964. Miller learned to ride in 1904 when he was fourteen years old, and just two years later won 388 of 1,384 races (28 percent), setting a national record for victories, a mark unmatched until 1950. He again won 28 percent of his races in 1907 (334 victories) and also in 1909. However, Miller outgrew his sport, reaching 5'8½'' and 160 lbs. (*EJS*, 320–22).

Jews were also very prominent in horse race gambling as wager-ers and as bookmakers. We have little data on the gambling pro-clivities of Jews at the turn of the century, although Barney Dreyfuss once pointed out that racetracks do little business on Jewish holi-days (Sachar 1992, 169; Dreyfuss to August Herrmann, AH, n.d.). At this time, Lower East Siders probably could not afford to go out to the Coney Island racetracks, and probably relied on local bookies to take bets. These working-class bettors probably considered gam-bling a highly rational activity for themselves (that is, a stock market for the poor). In the interwar era, Jewish celebrities such as Al Jolson and boxer Barney Ross were well-known racing aficionados. Studies of gambling behavior after World War II found that middle-class Jews went to the races and bet more heavily than most other middle-class groups (Kallick 1976, 178–82).

Although the legal and illegal taking of bets in late-nineteenth-century America was dominated by Irish members of early crime syndicates, Jews also quickly moved into the business. Sol Lichtenstein, Abe Levy, and Kid Weller were the most famous of the early Jewish bookmakers (*Spirit of the Times* 136, Nov. 12, 1898; 139, June 9, 1900). In subsequent decades illegal off-track betting was an important venue for Jewish crime syndicates who at first relied upon their own fellow ethnics for clients. Herman Rosenthal and Arnold Rothstein were among the most prominent protégés of Big Tim Sullivan, the number two man in Tammany Hall, and leader in the syndicate that controlled illegal off-track poolroom betting. Rothstein, who had reputedly made $12 million by 1906, became a minor folk hero in the Jewish community. He was generally thought to have established the system of laying off bets, although crime historian Mark Haller is skeptical of that (Haller 1976, 98–99; Katcher 1959, 100–103; Sorin 1992, 85; Sachar 1992, 169). Rosenthal was murdered in 1912 after he publicly admitted the existence of a police-protected gambling ring. His slaying led to one of the most notable murder trials in American history, resulting in the conviction and execution of police lieutenant Charles Becker (Sachar 1992, 171).

Several future bootleggers started off in gambling, such as Max "Boo Hoo" Hoff and Sam Lazar, who originally ran a string of South Philadelphia gambling houses, and Clevelander Morris Kleinman, a bookmaker before joining the infamous Moe Dalitz gang. By the end of the 1920s Meyer Lansky had recognized the potential profits from unifying many of the fifteen-thousand bookmaking operations around the country through the use of the racing wire. He became the nation's leading gambling entrepreneur (Sachar 1992, 348; Haller 1976, 91–92, 129–30).

After Prohibition ended, bookmaking remained a major criminal activity among Jewish hoodlums. Historian Marc Raphael found that in Columbus, Ohio, even synagogue leaders might be involved in bookmaking (1979, 329). In New York after World War II, Harry Gross, the "Mr. Big" of Brooklyn bookies, was the focal point of a major political scandal during which he admitted to annually making million-dollar payoffs to the police. The exposé discredited mayor William O'Dwyer, who subsequently resigned (Moore 1974, 40, 137, 176, 198).

A key figure in the highly profitable off-track betting business was Moe Annenberg, who controlled the racing wire during the 1930s. Moe and his family moved from East Prussia to Chicago in 1885 when he was eight years old. He dropped out of school at the age of twelve, and worked as a newsboy and held other odd jobs. Brother Max, who worked in the *Chicago Tribune*'s circulation department, was recruited to work for Hearst's *Evening American,* and hired his younger sibling as a solicitor of subscriptions. By 1904 the brothers were the circulation managers of the city's two Hearst papers. Their jobs included intimidating newsstand operators to sell their papers and boycott the competition. During the late 1920s and early 1930s Annenberg established a communications empire by securing control of racing's two major dailies, the *Racing Form* and the *Morning Telegraph,* along with various tip and scratch sheets. In 1927 he bought Mont Tennes's share in the General News Bureau (popularly known as the racing wire), which provided race results to bookmakers across the country. Annenberg and his associates (whom he bought out by 1934) developed a national monopoly, driving out independent wires. The key moment reportedly occurred at the Atlantic City meeting of gangland bosses in May 1929, when Annenberg agreed to supply their outlets with racing information. Annenberg's Continental News Publishing Company charged steep prices and further increased profits by sending data in code decipherable only to those betting parlors buying his daily wall sheets, which listed current races (Cooney 1982, 27–39, 54–55, 63–71, 77–80; Sachar 1992, 348).

In Annenberg's hometown of Chicago, off-track gambling during the 1930s and 1940s was largely controlled by Jake Guzik. Under his supervision, the old Capone gang coordinated handbooks and monopolized the distribution of racing information in the metropolitan area. When Annenberg went to jail in 1940 for tax evasion, his protégé, James Ragen, took over the racing wire. Guzik and his colleagues failed to gain an interest in Continental and instead established the rival Trans-America News Publishing Company with associates such as Bugsy Siegel who helped coordinate local distribution of racing news. In 1946 Ragen was murdered, and shortly thereafter Guzik took over the service. This monopoly enabled the mob, through Siegel, to gain control of legal bookmaking in certain Las Vegas casinos (Haller 1976, 101–3; Kefauver 1951, chap. 3).

The Jewish Sporting Woman

Although much attention has been given to manliness and Jewish sport, little attention has been given to the notable achievements of female Jewish athletes and promoters (Eisen 1990, 103–20). Among the first American women, renowned for her physical fitness, was Adah Isaacs Menken, the paramour of boxing champion James C. Heenan. Although married several times, she was an independent woman who in the 1860s gained worldwide fame as an actress, dancer, and acrobat (Guttmann 1991, 97; Dizikes 1981, 227–34). Among the most prominent Jewish women athletes were L. T. Neuberger, who won seven U.S. table tennis titles from 1951 to 1961, Tillie Eisen, star of the All-American Girls' Baseball League (1944–52), who stole 128 bases in 1946, and discus thrower Lillian Copeland, silver and gold medalist at the 1928 and 1932 Olympics. Copeland was undefeated in intercollegiate competition at USC, earned nine national championships in javelin, discus, and shot put, and held world records in all these events (*EJS*, 447–48, 441, 461–62). Jewish women have particularly distinguished themselves as promoters of women's sport. They include Senda Berenson, the founder of women's basketball (Spears 1991, 19–36), Charlotte Epstein, the mother of American women's swimming, who helped make it an Olympic sport in 1920 (Wettan 1977, 98–103), and Gladys Medalie Heldman, editor and publisher of *World Tennis Magazine,* established in 1953, and founder of the Virginia Slims professional tour that began in 1971.[27]

Linda Borish's seminal essay "Jewish American Women, Jewish Organizations, and Sports, 1880–1940" is the first comprehensive and analytical essay on Jewish American womens athletics. While recognizing the accomplishments of outstanding individual athletes, Borish's main point is that Jewish women participated in sport as fully as most other women, often under the auspices of Jewish organizations that sought to maintain their femininity and Jewish identity. Highly assimilated middle- and upper-class Jewish women, who were given more freedom than the daughters of recent immigrants, participated in the more prestigious sports at high schools, colleges, and country clubs. Second-generation young women from eastern Europe families had little parental support if they wanted to participate in sports. They relied on settlement houses, YMHAs, and summer camps established by philanthropists to help impoverished Jewish girls escape hot New York summers. Reformers sought to improve their health, provide uplifting recreation, and help Americanize them, just as they did for the boys. Settle-

27. Brief biographies appear in *EJS,* and the volumes on indoor and outdoor sport in *BDAS.* Levine (1992) devotes virtually no attention to women, and Jewish women are largely neglected in Gems's essay on ethnic women (1994).

ment house and YWHA leaders considered the physical training of Jewish girls and young women an important part of their mission. Their programs emphasized gymnastics, exercise, and adapted rules advocating a play spirit rather than competitiveness.

The Recent Jewish American Sporting Experience

Since World War II the extent of Jewish participation in sport at its highest levels has dramatically changed. There have been very few Jewish boxers, and fewer Jewish football players, and a precipitous decline in the number of Jewish basketball players to nearly none. The decline in baseball has been less sharp than most scholars have recognized. There were twenty-one players in the 1950s and eighteen in the 1960s, when Sandy Koufax was the preeminent pitcher in organized baseball. Koufax went 165-87 in his eleven year career, winning 129 games between 1961 and 1966 when he led the Dodgers to three pennants and two Series championships. The Hall of Famer went 25-5 in 1963, his best year, with 306 strikeouts and a 1.88 ERA. Koufax retired at 31 because of a sore arm. There were seventeen Jewish players in the 1970s, and thirteen in the 1980s. There has recently been a little-noticed revival of Jewish participation. In 1990–1996 there were twenty Jewish ballplayers, including thirteen in 1995 alone. Baseball scholars missed several players whose names are not obviously Jewish, or who had a non-Jewish parent. Jewish major leaguers today include both players with "traditional" Jewish names such as Levine, but also names like Amaro and Bautista. Spaner attributes their success primarily to assimilation in suburbia, now a prime locus for the recruitment of American-born players (1997, 179–80). A few Jewish big leaguers still come from Brooklyn, Philadelphia, and metropolitan Chicago, but the majority are raised in either California or Florida, where baseball is played year-round (*Baseball Encyclopedia* 1996; *Sporting News Official Baseball Register* 1996), undoubtedly supported by parents who are baseball fans. Their athletically gifted sons typically attended college on baseball scholarships and are now taking advantage of the lucrative salaries available to major leaguers.

Although Jewish participation in the major pro sports has been on a general decline, there was a significant rise in Jewish participation in the more elite individualistic sports, particularly golf, tennis, and swimming, and Jews have continued to enjoy some success in gymnastics. These developments were the product of Jewish economic success, the accompanying migration to suburbia and out of the inner city, and strivings toward structural assimilation among the third-generation Jewish Americans. Athletically gifted Jewish athletes grew up in families that stressed education rather than sports and lived in communities where sport achievement is not all consuming. Spatial limitations were no longer a problem, but aspiring ballplayers such as Art Shamsky, who played for the New York Mets, had relatively little encouragement for their athletic ambitions. The postwar generation was insufficiently motivated for the sacrifices necessary to improve their athletic skills.[28] There was little need for Jewish athletic heroes to prove Jewish prowess or fight anti-Semitism. The new manly and womanly Jewish heroes were Israeli pioneers and soldiers (Breines 1990).

Yet while Jewish participation in sports at the highest levels underwent noticeable changes, Jews continued to be very much involved in the sporting world as communicators and entrepreneurs. Jewish businessmen continued to play a disproportionate role in the commercial side of sport, ranging from the retail sporting goods business to boxing promotion and operating sports franchises. As we have seen, they were a dominant force in the NBA. Jewish entrepreneurs were also becoming increasingly prominent in major league baseball and the NFL, where they had been far less successful in securing franchises, probably because of anti-Semitism. The Jewish presence in the baseball business reached its nadir in 1946, after Bill Benswanger's sale of the Pittsburgh Pirates. The only Jewish owners in the majors that year were members of Bill Veeck's syndicate, which had just bought the Cleveland Indians; and Jews continued to play a prominent role in that club after Veeck sold out.

28. Koufax's primary sport was originally basketball, for which he earned a scholarship to Cincinnati. Actor Lou Gossett, who played basketball in college, said that when he grew up in New York, Koufax was the best player he ever faced. For a discussion of the decline in Jewish success on the diamond, see Levine 1992, 235–47. Levine (255) stresses, unconvincingly, the importance of the declining ethnic community as part of the reason for the declining Jewish success in basketball.

For the next few years, no other franchise had significant Jewish participation except for Baltimore, where beer baron Zanvyl Krieger shared control of the Orioles in the mid-1950s. In 1965 the team was sold to a competing brewer, Jerry Hoffberger. Shortly thereafter several other clubs were bought by Jewish entrepreneurs. Between the early 1960s through 1994, ten of the twenty-eight big league clubs have had Jews in controlling or significant ownership positions (Quirk and Fort, 391–408; Miller 1990, 35, 60, 97, 100–102).

In the National Football League, there were no Jewish owners at all in its first twenty years. Then in 1940 Fred Levy Jr. became co-owner of the Cleveland Rams, and Fred Mandel Jr. took over the Detroit Lions. Six years later the rival All-America Conference was organized, which provided new opportunities for investors. Its main backer was Benjamin Lindheimer, who also owned the Los Angeles franchise. By the 1950s, Jewish ownership in football became more commonplace, and since then nearly one-third (nine of twenty-eight) of the clubs have had Jewish ownership, including Carroll Rosenbloom, who owned the Baltimore Colts until he traded the team for the Los Angeles Rams (*EJS*, 284; Quirk and Fort 1992, 409–34).[29]

Sport and Communications

The fascination of American Jews with sports in postwar America was indicated by their eminence in sports communications, particularly sportswriting and radio and television, and also in belles

29. I have not uncovered any evidence of overt anti-Semitism. However, in 1944 Dodgers president Branch Rickey used some curious language in a confidential letter recently uncovered by SABRite Andy McCue. Rickey reviewed in his correspondence the efforts of the Ebbets and McKeever heirs to sell their stock in the Dodgers, which Rickey and his partner, team attorney Walter O'Malley, were trying to secure. One prospective buyer was "a Mr. Myers, of Jewish extraction, a manufacturer of fancy jewelry in Brooklyn," who got an option to buy one-half of the McKeever shares and the approval of most of the Ebbets heirs for another 50 percent share. However, the deal fell through. Another suitor was "a young chap named Osterman, of Jewish extraction and characteristics," who was prepared to spend one million dollars, and had made a solid offer for the Ebbets shares. Rickey's characterizations of his competition are insufficient to impugn him, but his words are suggestive (Letter to Roscoe Hobbs).

lettres. It would be simplistic to argue that this reflected their declining success on the playing field, and their felicity with the written and spoken word, but there is some truth in that. Sports fans who might not be good enough athletes to play at high levels can comment intelligently on it. In fact, Milwaukeean Albert Von Tilzer, a member of a prominent Jewish musical family, composed "Take Me Out to the Ball Game" in 1908 without ever having seen a major league game (Provizer 1993, 9).

There was a long tradition of Jewish sportswriters dating to at least 1883 when Jacob C. Morse became baseball editor of the *Boston Globe.* Five years later he authored one of the first histories of baseball, *Sphere and Ash: A History of Baseball.* The most eminent Jewish sports journalists in the pre-depression era were probably Nat Fleischer, founder of *Ring* magazine in 1922, and his partner, Dan Daniel, who wrote about baseball for more than fifty years beginning in 1909. Shirley Povich (father of Maury Povish), who first covered the Washington Senators from the late 1920s, is still active. After World War II, prominent Jewish boxing writers included Barney Nagler and Lester Bromberg, and the top baseball writers included Roger Kahn, Dick Young, Milt Gross, Leonard Koppett, and Jerome Holtzman. Furthermore, Jewish authors dominate the popular nonfiction genre of sports books as well as the scholarly literature on sport. Jewish prominence in radio dates to Bill Stern in the 1930s, who was followed by such eminent broadcasters as Marty Glickman (Glickman 1996) and Mel Allen. Since then, the tradition has been maintained by such notable television personalities as the late Howard Cosell, Marv Albert, and Warner Wolf. Furthermore, Jews play a prominent role in contemporary TV sports promotion, particularly Seth Abraham, head of HBO Sports, and his executive producer, Ross Greenburg.[30]

30. Prominent Jewish authors of popular baseball nonfiction include Eliot Asinof, Charles Einstein, Harvey Frommer, Peter Golenback, Roger Kahn, and John Thorn. On Kahn, see Solomon 1987a and F. Roberts 1995. For a recent bibliography of Jewish authors who have written nonfiction books on baseball, see Bjarkman, "Six-Pointed Diamonds," 333–36. The leading Jewish authors of scholarly sport histories include Adelman (1986); Warren Goldstein (*Playing for Keeps: A History of Early Baseball* [1989]); Gorn (1986); Guttmann (1985; 1984; 1978); George Kirsch (*The Creation of American Team Sports: Baseball and Cricket, 1838–1872* [1989]); and Levine (1995; 1992).

Sporting themes, especially baseball, has been a popular topic among Jewish American novelists (Bjarkman 1990, 331–32; Harrison 1981, 112–18; Solomon 1984, 43–66; 1985, 19–31; 1987b, 49–64; 1988, 106–27). Peter Bjarkman (1990, 313) has described baseball for them as "a perfect shiksa—mysterious, foreign, and altogether unintelligible to Old World parents; enticing, exotic, and full of endless pleasures for its new and fanatic devotee."

Allen Guttmann, author of seminal studies on sport history and Jewish American novelists, examines the fascination of Jewish literati with sport in his essay "Becoming American: Jewish Writers on the Sporting Life." Guttmann argues that the disproportionate Jewish literary production on sporting subjects is best understood by examining the sociocultural world in which second-generation Jewish Americans grew up. Guttmann believes that the fundamental influence was the concern of Jewish youth with assimilation, which he regards as the prevailing focus of post–World War II Jewish American fiction. Sport is perceived as an institution that was a part of assimilation and a gauge for evaluating one's acculturation. The authors he analyzes do not restrict themselves to studying sport in a Jewish context, but examine the athletic world in a broader setting because of sport's central place in American society and its importance in the lives of marginal Americans. Authors such as Bernard Malamud (Solomon 1984; Wasserman 1986, 47–64; O'Connor 1986, 37–42; Henry 1992, 110–29), Philip Roth (1975), and Mark Harris mainly focused on baseball (1988, 1–11), the game that best epitomized American culture, our society's traditional values and beliefs, and its future hopes. Baseball was very much a part of their youth, and provided them with a means of asserting their Americanization.

Guttmann considers boxing the second most popular sporting subject among creative writers because it provided a canvas for the analysis of realistic social conditions, such as ghetto poverty and inner city crime, that Jews and other impoverished immigrant groups encountered in urban America. Boxing provided a focus on a manly world, seemingly antithetical to the Old World Jewish ethos. Yet it was not far removed from the environment in which some Jewish authors grew up, and one that has continued to fascinate intellectuals such as Norman Mailer. Guttmann concludes by pointing out that Jewish authors' emphasis on sporting subjects has become less a quest for acceptance as Americans than as a metaphor for the search for human identity.

The final essay, literary critic Eric Solomon's "Eric Rolfe Greenberg's *The Celebrant:* The Greatest (Jewish) American Baseball Novel," is an outstanding exegesis of *The Celebrant* (1983). The novel is set in New York City in the early 1900s, focusing on the relationship between a young Jewish craftsman-entrepreneur in the diamond business who loves baseball, with the man he idolizes, Christy Mathewson. Matty, a real-life Frank Merriwell hero who epitomized muscular Christianity, won 373 games, the most in National League history. Solomon lauds Greenberg for capturing the grammar of the game through his use of oral history sources and traditional historical research and enriching the narrative with the text of Jewish American business fiction, and for eliciting the special role that fans play in the national game. The novel deals with such familiar themes as family, the loss of innocence, and the importance of the mind vis-à-vis the body. Baseball itself appears as a moral event demanding justice. Solomon considers the novel the finest fictional work ever written on the national pastime.

Many essential aspects of the American Jewish sporting experience remain to be fully explored, such as Jewish participation in sports gambling, the role of Jewish sports entrepreneurs, the Jewish experience in football, Jewish sportswomen, and the declining influence of ethnicity in postwar Jewish athletics. There is a need for comparative studies that consider the difference between Jewish suburban and urban sport, and between sport in New York and other cities. There is also a need to compare the Jewish athletic experience in the United States and abroad. Work needs to be done, for example, comparing the English and American boxing experiences. Besides the era of Anglo-Jewish pugilists of the Regency era, there was a second golden age of English Jewish boxers in the early twentieth century among the sons of recent Russian immigrants, including welterweight world champion Ted "Kid" Lewis. Another topic begging for comparative analysis is the less well known sporting experience of Jews in central Europe. Highly assimilated upper- and middle-class Jews were very active in central European sports in the first half of the century (Vertinsky 1995; Mayer 1980, 221–41), and were much more successful than American Jews. Between 1896 and 1964 Jewish Americans won merely eighteen of ninety

Olympic gold medals won by Jews, while Hungarian Jews alone won forty-eight, primarily in fencing and gymnastics (*EJS*, 393–96; Handler 1985). In Germany, where there was much Jewish involvement in sports, the rise of anti-Semitism in late-nineteenth-century German sports clubs hastened the rise of an alternative Jewish sports program. As late as 1933 there were forty-thousand participants in Jewish sports clubs in Germany (*EJS*, 401). The national record for the high jump was held by Gretel Bergmann, a Jewish woman, but she was barred from the Olympic squad (Bernett 1973, 93). Furthermore, the ethnic factor was important in the rise of "muscular Judaism," exemplified by the Maccabiah movement of the early 1900s and other Jewish sports programs (Eisen 1979). Max Nordau, the founder of muscular Judaism, wanted to build healthier Jewish bodies for physical well-being, to counter deleterious stereotypes and to prepare his fellow Jews to be full-scale citizens in every way (Gilman 1991, 53; Vertinsky 1995, 51–52).

The study of sport continues to offer valuable opportunities to better understand the Jewish American experience. Sport provides another window through which we can examine such familiar themes as the construction of social identity (assimilation, acculturation, community, and class), anti-Semitism, entrepreneurship, and social mobility, not to mention newer concerns such as gender, consumerism, entertainment, and crime. The analysis of sport particularly contributes to a fuller understanding of how second- and third-generation Jewish Americans found their niche in American society.

2

Tough Jews

The Jewish American Boxing Experience, 1890–1950

Steven A. Riess

Professional boxing has historically been a low-status sport that recruited its participants from among the poorest inner city youths
who had few or no alternate means of gaining fame and escaping
poverty. Prizefighting was proscribed virtually everywhere for most
of the nineteenth century, because it was a dehumanizing blood sport,
matches were believed to be fixed, and contests attracted disreputable
crowds. Yet despite the sport's ignominy, boxing had a great appeal
for impoverished second-generation Jewish youths, and it was the
first professional sport in which many Jewish Americans participated.
Their success in this sport surprised Gentiles who accepted conventional stereotypes about Jewish manliness and shocked first-generation
Jews who regarded boxing as antithetical to their religious teachings
and cultural traditions. Jewish Americans were not only prominent
as prizefighters but also became even more eminent outside the ring
in such supporting roles as trainers, managers, and promoters. This
essay examines why second-generation American Jews became a major
force in professional boxing, analyzes the decline and fall of the ethnic group as pugilists, and evaluates the extent of their success in the
sport both inside and outside the ring.

The Anglo-American Boxing Heritage

The prominence of Jews in prizefighting was not a new development, but dates to the late eighteenth century when poor Jewish residents of London's Whitechapel district became pugilists to gain respect, make money, and counter invidious racial prejudices that stereotyped Jews as weak cowards. The first noted Anglo-Jewish fighter was Daniel Mendoza, a 5'7", 160-lb. Sephardic Jew who was the English champion from 1791 to 1795. Mendoza introduced the elements of defense to a sport that had heretofore been dominated by sheer brute strength and endurance. He helped make the sport respectable and popularized boxing among the aristocracy. Among his patrons was the prince of Wales. He taught young gentlemen the rudiments of self-defense, hobnobbed with the elite, and played a crucial role in inaugurating the Regency Age of Boxing. Mendoza was a great hero in the Jewish community because he proved that Jews could be manly and courageous. He became a role model for other Anglo-Jewish fighters who followed in his footsteps, including "Dutch" Sam Elias, the reputed inventor of the uppercut, Barney Aaron, Izzy Lazarus, and the four Belasco brothers (*Jewish Encyclopedia* under "Sports"; *EJS*, 137–38; Endelman 1979, 219–23).

Despite the popularity of English boxing in the late eighteenth and early nineteenth centuries, there were few matches in the United States where boxing was illegal because of the brutality, gambling, and nefarious characters that made up the boxing community. It was mainly supported by members of the male bachelor subculture, often members of street gangs, who congregated at saloons, firehouses, and other male bastions. The first recognized American bout was the Jacob Hyer–Tom Beasley fight of 1816, but there were few bouts of any consequence until the American heavyweight championship fight of 1849, won by Yankee Sullivan over Tom Hyer. Boxing matches then were impromptu barroom brawls or contests surreptitiously arranged by fighters or their managers.

Most of New York City's leading midcentury pugilists were Irishmen or of Irish descent (56.3 percent), and nearly one-fifth (18.8 percent) were English. The English ones included "Young" Barney Aaron, the half-Jewish son of the English boxer of the same name, and Harry and Johnny Lazarus, also sons of an Anglo-Jewish fighter. Eighteen-year-old Barney Aaron came to the United States in 1854, and three years later won the American lightweight championship. Because there were few formal bouts, pugilists needed other sources of income, often as shoulder hitters who intimidated voters for political machines (Adelman 1986, 229–40; Adelman 1980, 563–64, 569, 601 n.109; Gorn 1986, 34–128; *EJS*, 138–39; Sportsman 1944, 17, 44).

In the 1840s formal matches were being arranged in sporting taverns and by the 1880s through the sporting press, particularly Richard K. Fox's *National Police Gazette*. Fighters competed for purses raised by their backers and for side bets. These bouts were held in secret in barns on the outskirts of town, on river barges, and in saloon back rooms. Especially important bouts were staged at obscure locations accessible only by specially chartered railroad trains. A crucial change in boxing promotion emerged in New Orleans, historically a wide-open city, where beginning in 1890, prizefights were permitted at athletic clubs. The Olympic Club organized matches between fighters who fought for a purse, and the club made money from box office receipts. The beginning of legalization and the innovations in promotion helped bring a degree of stability to the sport, and made it more enticing for rough young men who sought a quick route to fame and fortune (Adelman 1980, 560–81; Rader 1995, 38–39, 41–46; Somers 1972, chap. 8, esp. 174–91).

The Rise of Jewish American Boxing, 1890–1914

The Irish domination of the ring continued into the early twentieth century. In the 1890s, for instance, half of the world champions were of Irish descent, and as late as the second decade, nearly one-fourth were of Irish derivation. There were enough Jewish fighters in the 1890s for the press to acknowledge their presence, but only Joe Choynski achieved national fame. He was born in San Francisco on November 8, 1868, and worked in a candy factory before becoming a prizefighter. His father Isadore, the son of a rabbi, was hardly the stereotypical Polish immigrant, having graduated from Yale College. Isadore worked as collector of the Port of San Francisco during the Civil War and subsequently worked as a printer, antiquarian bookseller, and journalist for the city's English-language press. He also published the magazine *Public Opinion,* and for twenty years wrote the *Maftir* column for the *American Israelite,* the leading Jewish American publication. The family's high social standing, very atypical of prizefighters, was further reflected by Isadore's presidency of both the YMHA and a local lodge of B'nai B'rith (traditionally German-Jewish positions), and by the business and professional occupations of Joe's three brothers. Joe got his start in athletics at a local turnverein. He began boxing at sixteen, and won the Pacific Coast amateur championship three years later (T. Jenkins 1955, 15; Rischin 1991, 10; Kramer and Stern 1974, 333, 335, 343–44). As his father proudly reported to the *American Israelite*: "The Jews, who take little stock in slugging, are glad that there is one Maccabee among them, and that the Irish will no longer boast that there is not a Jew who can stand up to the racket and receive punishment according to the rules of Queensberry" (Kramer and Stern 1974, 336).

Choynski turned professional in 1888, winning $1,000 for a fourteenth-round knockout of Chicagoan Frank Glover at the California Athletic Club. His principal rival then was another local boy, James J. "Gentleman Jim" Corbett. They had three matches in 1889, the first on May 31, outside the city, in Fairfax, was stopped by the sheriff in the fourth round. They were rematched six days later on a barge near Benecia, where a desperate left hook by Corbett in the twenty-fifth round forced Choynski to quit the extremely violent bout. Their third contest on July 15 was a four-round benefit for Choynski at the Mechanics Pavilion in front of 2,110 fans that Corbett won by decision (Kramer and Stern 1974, 336–37).

Choynski boxed as a heavyweight for seventeen years although never weighing more than 172 lbs. During a 77-fight career, he had 50 victories (half by knockout), 14 loses, 6 draws, and 7 no-decisions. He was regarded as one of the most scientific boxers of his era and the originator of the left hook. He fought nearly all the leading heavyweights of his time, including future champions Bob Fitzsimmons in an 1894 no-decision five-round bout halted by the police, Jim Jeffries in a twenty-round draw three years later, and in 1901 knocked out an inexperienced Jack Johnson in three rounds. Corbett and Johnson were subsequently incarcerated for twenty-eight days for their interracial fight in Galveston, Texas. After retiring from the ring, Choynski was a chiropractor and the physical culture director of the Pittsburgh Athletic Club (Kramer and Stern 1974, 340–41, 344).

Choynski's middle-class background was unique, because nearly all other Jewish prizefighters were sons of impoverished eastern European immigrants who came to the United States between 1880 and 1914 and lived in indigent crowded slums where they struggled to make a living. The new immigrants from Russia and Poland were virtually all Orthodox and came from premodern sections of Europe where sporting institutions were undeveloped. In America these newcomers tried to maintain Old World customs, religious institutions, and traditions, along with a few new ones, such as the Yiddish-language press. Their limited leisure time was spent within the family circle, among *landsleit* at benevolent societies, clubs, and saloons, or at the Yiddish theater. The adult immigrant generation displayed no interest in American sports, which was typical of new immigrants coming from countries that lacked a sporting heritage. There were only rare exceptions to this generalization, such as Jake, the Americanized protagonist of Abraham Cahan's 1899 novel *Yekl: A Tale of the New York Ghetto,* who wanted to learn all he could about baseball and boxing so he could be a real "Yankee." His fellow sweatshop workers ridiculed his fascination with American sports such as baseball that they regarded as a children's game (Bernheimer 1905, 221–54; Rischin 1962, 141–42, 193; Howe 1976, 208–18; Burko 1983, 85–96; Mazur 1977, 270–72, 277–79; Cutler 1995, 133, 136–40, 155–58; Duis 1983, 162–64; Guttmann 1985, 274–86).

First-generation Jewish parents were as strongly opposed to athletics, if not more so, than any other immigrants. Not only were they unfamiliar with sports in the Old World but in America they regarded athletics as a waste of time that served no useful function. If anything, sport was a dangerous force that taught inappropriate social values, drew children away from traditional beliefs and behavior, and led to overexertion and accidents. Nevertheless, sports captured the attention of second-generation youths. Boys enjoyed talking about and playing different sports because they were fun, provided a means of gaining social acceptance, and demonstrated that they were not greenhorns. They read the sporting sections of newspapers as well as the juvenile sports literature, and used sports as a major topic of conversation. Jewish youths played ball games in city streets, participated in municipal recreation programs (most notably the New York Public Schools Athletic League), used settlement-house facilities, and took advantage of sports programs at the

YMHAs, organized by German Jews in emulation of the YMCA (Frank 1908, 477; "The Jewish Athlete" 1909; 1908b; Goodman 1979a, chaps. 1–3; *EJS*, 79; Rabinowitz 1948).

The athletic choices of Jewish youths were limited by environmental and social factors. The need to work part-time after school or full-time to help support the family left little discretionary time for recreation, especially during the shorter fall and winter daylight hours. Furthermore, because the new immigrants lived in the most crowded urban areas where there were few if any public parks and insufficient space for baseball diamonds or football fields, it became very difficult for Jewish youths to achieve proficiency in those sports, even if they became big baseball fans (Riess 1980, 36–37, 188–91).

If environmental conditions discouraged high-level achievement in baseball, they could encourage success in sports such as basketball and boxing that did not require much empty space but could be enjoyed year-round in the afternoon or evenings at neighborhood settlement houses and gymnasiums. Parents universally decried boxing as violent, dangerous, immoral, and dominated by bums and thugs, but many of their sons developed a keen interest in the

2.1. Boxing Club, Jewish Community Centers of Chicago, ca. 1910. Photograph no. ICHi-17315.

sport. The ability to box was a useful skill that promoted self-esteem, potentially a career, and prepared young fellows to defend themselves against young men from other ethnic groups. Inner city Jewish boys had to fight for space in parks and swimming pools, for places to sell newspapers, and even for access to sidewalks when they returned home from school. Ghetto lads saw fighting as a way to prove their bravery and manliness, protect the honor of their ethnicity, and counter old stereotypes that Jews were meek and cowardly. Their fathers in the old country had run away from the tsar's army and had not held "manly" jobs like farming, but were tailors and traders. Even their children were regarded as singularly unfit because of their crowded living conditions, limited play space, and bookish ways. This stereotype was accepted by German Jews and by Gentiles. German Jews established organizations in the 1890s such as the Jewish People's Institute and the Educational Alliance to improve the health and morals of inner city youth, teach them to be good Americans, and protect their religious and ethnic heritage. These institutions and the new settlement houses provided an important solution to the spatial needs of young inner city sportsmen (Riess 1980, 187–89; Berkow 1977, 142; *EJS*, 162–63; Goodman 1979, 37–40; Cutler 1981, 142–43, 158–59).[1]

Eastern European Jews achieved rapid success in prizefighting. By the turn of the century, Jewish American pugilists from inner city neighborhoods in Chicago, San Francisco, and especially New York were gaining recognition as notable professional pugilists. About two-thirds of the Jewish boxers between 1890 and 1940 were born in metropolitan New York, and most of the Russian-born fighters who came as children also grew up there (*TSN* 1896, Oct. 17; *NPG* 1903, Aug. 22; 1905, Sept. 30; *Cincinnati Enquirer* 1903, Nov. 17). Experts attributed their achievement to strong motivation. As Jimmy Johnston, a boxing promoter, Madison Square Garden matchmaker, and manager of Ted "Kid" Lewis (Gershom Mendeleff), an English Jew who was intermittently world champion welterweight (147 lbs.) between 1915 and 1919, noted, "You take a Jewish boy and sooner or later his race is decried. He tries so much harder to fight back for himself and for his people since

1. The rift between an immigrant family and their American-raised son who becomes a boxer was the subject of a short story at the turn of the century by Aaron Weitzman (Cahan 1914).

he regards himself as a representative of all Jews. The knowledge that more than one Jew is on trial when he fights gives him an incentive for training more faithfully and taking greater pride in his work" (S. Frank 1936, 98).

Among the first inner city Jewish prizefighters was Joe Bernstein, known as "the Pride of the Ghetto." Bernstein began fighting professionally in 1894 when he was seventeen years old, and during his sixteen-year career fought all the leading small men of his day, including champions George Dixon, Terry McGovern, and Young Corbett, but lost to all three. He fought McGovern for the featherweight title in Louisville on November 2, 1900, but lost on a seventh-round knockout (*EJS*, 149; Boxing Scrapbook 16: 85; Counter 1945).

Bernstein was succeeded as the pride of the ghetto by Leach Cross (Louis Wallach), a renowned lightweight club fighter who had 154 bouts. He won 43, lost 10, and the rest were no-decisions or draws. He is credited as the fighter most responsible for popularizing boxing among New York's Jewish population. The Wallachs were a large Viennese family that lived in the heart of the Lower East Side. Louis's first involvement in fisticuffs came when he was attending high school and had to walk through an Irish neighborhood to get to school. "I had to pass through either 2nd or 3rd Avenue and those who remember this district will recollect that a Jew was as welcome to the boys of that neighborhood as pork was in the home of our Orthodox Jews." He and his friends got into so many fights that they organized a gang to combat the Irish, and as the best fighter, Louis became their leader (Blady 1988, 84–85).

Louis attended NYU dental school and worked part-time in concessions at the Long Acre Athletic Club. It was a boxing club in the old Tenderloin district owned by a classmate's father. Even though he was a college man, Louis wanted to become a professional boxer, and after training with the renowned lightweight "Harlem" Tommy Murphy, turned pro in 1906, making six dollars for his first bout. Louis fought under a pseudonym so his parents would not find out what he was doing. If he came home late after a fight, Louis would tell his father that he had been involved in a dental school project. This went on for two years and twenty-six fights until he knocked out the community hero, Joe Bernstein, for a $100 purse. Then all the neighbors came by to congratulate his father. The elder Wallach berated his son when he got home: "So, a prize fighter you are. I believe you when you come home with a black eye and tell me you got it playing basketball at the Clark House. Now I learn you are a prize fighter. A loafer. A *nebish* [sic]." However, in due course, Chaim Wallach became a fan, which was just as well because three more Cross brothers became professional boxers, managed by their oldest brother Sam, a lawyer (*EJS*, 152–54; Rose 1952).

Cross had a reputation as an outstanding club fighter who always brought in the crowds and gave them their money's worth. He fought in the era of the "membership clubs" when prizefighting was illegal in New York. These clubs operated as subterfuges, promoting "exhibitions" for the entertainment of their members. Memberships were sold on fight night for one dollar, which entitled the buyer to attend the fights that evening. The most popular contests pitted fighters of different ethnic groups against each other, usually Jew against Irish, and each group would come out to support its hero. On St. Patrick's Day in 1908 Cross was matched against Frankie Madden in front of a largely Irish crowd that had kept out most of his Jewish supporters. The police received reports that a riot had started during the bout between spectators of rival nationalities, but when they came to investigate, the officers found Cross being cheered by the Irish spectators for his outstanding fistic display. Cross became an important role model for future Jewish fighters. The fighting dentist was a cagey pugilist who worked in a low crouch and always did a good job protecting himself. Cross never held a world's title, but did fight a ten-round no-decision bout for the lightweight title 1913 with champion Willie Ritchie at Madison Square Garden (*EJS*, 153; Rose 1952; Fleischer 1928; Fleischer 1947b; Fleischer 1958, 165–67).[2]

2. Fleischer claimed in his autobiography (1958, 165–67) that on the following day, Cross's picture appeared on the front page of the *Forward* with a story about the previous evening's events. Fleischer indicated that this was the first time that any mention of boxing had appeared in the Yiddish press. However, Jewish boxing historian Ken Blady could not verify Fleischer's story (Blady 1988, 86). On the membership days of boxing, see Riess 1985, 95–128.

According to Blady 1988, 80, Cross loosened most of K. O. Brown's upper front teeth in a ten-round no-decision fight at the Empire Athletic Club in New York on December 20, 1911. The next day manager Dumb Dan Morgan took Brown to the dentist, Dr. Louis Wallach, better known to the fistic fraternity as Leach Cross.

Although New York was the center of Jewish pugilism, the first Jewish American world champions were from Chicago and San Francisco. Bantamweight Harry Harris was of English ancestry and was born in Chicago in 1880. He stood over 5'10", yet fought at a mere 110 lbs., hence the nickname, "the Human Hairpin." Harry and his twin brother, Sam, both boxed as children and received their first gloves as Hanukkah presents. They learned to box by sparring each other, and later honed their skills at a boxing gymnasium where Harry came under the tutelage of newspaper artist Ed Carey and the cartoonist's friend, welterweight champion Kid McCoy, who taught the "Stringbean Kid" his famous corkscrew punch. Harry turned pro in 1896, dropping out of school and discarding his plans to become a window dresser. Sammy also turned pro and they mainly fought in the Chicago area. Harry's first big break came in New York in 1898 when he defeated highly rated bantamweight Charley Roden by a technical knockout in the ninth round of a card headlined by the match between former heavyweight champion Jim Corbett and the prominent contender "Sailor" Tom Sharkey. Harris won a $125 purse and a $250 side bet and received much favorable press attention (Harris Scrapbooks; Steiner 1973; *EJS,* 158; Sportsman 1947).[3]

In 1900 bantamweight champion Terry McGovern vacated his title, having outgrown the division, which was left without a clearcut successor. On March 18, 1901, Harris won the bantamweight championship in London by defeating the British champion, Pedlar Palmer, in a fifteen-round fight. Just moments before the bout, Harris had been informed of the death of his twin brother, but chose to fight on, using his grief to motivate himself. Harris's tenure as champion was brief because he likewise outgrew the division. He fought five more times as a featherweight and then in 1902 went into the entertainment business. Harry became the manager of the New Amsterdam Theater in New York, having

3. On one occasion Sammy was matched with Johnny Whitecraft, but got sick. Manager Ed Carey secretly substituted Harry, and he knocked out Whitecraft in the third round (Blady 1988, 59).

Bantamweight Morrie Bloom had his first professional bout in 1904 when he was just fourteen. He and his peers started fighting in backyards or empty lots by the time they were as young as six or seven (Blum interview, 1984; Bloom scrapbooks).

been friends with A. L. Erlanger, the theatrical impresario. The "Human Hairpin" made a brief comeback in 1907, and ended with about sixty career victories and just two defeats. He later became a successful broker on the New York Curb (now the American Stock Exchange), buying a seat in 1919 for $30,000 (Harris Scrapbooks; Steiner 1973, 65–66; *EJS,* 158).

The preeminent Jewish boxer of the early 1900s was San Franciscan Abe Attell, the sixteenth of nineteen children of Russian immigrant parents who owned a jewelry store in an Irish neighborhood. Like most future professionals, Abe had been a street fighter and a poorly behaved child. "I had to fight or be figuratively murdered," he reminisced. "I either had to hold my own with those tough Irish lads or be chased off the block." Abe's father died when the boy was just thirteen, and he was sent to live with an uncle in Los Angeles to learn some discipline. When Abe returned a year later, he became an amateur fighter, selling the medals he won as an amateur for fifteen dollars to help support the family. His mother opposed his fighting, but after he brought home $15 with his face unmarred, she changed her mind: "Abie, when are you going to fight again?" Abe turned professional in 1900 when just sixteen, and within a year was fighting twenty-round main events (*EJS,* 144–46; *NYT* 1970, Feb. 7; *NPG* 1920, Oct. 9; *Milwaukee Sentinel* 1911, Feb. 12; Blady 1988, 42).

The 5'4" Attell first claimed the featherweight championship in the fall of 1901, despite his youth and inexperience, when titleholder Terry McGovern apparently gave up prizefighting for the stage. "The Little Hebrew" based his claim on two fights with former champion George Dixon, a draw on October 20, followed by a fifteen-round victory by decision eight days later. However, McGovern returned to the ring on Thanksgiving Day, but was defeated by Young Corbett. One year later Corbett relinquished the title when he outgrew the division and became a lightweight. This threw the featherweight division in disarray, because there was no boxing organization that could determine a successor.

Attell again put in his claim for the title, as did several other ranking featherweights, and received considerable support in the sporting press. His championship claims were weakened three years later when he was knocked out in a title match by Tommy Sullivan on October 13, 1904. However, the challenger had failed to make the 126-lb. weight limit, and so the press continued to recognize "the Little Hebrew" as champion. Attell's hold on the crown was solidified four years later when he knocked out Sullivan in the fourth round of their rematch (Andre and Fleischer 1981, 325–27).

Attell fought a number of classic bouts as champions, most notably with the great English pugilists Owen Moran and Jem Driscoll. Moran had previously defeated Abe's brother, Monte, and on January 1, 1908, the champion sought his revenge. They fought a twenty-five-round draw, and a rematch that went twenty-three rounds also ended in a draw. Attell fought Driscoll in New York on February 19, 1909, to a ten-round draw, although the ringside consensus was that the Englishman had outclassed him (Andre and Fleischer 1981, 326, 327; Daniel 1945; Daniel 1946; *NYT* 1970, Feb. 7).[4]

Attell was a highly regarded pugilist who was usually much craftier and quicker than his opponents. Nat Fleischer rated him the third greatest featherweight of all time. He was so superior to most featherweights that he often fought much heavier men, such as "Battling" Nelson, a future lightweight champion, with whom he fought a draw in 1908. Sportswriters often accused Attell of stalling, carrying weaker opponents, and of even throwing nontitle fights to secure a lucrative future rematch (Daniel 1946, 24; Daniel 1945, 14–15; *EJS*, 145; Boxing Scrapbook 16: 38, 59). "The Little Hebrew's" integrity was not of the highest order. As one journalist attested: "During the time Attell held the title he engaged in more crooked bouts than all the champions in the country put together in the last decade. It got so during the last four or five years that no one could tell what was going to happen when Attell was in the ring" (Boxing Scrapbook 16: 38).

In 1911 boxing was legalized in New York State by the Frawley Act (repealed in 1917), which placed pugilism under the supervision of the New York State Athletic Commission. One year later Attell became the subject of one of the commission's first major investigations after his poor fight in New York City on January 18, 1912, with "K. O." Brown. The investigation revealed that a doctor had given him an overdose of cocaine to ostensibly relieve pain

---

4. Attell later implied that he was setting up Driscoll for a rematch in which he had placed a $20,000 bet. However, the rematch was canceled when Driscoll claimed he was ill (*EJS*, 145).

from a previous accident. Attell was suspended for six months (*NYT* 1912, Jan. 19, 23, 25, 26).

The NYSAC's action had little impact because Attell could still fight in California where the commission's rulings carried no weight. Abe unsuccessfully defended his crown on his birthday, February 22, 1912, against Johnny Kilbane in a twenty-round fight at Vernon, a Los Angeles suburb, in front of ten-thousand spectators, losing by decision. Attell fought for three more years, ending up with 168 recorded contests, winning 91 (47 by knockout) and losing just 10; 67 ended with no decision. He earned about $300,000 in the ring but was a heavy gambler and had almost nothing left when he retired. Attell found it difficult to drop out of the limelight and became a hanger-on with the infamous gambler Arnold Rothstein. He used this connection to help cut himself into the World Series fix of 1919 by promising the conspirators that Rothstein would bankroll the action. Attell ultimately became the manager of an East Side tavern in New York, a common retirement occupation of former prominent prizefighters (*NYT* 1912, Feb. 23; 1970, Feb. 7; Katcher 1959, 142–45, 147, 148; Seymour 1971, 300–303, 307–9, 325–27, 329, 336–37).

The Era of Benny Leonard

During the second and third decades of the twentieth century, tough second-generation eastern European Jewish youths who were not well educated had few valuable social contacts and had no bent for commerce looked to the ring as an alternate avenue of social mobility. Boxing remained popular among inner city Jewish boys because it was an accessible sport that was inexpensive, required little space, and was based on skills acquired on the street. It was a good physical conditioner, a means of gaining self-confidence, and provided a route to escape from the inner city. Boxing also was the rare sport in which champions came in all sizes, because pugilists boxed only men of similar stature. This restriction was particularly important among second-generation newcomers who were typically of smaller build. Furthermore, role models of earlier Jewish boxers such as Abe Attell and Leach Cross, who were famous, had money, and were idolized by women, encouraged younger Jewish boys to become professional boxers. Aspiring boxers had other role models too, such as older brothers or neighborhood lads who had fought in the ring. The growing number of top-notch Jewish fighters was reflected by the increased proportion of Jewish contenders and champions. There were just two Jewish champions in the early 1900s out of thirty-five titleholders, but there were four Jewish American champions in the next decade out of thirty-five titlists. This was equal to the German representation, and exceeded only by the eight Irish champions. As late as 1916, Jews did not rank among the top three ethnic groups in contenders (Irish, German, or Italian), but that soon changed, reflected by the presence of five Jewish boxers on the 1920 Olympic team and six in 1924. By 1928, Jews made up the largest number of contenders, followed by Italians and Irish. In the 1920s there were eight Jewish American champions out of forty-nine, placing them third behind Italians (twelve) and Irish Americans (twelve). The only year between 1910 and 1940 when there was no Jewish champion was 1913. There were often multiple Jewish titleholders, and in 1934 half of the eight divisions had Jewish champions (Levine interview; Riess 1980, 187–88; Weinberg and Arond 1952, 460; Simri 1973, 83).[5]

The first Jewish champion after Abe Attell was Al McCoy, the son of a Brownsville kosher butcher, who won the middleweight championship (160 lbs.) in 1914. His real name was Harry Rudolph but, like many other Jewish prizefighters, he fought under a pseudonym to escape parental disapproval and advance his career. McCoy

5. Data on world champions are taken from Sugar 1981. For this study, a titlist whose reign overlapped two decades was counted for each ten-year period in which he fought. A champion who lost and regained his title was credited with holding the title twice.

Between 1910 and 1915 the welterweight division was in confusion and the championship was disputed. I followed the *Ring 1981 Record Book* for titleholders for this era. Among the claimants to the crown was Harry Lewis of New York (1908–11), but he was not widely recognized as champion. A previous study (Jenkins 1955, 190–97) of ethnic succession used a slightly different list of champions. Besides the four Jewish American champions, there were two English world welterweight titlists. Matt Wells held the welterweight title from 1914 to 1915, and "Kid" Lewis held the welterweight title from 1915 to 1916 and from 1917 to 1919. For a useful examination of the Jewish boxers of the 1920s and 1930s, see Levine 1992, 144–89. The four Jewish champions in 1933 were Ross (lightweight), Jackie Fields (welterweight), Ben Jeby (middleweight), and Maxie Rosenbloom (light heavyweight).

was a relative unknown when the southpaw gained the crown with a shocking knockout of titleholder George Chip in fifty-four seconds of the first round. McCoy had been matched against Joe Chip, who fell ill, and his brother substituted for him at the last minute. The champion felt safe about putting up his title, because under the Frawley Law, bouts going the limit were automatically no-decision contests. Thus, in New York, a challenger had to knock out the champion to dethrone him. Because McCoy was primarily a defensive boxer without a strong punch (23 KOs in 99 fights), Chip thought there was little to worry about. McCoy was never considered a great fighter but from his debut in 1908 at age fourteen, he was undefeated in 139 straight fights until he lost the championship in 1917 (including forty-two bouts as titleholder). The streak included 92 no-decision fights.

Besides Attell and McCoy, the other undisputed Jewish American world champions from 1910 to 1919 were "Battling" Levinsky, a Philadelphia light heavyweight (175 lbs.), who reigned from 1916 to 1920, and Benny Leonard, the lightweight titlist from 1917 until his retirement eight years later. Their success reflected the coming to manhood of a large cohort of second-generation eastern European Jews who had grown up in poverty and deprivation and were prepared to use whatever means necessary to escape the inner city, including violent careers in prizefighting or even crime (*EJS,* 162, 164–65, 167–68; Andre and Fleischer 1981, 182, 185, 220; Landesman 1969, 359; Haller 1971–72, 221–27; Bell 1960, 127–50).[6]

The conventional wisdom at this time was that Irishmen made the best fighters, and consequently ambitious young fighters who were not Irish often chose Irish names in the hope of getting more public recognition, such as Jewish fighters "Ring" O'Leary and "Mushy" Callahan (Vicente Morris Scheer), the second junior welterweight champion (1926–30). As Jews gained recognition as boxers, men from other backgrounds might take Jewish names.

---

6. Levinsky was Beryl (Barney) Lebrowitz, who had started out in boxing as Barney Williams. His manager, "Dumb" Dan Morgan, had him change to a more Jewish-sounding name to attract the New York boxing fans, and gave him a nickname that would mislead people into thinking he was a slugger rather than a counterpuncher (Blady 1988, 100–101).

Italian Sammy Mandella, who won the lightweight championship in the late 1920s, fought as Sammy Mandell. And Jews whose name did not sound particularly Jewish might take on more ethnic names. Hence, Jack Dudick, the junior lightweight champion in 1923, fought as Jack Bernstein. The growing awareness of the tough Jewish fighter was even reflected in Ernest Hemingway's *The Sun Also Rises,* in which one of the main characters, Robert Cohen, was a former college fighter (Blady 1988, 134–38, 169–73).[7]

The adoption of non-Jewish names by Jewish fighters resulted in some humorous consequences. One of the great Benny Leonard's early fights was against "Irish" Eddie Finnegan. During the fight Leonard became angered by an anti-Semitic crowd yelling "kill the kike" and "murder the Yid." He began pummeling his opponent, who held on in a clinch, and asked, in Yiddish, for mercy because he was really Seymour Rosenbaum. A similar story was reported in the *American Hebrew* on June 6, 1919 (96) of a Jewish fighter being urged on by his fans to destroy his Polish opponent in response to the ongoing pogroms in Poland. Again it turned out that the battered opponent was also Jewish. The tale, entitled "Irony," indicated how the respectable Jewish American media could appreciate the value of boxing as a means of combatting anti-Semitism and negative Jewish stereotypes, despite their general distaste for prizefighting (Levine 1992, 162).[8]

Benny Leonard, the most exalted of all the Jewish boxing heroes, was born on April 7, 1896, on the Lower East Side. By the time he was done, he was second only to Joe Gans in the history of the lightweight division, and was the outstanding Jewish American athlete of the first third of the twentieth century. The Jews of his day adored "the great Bennah." He could outfeint, outhook, and outdance any pugilist. No fighter had more "form," by which was

7. Many young men on their way to college boxed to earn money, and several colleges at this time had boxing teams because of the widespread belief in the efficacy of the sport as a builder of bodies and promoter of manliness.

8. On September 2, 1913, Leonard fought a boxer named Ah Chung, supposedly the only Chinese fighter in the world on the Chinese New Year in New York's Chinatown. The boxer was a heavily made-up Jewish fighter named Rosenberg, who would presumably appeal to the local audience. A temporary truce had been arranged between the On Leong Tong and the Hip Sing Tong that lasted until the match was over (Levine 1992, 144).

2.2. Benny Leonard. Lightweight champion of the world, 1917–25. *Courtesy of George Eisen.*

meant "skill, speed, wariness, agility . . . the fullest use of your powers, it meant movement and exertion proper to the ever-changing situation" (Liben 1967; *EJS*, 163–64). *Ring* magazine recently rated him the best boxer (ring general) of all time.

Leonard lived near the public baths in Harlem, and remembered that "you had to fight or stay in the house when the Italian and Irish kids came through on their way to the baths." He and his pals fought in the streets and also had gloved matches in back alleys. Minnie Leiner opposed her son's interest in fisticuffs, and tried to get him interested in the printing trade, but to no avail. Benny turned professional in 1911 under a pseudonym so his parents would not find out he was fighting. His professional career started slowly as he lost his first bout under manager Buck Areton. Benny was then so frail and his punch was so weak that he was known as the "Powder Puff Kid" (Fleischer 1947a, 30–32; *EJS,* 164; Blady 1988, 116–18).

There are many stories of how Benny's parents learned he was a fighter. According to one version, his mother noticed a bus loaded with fight fans with a big sign: Benny Leonard, Our Champion, although he was just fighting six-rounders then (Fleischer 1947a, 22–27; *New York World* 1916, Jan. 2; Carroll 1947b). His mother asked a neighbor what was going on, and then she nearly fainted—"*A charpeh un a shandeh*" (a tragedy). When Benny came home, "My mother looked at my black eye—and wept. My father who had to work all week for twenty dollars, looked at the twenty dollars. 'All right Benny, keep on fighting, he said. It's worth getting a black eye for twenty dollars. I am getting *verschwarzt* for twenty dollars a week' " (Barzell n.d.).[9]

Leonard's career picked up in 1914 under a new manager, Billy Gibson, a prominent Bronx politician and the owner of the Fairmont Athletic Club. Gibson's trainer, George Engle, built up Benny's strength and improved his speed and timing (Fleischer 1947a, 32–39; M. Fried 1991, 238). As Mannie Seaman (Mandel Simenovitch), Leonard's future trainer pointed out years later, "Benny wasn't strong, and knew it. He was easily hurt with good punches. In fact, he could be hurt a little more than the average fighter. That's what made him such a great boxer. He knew he had to be clever to keep out of trouble, and so he spent many hours learning to 'hide' and get away" (M. Fried 1991, 238). He would sometimes train by fighting two men at once. Leonard developed into a successful club fighter who attracted large crowds that admired his stylish ring manner.

Benny's big break came in New York on March 31, 1916, when he fought world champion lightweight Freddy Welsh. The bout went the ten-round limit, and to everyone's surprise Leonard dominated the bout and the press acclaimed him the winner. His fine showing led to a rematch on July 28, but this time the Englishman had the better of the no-decision fight. One year later, on May 28, they had their third fight in New York. Welsh was sent to the

9. According to Ray Arcel's version, Leonard brought home $35. Mr. Leiner asked, "*Vos iz dos?*" His son replied, "That's what I got for the fight." Then his father said, "That's what you got for the fight? One night? You got that for the fight? Benny, ven are you going to fight again?" (Arcel Interview, 66–67).

canvas three times in the ninth round, and when the referee refused to let him come out for the tenth round, Leonard became the new champion (Fleischer 1947a, 49–50; *EJS*, 163; *New York World* 1916, Jan. 2; Daniel 1944).

Leonard was known as a fighting champion who ducked no one, and fought more than eighty contests while titleholder. He had several stirring title defenses in which he relied on exceptional guile and skill to save his crown. Among his most memorable was a fight against Rickie Mitchell on January 14, 1921, in which he had bet heavily on himself to achieve a first-round knockout. Leonard knocked the challenger down three times in the first round, only to be floored himself for a nine count. Leonard won that battle with a sixth-round knockout (*EJS*, 164).[10]

Leonard had several great fights against other Jewish lightweights who seemed to dominate the division, including Charley White (Anschowitz). White was born in Liverpool in 1891 but grew up in Chicago, where his father was in the clothing business. He was a superb fighter, but not the quickest thinker on his feet, a flaw that had cost him a potential knockout in a championship fight with Freddy Welsh in 1916. On July 5, 1920, White fought Leonard for the lightweight title in Benton Harbor, Michigan. He had the champion all but out in the fifth round but let Leonard outwit him to survive the round. Benny discovered during the fight that White "telegraphed" his vicious left hook by raising his left leg. In the ninth round Leonard beat him to the punch and knocked White out (*EJS*, 164; Andre and Fleischer 1981, 294).

Leonard's principal nemesis among the lightweights was Philadelphian southpaw Lew Tendler. A future member of boxing's Hall of Fame, Tendler came from an impoverished family whose father had died, and became a newsboy at the age of six to help out. He learned that fighting was a valuable skill for newsboys, because they had to protect their territory against interlopers (Daniel 1959, 17–18; Leseman 1947b, 22–23). A long tradition of newsboys becoming boxers went back at least to Russian-born welterweight

10. Leonard reputedly bet $1,000 against $10,000 with Arnold Rothstein that he would win by a knockout in the first round (Albertanti 1948, 22). In another version of the same incident, Rothstein bet $25,000 on a first-round knockout, 10 percent for Benny, and the champ added $10,000 of his own money as well (Blady 1988, 123).

Abe "the Newsboy" Hollandersky, who in 1894 at age six peddled newspapers to help support the family, whose father had gone blind (Hollandersky 1943; Blady 1988, 71–76) Another former Jewish newsboy was Kid Herman, an outstanding Jewish lightweight who fought the great Joe Gans for the championship in 1907. Once when another boy showed up and tried to take his spot, "I told him to move on, that this was my block. Then he wanted to fight me. I hit him and he ran away. That's how it was all the time. We had to learn to fight in those days if we wanted to hold our business" (Leseman 1947a). When Tendler eventually got his start in boxing, he worked under boxing manager Phil Glassman, who was the head of the Philadelphia Newsboys' Association (Daniel 1959, 17; *EJS,* 175–76; Leseman 1947b, 23).

On July 27, 1922, Tex Rickard matched Tendler against the champion at Boyle's Thirty Acres in Jersey City, the site of the record-breaking Dempsey-Carpentier fight a year before. The pairing was an outstanding attraction, bringing in a gate of $368,000, then the third highest in boxing history. The challenger floored Leonard in the eighth round, but Benny had the fortitude to hang on and the shrewdness to talk to the southpaw and disrupt his concentration. Leonard recovered and went the distance as required under New Jersey rules to keep his title. The public demanded a rematch, which was staged at Yankee Stadium on July 24, 1923, and brought in $453,000. The rematch went the fifteen-round limit, but Leonard had matters well in hand and easily won the decision (Fleischer 1947a, 82–84; Andre and Fleischer 1981, 295).

Leonard trained at Grupp's Gym at 116th and Eighth Avenue in Harlem, the preeminent New York gym after World War I, along with most of the other top Jewish fighters going back to Leach Cross and Benny Valgar. However, after the war, owner Billy Grupp began blaming Jews for World War I and his anti-Semitism began to hurt his business. In 1920 a 125th Street gym was opened by philanthropist Alpheus Geer for the use of his Marshall Stillman Movement to help rehabilitate criminals. Managed by Lou Ingber, the gym had nothing to do with boxing. However, its original mission quickly failed because its clients stole the equipment. Benny Leonard at this time recommended his friends go to Stillman's Gym and leave the anti-Semitic Grupp. Ingber recognized the commercial potential once Leonard moved in, and began charging fans fifteen cents admission to watch the champion train. After the passage of the Walker Act, which made prizefighting legal, the sport became increasingly popular in New York, and Ingber (now known as Lou Stillman) moved operations to a hall he and a partner rented for $1,000 a month at Eighth Avenue between Fifty-fourth and Fifty-fifth Streets near Madison Square Garden. Stillman's Gym became the most famous boxing gym in the world with as many as 375 fighters training there for $6 a month. Spectators were charged just twenty-five cents admission (M. Fried 1991, 41–44; *NYT* 1959, Feb. 8, July 26; Liebling 1990, 21).

Leonard retired as champion in 1925, the only loss during his reign coming in a welterweight champion fight with Jack Britton in New York on June 26, 1922. Titleholder Britton was then thirty-seven, and did not compare with Leonard, a 3–1 favorite, in fitness, speed, and punching power. Leonard used a counterpunching style that night, and trainer Mannie Seamon felt that his fighter did not fight well. Nonetheless, in the thirteenth round, Benny knocked down Britton, who claimed a foul. Leonard then walked across the ring and hit Britton on the head as the referee's count reached nine, which resulted in an automatic disqualification. This unsportsman-like action shocked everyone in the arena, and led to much public discussion of Benny's ties to organized crime (Andre and Fleischer 1981, 293; Fleischer 1947a, 59; M. Fried 1991, 247–48). Twenty-six years later, in 1948, Seamon revealed to the press that "for some reason which I do not know to this day he just didn't have to [win]. Manager Billy Gibson had told Leonard after the weigh-in, 'I'm sorry I've got to say this, but you can't win this fight tonight'" (M. Fried 1991, 248). Despite this blemish Benny left the ring with a million dollars and the universal respect of boxing fans for his integrity and gentlemanly conduct. He was the proverbial credit to boxing and his race. Hearst editor Arthur Brisbine declared, "Benny Leonard has done more to conquer anti-Semitism than a thousand textbooks" (*EJS,* 164).[11]

Upon his retirement, the *New Warheit* rated him greater than Einstein:

---

11. The defeat did not cost Leonard's backers any money because 99 percent of the wagering was on the terms "foul, no bet" (M. Fried 1991, 248).

[F]or when Einstein was in America only thousands knew him, but Benny is known by millions. It is said that only 12 people or at the most twelve times twelve the world over understand Einstein, but Benny is being understood by tens of millions in America, and just as we need a country so as to be the equal of other people, so we must have a fist to become their peers. (*Jewish Daily Bulletin* 1925, Mar. 25, in Blady 1988, 125)

Benny left the ring with one million dollars in earnings, but the stock market crash wiped him out. He returned to the ring in 1931 as a welterweight. He was trained by Ray Arcel, who also booked the fights. As Arcel reminisced,

I knew he had nothing. He was washed up. But he was dead broke. I knew he wasn't gonna make any money, so I figured if he was that great a fighter, he rates much consideration. As fast a thinker as he was and as good a fighter as he was, his reflexes were gone and his coordination was way off, and he had to have constant work in order to be able to reestablish himself mentally and physically—and regain his confidence. (M. Fried 1991, 76–77)

Leonard fought in small clubs and was only a shadow of his former self. Fighting carefully selected opponents, he won eighteen matches (seventeen in a row) and drew once. The Boxing Commission did not want him to fight, and told him to get a payday and get out. He received $15,000 to fight Jimmy McLarnin, the future welterweight champion on October 7, 1932, at Madison Square Garden, which sold out that night. Benny lost in the sixth round on a technical knockout, the last of his 209 fights. He had a remarkable record of 88 victories (68 by knockout), a mere 5 losses, and 1 draw (115 fights were no-decision bouts). Benny subsequently ran a boys camp, was part owner of a Pittsburgh hockey team, and after World War II was a partner in a dress business. He maintained his ties to boxing by refereeing, and died in the ring in 1947 while working a fight (*EJS,* 162–64; Fleischer 1947a, 92–95, 113–19; M. Fried 1991, 78).

Leonard's retirement left a void that was never filled, but Jewish fighters continued to dominate prizefighting, especially in the lower-weight classifications with world champions such as "Kid" Kaplan (1925–27) and Benny Bass (1927–28) in the featherweight division,

Abe Goldstein (1924) and Charley Phil Rosenberg (1925–27) in the bantamweight class, and "Corporal" Izzy Schwartz in the flyweight (112 lbs.) ranks. They were all outstanding boxers yet lacked the charisma and extraordinary boxing skills of Leonard. The heir apparent to Leonard as the pride of the ghetto when he retired in 1925 was Reuben "Ruby" Goldstein, an eighteen-year-old lightweight from the Lower East Side who won seventeen straight matches that year. "Jewish fans . . . stormed the doors whenever he appeared," remembered one old-time boxing writer. "His name on a card came to mean a complete sellout" (Carroll 1942). Goldstein never fulfilled his promise in the ring, but he did become one of the great referees of all time.

Goldstein's career provides a good example of important trends in the Jewish American boxing subculture, particularly his connection to organized crime. Reuben was a poor boy who grew up on the Lower East Side with three older siblings in a household headed by his mother, who took in sewing and washing. Reuben had his first fight at age ten when someone stole his sneakers while he was sleeping in the park one summer evening. He learned to box at the Henry Street Settlement and by the time he was fourteen was practicing nightly the skills he learned by watching professionals train at Grupp's Gym in Harlem. Ruby soon became a highly regarded amateur. He got a watch every time he won, and then would sell it for twenty dollars at the Jewelry Exchange in the Bowery. Ruby's instructor at the Educational Alliance was Hymie Cantor, a former professional fighter, who took him under his wing. In 1924 seventeen-year-old Ruby turned professional under Cantor's management, lying on his application that he was eighteen as required by law (Carroll 1942; Goldstein and Graham 1959, 4–27).

Ruby was a hit right from the start, receiving fifty dollars for his first pro fight, an unheard-of amount for a novice. Cantor soon sold half of his interest in the young fighter to Charlie Rosenhouse, a gambler associated with Arnold Rothstein, who was himself very much involved in prizefighting (Goldstein and Graham 1959, 29, 31; Katcher 1959, 304–6; Walker 1961, 52–53, 58–59). Goldstein was worried about this move but was advised by trainer Joe Gross that it was a good idea: "Rosenhouse has a lot of friends and can do a lot for you in the [Madison Square] Garden and sell a lot of tickets for you" (Goldstein and Graham 1959, 31). Late in 1924 Rosenhouse was murdered, but Cantor was not without a new partner for long. Among the spectators at Goldstein's fight on May 20,

1925, at the Manhattan Casino, a noted sporting resort across the street from the Polo Grounds, was Waxey Gordon (Irving Wexler), one of the leading New York bootleggers. One of his men visited Cantor after the fight, and a day later Ruby was told that Gordon had a piece of him. Cantor advised his lightweight, "Don't worry about it. If it wasn't all right, I wouldn't do it. He can help us. He's got power in this town. People listen to him when he talks" (Goldstein and Graham 1959, 32, 35).

Fighters frequently fell under the spell of the glamour and glitz supplied by the underworld. "The Jewel of the Ghetto" became the darling of the mobsters, who would think nothing of betting $2,500 to $10,000 on him, and rewarded him with lavish gifts. Ruby enjoyed their attention, including the chauffeured cars sent to pick him up after training to take him to dinner at a top restaurant or a speakeasy (Goldstein and Graham 1959, 47–48). Charley Phil Rosenberg, who became bantamweight champion in 1925 at age twenty-one, also enjoyed life in the fast lane.

> I met fabulous people. I met judges, I met the underworld charac-ter, I met everybody. I was a [guest] of all the hoodlums in Chicago. Capone was a great host. After every fight he entertained us royally. I was boxing in East Chicago. Capone used to take fifty tickets . . . I rode home with him after the fight. . . . Fabulous parties, I'll tell you. A great host. I mean, I don't know nothing about his personal life. I'm not interested. Great Host. I'm proud to say that I knew him. A fine man. . . . To me a fine person. He never stood me five cents. I mean, girls, everything. Everything went. Wine, whiskey, women, and song. He was a great host. (Heller 1973, 92–93)[12]

12. For an interview with Rosenberg, see Heller 1973, 86–95. Born on the Lower East Side, Rosenberg (né Charles Green) had a difficult childhood. One of nine children in a single-parent household, his father died before he was born from an accident at work. At sixteen Green took the name of a fighter named Rosenberg who was ill, and he secretly substituted for him in a match to make $15 (Heller 1973, 87). Rosenberg had never fought in the ring before, and lost his first eight fights. Yet in 1923, at age nineteen, he was making $1,000–$1,500 a fight. Rosenberg won the championship two years later.

On February 4, 1927, Rosenberg was matched to defend his bantamweight title against Bushy Graham, but failed to make the weight. The New York Boxing Commission declared the title vacant even though Charley defeated Graham in fifteen rounds. The commission discovered some questionable outside influences, and suspended both fighters for a year (Heller 1973, 86).

Waxey Gordon's connection with Goldstein was not aimed at fixing fights, although he did hope to make money, but more important was his desire to mix in the exciting sporting world. It typified how bootleggers collected women, horses, and fighters as a conspicuous display to show off their success. Ruby's bubble burst in 1926 when he fought "Ace" Hudkins, a much underrated pugilist who later fought for the middleweight championship, in what was supposed to be a tune-up for a championship fight with Italian lightweight Sammy Mandell. Gordon and his friends bet heavily on Goldstein to win in the first round, and Ruby tried to oblige them. He knocked down Hudkins in the first round, but overextended himself, and was knocked out himself in the fourth round. Waxey Gordon reputedly lost $45,000 that night, and other big losers included Mayer Boston and Sam Boston, associates of Rothstein, who dropped $35,000, and singer Al Jolson, who squandered $5,000. Goldstein was never the same after this fight and, although he continued to fight main events, had yielded his aura of invincibility. The "Jewel of the Ghetto" would occasionally sparkle but he had lost his brilliant glow (Goldstein and Graham 1959, 56, 60, 65–66).

Barney Ross and Jewish Fighters in the Depression

The level of competition in professional boxing was extraordinary during the depression as hungry young men of all ethnic groups sought whatever means they could to put money on the table. Nat Fleischer of *Ring* magazine estimated that there were eight-thousand professional boxers in this era. Despite fierce competition, Jews continued to produce an important share of the best prizefighters. One-sixth (15.9 percent) of the sixty world champions in the 1930s were Jewish, slightly below their representation of the previous decade (16.3 percent). There were seven individual Jewish American champions, including Barney Ross, who held two major titles simultaneously. The proportion of Jewish titleists was second only to the Italians, but there was a decline in the number of contenders, with the Jews falling to third place behind the Italians and Irish.[13]

13. Ross also held a third title in the junior welterweight division. Ross and fellow Chicagoan Jackie Fields were Jewish champions who lost, and later regained, world championships. Fields was welterweight champion in 1929–30

American-born Jewish fighters in the 1930s continued to come primarily from New York City, the national center of prizefighting, and still the site of the largest and poorest Jewish communities. The greatest Jewish fighter from New York during the depression was "Slapsie Maxie" Rosenbloom of Harlem, a much underrated pugilist, whose nickname came from his habit of slapping opponents with open gloves. Rosenbloom started boxing in 1923 and became undisputed light heavyweight champion in 1930. Maxie kept the title for four years until he was dethroned by Bob Olin, another Jewish fighter. During his fifteen-year career he had 289 matches with 203 victories, a remarkable achievement, especially considering his unorthodox training (or lack of training) techniques. But he fought so often that he didn't have to train. Known as the "Playboy of the Ring" for his active social life, Max later became an actor in grade B Hollywood movies (Albertanti 1926; Fleischer 1932; Carroll 1936; Carroll 1947; *NYT* 1976, Mar. 8; *EJS*, 170; Sammons 1988, 92).

Much media attention was given heavyweight fighter Max Baer, a handsome 6'4", 220-lb., finely chiseled athlete, who was at best nominally Jewish (paternal grandmother). As Peter Levine points out, however, the significance of Baer's ethnic identity was how he encouraged it, and how others saw him as a symbol of the tough Jew to challenge anti-Semitic stereotypes. On June 8, 1933, in New York, when Baer won a surprising victory over former champion Max Schmeling, he wore a Star of David on his trunks for the

and in 1932–33. There was much confusion in the middleweight ranks after the relinquishment of the crown by Mickey Walker in 1931, when he moved up to a heavier division. *Ring* credits Marcel Thil of France as champion from 1932 to 1937 but acknowledges the widely accepted claims of other men during this period. The highly regarded New York Boxing Commission recognized Ben Jeby as their champion in 1932–33. Late in 1938 Solly Krieger gained the National Boxing Association championship until he lost his crown in a rematch eight months later with former champion Al Hostak. Undisputed Jewish American champions in the 1930s included light heavyweights Maxie Rosenbloom (1930–34) and Bob Olin (1934–35), welterweights Jackie Fields (1929–30, 1932–33) and Barney Ross (1934, 1935–38), and lightweights Al Singer (1930) and Ross (1933–35). Flyweight champion Young Perez (1931–32) of Tunis was also Jewish (*EJS*, 170). On the proportion of Jewish contenders, see Weinberg and Arond 1952, 460.

first time in his career, a ploy, according to a trainer, to attract Jewish fans. Yet Baer later argued that as far as Hitler was concerned, he was a Jew. One year later, on June 14, Baer took the heavyweight crown from Primo Carnera, the huge Italian title-holder who had won the championship through the connivance of his underworld management (Levine 1992, 180–83; Fleischer 1942; Sammons 1988, 94–95). Baer claimed to be "the first bona fide heavyweight champion of the Jewish race," and many Jewish periodicals happily identified him as one of their own. He sought a rematch with Schmeling in Hamburg, but Hitler balked. Max declared, "Every punch in the eye I give Schmeling is one for Adolf Hitler" (Sammons 1988, 106). Baer quickly made money from endorsements and radio and film appearances. He lost his only title defense on June 13, 1935, by decision to journeyman Jimmy Braddock, which up to then was one of the greatest upsets in the heavyweight championship. Contemporary boxing experts often belittle Baer's achievements because he seemed to waste his talent with a devil-may-care attitude, but Max did win seventy of eighty-three matches (fifty-two by knockout) and was elected to boxing's Hall of Fame in 1968.

The preeminent Jewish fighter of the 1930s was Barney Ross (born Barnet David Rosofsky), outranked only by Joe Louis and Henry Armstrong among all depression-era fighters. *Ring* magazine recently rated him one of the three gutsiest fighters of all time. He was born on the Lower East Side in 1909 to Orthodox Russian immigrants. They moved to the impoverished Maxwell Street area in Chicago's Near West Side two years later, where the father opened a general store. It was next door to the home of the notorious gangster Nails Morton, who was unwelcomed as a patron (Ross and Abrahamson 1957, 11, 21, 65; *EJS*, 171–174). The neighborhood was home to Orthodox Polish and Russian Jewish immigrants who tried to reestablish as much of the old shtetl lifestyle as they could (Wirth 1928, 171–292; Mazur 1977, 273–81; Cutler 1995, 131–46, 151–60; Berkow 1977). The ability to fight well was a highly respected skill among second-generation West Siders, especially during the Prohibition era, because it showed Gentiles that Jews were as brave and manly as anyone. Tough Jews fought to defend life, limb, property, and turf in an area surrounded by poor Irish, Polish, and Italians with whom they did not enjoy cordial relations.

2.3. Barney Ross, lightweight champion
of the world, 1933–35; welterweight
champion of the world, 1934, 1935–38.
Courtesy of George Eisen.

West Side Jews were periodically terrorized by toughs from other
groups, particularly Poles. Their protection came from social and
basement clubs (also known as social and athletic clubs). The best-
known protectors included men such as the gangster Nails Morton,
whose funeral was attended by five-thousand people, and the Miller
brothers. The Millers had a reputation for being roughnecks who
should not be crossed, but were also regarded as heroes who shielded
the community against its enemies. Five of the seven Miller brothers were tough guys, who put their street-fighting skills to ample
use. The Miller's gang, one-fourth of whom were reportedly
prizefighters, was led by Davey, himself a former boxer and nation-
ally renowned referee. His rough siblings included Al, a sometime

boxing manager; Harry, a policeman with underworld connections; Hirschie, a prominent underworld figure who imported liquor from Canada; and Max, a liquor distributor. Both Hirschie and Max faced murder charges but were acquitted (Thrasher 1963, 12, 150; Haller 1971–72, 221–27; Levine interview; Ross and Abrahamson 1957, 38; Cutler 1995, 157–58; Bernstein 1991; Roth 1991, 1, 7–9; "Runyon on Davey Miller" 1993; Miller scrapbook; Landesco 1929, 155, 157, 198, 228, 231–32).

Barney Ross grew up in this rugged West Side environment where boxers were idols. During the 1920s even the Yiddish press published articles on the exploits of Jewish boxers. Yiddish papers symbolically legitimized the ring by publishing cigarette advertisements that depicted sparring heavyweights discussing (in Yiddish) the superior quality of "Old Golds" (Levine 1992, 148ff.). Barney fought in the streets along with his friends, but his father hoped to cure him of that habit. "Let the atheists be the fighters, the trumboniks, the murderers," he told his son. "We are the scholars." In 1924 Barney's father was murdered in his store by hoodlums, and the fourteen-year-old was badly scarred by this tragedy. The family was broken up after his mother's nervous breakdown. Barney and a brother moved in with cousins, and the younger siblings went to an orphanage. He quit school and left the synagogue. "I wanted to be as bad as bad can be. I felt as if I wanted to knock over anybody who walked in front of me." He became a participant in street gang fights. Barney applied for a job in Louis "Two Gun" Altarie's gang but was rejected out of respect for his deceased pious father. Altarie sent him to Al Capone's nightclub, The Four Deuces, and Capone gave Barney odd jobs, mainly as a messenger boy (Ross and Abrahamson 1957, 22, 41–65).

Barney's next job was as a stock boy at Sears, Roebuck, when, encouraged by his friends, he began to cultivate his fistic ambitions, frequenting Kid Howard's Gymnasium, just outside the Maxwell Street neighborhood. Like his peers, he was familiar with the exploits of Jewish heroes such as Benny Leonard and idolized a boy from the neighborhood, Jackie Fields, who had won an Olympic gold medal in the flyweight division in 1924 when he was sixteen years old, the youngest in history (Heller 1973, 129–39; Berkow 1977, 141–49). The previous Jewish Olympic boxing champions had been heavyweight Sam Berger in 1904 and lightweight Sam Mosberg in 1920.

Barney developed into an excellent amateur bantamweight once he was discovered by Davey Miller, who got him into the Golden Gloves, a national amateur boxing competition. Barney fought under a pseudonym so his mother would not find out what he was doing. Although professional boxing was prohibited in Chicago until 1927, there were many small boxing clubs all over the city where amateurs fought. Even before he was sixteen he would fight two or three times a week, winning medals, shoes, shirts, ties, and other prizes that he pawned (Ross and Abrahamson 1957, 41–65; Roth 1991, 7). When his mother discovered that her boy was boxing, she berated Barney. "No son of mine is going to be a fighter, a bum! You are shaming your father's name. Your father wanted you to be a Hebrew teacher, someone to be proud of. Isn't it bad enough you have gone away from his teachings. . . . Now you want to be a fighter. . . . Never, never . . . I forbid it! (Ross and Abrahamson 1957, 80). But in the end there was nothing she could do about it. Sarah Rosofsky sewed a Star of David on his trunks so he would "have protection from God." Barney promised to stop fighting once he got the family together. When Barney became a pro, she would get ill waiting for the phone call reporting the outcome of the fight. So he persuaded his mother to attend the matches instead. They were usually on Friday evenings, and Mrs. Rosofsky would walk to the neighborhood boxing clubs or five miles to the Chicago Stadium, usually accompanied by local children (Ross and Abrahamson 1957, 86, 115).

Barney was a great draw as an amateur, and the neighborhood youth followed him all over the city. His fans included the gangsters for whom he had once run errands, and one night Al Capone bought out Kid Howard's Gym so he and his friends could see Barney in action. Ross's amateur career climaxed in 1929 when he won the featherweight title at the national Golden Gloves championship (Ross and Abrahamson 1957, 82–86).

Barney's professional career started off poorly under Davey Miller, who was very busy at the time, and gave his young fighter to Gig Rooney, the manager of Jackie Fields, now welterweight champion of the world. Under Rooney, Ross suffered from poor training habits, a fascination with night life, and sloppy gym work. His third manager, the well-known Sam Pian, and his new trainer, Art Winch, persuaded Ross to turn himself around, and he began to realize his potential. Ross's big break came early in 1932 when he defeated lightweight contender Ray Miller, also a West Side Chicago Jew, and earned a championship bout against Tony Canzoneri, holder of the lightweight and junior welterweight titles. On June 23, 1933, some thirteen-thousand fans at the Chicago Stadium saw the hometown boy win by a decision and thereby gain two championship crowns. Ross became a great hero in the Windy City, especially on the West Side. Boys followed him in the street, girls wrote him romantic letters, and civic leaders invited him to public functions (Ross and Abrahamson 1957, 91–125; Roth 1991, 7; "Runyon on Davey Miller" 1991; *EJS*, 172–74).

In 1934 Ross stepped up in class to challenge welterweight champion Jimmy McLarnin, an Irishman renowned for his victories over prominent Jewish fighters such as Ruby Goldstein, Benny Leonard, Kid Kaplan, and Al Singer. Ross was spurred on to avenge those defeats, and to stand up for all Jews against their growing mistreatment in Germany. The fight at the Long Island Bowl on May 28 was attended by forty-five-thousand fans who saw the underdog Ross knocked down in the ninth for the first time in his career. Yet Ross responded, and knocked McLarnin to the floor later that round. He kept the champion off balance, and won a fifteen-round split decision. Ross became the first fighter to simultaneously hold three championships. American Jews, including Sarah Rosofsky, thought this victory would show Hitler that the Jewish people could not be pushed around.

On September 17 Ross and McLarnin had a rematch that McLarnin won by a decision, regaining his title. The two pugilists had a third and final match on May 28, 1935, at the Polo Grounds, with Barney coming out on top with a unanimous fifteen-round decision. Ross outgrew the lightweight and junior welterweight divisions, but remained welterweight champion for three years. In one of Ross's greatest fights a few months later, he defeated Ceferino Garcia, after breaking his right thumb two days earlier, by fighting exclusively with his left hand. On May 31, 1938, he lost his title to the great Henry Armstrong, who gave Barney an awful beating, but pride kept Ross on his feet until the final bell. He subsequently retired with a record of 74-4-3 and one no-decision (Andre and Fleischer 1981, 258–62, 297; Ross and Abrahamson 1957, 140, 150–59; M. Fried 1991, 87; Levine 1992, 178).

Ross earned about $500,000 in the ring, but his inveterate gambling, particularly at the track, left him virtually broke. He had a hard time adjusting to retirement and opened a cocktail lounge to take advantage of his fame. When World War II broke out, he volunteered for the Marine Corps, becoming a heavily decorated hero at Guadalcanal. Ross was severely wounded and while recuperating developed an addiction to his medicine that continued for several years after his discharge. Barney's life was portrayed in two movies, *Body and Soul* (1947), and *Monkey on My Back* (1957), which dealt with his drug addiction (*NYT* 1967, Jan. 19; Ross and Abrahamson 1957, 159–71; *EJS,* 172–74).

Ross's retirement virtually marked the end of the Jewish boxing era in America. The last Jewish American champion for forty years was Solly Krieger, who won the middleweight championship on November 1, 1938, and held it until June 27, 1939. Krieger was controlled, like most middleweights, by mobster Frankie Carbo, a dominant force in the sport from the mid-1930s until about 1960. There were few Jewish fighters of note after Krieger, and during the 1940s it became increasingly rarer to see Jewish names on boxing cards ("Thumb Nail Sketches" 1939, July 15; *EJS,* 162; Coughlan 1955, 17).[14]

Retired Jewish boxers were more successful out of the ring compared with most professional fighters who historically fared poorly outside the ring. Fighters left boxing with no skills (unless they became trainers), no education, and varying states of brain damage. Even the greatest champions suffered sharp falls. Abe Attell, Benny Leonard, and Barney Ross all lost fortunes, Leonard because of the depression, and Attell and Ross because of high living. It was not uncommon for fighters, especially the less successful, to end up back where they started. Kirson Weinberg's classic study of ninety-five former contenders and champions reported that most suffered a severe decline after retirement, with one-fourth ending up blue collar. By comparison a survey of thirty-six notable Jewish fighters found only one who ended up with a manual job. Although this crude sample probably overestimates their success, they did fare

14. Robert Cohen (1954–56) and Alphonse Halimi (1957–59, 1960–61) were Jewish Algerian bantamweight champions (*EJS,* 152, 157; Blady 1988, 285–92). After Krieger, the next Jewish American boxing champion was Mike Rossman (Jewish on his mother's side), who held the light heavyweight championship from 1978 to 1979. The next, and last, Jewish champion was Saoul Mamby of the Bronx, the WBC junior welterweight champion (1980–82) (Blady 1988, 295–302).

much better than most fighters and were unlikely to end up down and out as did former lightweight champion "Beau" Jack, who became a shoeshine boy. Former Jewish fighters were more likely to remain in the sport (27.8 percent compared with 21.1 percent of Weinberg's cohort), particularly in a leadership position. They were much less likely to end up in the restaurant or tavern business (11.1 percent compared with 27.4 percent), where successful former athletes often seemed to end up. On the other hand, one-third of the former Jewish boxers were either in other businesses or had a high white-collar job compared with merely 2.1 percent of Weinberg's group (Weinberg and Arond 1952, 469; Hare 1971).

The Jewish Impact Outside the Ring

The influence of Jewish Americans on boxing in the early twentieth century was hardly limited to the principals in the ring. By the 1920s Jews were active in all aspects of the boxing business, just as they were heavily involved in aspects of the entertainment business that were shunned by the more established ethnic groups. A Jew, for instance, Sol Levinson of San Francisco, invented the modern boxing glove, and the Everlast Company, the leading manufacturer of boxing gloves, trunks, and other equipment, was founded and operated by Russian Jewish immigrants. *Ring* magazine, the principal periodical in boxing, was established in 1922 by boxing writer Nat Fleischer, the preeminent journalist in the field, in association with sportswriter Dan Daniel. The monthly was a great source of information about the background of prizefighters and the history of boxing. Its monthly rankings of fighters was considered definitive. In 1941 Fleischer introduced the annual *Ring Record Book,* and it quickly became the bible of boxing fans. Fleischer was the leading popular historian of boxing and wrote many books, including a biography of Benny Leonard and a five-volume collective biography of African American fighters called *Black Dynamite* (Fleischer 1958; *EJS,* 155–56; Blady 1988, 63; *NYT* 1983, July 10; 1972, June 26). After World War II, Barney Nagler and Lester Bromberg were among the most eminent boxing writers.

Jews were also notable writers of fiction employing boxing themes. In 1937 Clifford Odets wrote the play *Golden Boy* about a second-generation Italian American prizefighter who gave up his violin to become a fighter. Boxing was going to be his route to the American dream, but in a Faustian bargain, protagonist Joe Bonaparte sells his soul to become "somebody." There were a lot of risks in the deal, however, beginning with the fighter/violinist damaging his hands while punching. Joe subsequently kills an opponent in the ring and later dies in a car crash. The role of Joe was originated on Broadway by John Garfield (the 1939 movie featured William Holden), who later starred in the aforementioned *Body and Soul* (1947), which was loosely based on Barney Ross's life; Midge Kelly, the protagonist of *Champion* (1949), based on a story by Ring Lardner, was portrayed by Kirk Douglas. Jewish novelists who have used boxing as their theme include Budd Schulberg's *The Harder They Fall* (1947) and Harold Robbins's *A Star for Danny Fisher* (1951). Norman Mailer did not write any boxing novels but was himself an amateur boxer, and wrote a biography of Muhammed Ali. Schulberg's novel told the story of Toro Molina, a circus strongman, nearly seven feet tall, who has no fighting talent, but became a contender because a gangster fixed all his matches. When Molina finally fights a legitimate bout, he is badly injured, and gets paid, after expenses, $49.07. Schulberg also wrote much boxing nonfiction, including important investigative articles on the influence of organized crime for *Sports Illustrated* in the mid-1950s. Rod Serling treated boxing like Schulberg in his pithy "Requiem for a Heavyweight" (1956), a powerful TV drama that vividly portrayed the depravity and degradation of the ring (Weaks 1985, 129; Brenman-Gibson 1981, 465–68, Bergan 1982, 34–36).

Just as Jewish fighters succeeded Irishmen into the ring, they also followed the Irish into jobs as referees (a part-time job), trainers, managers, and promoters. Among the most famous referees between the 1930s and 1950s were Davey Miller, Benny Leonard, and especially Ruby Goldstein, all former fighters. Miller began refereeing amateur bouts sponsored by the *Chicago Tribune* in 1923 when there were no pro bouts in Chicago. He refereed about five-thousand bouts until he retired in 1950. Miller was the scheduled referee for the 1927 Dempsey-Tunney championship fight that marked the return of pro boxing to Chicago. However, minutes before the fight the Illinois Boxing Commission replaced him with Dave Barry, who worked the famous "long count" fight (Goldstein and Graham, 1959; Roth 1991, 1, 7–9; Roberts 1979, 258–63). At a retirement dinner in the early 1950s, Miller revealed that he had been beckoned the night before the fight and driven to a South Side hotel where Al Capone joined him in the car. Capone told him he was betting $50,000 on Dempsey. "Dave, all I want you to do tomorrow night is to give Dempsey an even break." Miller told the press that "there were no actual threats, but. . . . " (*Chicago Herald-American* n.d., in Miller Scrapbook).

Trainers were also former pugilists. They learned their trade from their boxing career and by apprenticing with experienced trainers who taught them their secrets. There were many noted Jewish trainers in the 1920s and 1930s, including Heinie Blaustein, who trained five world champions; Izzy Klein, who worked with Barney Ross and Max Baer; and Mannie Seamon, considered among the slickest and fastest thinkers, who worked with Leach Cross, Benny Valgar, Ted "Kid" Lewis, Benny Leonard, and Joe Louis. In one bout, when Mannie's fighter was nearly knocked out, he surreptitiously cut the ring ropes. The thirty minutes needed to fix the ropes enabled his fighter to recuperate. In another bout, in which his fighter Archie Bell had a bad eye cut, Mannie gashed a glove causing the referee to stop the fight to switch equipment, which gave him time to repair the wound so that Bell could continue (M. Fried 1991, 74, 235–36).

Successful trainers, such as Seamon, Ray Arcel, and Charley Goldman, had very long careers. Israel "Charley" Goldman was born in Warsaw in 1888, and came to America two years later. He dropped out of school in the fourth grade after his teacher slapped him, and Charley slapped him back. "Then I ran out of the class and never came back. I'd leave the house every day and go to the back of a saloon and fight for change, and then come back home and say I went to school all day." He was taught to fight as a boy by Terry McGovern, but the bantamweight never made more than $900 in any of his four-hundred-odd fights. He started training fighters in 1914, and eventually worked more than two-thousand fights. He trained five world champions—Al McCoy, Joey Archibald, Lou Ambers, Marty Servo, and Rocky Marciano. Marciano came to him as a very crude brawler, but Goldman saw his potential and desire, and taught Rocky the balance and leverage needed to become a great boxer. He instructed him how to fight from a crouch, how to slip punches, and how to use his left hand. Goldman put towels under Rocky's arms to make him throw straighter punches, tied his right hand behind his body to develop the left, and corrected Marciano's poor footwork by tying his shoelaces together (Goldstein and Graham 1959, 23–29, 182–83; B. Miller 1932; Lesemen 1947c; Jones 1948; Grombach 1977, 186; Blady 1988, 67, 69; M. Fried 1991, 167; Liebling 1990, 40–42).

The most outstanding Jewish trainer was Ray Arcel, honored in 1988 by the Downtown Athletic Club as "Boxing Man of the Century" (Anderson 1991, 120). Arcel trained fighters from the late teens until 1954, when he retired after training Ezzard Charles for his rematch with Rocky Marciano. A. J. Liebling in *The Sweet Science* described him as "severe and decisive, like a teacher in a Hebrew school." Arcel was born in 1899 to an immigrant from Odessa who married a New York girl and settled in Terre Haute, Indiana, where he was a wholesaler of candies, fruits, and nuts. The family relocated to New York in 1903, going into the dairy business shortly before his mother died of diabetes. The family moved from the Lower East Side to Italian Harlem after the business failed. Young Ray got into many fights with the Italians, who referred to him as a "masacristo" (Jew Killer). "You had to fight in those days. You lived in a neighborhood where you were challenged every day. We were the only Jewish family there. . . . If you didn't fight you were yellow" (Fried 1991, 62). His family was so poor that when he went to Stuyvesant High School, five miles away, he rollerskated to school. Ray learned to box at the Union Settlement, and at fifteen had twelve professional fights for which he earned up to three dollars. After graduating from high school, he spent most of his time at Grupp's Gym learning to become a trainer (M. Fried 1991, 56).

> In those days the trainer was the boss. The trainer took control of the fighter and we didn't have to have any bodyguards, we didn't have to have anybody. We just did our business, went in there, the trainer made out the schedule, he took control of the whole program. What to eat, when to eat, when to sleep, when to work, how much to work, and all of that, and that was your responsibility. (Arcel interview, 134)

Ray learned the craft from noted trainers Doc Bagley and Dai Dollings and by watching and listening to boxers, particularly Benny

Leonard. As Arcel remembered, "His main asset was his ability to think. He had the sharpest mind. He was the one fighter that I saw who could make you do the things he wanted you to do. He could feint you into knots. He was a master of the feint" (62). Arcel considered himself a teacher rather than a trainer, and learned to treat each fighter as an individual. "I had great patience. I never scolded a fighter, especially a young fighter because I learned early in my career that that's the easiest way to discourage a fighter" (72). He believed in positive reinforcement. He would start about eight or nine in the morning and not leave the gym until seven or eight. Then as often as six nights a week he would work at local arenas in his fighters' corner. He lived modestly and completely devoted himself to his boxers. During the depression he often walked home to Queens, fifteen miles from Stillman's Gym to save money, which he often ended up giving to a fighter (17, 71–73).

Arcel trained eighteen world champions, beginning with bantamweights Abe Goldstein in 1924 and Charley Phil Rosenberg one year later. He stressed conditioning in half-mile to mile intervals ("Walk, jog, sprint") and developing the traits needed for success: "Mental energy. Self-control. Determination" (Anderson 1991, 121, 122). His most outstanding achievement as a trainer probably occurred in 1925 when he helped Rosenberg drop from 155 to 116 lbs. (two pounds under the bantamweight maximum) in three months and then win the title from Eddie "Cannonball" Martin. Besides Rosenberg's normal sparring and training regimen, the two walked ten miles a day together, shared a spartan diet, and slept in the same room so that Arcel could keep an eye on his champion (Blady 1988, 187).

Arcel's partner for nine years (1925–34) was Whitey Bimstein, but they never made much money, usually twenty to twenty-five dollars a night. (Anderson 1991, 123). Known as "the Siamese Training Twins," their fighters included junior welterweight champion Jackie "Kid" Berg ("the Whitechapel Whirlwind"), middleweight champ Lou Brouillard, and bantamweight champion Sixto Escobar. Kid Berg (Judah Bergman) was known for carrying tzitzis (fringed garments worn by Orthodox Jews) into the ring and waving them. As Arcel remembered,

Most of the fight fans were Jews. They used to go crazy. And he used to take the tzitzis and put 'em right on top of the ring posts.

And the commission called me down one day, and they said to me, "We can't allow this." I says, "Well, Commissioner, he does this the same way as a Catholic boy would go to a corner, kneel and bless himself. It's the same thing," I says, "only he does it to get the crowd cheering him." (M. Fried 1991, 87)

In all, Arcel trained twenty-one champions including Corporal Izzy Schwartz, Jackie Fields, Barney Ross, Tony Zale, Jackie Fields, Bob Olin, and Ezzard Charles. Arcel was such an extraordinary teacher and conditioner that he was brought out of retirement to periodically work with Roberto Duran, particularly his two bouts with Sugar Ray Leonard in 1972 and 1980. He was renowned for his full bag of tricks that included reviving a fighter by biting his ear or lighting a match to his spine (Arcel telephone interview; Arcel interview, 2–3, 6–9, 17, 18, 23, 25, 46–48, 94–100, 152–54).

In 1953 and 1954 Arcel promoted "Saturday Night Fights" on ABC-TV at 9:00 P.M. EST. Arcel's matches were often held in the hometown of one of the fighters, which would be blacked out (no local TV) to build up a large studio audience. Arcel's venture met much opposition from the International Boxing Club that monopolized championship fights, and probably from other rivals as well. He received threatening phone calls urging him to get out of the business. In March 1953 he picked up a telephone from a caller who told him, "Get out of the TV racket, if you know what's good for you!" Ray was attacked in Boston in the middle of the afternoon on September 19, 1953, by a thug with a crowbar in front of the Hotel Manger next to the Boston Garden while chatting with fight manager Willie Ketchum. Ketchum, who had underworld ties, could not identify the assailant. Ray was hospitalized for nineteen days (Arcel interview, 79–86, 126–28; Cohane and Grayson 1954; M. Fried 1991, 97–98).[15]

While a successful trainer needed to have much specialized knowledge, anyone could become a manager, although it was obviously

15. Arcel was candid in his interview with me about all subjects, but would not discuss the attack, which the police never solved. A similar attack had befallen on promoter Sam Silverman a few years earlier. Silverman was beaten by an attacker with brass knuckles who was arrested and sent to prison. He later collaborated with Arcel in the "Saturday Night Fights" (Cohane and Grayson 1954, 42).

advantageous if they had expertise in the sport. The manager's job was to hire a trainer for his fighter, arrange matches, and negotiate contracts. It was potentially a lucrative job because the manager got one-third of his fighter's purse after expenses (or one-half before expenses). The occupation attracted Jews with an entrepreneurial bent, typically men who had grown up in poor neighborhoods with fellows who would become prizefighters. Jewish managers usually started out with the contracts of Jewish boxers they had recruited as novices who showed potential in the streets, at settlement houses, or boxing gymnasiums.

The first prominent Jewish manager was Sam Harris, whose prizefighter was "Terrible" Terry McGovern, world champion bantamweight (1899) and featherweight (1899–1901). Harris not only arranged McGovern's fighting schedule but also tried to help him benefit from his fame by putting Terry on the stage in plays such as *The Bowery after Dark*. Harris subsequently became a famous theatrical impresario in partnership with George M. Cohan. He owned three theaters in New York, two in Chicago and Boston, and produced the Irving Berlin Music Box reviews (Fleischer 1943).

By the early 1930s there were more than twenty prominent Jewish managers. Among the best known were Sam Pian, the manager of Barney Ross; Frank Bachman, who directed the affairs of Maxie Rosenbloom; Al Weill, whose fighters included Tony Canzoneri, Lou Ambers and Rocky Marciano; and Max Waxman, a Baltimore restauranteur who was Jack Dempsey's business partner for many years. Waxman had managed fighters since he was nineteen years old in 1910, when he started with Young Italy (Meyer Horowitz), and was the only manager to take brothers (Vince and Joe Dundee) to championships (Grombach 1977, 176, 178–79; Goldstein and Graham 1959, 23–62; B. Miller 1932).[16]

The most colorful manager was probably Lena Levy, who managed her brother, "Kingfish" Levinsky (Harry Krakow), a leading heavyweight contender by the time he was twenty-one. She was known as "Leaping Lena" because of her agitated state during his fights. Lena took over her brother's affairs because she felt his

16. Hirschberg and Aaronson (1957) focuses more on Aaronson's youthful days in Brownsville and his efforts to use boxing to save inner city young men than on his work as a boxing manager.

managers had undervalued him. In 1931, for instance, he got $4,000 for a ten-rounder in Chicago, while his opponent got $25,000. She got him better contracts, but often put Kingfish in the ring with fighters above his class. For example, she got him a nontitle bout with champion Max Baer in 1934 and a match with the up-and-coming Joe Louis in 1935, and Levinsky was pummeled in both fights. Lena retired in 1936 after she was slapped with a suspension for misconduct after one of her brother's defeats.[17]

The best-known Jewish manager in the 1920s and 1930s, and certainly the most remarkable, was Joe "Yussel the Muscle" Jacobs, whose ethnicity was important in his career. In 1924, for instance, he took his world champion light heavyweight Mike McTigue to Columbus, Georgia, to defend his crown against local favorite "Young" Stribling. A prominent local resident visited them before the bout and warned them that the Ku Klux Klan "had little patience with un-American or unsportsmanlike tricks." The gentleman then pointed out the window and told Jacobs and McTigue that "there is one tree apiece, and there is plenty of rope. May the right man win." The referee was also intimidated. He gave McTigue the decision, then reversed himself twice, first calling the challenger the victor, and finally declaring the bout a draw. The next day, after escaping town, the referee proclaimed McTigue winner and still champion (Sports Files, AJA; Andre and Fleischer, 1981, 186).

Jacobs was a skilled boxing coach who could make a contender out of portly "Two Ton" Tony Galento, but was best known as the manager of Max Schmeling, the noted German heavyweight. In 1930 Schmeling fought Jack Sharkey in an elimination contest to determine the successor to retired champion Gene Tunney. Schmeling was knocked down in the fourth round, but Jacobs jumped into the ring claiming his man had been fouled. The referee upheld his

17. Krakow originally wanted to take an Irish name like Knockout Hogan, but his manager (probably Al Miller) told him that a Jewish name was better box office, especially because there had never been a Jewish heavyweight champion. Sources disagree on how Levinsky got his fighting name. Some claim it was from the family fish business (though some sources say it was taken from a character in *Amos 'n' Andy*) and from "Battling" Levinsky, the light heavyweight champion from 1916 to 1920. One of his first managers was Al Miller, one of the famous Miller brothers (Roth 1993, 9–11; Blady 1988, 213).

claim, and Schmeling became champion. Two years later, they had a rematch that Sharkey won by a controversial decision. Schmeling was able to keep Jacobs as his American manager even after the rise of the Nazis, because Hitler and his crowd wanted the German to recapture the title for the glory of the Fatherland, and felt they needed Jacobs's help. Four years later Jacobs got Schmeling a fight with the up-and-coming Joe Louis on June 19, 1936, at Yankee Stadium, and to everyone's surprise the former champion fought brilliantly and won with a twelfth-round knockout. After Louis became champion in 1937, there was much public interest in a possible rematch that Louis wanted to vindicate himself and avenge his previous humbling defeat. Jewish groups put pressure on the Jewish promoter Mike Jacobs to block the championship fight, and their efforts only increased after Yussel Jacobs went to Germany where he purportedly saluted Hitler. He reported that conditions were good for Jews in Germany and blamed their problems on American Jews. Promoter Mike Jacobs was also strongly castigated by Jewish groups, who called him a traitor for bringing over Hitler's favorite boxer for a championship fight. The Louis-Schmeling match took place June 22, 1938, as seventy-thousand fans packed Yankee Stadium. It lasted merely 124 seconds as Louis pulverized his contender in the second shortest battle in heavyweight championship history (AJA; Andre and Fleischer 1981, 113, 121; Sammons 1988, 115; *EJS,* 160).[18]

The Jewish entrepreneurial tradition was particularly reflected by their prominence in boxing promotion. Most promoters at the turn of the century were Irish politicians (Riess 1985, 97–98, 109), but by the early 1930s there were about two dozen Jewish promoters of note across the country. In Chicago, for example, most of its major clubs and arenas were operated by Jewish businessmen, including Maurice Feldman at the Rainbow Fronton, Irv Schoenwald and Jack Begun at the Marigold Gardens, and Nate Lewis at the Chicago Stadium. Major Jewish promoters then included Sam Silverman in Boston, Benny Geigerman in New Orleans, and Larry Atkins in Cleveland, all of whom were closely connected to Frankie

18. There is little evidence that Schmeling was anti-Semitic, and he saved the lives of a Jewish friend's children during Kristallnacht (Weisbord and Hedderich 1993, 36–41).

Carbo, the underworld's tsar of boxing. Some promoters, such as Max Waxman and Al Weill, the matchmaker for Madison Square Garden in the early 1950s, were also managers. Weill circumvented this clear conflict of interest by getting relatives or associates to "front" for him. The friends and business associates of certain promoters were not necessarily the most honorable. Herman Taylor, a notable Philadelphia boxing figure for more than forty years, who was an important manager and the city's leading promoter, admitted in a 1951 Senate investigation of organized crime that he knew such noted gangsters as Carbo, Capone, "Lucky" Luciano, Frank Costello, and Jake Guzik. Investigators at the 1960 hearings into prizefighting claimed that Taylor operated under the influence of Carbo and former bootlegger Nig Rosen (Bentley interview; B. Miller 1932; Grombach 1977, 233; *EJS*, 179; Fleischer 1946; Fleischer 1951; Brenner and Nagler 1981, 21–24, 29; U.S. Cong., Senate Judiciary Committee 1961, 114, 348).

Mike Jacobs was the preeminent Jewish boxing promoter and the successor to Tex Rickard as the leading entrepreneur in the sport. Mike was born March 17, 1880, and reared on the Lower East Side. He got his start in the entertainment business scalping tickets and did so well that he helped finance such sports promotions as the six-day bicycle races in return for the best seats. Jacobs was a boxing fan who first became directly involved in the sport in 1915 when Tex Rickard came to New York to promote the Jess Willard–Frank Moran heavyweight championship fight. Rickard needed a local backer to help finance the fight and resolve his political problems with Tammany Hall, and Jacobs proved to be his man. Six years later Jacobs made his first major boxing deal when he helped Rickard promote the Dempsey-Carpentier fight by raising $100,000, and in return was given an opportunity to buy a huge number of expensive ringside seats that he resold at a premium. Rickard later relied on Jacobs for assistance in some of his biggest fights, such as the Dempsey-Firpo match at the Polo Grounds in 1923 and the two Dempsey-Tunney championship fights (Daniel 1950, 18–50; Fleischer 1958, 138; Kearns 1963, 142; Albertanti 1936).

When Rickard died in 1929, Jacobs was disappointed he was not selected to replace him as the Garden's boxing promoter. In 1933 Jacobs began organizing matches when he established the Twentieth

Century Sporting Club in partnership with Damon Runyon and two other prominent Hearst journalists. Their first big client was the Hearst Milk Fund, which had sponsored fights at Madison Square Garden to raise money for its charities, but had left in 1934 when the Garden raised its rental fees. The Milk Fund turned to Jacobs for help, and he arranged their bouts at the Long Island Bowl, the Bronx Coliseum, and the midtown Manhattan Hippodrome (Daniel 1950, 53–54; Albertanti 1936; Grombach 1977, 71–72).

Jacobs's success as a promoter resulted from his foresight in signing Joe Louis to an exclusive contract in 1935, before the Brown Bomber had become a household name. Their first great event came on June 25, 1935 at Yankee Stadium, when Louis fought former champion Primo Carnera. The bout drew a $328,655 gate, or about $120,000 more than the Baer-Braddock world championship fight staged a few weeks earlier. On June 22, 1937, Louis got a shot at Braddock's title, despite his earlier loss to Schmeling, because Jacobs promised Joe Gould, Braddock's manager, that the champion would get 10 percent of Jacobs's profits from Louis's future defenses should he lose the title (Fleischer 1958, 139; Grombach 1977, 72–73; Edmonds 1973, 31–33; Andre and Fleischer 1981, 125–30).[19]

By then Jacobs was in total control of the Twentieth Century Sporting Club, which he ran with ruthless vigor. Shortly after the Louis fight, he ended his long dispute with Madison Square Garden when its management agreed to rent him the arena for fights. One year later he took over control of its boxing program. Jacobs developed a near monopoly over major fights in the United States, with, some critics claimed, the support of such underworld characters as Owney Madden, Frankie Carbo, and "Blinky" Palermo. Jacobs required all challengers to agree that he would promote their future title defenses should they win before they could get a championship match.

From 1937 to 1947, Jacobs staged sixty-one championship fights, 320 boxing shows at Madison Square Garden, and countless cards

19. Levine argues (1992, 186–87) that the Non-Sectarian Anti-Nazi League, led by Mayor Fiorello LaGuardia, threatened to boycott the proposed Schmelling-Braddock title fight, and that their pressure had some influence on Joe Gould deciding to fight Louis instead. Many Jewish organizations sought to have Louis's defense against Max Schmeling canceled. Jacobs responded by offering to donate 10 percent of the gate to assist Jewish refugees.

elsewhere. Joe Louis, his biggest draw, fought twenty-five defenses under Jacobs's aegis. Mike's most famous promotion was the second Louis-Schmeling fight that brought in more than a million-dollar gate. However, his most profitable bout, which earned $1.9 million, was Louis's first postwar defense against Billy Conn, who had nearly defeated the Brown Bomber in 1941. A severe illness in 1949 forced Jacobs to relinquish control of the Twentieth Century Boxing Club, and he died later that year. The company was lost without his leadership, and the new, mob-riddled International Boxing Club of James Norris and William Wirtz became the dominant force in boxing promotion (Fleischer 1958, 150; Grombach 1977, 74–75, 220–22; Daniel 1950, 125; Nagler 1964).

• • •

The Jewish American boxing experience reflected the social conditions of a subcommunity of marginal second-generation new immigrants growing up in urban slums in the first third of the twentieth century. Pugilism provided a means for impoverished Jewish athletes, regardless of size, to gain fame, earn money, and stand up for their race. Unlike most Jewish males, who used traditional means to get ahead and become businessmen and professionals (75 percent of Boston's second-generation Jews were white collar, compared with 25 percent of the first generation), a small but significant cohort of the most disadvantaged sought alternate means to escape poverty. These men sought a quick exit from their poor neighborhoods by using what they had learned in the streets and local gymnasiums to become boxers. However, the high rate of social mobility among the well-educated second-generation Jews obviated the need for the third generation to seek alternate routes for success, particularly the violent sport of boxing. As fewer Jews were left behind in the old inner city neighborhoods, and as Jews became more accepted by mainstream society, prizefighting became an anachronism even among athletically talented Jews. Jewish youngsters living in suburbia and the urban fringes had other sporting choices, and they became increasingly successful in more bourgeois sports, such as tennis and swimming. In postwar America, Italians and other tough new inner city residents, particularly African Americans and Latinos, replaced Jews in the ring. Jews continued to play a significant role in the sport, but it was outside the ring,

as trainers, managers, and promoters. The enduring Jewish prominence in the business aspects of the sport reflected the historic
Jewish entrepreneurial tradition that had prepared them so well for
life in America (Thernstrom 1973, 131, 136–37; Kessner 1977).

3

Jewish American Women, Jewish Organizations, and Sports, 1880–1940

Linda Borish

Despite the significant achievements of contemporary Jewish American female athletes in such sports as tennis, golf, and basketball, their historic role in American sport has not been examined (Riess 1995, 7; Borish 1994, 410–11). In tennis, for instance, Jewish women have achieved impressive results in national competitions. In the 1940s Helene Irene Bernhard earned the No. 4 ranking in U.S. singles, one of the highest rankings achieved by an American

Research for this essay has been assisted by the Research and Development Award Program, Western Michigan University. I want to thank Ronald Davis, Chair, Department of History at Western Michigan University, for his support of this research, and Cheryl Lyon-Jenness for her bibliographic assistance. Barbara Melosh provided beneficial comments on historical resources for this project, and Hasia Diner gave me her intellectual support in pursuing this research. Steven Riess offered helpful suggestions and critical comments as I developed this manuscript. I am grateful to Steven Siegel, of the 92d Street YM-YWHA Archives, Lily Schwartz, of the Philadelphia Jewish Archives Center, Preston Levi, of the Henning Library, International Swimming Hall of Fame, and the archives staff at the YIVO Institute for Jewish Research and at the Spertus Institute/Chicago Jewish Archives for their valuable assistance with records consulted for this research project.

Jewish woman. Julie Heldman, a national junior champion and one of the top-ranked players in the United States in the late 1960s and early 1970s, achieved a No. 5 world ranking. Gladys Heldman, Julie's mother, who played some competitive tennis, founded the Virginia Slims Women's Professional Tour in 1971 and served as editor and publisher of *World Tennis,* beginning in 1953 (Slater 1992, 94–97, 241; *EJS,* 443, 447–48). Amy Alcott, since the mid-1970s, has earned victories and prize money on the Ladies Professional Golf Association tour. Nancy Lieberman dominated women's college basketball in the 1970s as an all-American at Old Dominion University. Lieberman made the 1980 Olympic squads, and played in the women's professional basketball league in the 1980s (Slater 1992, 140–43). Yet before these mid- and late-twentieth-century athletes, Jewish American women participated in sports.

This essay examines Jewish American women in sport from 1880 to 1940, exploring the role of various institutions and individuals in shaping the sporting practices of Jewish American women. A historical inquiry of Jewish women in America with a focus on sports yields valuable information about how gender, ethnicity, religion, and social class have shaped the opportunities and constraints of Jewish American women and sports. In particular, this essay investigates how German Jews sought to influence the sporting practices of eastern European Jewish immigrant women and girls. This research explores Jewish settlement houses and the sport and recreation programs for Jewish working-class young women and girls, often promoted by upper- and middle-class Jewish women in urban areas.

Historical research on Jewish American women and sport drawing on various primary sources, such as archival materials, newspaper accounts, American Jewish periodicals, institutional records of Young Men's Hebrew Associations, Young Women's Hebrew Associations, and Jewish settlement houses, documents about Jewish camps for girls, and material culture, offers a rich view of sport in the lives of Jewish American women. Archives of the Young Women's Hebrew Association of New York City, founded in 1902, reveal that the YWHA Jewish female leaders enthusiastically endorsed sports as a valuable part of Jewish working-class females' use of leisure time; a *Bulletin of Classes* for the 1920s communicated to Jewish females, "Maintain your physical fitness by joining our class in Gymnastics. Play Basket Ball! Use our Swimming Pool!" In short, Jewish women ought to partake of sports and "combine health-building exercise with a good time!"

To varying degrees in time and place, Jewish American women participated in sport and physical recreations in Jewish institutions and programs designed to promote Jewish women's spiritual and physical well-being. As American Jewish historian Paula Hyman has maintained, "The complex interplay of gender, social class, and religio-ethnic culture shaped the ways in which Jewish women participated in the economic, cultural, religious, and political life of the immigrant Jewish community and U.S. society" (1995, 223). Likewise, the exploration of the ways Jewish women participated in the sporting life within the immigrant and larger American culture indicates gender, class, ethnic, and religious considerations. Indeed, Hyman has written that "in some ways Jewish women were agents of assimilation; in others, buffers against the disruptive influences of the new society" (Hyman 1995, 97). In the venue of sports, some German Jewish women desired to assimilate new eastern European immigrant females in supervising organized play and exercise programs; at other times, Jewish young working-class women and girls might generate conflict with adult women based on a different outlook on sport and leisure in American culture (Eisen 1991; Goodman 1979; Peiss 1986; Schreier 1994). Although historian Peter Levine remarks that Jewish women's "participation in sport, especially prior to World War II, remained severely limited" (1992, 8), research on Jewish women's sport and physical activity suggests another perspective.

For Jewish immigrant women, exposure to American life and sporting forms often occurred at settlement houses and immigrant aid associations in the latter decades of the nineteenth century. As east European immigrants came to America and populated urban areas such as New York and Philadelphia, frequently the earlier nineteenth-century immigrants, German Jews who by the 1880s became wealthier and oriented to American culture and institutions, sought to assist the newest Jewish immigrants to American culture and customs; many German Jews chose to promote assimilation rather than nurturing the ethnic identities and religiosity of these Jewish immigrants (see e.g. Glanz 1976; Diner 1995; Ewen 1985). During the 1880 to 1920 period of widespread Jewish immigration to the United States, various institutions spearheaded by wealthier German Jews labored to assimilate Jewish people. Historian Gerald Sorin writes (1990, 62–63), "German Jews continually coaxed and prodded the immigrants to Americanize as well as to disperse. These established Jews, often mirroring values current in the Progressive era," Sorin explains, "wanted their Old World coreligionists to discard social habits that made them embarrassingly visible and that stood in the way of rational and efficient adaptation."

In the Progressive era, middle-class social and educational reformers desired to solve urban problems of poverty, poor sanitation, and overcrowding of immigrants in urban areas, and some reformers organized playgrounds for city immigrant children. Reformers Jane Addams and Lillian Wald, and other Progressive era commentators, believed sporting activities a better use of immigrants' leisure time than street activities and the commercial lure of big cities such as Chicago and New York (Addams 1923; 1910; Wald 1915; Davis 1973; Eisen 1991; Nasaw 1985; Riess 1989). Reform-minded German Jewish philanthropists in major cities sought to provide for the educational, social, and physical welfare of Jewish men and women at institutions such as the Young Men's Hebrew Association and auxiliary Women's Hebrew Association and the Educational Alliance in New York City.

The Educational Alliance, founded in 1889, evolved from the merger of the Hebrew Free School Association, the Young Men's Hebrew Association, and the Aguilar Free Library Society, three agencies led by German Jews. The Educational Alliance proclaimed its mission was to help eastern European immigrants in the transition to American society (Sorin 1992, 86–87; Rabinowitz 1948). The Americanization program envisioned by German Jews "sought to inculcate a mixed sensibility, at once American and distinctively Jewish. Acting under the prevailing environmentalist assumptions of the Progressive Era," a historian of the Educational Alliance observed, "the German Jews sought to replace the old forms of Jewish life with new ones, forms that would create a new American Jewish 'content'" for the flood of immigrants pouring in to the Lower East Side of New York (Bellow 1990, 70–78). The ideology of reform and Americanization could and often did generate conflict between German Jews and the eastern European Jews desiring to preserve their Jewishness and ethnic identities. For example, the uptown Jews desiring to Americanize the downtown immigrants believed that the Educational Alliance should discourage all the " 'isms'—socialism, anarchism, Zionism, Bolshevism, unionism, Yiddishism" and the directors promoted the view of Americanizing Jews as the function of the alliance (Bellow 1990, 75–76, 78; Goodman 1979). Some immigrants objected to upper-class German Jews instituting programs aimed at changing the language and habits of eastern European Jews. As Gerald Sorin explains (1992, 87–88), "From its inception, the Educational Alliance came under attack from immigrants of every stripe, who felt they had a culture of their own."

New York City's Educational Alliance considered physical training and sporting experiences for immigrant Jewish females as well as males part of its mission. *The Souvenir Book of the Fair of the Educational Alliance and Hebrew Technical Institute* (1895) stated in its section on "Physical Work" that "the usefulness of the gymnasium has been extended. Competent instructors have been engaged both for the male and female classes, and now both young men and young women and children receive the benefits of well-regulated physical exercise" (13, 23). The Physical Culture Department provided courses for young women and children in the gymnasium two afternoons and one evening during the week in 1899 when the Educational Alliance was incorporated (EA 1900, 32–33). The Women's Section of the alliance was active in shaping the training for working girls. An 1898 House Committee Meeting indicated the need for improved space for women's physical training equipment. "Petition from the Physical Culture Instructor of the Young Women's Section for a closet in Gymnasium" had been accepted by the committee. Female gymnasium activities consisted of "free developing exercises, marching, fancy steps and work with bells, wands, clubs, balls, hops, horse rings, rope and jumping." Physical culture teachers emphasized health-building sporting activities rather than competitive contests. In a report of the Women's Auxiliary Society in March 1902, the chair of the Committee on Physical Culture "urgently recommends that a lady physician be present to examine the girls and women on admission to the gymnasium classes." Thus, the stated goal of such physical exercise was "the cultivation of a good carriage, and the training of muscles and nerves, the bringing the body under control of the will and the reproducing of better health" (EA 1898; EA; 1900; EA 1902; Glanz 1976, I: 44–46).

Physical culture formed a key part of the Americanization plans of the Educational Alliance in its early years. In 1905 the chair of the Special Committee on Reorganization to bolster programs reported that the School of Physical Culture should continue and the "work will furnish a new means for the Americanizing of immigrants" (EA 1905). Women social workers and trainers seemed to heed this counsel in their reports on Jewish girls' activities. Commenting on an athletic meet of the girls, a social worker termed it "a great success, there being about 250 persons in attendance, 100 of whom were mothers of the girls." Increasing the girls' use of the gymnasium appeared in the alliance records. In 1911 Miss Julia Richman, active in philanthropic endeavors, reported to the Committee on Education the suggestion for the gym to be opened on certain afternoons for "girls between the ages of eleven and fifteen, who are wandering aimlessly about the streets and who might be attracted to amusement halls and other places of doubtful influence" (EA 1911; EA 1912). As a counterpoint to the dance halls, saloons, and street life, believed to be dangerous and unhealthy for Jewish girls, the alliance's physical culture promoters wanted girls to participate in sport and exercise. Women physical culture trainers praised "The Walking Club" with the purpose of "arousing girls' interest in city history and at the same time stimulating in them a desire for healthful outdoor exercise." Moreover, the director of Girls' Clubs stated in 1916 that "the Athletic Club . . . is doing excellent work." An effort occurred in 1917 to "secure the pool at the Hebrew Technical Institute School for Girls for a swimming class for our seniors." These athletic pursuits formed part of the Educational Alliance's purpose to "help the newly arrived Jewish immigrants and their immediate descendants to an understanding of the English language" and "customs of the United States" in offering "them opportunities for self-betterment" (EA 1916; EA 1917; EA 1919).

Some upper-rank Jewish women in New York City wanted to increase the sporting facilities for Jewish people in their benevolent and philanthropic work. The corresponding secretary of the YMHA of Harlem, New York, Mr. S. N. Carvalho, in July 1880 expressed the appreciation he and fellow Jewish male sports enthusiasts felt for the assistance given by "the Hebrew ladies of Harlem, who donated the handsome sum of three hundred dollars for the establishment and equipment of gymnasium." The Hebrew ladies held a strawberry festival to raise money to achieve the "great advantages which would accrue to their brothers of the YMHA of Harlem, by their participation in varied athletic exercises as a means of physical culture." The men stated their gratitude of the women's charitable efforts in gender terms expressing expectations of male and female roles in the Progressive era in American society: "That in whatsoever aspect Woman manifests herself to Man, either as mother, wife, daughter, sister or benefactress, she communicates wisdom, admiration and delight, erects a throne in every heart, dispenses with a most gracious and benignant power, a combination of beautiful influences" (Carvalho 1880). Jewish women might participate in fund-raising for sports equipment for Jewish men, but others desired to use athletic facilitates at YMHAs. To acknowledge women's valuable contribution, the YMHA therefore resolved, "That the Hebrew Ladies of Harlem shall always have exclusive and free access to the gymnasium for their own practice at such times as may be decided" by the regulations of the Athletic Society members (Carvalho 1880).

At Young Men's Hebrew Associations, where women could gain access to facilities as affiliated members, designated times for admittance to the gymnasium by men, boys, women, and girls generally appeared in the schedule of activities. The Young Men's Hebrew Association of Louisville, organized primarily for the assistance of eastern European immigrants by well-established Jews led by Isaac W. Bernheim, a Kentucky distiller and philanthropist, completed the gymnasium in 1890; the Louisville YMHA conducted separate classes for women one year later. Girls' and ladies' classes were on Tuesday and Thursdays, and boys' and men's classes on Monday, Wednesday, Friday, and Saturday; the Saturday gymnasium schedule, however, was from 8:00 P.M. to 9:30 P.M. to avoid religious conflicts on the Sabbath. The New York YMHA instituted a similar policy of scheduling separate gymnasium classes for males and females in the 1890s (Weissbach 1995, 266; Rabinowitz 1948, 52, 62, 90). Men usually dominated the use of gymnasiums and sports equipment. An account of the history of the St. Louis

YMHA, established in 1880, related that "the 'W' part of the 'Y' had little or no activity in the old days with the Physical Department being strictly male territory" before a new gymnasium opened with greater opportunities for women ("Physical Department Increases Its Facilities" 1952, 10–11).

Nevertheless, in cities with a significant immigrant Jewish population, several middle- and upper-class German Jewish women created programs of sport and physical education primarily for eastern European Jewish women and girls. Jewish females partook of sporting and recreational pursuits in Jewish settlement house programs. At the Young Women's Union in Philadelphia, founded in 1885 by Miss Fannie Binswanger and other young Jewish philanthropically oriented women who sought to serve the social needs of Russian Jewish immigrants, the women at first opened a kindergarten. Soon other programs followed at this oldest Jewish settlement house in America, including a school for domestic instruction, classes in English and reading, and recreation and sports to give city children a chance to escape the congested city (Young Women's Union, "History"). Young Jewish women and girls were instructed in calisthenics and gymnastics and when the new building opened in 1900, "the gymnasium was used by girls as well as boys" with "Gymnasium Class" conducted by "Miss Caroline Massman and Miss Sadie Kohn" (Young Women's Union, *Twenty-fifth Anniversary Report*, 7–8, 28). Sporting activities continued to be popular with young women and girls; when the Young Women's Union moved into a larger facility in 1900, the president reported the need to construct a new gymnasium.

The Young Women's Union expanded into a settlement house during the first decades of the twentieth century with an emphasis on greater educational and social programs for Jewish immigrants. President Gertrude Berg explained in the *Twenty-seventh Annual Report* (Young Women's Union, 1912) that the Young Women's Union began directing its efforts to "the safe-guarding of our people by giving them in wholesome environment opportunities for recreation," and continued, "We have opened wide our doors to the children of the neighborhood, taking them out of filthy alleys and crowded tenements, and keeping them off the dangerous streets— dangerous to life and limb and dangerous to character" (Greifer

1948, 249–50). Reorganized as the "Neighborhood Centre" in 1918, the director of the agency stated "a recreational program in the settlement was carefully outlined; one which made a ready appeal to groups of unorganized boys and girls." The change in the center's schedule featured added activities in art, dramatics, embroidery, cooking, and athletics (Young Women's Union, *Annual Report, 1916–1917, 6–7;* Young Women's Union, *Director's Report, Apr. 1917 to Apr. 1918, 1–2*).

To promote spiritual and bodily well-being of Jewish females, philanthropists who founded the Irene Kaufmann Settlement House in Pittsburgh in 1895 incorporated "many social, civic, health, recreational and educational activities." The Council of Jewish Women of Pittsburgh, following the suggestion of Rabbi Mayer, organized the first activity of this influential institution for Jewish immigrants first known as the "Columbian School"; through the generous gift of Mr. and Mrs. Henry Kaufmann, who gave the building and equipment as a memorial to their daughter, Irene, the Irene Kaufmann Settlement House integrated women's sport and physical education with their program offerings ("1895-GREETINGS-1925" 1925, 1–3). Known as the IKS, the settlement conducted activities in wholesome physical exercise and athletics. In particular, the Irene Kaufmann Settlement Girls Clubs promoted sport and exercise for the benefit of the girls at the settlement. In the settlement's house organ, the *I.K.S. Neighbors,* an article in 1923, "Gym Work for Girls," revealed the keen interest of Jewish girls in bodily exercise; "Many of our girls have asked for the use of the gymnasium and their requests have been granted." For girls of various age levels, classes were held in "dancing, gymnasium, and swimming" including "Basketball" and "Aesthetic Dancing" in the program ("Dancing! Gymnasium! Swimming! 1923).

Several articles in *I.K.S. Neighbors* heartily recommended certain athletics for Jewish females. For example, in "Girls Play Volley Ball (1926)," girls interested in "athletics are invited to join Miss Sniderman's class in the gymnasium." After the gym class, swimming followed. Instructors of IKS endeavors urged girls to exercise year-round in 1925, even after the summer when "outdoor sports" would not be pursued when the weather got cold in October. To maintain fitness and "keep ourselves in trim all through the year,

is to make it a regular habit to go to the Gym and to take a swim."
In short, for the IKS females, "Gym and a Swim for Vigor and
Vim" (1925).

The ideology of sport and physical culture for Jewish women
immigrants expresses gender, class, and ethnic concerns of Progressive era middle-class reformers. Female social reformers, alarmed at
the vice and danger they perceived in the chaotic city culture and
street life of lower-class eastern European Jewish immigrants, sought
to offer an alternative and inculcate youth into middle-class cultural roles and values. Progressive reformers who believed that
women needed physical stamina to fulfill domestic roles and to
offset the negative influence of urban conditions on women's health
thought that some kinds of physical training and sports belonged
in women's sphere, as well as men's.

At the Jewish Training School of Chicago, founded in 1888 by
wealthy German Jews led by Leon Mandel, who donated money to
"equip the sons and daughters of our Jewish poor with the power
of making a healthy, honest, and honorable livelihood," physical
training for new immigrants formed part of the Americanization
curriculum. Directed by Prof. Gabriel Bamberger, the school's first
superintendent, the training for Jewish European immigrants included physical exercises along with the kitchen-garden, industrial
class, and manual training departments (Jewish Training School,
Second Annual Report, 11). Jewish immigrant Hilda Satt Polacheck,
who came from Poland to Chicago, remembered her physical training at the school in 1892–93. As a young girl Hilda recollected
that "gymnastics were taught in a real gymnasium" (Polacheck
1989, 36). Professor Bamberger praised the efforts of Miss Antoinette
Belitz, gymnastics teacher. In the *Ninth Annual Report of the Jewish
Training School of Chicago, 1898–1899,* he thanked "the teachers for
their devotion and earnest work, and especially Miss Belitz who
besides teaching in the Gymnasium, had done a great deal for our
Alumni Association." In fact, graduates of this school hoped to
increase sports in the school's curriculum. The graduates of 1898
desired to donate money to the school that would in "a few years
accumulate and might be used for the establishment of a Natatorium" (Jewish Training School, *Ninth Annual Report*, 12, 24). After
her stay at the Jewish Training School, Hilda then became a Hull-
House Girl. She recalled in her memoirs how at Hull House she

and her sister "joined the gymnasium. We managed to scrape together enough money to buy the regulation gymnasium suit—wide
bloomers and blouse—though if anyone could not afford the suit,
she could attend anyway." With calisthenics and basketball games
going on at Hull House, Hilda reminisced that "the gymnasium
was like an oasis in a desert on Halsted Street" (Polacheck 1989,
76–77). Hull House women's basketball clubs brought acclaim to
the settlement house, and the reformers hoped recreation provided
youth an alternative to the play on the city streets (Davis 1973,
67–71, 150; Riess 1989, 164–65).

The Young Women's Hebrew Association of New York City, one
of the most important organizations at the turn of the century,
offered physical education and sports opportunities to immigrant
Jewish women. Jewish women from prominent backgrounds spearheaded the leadership and administration of programs at this YWHA
supporting both Jewish culture and sporting culture. Founded in
1902 under the leadership of Mrs. Israel Unterberg and a small
group of women active in community affairs and Jewish philanthropy, the dedication of the first building for the New York Young
Women's Hebrew Association took place February 1, 1903; the
board of directors touted the motto "Reverence and Modesty" for
their Hebrew Association for females (YWHA, *Twenty-fifth Anniversary, 1902–1927;* YWHA, *Twenty-fourth Annual Report* 16–17). The
large numbers of Jewish young women and girls using the facilities
at the Lexington Avenue home, which rose from 30,000 in 1906 to
102,000 in 1913, led the YMHA to undertake a campaign for a
new building. In 1914 the impressive new YWHA opened at 31
West 110th Street (*NYT* 1914, Apr. 26). From the beginning, the
Jewish ladies spearheading the YWHA incorporated sport and
physical education into the institution's mission. Its president reported in 1916, "The Young Women's Hebrew Association is unique.
It is the largest if not the only association of its kind that is devoting itself exclusively to the religious, mental and physical life of the
Jewish young women of our city," and she professed it "is carrying
on the work so effectively that it has become the centre of inquiry
and source of inspiration for work of a similar nature throughout
the whole country." At the YWHA, "religious work, gymnasium,
social work and educational work are the four main headings under
which our activities may be classified." Moreover, she asserted in

the president's *Annual Report* (Young Women's Union, 1916–17), "the athletic work is not merely confined to the gymnasium; there are health talks, meets, games, and special classes that look to the individual as well as to the group development" (YWHA, *Thirteenth Annual Report* 12–13; YWHA, *Twenty-fifth Anniversary, 1902–1927*).

Records of the YWHA reveal the sport and physical training activities available to Jewish young women and girls. Administrators promoted Americanization and domestic classes, as well as physical education classes. In the 1911 Class Report, the chairlady stated, "The gymnasium class which meets twice a week, on Monday and Thursday evenings, always attracts many visitors. The full attendance at the sessions and the splendid work of the girls fully justify our devoting a second evening to this class." On Monday evening the girls devoted time to "apparatus work, jumping, and folk dancing, and Thursday evening to basket ball, athletic games and drills" (YMHA "Class Report" 1911). The popularity of the gymnasium activities added to the YWHA officials' decision to seek larger quarters in their new building in 1914. Thus, the new home featured "a swimming pool, 20 feet by 60 feet, a gymnasium [and] a roof garden with tennis courts." In fact, the president, Mrs. Israel Unterberg, emphasized the importance of physical culture in describing the athletic equipment. She stated, "We have made ample provision for the physical welfare and the recreation needs of our girls." Mrs. Unterberg detailed the features in the association's new home: "The large gymnasium, connecting lockers and the shower baths in the basement, will hold a class of 200, in, say, Swedish floor work. We are planning regular gymnasium classes under competent instructors, and there will be organized sports, activities that were not possible in our former crowded quarters" (*NYT* 1914, Apr. 26). Mrs. Unterberg also praised a novel feature of the gym. "All the equipment in our gymnasium is to be movable—such things as travelling rings being suspended over the swimming pool—so that this big hall may be turned into a ballroom" (*NYT* 1914, Apr. 26).

The staff of the YWHA and Jewish female residents commended the sports facilities. The physical director of the YWHA, Frances Kahn, in 1915 urged Jewish females in the dormitory girls' publication *Kol Alamoth* (Voice of the girls), to "live a Little Longer" by exercising in the YWHA gymnasium. Kahn described a range of

3.1. Young Women's Hebrew Association, Commercial School exercise class, early 1920s. *Courtesy of the 92d Street YM-YWHA Archives.*

physical exercises from gymnastic drills to ball game variations offering "plenty of laughter, which is needed after a hard day's work" (Kahn 1915).

Gym exhibitions also served as fund-raisers for the construction of the indoor swimming pool, hailed as one of the best pools available to women when it opened in October 1916. A swimming pool committee, composed of chairwoman Mrs. Moses Hyamson and four other ladies, was organized to secure the completion of the pool at the Y's 110th Street location. On the building of the swimming pool, the 1916 *Thirteenth Annual Report* (YWHA, 36–37) communicated, "Unquestionably, nothing has been of such interest to the young women of the Association as the prospect of this delightful and health-giving addition." The swimming pool definitely appealed to the Jewish women; the pool attracted "large crowds for instruction and for the refreshing and stimulating opportunity it gives for exercise," described YWHA president Bella Unterberg in surveying the institution's activities in the 1920s. " 'Meets' are planned and contests in water sports and individual

3.2. Young Women's Hebrew Association swimming pool, early 1920s, 31 West 110th Street, New York. *Courtesy of the 92d Street YM-YWHA Archives.*

supremacy tests are held, all of which call forth a lively interest" (YWHA 1924, 21).

The director of the swimming pool clearly expressed the need to see that females were not suffering from health problems before being allowed to swim. Concerns that women might harm themselves with too much physical exertion shaped the requirement that they have medical clearance before they used the swimming pool. A 1916–17 *Bulletin of Classes* (YWHA) indicated, "Physicians's certificate is required of all those using the pool," costing twenty-five cents for the examination. Moreover, girls needed to wear suitable clothing for the pool. Each swimmer "must bring a plain, rubber bathing cap. Silk and fancy caps are not permitted," the Physical Education Department notified women, but "suits may be purchased for 50 cents at the Association Building." The swimming pool rules also stated that suitable bathing suits must be used, that is, "only gray Annette Kellermans are permitted" and "all suits must be left at the building to be sterilized." An extensive swimming program could be pursued by Jewish girls with swimming lessons, "plunges" (dives), and the competitions at the natatorium. The YWHA boasted, "The girl who can SWIM is in the 'SWIM' " and swimming promoted "Health-Sport-Safety" (YWHA, Scrapbooks 1920s and 1930s).

The swimming pool represented a major component of the YWHA facility to promote sport and fitness for working girls and women. This excellent pool hosted not only recreational classes but also national competitive swimming championships featuring outstanding national and Olympic champions such as Aileen Riggin and Gertrude Ederle in the 1920s. Aileen Riggin, 1920 gold medal diving and swimming champion at the Antwerp Olympics, recalled how as a member of the Women's Swimming Association of New York she swam at the YWHA facility. The Women's Swimming Association (WSA) was founded in 1917 by Charlotte Epstein and a few other businesswomen interested in swimming for exercise. Charlotte Epstein became prominent as the WSA club manager and 1920 and 1924 Olympic women's swimming team manager; she needed a pool to host national championship events. Aileen Riggin remarked that the WSA team members "went to the Young Women's Hebrew Association and had meets there—they had a standard pool" (Soule telephone conversation; Borish, forthcoming). In the Women's Swimming Association newsletter, the *W.S.A. News,* in March 1921 the swimming club offered "a Word of Thanks" to "acknowledge a debt of gratitude to the officers of the YWHA for their generosity in allowing us the use of their handsome natatorium for our swimming meet of March 12th" (WSA 1921). The WSA held National Swimming Championships in the early 1920s governed by the Amateur Athletic Union rules at the YWHA pool; this highly competitive swimming meet included prizes for the champions (W.S.A. 1920; YWHA Scrapbook 1923). The Young Women's Hebrew Athletic League, too, hosted swimming meets at the pool of the YWHA at 31 West 110th Street.

The New York YWHA offered a wide range of sporting pursuits for women. This association housed what one New York newspaper hailed as "the most comprehensive program of physical education in the country for Jewish women and girls," with the pool open all the time, and working girls using the gym for basketball, gymnastics,

3.3. Young Women's Hebrew Association tennis class, late 1930s. *Courtesy of the 92d Street YM-YWHA Archives.*

fencing, tennis, and dancing classes ("Hows and Whys of Big Burg's Y's"). Program administrators sanctioned sports such as swimming and tennis for females to maintain femininity and fitness, similar sports encouraged for gentile females in the first decades of the twentieth century.

In the early twentieth century, Pittsburgh's Irene Kaufmann Settlement, too, sponsored several sports deemed suitable for girls. The *I.K.S. Neighbors* reported that "every girl may be as slender as the fashion demands if she will take advantage" of such physical recreations as gym, swimming, and basketball. And if the girls needed the appropriate gym costume, that might also be part of their domestic training: "Dig up your bloomers and middies and c'mon! If you want to make new bloomers, you can do it in the sewing class," the IKS commentator urged in 1923 ("Dancing!" 1923). Wearing a proper swimming suit and cap, a Jewish girl might be interested in joining the "Little Ladies' Swimming Club" of the settlement house ("The Water Is Fine on Mondays" 1927, 34). One journalist related to girls, "Don't forget the boys are making good use of the Pool and have won several Swimming Meets. If you want to do the same, you'll have to swim at the IKS as often as they do." The cultural messages about sports expressed to Jewish females echoed those messages disseminated to Gentiles in the larger American culture. An IKS sports columnist wrote that swimming benefited young and older women alike; girls ought to tell their own mothers that "mothers swim nowadays, as well as the daughters. This keeps them in good form and—here's a secret—thin also" ("Girls, Use the Shower Baths and Swimming Pool" 1925).

When Jewish females excelled in athletics, gendered language often appeared in accounts of their feats. Jewish girls highlighted for sports success were characterized in feminine ways, like gentile girls. For example, Ethel Bilson, called a " 'Medal-Some' Mermaid," who won several swimming races and diving contests in 1919–20, swam for the Emil G. Hirsch Social Center of Sinai Temple in Chicago. She competed in AAU events as a "proficient water nymph," earning medals for her swimming and diving prowess, and added "more 'jewelry' of sport to her prize collection," reported the *Chicago Tribune* (1920, Dec. 19). Another press account, "A Harlem Mermaid Scores in a Metropolitan Swimming Meet," recounted how Miss Eugenia Autonof won the 100-yard freestyle and other events at the YWHA "Aquatic Carnival." Several YWHA girls pictured at the swimming pool in 1933 revealed the feminine physique in sport: "It's a daily plunge in a cold pool that helps these girls retain that admirable figure. They recommend it as an efficient substitute for dieting" (YWHA, Scrapbooks 1930, 1933).

Besides swimming, some Jewish organizations promoted women's basketball in intramural and team competition. The women's game differed from the men's version to accommodate concerns of basketball being too physically rough on woman's constitution. The head of women's work in 1910 at the Educational Alliance stated that the "basketball club is composed of some of the roughest girls in the schools of the neighborhood" (EA 1910). Adapted women's basketball rules avoided physical contact and ensured a team-oriented philosophy, with more females playing cooperatively on each team. Jewish American immigrant Senda Berenson, born Senda Valvrojenski near Vilnius, Russia, in 1868 until her father changed his name when he immigrated to America in 1874, was known as the "Mother of Women's Basketball." Berenson became a leading woman physical educator at Smith College, endorsing women's sporting activities in the 1890s within a female context (Spears 1991, 19–36). She authored rule books on women's basketball to promote physical vigor and womanly athletic skill. In the 1901 *Spalding's Athletic Library Basket Ball for Women,* edited by Berenson, she wrote an essay, "The Significance of Basket Ball for Women." She remarked (24–25), "The two important changes are the division of the playing field and the prohibiting of snatching or batting the ball from the hands of another player." Dividing the basketball court into three zones and prohibiting players from running into another zone in the field of play made this game suitable for women. Berenson explained these rules did "away almost entirely with 'star' playing, hence equalizes the importance of the players, and so encourages teamwork." Women's basketball not only gained popularity in collegiate institutions but also spread to other schools, youth groups, YWCAs, and YWHAs. Jewish organizations for female youth promoted basketball in their programs. The New York YWHA promotion for girls' classes asserted: "Basketball—Enjoy a weekly work-out playing the greatest of all indoor games" (YWHA, *Printed Materials of Class Activities,* 1934). A basketball game followed by a dance in the gymnasium offered recreation for players and spectators alike at the association. Likewise, in the *I.K.S. Neighbors* a call for Pittsburgh Jewish girls to play claimed, "Basket ball has become the national game for all girls. Everyone is doing it!" Securing a coach, Miss Komar, the settlement house publication urged, "Let us have an I.K.S. Girls' Basket Ball Team and show others how full of pep and very much alive we are!" ("Basket Ball" 1923). At the Jewish People's Institute in Chicago, girls played basketball proficiently winning three girls' basketball championships in the early 1920s (Meites 1924, 472–73).

In keeping with the rhetoric of female physical educators, the YWHA hoped to promote Jewish womanhood and the spirit of play rather than a male competitive ethic on the basketball court. On the twenty-fifth anniversary of the New York YWHA, the president remarked, "We have several Basket Ball teams which are making excellent records in inter-association games," but added,

"We teach them that the games is the thing—not the victory" (*Twenty-fifth Anniversary,* 22).

Competition for Jewish girls within the bounds of Jewish organizations seemed to be acceptable in basketball contests. In Detroit, the Jewish *Center News* "Calling All Girls!" (1936) not only exhorted them to pursue basketball "to keep that lovely figure by keeping in good shape" but also asked girls, "Do you want to feel the glory of winning a thrilling game?" And the sport enthusiast urged, "Keep pace with the boys. There has always been a league for the girls, you owe it to yourself to organize a team in your club and enter into competition" (2). Apparently, the Philadelphia Neighborhood Centre Jewish girls responded to such a call; Miss Beatrice Rubinson, chair of the Committee on Clubs and Athletics, stated that at the basketball banquet, awards would be given to "the winning clubs" including "the girls basketball group" (Young Women's Union 1941). Jewish girls, too, might excel in basketball games at non-Jewish institutions in developing physicality and competitive experience. Some Jewish women exhibited their basketball skills in college. For instance, the *American Hebrew,* in its "Personalities in Sports" column in 1924, wrote about Miss Claire Strassman, varsity forward of the New York University Girls' Basketball Team, recently granted full varsity sport status (126).

In the early twentieth century, outdoor sports also yielded health dividends for Jewish young women and for girls generally confined indoors. Jewish vacation homes and summer camps for working-class young women and girls developed under the auspices of Jewish institutions to provide them with an opportunity to enjoy time away from the city participating in outdoor sports in the summer. YWHA president Bella Unterberg described the YWHA Country House at White Plains, New York, the forerunner to the association's summer camp, Ray Hill Camp in Mt. Kisco. She remarked, "For many years we have had a vision of the possession of a country home where tired girls leaving the hot and noisy city might play outdoors and go back to their daily jobs with renewed hope and vigor." At Ray Hill Camp, dedicated in May 1922, "during July and August, ninety girls every week have filled the camp to capacity. The splendid opportunities for rest and recreation that it affords must unfortunately be limited to this number and many applicants have to be turned away" (YWHA 1924, 37–38). Sports constituted a popular attraction of the Jewish summer camp. The minutes of a meeting of the Ray Hill Camp Committee in May 1926 revealed that a donation of one hundred dollars "was to be used to pay for fixing the tennis courts, and it was believed that this amount would also take care of the basket ball court." In 1927 camp girls started a weekly paper, *The Buzzer,* which featured a "Sport News" column (Minutes of the Ray Hill Camp Committee; Joselit 1994, 19–22).

Sports for Jewish' girls formed a significant part of the camp-going experience as detailed in documents and photographs of the YWHA Ray Hill Camp. The "Report of the executive director for the Season of 1928" vividly linked sports with the enjoyment of the 516 Jewish girls who spent part of their summer at rural camp. The athletic facilities, newly renovated, proved "a great boon to our guests." Camp Executive Director Minnie E. Freeman elaborated on the benefits of such wonderful spaces for sport. Freeman even illuminated the influence of a 1920s popular female tennis star in her spirited account.

> The swimming pool, in her aquamarine dress, was ever busy. The resurfaced tennis court was appreciated by the Helen Wills's. . . . Archery was indulged in twice a day, and many a Miss William Tell is in the making. Basketball and baseball claimed some of the athletes' time. Our three sets of croquet were used at all hours of the day by the girls who could not swim or play tennis. (Freeman 1928, 1)

Jewish girls enjoyed playing baseball at camp, typically perceived as a male sport. Ray Hill Camp counselors reiterated the director's comments in describing the enthusiasm for sport exhibited by young women. The 1920s sport heroines again appeared in camp correspondence in the "Report of Counsellor in Charge of Archery, Sewing and Picnic Lunches." Counselor Helen Lewis described clues for a treasure hunt: "Search with care from side to side. May Gertrude Ederle be your guide (Swimming Pool.)"; "The centers pass the ball with vim, to the sprightly ends who get it in. (Basketball Court.)" (Lewis 1928, 1). According to Rose Feldman in her "Report of Athletic Counsellor—Tennis, Basketball, Baseball," (1928) more tennis courts would "aid our budding champs" and, she recommended, an "acre of flat ground would be appreciated, as it would enable us to extend our activities to include an outdoor baseball diamond, a handball court, a hockey field."

3.4. Women playing baseball, Young Women's Hebrew Association Country House, White Plains, New York 1920 or 1921. *Courtesy of the 92d Street YM-YWHA Archives.*

At Camp Council for Jewish girls in Phoenixville, Pennsylvania, founded by members of the Council of Jewish Juniors, sports likewise dominated many camp functions. In the summer of 1928 Camp Council provided vacations for two hundred girls. Besides playing "baseball, kickball, volleyball and basketball, the innovation of Hockey was a big success," related Janice Smith Bers, directress of Camp Council. The head counselor, Dellie Sigmund Klein, planned "some fine athletic meets this summer, in which the entire camp participated" (Bers, 3). These kinds of athletic events perhaps influenced Camp Council administrators to report in the 1930s, "Staff was given permission to wear shorts instead of bloomers" (Camp Council, Inc., "A Brief History"). Emma Farm Camp, also in Pennsylvania and run by the Irene Kaufmann Settlement, provided girls with summer fun. The "Emma Farm Camp News," in the 1924 *I.K.S. Neighbors,* featured a picture portraying girls enjoying swimming, with the caption "Swimming Pool, Emma Farm Camp As popular as the Dining Room." Year-round, indoors or out, increasingly a wide range of sports and physical education opportunities for Jewish women and girls, from bowling to volleyball, went together with activities at Jewish camps and center programs (Lloyd 1931, 6–10).

Some Jewish females vied for victory and medals, like other non-Jewish females, in highly competitive sporting events in the first decades of the twentieth century. For example, in track and field, Lillian Copeland was a superb athlete at the University of Southern California and won many national titles in the discus and shot put in the 1920s and early 1930s before achieving victory at the Olympic Games. As a track and field star Lillian Copeland earned Olympic medals for her feats in the 1928 and 1932 games. In the 1932 games she won the gold medal for the discus, setting a world's record; in the 1928 games she earned a silver medal in the discus competition. She broke world records in the javelin in 1927, and in 1928 broke the world record in the eight-pound shot, but the 1928 Olympics did not schedule the shot event for women. She was considered one of the world's great woman athletes (*NYT* 1964, July 8, 35; Slater 1992, 53–54). Whether Copeland's Jewish identify was an issue requires additional research. In the Chicago Women's Olympic track meet, Edith Marshak of the Jewish People's Institute won the shot put and hurdles. Another accomplished track athlete, Edith Chaiken, while at Northwestern University in 1914, won the national championship in the 440-yard dash for girls (Meites 1924, 473–75; Gems 1995, 20).

In tennis, considered a suitable feminine sport in the 1920s for women, Jewish and gentile, some Jewish female tennis stars achieved success on the courts. In August 1928 a piece in the *American Hebrew* featured Clara Greenspan, the captain-coach-manager of the Hunter College tennis team, and winner of the Women's New York State Doubles Championship, Eastern Clay Court Championship, and other tournaments. The article, written by a male journalist, praised Greenspan as displaying the feminine body he thought fitting for Jewish girls in the "sportlight"; he described Miss Greenspan as "pretty of face" with the "fine complexion that comes with a healthy outdoor life," concluding she "makes a picture equally attractive on the court or in a ballroom." Greenspan's wholesome athletic life appealed to Jewish sports enthusiasts. That "Miss Greenspan does not smoke" because she "simply does not like Lady Nicotine" provided a good example for other Jewish youth. She keenly observed the feats of Jewish male athletes. Rather than the great ambition to defeat Helen Wills, the celebrated women's tennis champion, "though, of course, she would relish that," more than "anything else in the world, Clara Greenspan wants to meet Andy Cohen!" (Gumpert 1928, 389; Levine 1992, 204).

To promote tennis participation of Jewish girls, middle-class women of the Council of Jewish Women, Junior Auxiliary, sponsored tennis tournaments in New York. The author of "Junior Jottings—and—Golf and Tennis" in the 1924 *American Hebrew* commented, "In years gone by a women's organization began its year with a bridge or a tea or something equally feminine. Not so the Juniors, this year," and she expressed how the juniors started with "a series of tournaments which proved conclusively that this year's Juniors have pep and grit and the other qualities that will go to make them a really live and active organization." Moreover, the girls incurred no expenses for playing in the tennis won by Miss Elsie Flank, and "even the prizes were donated—two bottles of Golligowg perfume, which made the contest really worth winning" (Blitzer 1924). An appropriate reward for a female, indeed.

Although some Jewish female athletes gained experience in sport through collegiate and Jewish Y programs, women and girls of the middle and upper ranks participated in more elite sports, such as tennis and golf, at Jewish country clubs. By the 1920s several Jewish clubs with wealthy German Jews as prominent members became places for social, recreational, and competitive sports for women as anti-Semitism prohibited Jews from Anglo-Saxon, Protestant country clubs. To join a country club required money and social status. The Jews, "the one ethnic group in this country that had families as wealthy and educated as those of the WASP establishment," formed their own country clubs in major cities such as New York, Chicago, Philadelphia, and Los Angeles (Levine 1995, 27–49; Gordon 1990, 81–82). Jewish female golfers at times confronted anti-Semitism by official organizations of golf. In this regard, women, like Jewish men, experienced exclusion by the wealthy Gentiles administering golf tournaments. In Chicago, where fine Jewish women golfers gained some victories on the links, the Women's Western Golf Association in 1923 failed to invite any Jewish golfers out of the ninety-one competitors for a Chicago city tournament (Levine 1995, 44–45).

The *American Hebrew* frequently printed articles on sports at country clubs and cited the accomplishments of Jewish female golf stars, but their gender roles as wife, mother, or daughter shaped the descriptions of athletic prowess. Elaine Rosenthal Reinhart exhibited talent on the golf links winning the Women's Western Golf

Championship for the third time in 1925, after her 1917 and 1918 victories en route to her "triple crown." It appears that the Women's Western Golf Association deemed her talents outstanding and invited her to play in their tournaments, with no anti-Semitism reported in the *American Hebrew*'s 1925 article about Mrs. Elaine Rosenthal Reinhart, the best Jewish female golfer in the United States. Nonetheless, journalists in the American Jewish press tended to comment on her husband's good golf, and discussed her marriage. "How often Mr. Reinhart was a golf widower is not in the records, but that Mrs. Reinhart lost neither heart nor cunning in the games was again proved" when she repeated as Western Women's Golf Association champion in 1918 ("Thrice Western Women's Golf Champion.")

When the American Jewish press featured articles on female golf champions, considerable attention centered on their domestic roles. Another woman golf champion, Mrs. Louis Lengfeld, won the Northern California crown in 1927, and was a member and golf captain of the Beresford Country Club, in San Francisco, California, one of the most exclusive Jewish clubs in the West. The *American Hebrew* issue of June 1, 1928, described "at the risk of mixing family and golf history . . . the facts" of Mrs. Lengfeld's accomplishments expressed in gender terms.

> In August 1926, Mrs. Lengfeld won the championship of the City of San Francisco. From that tournament to the Northern California match, she had played less than a dozen rounds of golf. A large part of that year and a half was claimed by Miss Kathleen Margaret Lengfeld. That young lady is just nine months old now. Most women golfers would consider a daughter of that age rather an obstacle to golf greatness. To Mrs. Lengfeld, apparently, she was an inspiration. ("Highlights on Links and Polo Fields," 94–95)

This piece detailed even more family history about Mrs. Lengfeld, revealing she had two older children, a son and a daughter, besides daughter Kathleen Margaret, and she "has a lovely country home at Menlo Park, a fashionable suburb of San Francisco" (95).

A Jewish female golf champion, Mrs. Harry Grossman, earned the 1929 Women's Golf Championship of Los Angeles and belonged to the well-known Jewish club, Hillcrest Country Club.

However, the Jewish press highlighted her family ties, noting she "is the mother of a 14-year-old son" who plays a good golf game. A New York golfer winning laurels on the link, Mrs. Leo G. Federman enjoyed playing golf with her daughter Jean, nine years old. Mrs. Federman believed gender lines should remain in force on the golf links. Mrs. Federman remarked that "women will never be able to compete with men in golfing laurels—they are so much more temperamental and so easily affected by the intricacies of the game." The 1929 *American Hebrew* identified such outstanding Jewish ladies on the links as some of the personalities who "enliven American Sports" (Rosenberger 966).

To look their best on the links, sportswomen read the *American Hebrew* to learn about the latest sporting fashions. In a 1920s Arnold, Constable and Company advertisement, sportswomen could glimpse the "Summer Sports Attire Seen on the Links." From the "Vogue of Flannel" to the "Overblouse and Skirt Costumes," wealthy Jewish female golfers could dress as champions even if their golf score did not earn them victory ("Summer Sports Attire" 1924). Whether for leisure or competition the Jewish country club for middle- and upper-class Jewish females provided a setting to develop athletic skills in golf, tennis, and swimming.

Even though only the wealthier Jewish females might spend time playing sports as members of country clubs, Jewish vacation resorts combined social and sporting activities for women of the more ordinary ranks by the turn of the century. More than other immigrant groups, Jews adopted the enjoying of an American vacation. They envisioned the summer resort as a suitable place for average people, and escaping the work routine represented the consumer ethic of American society. Moreover, coeducational leisure pursuits emerged for young women who spent some summer days on vacation, and girls could display stylish sports fashions for an outing by the sea. Jewish resorts by the sea or in the mountains offered another means for experiencing a sporting culture away from the crowded city. Jewish resorts and hotels in a rural atmosphere flourished at the Catskill Mountains for Jewish immigrants seeking the pleasure of a vacation (Heinze 1990, 124–32; Schreier 1994, 140–41). And for women desiring to augment their sports skills in a holiday outing, the YWHA suggested lessons in tennis, "the popular sport," and in "Bicycling, Come here before going to

Bermuda, or to be practical, the road in Central Park" (YWHA, *Program of Activities*, 1938). For working and middle-class Jewish urbanites in places such as Chicago and Detroit, summer resort and vacation spots such as South Haven, Michigan, provided sports and recreation as well as escape from summer heat. Kosher food and fun awaited working girls taking a respite from their jobs (Kraus 1994). At resorts and hotels with recreational amenities, married and single Jewish women of various social classes and religiosity could enjoy swimming, tennis, golf, bicycling, dances, and other leisure endeavors within a Jewish context.

Jewish women and girls participated in sport and physical education activities various contexts, such as Jewish settlement houses, Young Women's Hebrew Associations, Jewish youth and social clubs, high schools, colleges and universities, summer camps, and elite country clubs. The goals of organizations sponsoring sports for Jewish women and girls might differ; whether to foster Americanization for eastern European immigrant females, increase physical health, provide social activities in a wholesome atmosphere for working-class young women, or maintain Jewish identity within a physical education program, Jewish women and girls pursued a range of sporting practices. Therefore, in response to "How We Serve the Community" in 1922, the New York Young Women's Hebrew Association identified their aim of "Physical Education" along with "Dormitory," "Religious Work," "Education," "Commercial School," and "Trade and Domestic Arts." The association's "Swimming—Tournaments and Contests, Gymnastics, Athletics" presented sports to Jewish women and girls as one element of American culture (YWHA, *Twentieth Anniversary Luncheon and Annual Meeting*, 5).

Yet in the November 1942 volume of *The Y.M.H.A. Bulletin,* the official organ of the New York Young Men's Hebrew Association, the sports editor, Joel Friedman, gave his "expert" advice to "Female Gym Enthusiasts" but he neglected to acknowledge the sporting heritage of his Jewish sisters. For the first time since the Young Men's Hebrew Association at 92d Street had begun sixty-eight years earlier, in 1942 women could use the YMHA's gymnasium and swimming pool with the merger of the Young Men's and Young Women's Hebrew Associations. The columnist gave special instructions to Jewish females on how to properly play sports and use the athletic facilities. "When girls invade the gym, they might not know what all the apparatus is for, we'll try to explain." Friedman informed females that in the gym, "you might see a number of baskets without bottoms attached to a wooden board" and, girls, *"do not jump through the baskets yourselves."* In his tongue-and-cheek advice, instead he told them to throw a ball through it, after all, "it's safer." Before the young Jewish women played baseball, the editor recommended that he teach them some basic rules. "Throw the ball at the bat, not the bat at the ball." He also reminded Y members that in the swimming pool, both male and females "will now be required to wear bathing suits" (Friedman 1942). The commentator completed his lesson to the girls and women on the use of the gym and pool, insinuating that Jewish females lacked experience in sports and physical education activities until the YMHA and YWHA merged. The exploration of Jewish American women, however, reveals a historical record of their sporting practices, and in turn, advances the historical understanding of American sport and American Jewish life.

4

Jews and the Making of American Marathoning, 1896–1960

Pamela Cooper

From the introduction of the marathon footrace to America, Jews made important contributions to the events not only in participation and competition but also in bringing organization and access to the sport. Important leaders of the "running boom" of the 1970s and 1980s, men such as Fred Lebow, who popularized the mass marathon in New York City, came from the tradition of Jewish American marathon running that can be traced to the first marathon in the United States.

In 1896 the American team brought the idea of the marathon home from the first modern Olympic Games. The first United States marathon, a twenty-five-mile footrace from Stamford, Connecticut, to the Columbia Oval in the Bronx, was held September 19, 1896, as an event in the Knickerbocker Athletic Club annual games. John J. McDermott won in 3:25:55, Hamilton Gray of St. George Athletic Club was second in 3:28:27, and Louis Liebgold of the New Jersey Athletic Club was third in 3:36:58. McDermott belonged to the Pastime Athletic Club, a club without the social pretensions of the New York Athletic Club or the Knickerbocker Athletic Club but with a strong tradition of fine cross-country performances (*Spirit of the Times* 1896, Sept. 26). A few months after the New York City event, the Boston Athletic Association established its annual marathon. In 1904, twenty-one-year-old Michael Spring, who designed powerhouses for the Edison Company in New York, won the Boston Athletic Association marathon. Spring and teammates Arthur Ziegler and Louis Marks wore the Maltese cross of the Pastime Athletic Club. The Jewish presence in the Boston marathon originated in New York City (*Boston Evening Transcript* 1904, Apr. 20; 1905, Apr. 20; *Boston Daily Globe* 1904, Apr. 19; Derderian 1993, 26, 28).

Jewish participation in the marathon was encouraged by several factors. The settlement houses that aided in the adjustment of the new arrivals endorsed sports as a catalyst for Americanization and as a way of bringing people of diverse backgrounds together. Settlement house clubs and other working-class sport clubs abounded in New York City during the first decade of the twentieth century. Mostly small in membership and with limited athletic facilities, these clubs found footracing events their first opportunities to compete. The marathon footrace was quite compatible with their high athletic potential and limited resources (University Settlement Society 1893, n.p.; Cole 1910, 18–19, 21–22; Riess 1989, 109; Rader 1977, 361). Runners competed as representatives of their ethnic groups, as members of an ethnic sports club, or as representatives of the corporation.

The appearance of the marathon on the athletic agenda coincided with the great eastern European immigration to American cities. Ethnic groups seeking acceptance from the broader society found that the successful marathoner served their purpose by embodying the characteristics valued by the dominant American culture. The marathon runner was perceived as an energetic, active individual who showed assertiveness and self-confidence by running in the marathon, and willpower and self-control by staying the course. Jewish sports participation filled a specific need to efface the stereotype of the slope-shouldered yeshiva scholar. The perception of the new Jewish immigrants as physically weak, preferring religious study to athletics, produced uncertainty about their potential to become assimilated. In contrast, the ethnically identified marathon runner symbolically demonstrated the compatibility of his group with American ideals (Conzen 1992, 5–6; Mrozek 1983, 167–69; Levine 1992, 7, 162, 167). The significant ethnic participation contributed to the identification of the marathon as a working-class event.

Working-class runners often received some support from their employers. This support could be in the form of the company team, meant to be a focus of loyalty and a source of pride to the employees (Brandes 1976, 12, 78, 82). In 1908, at the behest of their employer, the employees of John Wanamaker's department store in New York formed the Millrose Athletic Association (MAA). Wanamaker donated a Brooklyn clubhouse with facilities that included a running track, and the club quickly achieved stature in athletics. Started in 1914, the Wanamaker Millrose Games eventually became the nation's premier indoor track meet, featuring such events as the Wanamaker Mile. The MAA promoted Wanamaker's department store to potential athletes as well as to workers; high-performing working-class athletes sometimes received jobs at Wanamaker's in the expectation that they would join the MAA. Abel Kiviat, the great Jewish miler, was already known as a competitive runner when, through the efforts of some track friends, he got a job in Wanamaker's sporting goods department (Schmertz n.d., 8, 11–12, 19; Simons 1986, 242, 252).

Fred Schmertz, a Jewish youth working in Wanamaker's delivery department, became a charter member of the MAA. As a student at Dewitt Clinton High School, Schmertz had acquired experience in athletic administration as manager of the Clark Settlement House track team, and he put the knowledge to use in helping present the first Millrose indoor track meet. Schmertz continued with the Millrose Athletic Association to become meet director of the Millrose Games in 1934, retaining this position until his death in 1976. He also stayed on with John Wanamaker. He attended New York University law school at night and became an attorney for John Wanamaker, eventually retiring after fifty years on the staff (Schmertz n.d., 8, 11–12, 19). When issues of anti-Semitism influenced the decisions of athletic clubs, particularly in the 1920s and 1930s, Schmertz's position on the MAA assured fair consideration of Jewish athletes.

Jewish athletes were also welcomed by the Irish American Athletic Club (IAAC) in the early twentieth century. The IAAC was organized in 1878 as a working-class sports club and a vehicle to help Irish immigrants assimilate. The IAAC now reached out to the later immigrant groups; faced with shifting boundaries in traditional ethnic communities and the continuous influx of new immigrants, the Tammany politicians who supported the IAAC courted the Jewish vote. At one time or other before the club was disbanded in 1917, Jewish athletes Abel Kiviat, Alvah Meyer, Myer Prinstein, and Charles Pores became national AAU champions while wearing the green shamrock emblem of the Irish American Athletic Club (Riess 1989, 72–82; Levine 1992, 190; Miller 1985, 536; Frank 1936, 247).

Although Boston had established the tradition of an annual marathon footrace, New York City was establishing a marathon culture. In 1908–9, New York City experienced a marathon boom, precipitated by the close marathon finish between the Italian Dorando Pietri and Irish American Johnny Hayes of New York, who was declared the winner. Increased marathon participation by Irish Americans and Italian Americans characterized the marathon boom, but a few Jewish marathon runners, such as Harry Goldberg, emerged as significant competitors. More important, the 1908–9 marathon boom left a legacy of increased interest in the event in metropolitan New York. A Yonkers marathon was held annually from 1907 to 1917. The Brooklyn–Sea Gate Marathon celebrated Lincoln's Birthday from 1909 to 1914, with a race over the marathon distance of 26 miles, 385 yards (*Brooklyn Daily Eagle* 1909, Feb. 12). In 1915 bad weather caused officials to postpone the marathon to Washington's Birthday and shorten the course to twenty miles. Charles Pores won the race and the prize of a trip to San Francisco for the Panama Pacific Exposition Marathon on August 28, 1915. Pores traveled to San Francisco as part of the Millrose Athletic Association marathon team, which included Willie Kyronen, Nick Giannakopulos, and John Cahill, accompanied by coach Mel Sheppard (*NYT* 1914, April 26; 1915, Feb. 23; May 3).

After World War I, the Millrose Athletic Association supplanted the Irish American Athletic Club as New York City's preeminent multiethnic working-class sports club, and in the 1920s became one of the two most important clubs in New York City. Its chief rival was the New York Athletic Club, whose members infrequently ran marathons. The winner of the 1920 Boston Marathon, Greek-born New Yorker Peter Trivoulidas, was employed in John Wanamaker's department store restaurant. He represented Greece in the 1920 Olympic marathon, and then joined the Millrose Athletic Association (*New York Tribune* 1920, Apr. 20; *NYT* 1921, Apr. 20).

In October 1925, an annual marathon was started in the town of Port Chester in Westchester. A New York University freshman named Arthur Gavrin finished twenty-seventh, in 3:32:34⁴/₅, but he would soon improve. Gavrin had come to the United States in 1921, and finished high school in New Rochelle before entering the university. In June 1926, against the advice of his track coach, Gavrin entered Philadelphia's Sesquicentennial Marathon and finished fifth in 2:53:53. He was a serious contender for the 1928 Olympic marathon team, but was not selected. On a hot October day in 1928, Gavrin won the Port Chester Marathon (*NYT* 1925, Oct. 13; *NYHT* 1926, June 3; *Port Chester Daily Item* 1926, Oct. 13; Amateur Athletic Union 1928, 58–59).

As different groups competed for the few available jobs during the Great Depression, ethnic and racial antagonisms increased. The long history of Irish American anti-Semitism was manifest in New York City by street violence and vandalism. The 1933 election of Fiorello LaGuardia as mayor of New York threatened Irish dominance of politics and the civil service as LaGuardia opened more appointments to Jews and Italians. Of the resulting ethnic conflicts, the Irish-Jewish was the more severe (Bayor 1978, 24–25, 27, 156, 165–67; Capeci 1977, 3). The deteriorating European political situation of the 1930s further sharpened American ethnic rivalries. The Nazi movement in America centered in New York City, home of the nation's largest Jewish community. In July 1933 several small Nazi groups in New York City united to form Friends of the New Germany, later known as the German American Bund. The bund extended its influence to German American cultural and sporting societies with offers of money (Bayor 1978, 59–60, 68–69, 71, 165–67). Nativist anti-Semitism and Irish American anti-Semitism converged in the sports world, most noticeably in the New York Athletic Club (NYAC), the single most powerful club in the Amateur Athletic Union. Irish Americans had first entered the NYAC as active athletes, and rose to administrative posts and social acceptance as their group became established in American society. The president of the NYAC from 1926 to 1932, Maj. William Kennelly, sometimes led New York City's St. Patrick's Day Parade on Fifth Avenue (Considine and Jarvis 1969, 78–79). Irish Americans were openly accepted, but the rules of the NYAC scorned Jewish members (Wapner 1937, 11).

William Steiner, winner of the May 8, 1932, AAU Metropolitan Marathon Championship, may have been the greatest Jewish marathoner. For example, in 1935 he won the Jewish marathon championship held as part of the Maccabiah Games in Tel Aviv, Israel. Steiner was considered a strong contender for the 1932 United States Olympic Marathon team, but he was not chosen. The 1932 team was selected from the runners at Boston on April 19, 1932; at a marathon from Cambridge to Salisbury, Maryland, won by Hans Oldag of Buffalo, New York, on May 28, 1932; and at a marathon held shortly after, in Los Angeles, won by Albert Michelson. The final team comprised Michelson, Oldag, and James Henigan, who was second at Boston. The winner of the Boston Marathon, Paul de Bruyn, a member of New York City's German American Athletic Club who had finished a far second to Steiner in the 1932 Metropolitan Marathon, went to the 1932 games as a member of the German Olympic team (*Port Chester Daily Item* 1931, Oct. 10; Amateur Athletic Union 1932, 60; *Boston Evening Transcript* 1932, Apr. 19; Martin and Gynn 1979, 108, 112; *NYT* 1932, Aug. 21; Daley 1932, 22).

Members of the German American Athletic Club started entering long-distance competitions in the early 1930s. Founded in 1884, the German American AC disbanded in 1917 in response to anti-German sentiment accompanying World War I. Dietrich Wortmann, a member of the German American AC since 1901, revived the club in 1927. The club absorbed a smaller ethnic German athletic club in 1928 and bought a clubhouse, the Scheffelhalle, a German American landmark in Manhattan. The club apparently had substantial discretionary funds, important in attracting top athletes who might need subsidies for travel and for other competitive and training expenses. Many of the German American AC's active members, especially its track and field competitors, were Jewish, including the great track coach Max Silver and the long-distance runners Joseph Kleinerman and William Steiner (Frank 1935, 20).[1]

1. Max Silver died in the early 1960s. William Steiner is currently living in Lakewood, New Jersey. Joseph Kleinerman is still very active in long-distance running, having served for decades as the registrar of the New York Road Runners Club.

The German American AC became a major power in American marathoning with Paul de Bruyn's win at Boston in 1932. De Bruyn won the 1933 Port Chester Marathon, and along with William Steiner and Harvey Lichtenstein captured the team trophy for the German American AC (Abramson 1933, 23). In the March 25, 1934, AAU Metropolitan Marathon Championship, Steiner and de Bruyn finished first and second respectively. The German American AC won the team trophy with a perfect score when teammate Russell Jekel finished third (Effrat 1934).

Traditionally, German American–Jewish relations in New York City were amicable (Bayor 1978, 4–6). Stanley Frank of the *New York Post* wrote a January 3, 1935, article that emphasized the German American AC's abhorrence of religious and political polarization. On January 10, 1935, German American AC officials replied to the Frank article in the *Deutscher Weckruf und Beobachter,* the American Nazi German-language newspaper. Dietrich Wortmann, president of the German American AC, was one of the signers of this reply: "[The *Post* article] was published without our agreement and was aimed at the creation of dissensions in the ranks of German-American sports. . . . our sympathies belong to 'New Germany.' All our performances took place under the sign of sovereignty of Nazi Germany" (*Columbia Daily Spectator* 1935, Dec. 3).

When Jewish members of the German American AC threatened to resign, Wortmann asked them to stay. Max Silver and other Jewish athletes stayed, even after the swastika was displayed at the German American AAU Championship on September 8. Silver, who volunteered his services as coach, did not want to desert his long-distance runners before the important Port Chester Marathon and the Thanksgiving Day cross-country meet. After the German American AC team won both events, Silver resigned, stating that Wortmann was a Nazi sympathizer (*Columbia Daily Spectator* 1935, Dec. 3).

The conflict within the German American Athletic Club took place within the context of the larger conflict over the AAU's certification of American athletes for the 1936 Berlin Olympic Games. In 1931, before Hitler came to power, the International Olympic Committee had granted Garmisch-Partenkirchen, Germany, the 1936 winter games, and Berlin the 1936 summer games. By 1934 Jews in Germany experienced increasing discrimination, and American Jewish groups demanded a boycott of the 1936 Olympics. Concern about Jewish athletes in Germany reached the December 1934 AAU convention, delaying AAU acceptance of Germany's invitation to the games. The boycott campaign increased in momentum throughout 1935, and several AAU associations instructed their delegates to vote against American participation at the next AAU meeting (Guttmann 1984, 62, 70–71; Abramson 1935a, 26).

At the October 8 meeting of the Metropolitan Association of the AAU, Charles L. Ornstein presented a resolution condemning the Nazi government and requesting that the national AAU refuse certification for the Berlin Olympic Games to American athletes. The resolution was favored by national AAU president Jeremiah T. Mahoney, a member of the Metropolitan AAU and a former state supreme court justice. However, the Metropolitan Association voted by secret ballot, 77 to 32, to table it. The choice of a secret ballot was unusual for the Metropolitan Association, and, according to noted track writer Jesse P. Abramson, Mahoney accused Metropolitan Association president Patrick J. Walsh "with attempting to railroad the resolution out of the meeting" (Abramson 1935a, 26).

The meeting ended with the selection of Metropolitan Association delegates to the national AAU convention in December 1935. Both Jeremiah Mahoney and Patrick Walsh were selected, along with Wortmann of the German American AC and Charles L. Diehm, vice president of the Metropolitan AAU (Abramson 1935a, 26). A January 10, 1936, letter from German American AC officials to the *Beobachter* claimed that Brundage, Walsh, and Diehm agreed with Wortmann's position (*Columbia Daily Spectator* 1935, Dec. 3). Other Metropolitan AAU delegates included Charlotte Epstein, Charles A. Elbert, Frederick W. Rubien, John J. Flaherty Jr., Roy E. Moore, Arthur M. Wehrmann, Melvin W. Sheppard, and Thomas T. Reilley (Abramson 1935a; Considine and Jarvis 1969, 75, 127). Reilley, a city court judge and chairman of athletics at the New York Athletic Club, strongly favored American participation in the 1936 Olympics (Abramson 1935a; Considine and Jarvis 1935a, 107).

Responding to a motion by Patrick Walsh, the national AAU convention voted on December 7, 1935, to table a resolution to boycott the 1936 Olympic Games. On the following day the AAU associations and the allied organizations voted for American participation in the Berlin Olympics; the vote of the Metropolitan AAU was overwhelmingly in favor of Olympic participation. On December 9 Mahoney resigned from all AAU committees. Avery Brundage was elected national president of the AAU and Patrick Walsh was elected first vice president (Abramson 1935b; 1935c; 1935d).

The dispute subtly undermined long-distance running in metropolitan New York for years. The German American Athletic Club had one of the most important marathon teams in the United States. The dispersal of that team meant the loss of its leadership in marathon training and competition. Jewish athletes felt obvious repercussions by February, when Abel Kiviat and Max Silver, Jews who had been against Olympic participation, were summarily dropped as AAU officials. Kiviat had been the press steward for most of the major metropolitan track meets; Silver had been an official at every local meet since the war. Charles A. Elbert, secretary of the Metropolitan AAU, claimed, "They were accidentally overlooked, yes, accidentally overlooked, that is all" (Abramson 1936). At the 1936 AAU National Marathon Championship, William Steiner was once again a member of the winning team; this time, he ran for Millrose. And Max Silver had returned as a race official for the thirteenth annual Port Chester National Marathon (Amateur Athletic Union 1936, 50; *NYT* 1936, May 31; *Port Chester Daily Item* 1937, Oct. 13).

In New York City, the Millrose Athletic Association, already established athletically if not socially as an equal of the New York Athletic Club, increased its power as a marathon team. Millrose members Pat Dengis and Mel Porter were the first- and second-place finishers in the 1938 Lawrence-to-Salisbury Beach marathon, and Millrose won the championship. Millrose also won the team prize at the October 12, 1938, Port Chester Marathon. In November Pat Dengis won the AAU National Marathon Championship at Yonkers (*NYT* 1938, May 31; *Port Chester Daily Item* 1938, Oct. 13; Worner 1938). The Millrose AA supported the marathon, but accepted only runners who had already proven themselves in competition. If New York were to maintain a strong presence in the marathon, it needed a way for potential long-distance runners to enter the club system and get coaching for high-level competition. Furthermore, especially during the depression, many young men did not have the transportation and entrance fees that a club could provide. New York City needed a grassroots athletic club that was readily accessible to many boys to ensure the continuation of its marathon culture. Such an organization developed in Harlem.

The depression had hit Harlem more severely than any other part of New York City. Racial discrimination as well as soaring unemployment jeopardized the jobs of many African Americans, including those in the professions. Residential segregation resulted in overcrowding as well as high rents and food prices. Even with the New Deal, services and public assistance available to African Americans remained inadequate (Greenberg 1992, 398–99; Capeci 1977, 38). Harlem's children needed after-school supervision and recreation, a priority when both parents of a Harlem family worked long hours at menial jobs far from the home (Greenberg 1991, 138, 190–91).

In 1936 three Harlem businessmen—Joseph Yancey, Robert Douglas, the owner of the Renaissance Ballroom, and William Culbreath, a trainer at New York University—started the New York Olympic Club, which was registered with the AAU. The name was soon changed to the New York Pioneer Club (Booker 1951). Yancey was involved in athletics during high school and college, and later ran for the Mercury AC of Harlem. The Pioneer Club began on the sidewalks of New York as a track club for Harlemites who had neither the money nor expertise to join a top city club (Booker 1951, 7). The club accepted any athlete who wanted membership. According to Ed Levy (interview 1992), manager of the Pioneer Club and later a school principal:

> The message was that we were open to this. Others' message was that they were not open to this. You know the organizations I could refer to that were very restricted at that time. And some other organizations only wanted the top five athletes. They weren't interested in development, they wanted ready-made people. But [Yancey] was always a grass-roots person, the club was always grass-roots. The newspapers referred to us as the "Sidewalks of New York Club." So that's where we were. That was the focus of the organization, not in the elite, but it was everyman's club.

The Pioneers had no clubhouse, but Yancey, a reserve captain in the 369th Regiment, got the club access that winter to the regiment's armory at 142d Street and Fifth Avenue. The Pioneers ran the rest of the year at McCombs Dam Park in the Bronx, a popular training venue for cross-country and long-distance runners, where white runners began training with them (Booker 1951, 7). Besides promoting athletics, the Pioneer Club also had a political agenda. Yancey planned to use the club to advance racial understanding and to promote higher education for Harlem youth (Booker 1951, 7; Levy 1992). In 1942 the members decided to change the club's constitution so that white athletes could become official members (Abramson 1945, Sept. 11). A handwritten copy of the 1942 constitution stated:

> The objects of this organization are to support, encourage, and advance athletics among the youth of the Metropolitan District, regardless of Race, Color, or Creed. To encourage and further the ambition of our youth for higher education that they might become intelligent, civic-minded citizens, and to work toward a better racial understanding through the medium of education and sports.

The Pioneer Club's liberal admission policy did not constrain the most talented members; Yancey produced several national-class athletes. By 1945 the Pioneers had won several individual metropolitan and national AAU championships; two metropolitan junior championships, one national junior championship, and national 400 and 1600 meter relays (Abramson 1945, Sept. 11). But Yancey continued to offer training to any athlete who wanted to run. Murray Melnick, a high school runner in the 1940s, explained Yancey's impact on local high school athletes.

> I first heard of the club when I was a student at the Bronx High School of Science. That must have been about 1946. . . . It was my understanding that the club was largely Black but that was not particularly significant for me at the time. What was important was that it was possible for us high-schoolers to have access to a kind of organized running outside of the high school. . . . The thought that regardless of how we did on the school team we would be welcome at the Pioneers was a great, great infinitely pleasant and intriguing opening for me. It represented the possibility that I was not stuck, that I was not mediocre, that I too could move beyond. (Melnick Correspondence 1994)

In the 1940s and 1950s, the Pioneer Club became a vehicle for integration by bringing white athletes into a black club, and by indoctrinating in both black and white youths Yancey's middle-class values. Yancey was able to reach young men by creating the New York Pioneer Club as "everyman's club." Some of the new members were second-generation Jewish children who lived in Jewish ethnic neighborhoods. Joe Yancey introduced them to the manners and culture of middle America.

> [Yancey] did a lot of talking about being a gentleman first, and the values of sportsmanship and growing up to become good citizens. And much of the talking and teaching that we had every night was a lecture of some kind. And these are the topics that we covered in addition to how to run, how to strategize your races and so on. But a great amount of time was spent in personal development and subjects to that nature. And many, many people began to come down and join. We would have nights when in the Armory here you might have 150 kids, training and learning. Outside during the summer months it swelled to even greater numbers. A lot of this was due to the fact we had a very large and integrated team. We never turned anyone away because of any racial or ethnic consideration. At that time, the country was largely segregated right down to the social aspects. (Levy interview 1992)

Racial discrimination had never taken hold in the marathon, for the AAU neglected both white and black long-distance runners equally. The AAU still maintained close ties with the anti-Semitic and anti-black New York Athletic Club. These conditions prompted black and Jewish athletes to consider changes in the marathon bureaucracy (Wapner 1937, 11; *NYT* 1951, Mar. 5; Brooks 1974, 59; *NYT* 1949, Oct. 16). With Louis White's fifteenth-place finish at the 1946 Boston Marathon (*NYT* 1946, Apr. 21), the Pioneers officially moved into the event, bringing the tremendous energy of 1940s Harlem into the stagnant New York City marathon culture. In the 1950s the New York Pioneer Club fielded one of the top national marathon teams, winning the team title in the AAU National Championships in 1954 and 1955, and winning the team title at the Boston Marathon in 1955 (*NYT* 1954, May 17; Flynn 1955; *Ebony* 1955). New York marathon runners were ready to wrest control of their event from the AAU.

Browning Ross, a 1952 Olympic steeplechaser who continued in long-distance competition, directed athletes toward a new marathon administration. Ross suggested a structure like England's Road Runners Club, with district representatives, volunteer coaching, and fund-raising dinners, but his intention was the creation of an organization that "could exercise full control of our branch of the sport" (Scandurra 1981, 10, 18; *New York Times* June 20, 1954; Ross 1957, 2) On December 22, 1957, Browning Ross organized the Middle Atlantic Road Runners Club in Philadelphia. The New England Road Runners Club started two months later. The national organization, the Road Runners Club of America (RRCA), began on February 22, 1958, when Ross met with nine other runners at the Paramount Hotel in New York City (Williams and Darman 1978, 208; Scandurra 1981, 11).

New York City, where established marathon teams had a history of friction with the AAU, gave vital support to the RRCA goal of a new long-distance bureaucracy. Most of the leaders of long-distance running came from the New York City clubs such as the Millrose and the New York Pioneer Club. John Sterner of the Pioneers established the Road Runners Club New York Association (now the New York Road Runners Club [NYRRC]) in June 1958 (Scandurra 1981, 12). On February 22, 1959, the NYRRC sponsored its first marathon at McCombs Dam Park in the Bronx. There were twelve competitors. Ted Corbitt won; Nat Cirulnick, also a member of the Pioneer Club, was second (Scandurra 1981, 12; *NYT* 1959, Feb 23; *Long Distance Log* 1959).

Jewish runners supplied pivotal guidance during the early years of the RRCA and the NYRRC. Joseph Kleinerman, a charter member and frequent officer of the NYRRC, was elected vice president of the RRCA in 1960 and again for the 1963–64 term. In 1966 Nat Cirulnick served as RRCA vice president; he also was vice president and then president of the NYRRC. Cirulnick and Kleinerman, along with Barry Geisler and Cirulnick's wife, Ann, set up the New York Road Runners Club's Run for Fun program in the mid-1960s. Because mothers were encouraged to jog with their young children in noncompetitive events, the Run for Fun program was significant in introducing women to recreational long-distance running (*Road Runners Club New York Association Newsletter* 1965; 1966; 1967; 1968; 1970; Williams and Darman 1978, 208–12; Scandurra 1981, 16).

4.1. Fred Lebow, founder of
the first New York City Marathon in 1970. *Photograph by
Nancy Coplon, courtesy of* Running News.

In 1970 Fred Lebow, a Romanian Jewish immigrant, directed
the first New York City Marathon. Lebow was elected president of
the NYRRC in 1972, and held that post for twenty years, until he
advanced to chairman of the NYRRC. In 1976 he moved the
marathon out of Central Park and onto the streets of all five bor-
oughs of New York City, turning it into an international race that
became the showcase event of the New York Road Runners Club.
Lebow's accomplishments built on the work of men such as Fred
Schmertz, Max Silver, Bill Steiner, Joe Kleinerman, and Nat
Cirulnick, who ensured the place of the Jewish athlete in the
American marathon footrace (Cooper 1992).

5

The Rise of Sport at a Jewish Settlement House

The Chicago Hebrew Institute, 1908–1921

Gerald R. Gems

Being Jewish has never been easy. Pogroms, the Diaspora, and the Holocaust present ample evidence of the persecution of Jews throughout history. But in America, a land founded on the ideals of freedom and democracy, many Jews believed that they had found the new Jerusalem. Although their lifestyle differed from that of most settlers, Jews found freedom to practice their religion and enough economic opportunity to attain a degree of success in the United States. By 1890, 40 percent of American Jews even had house servants. As more Jews sought refuge in America, the established Jewish Americans felt their social status threatened by the immigrants from eastern Europe. Differences in class, language, religious, and leisure practices fractionalized the Jewish community and accentuated the differences between all Jews and non-Jews. By the end of the nineteenth century, the established Jewish Americans attempted to resolve such differences with their brethren through widespread Americanization programs in the largest Jewish communities, particularly New York and Chicago. They accomplished the task within a generation by emphasizing not only

American patriotism and the use of English but also adoption of sports and games that fostered physical prowess and a competitive spirit (Rawidowicz 1952, 133; Mazur 1990, 22, 25–26, 43–44, 65–68; Steinberg 1989, 82–105).

The first Jews who settled in Chicago migrated from southwest Germany in the 1840s. They had a history of commercial enterprise and established themselves as merchants, sharing the commercial values of the native leaders. But despite their commercial interests, they set up distinctly different cultural institutions in synagogues, separate cemeteries, hospitals, and fraternal associations. The German Jews shared a common language and interacted well with other Germans, using turner halls and the Concordia Club to hold their meetings. Within the commercial world some of these early Jews attained prominence. Henry Greenbaum, president of the German National Bank, served as the Sixth Ward alderman, and his brother, Elias, became a school agent. In 1869 wealthy Jewish businessmen, who had been barred from native clubs, formed their own Standard Club, a social organization that became one of the city's most prominent commercial fraternities.

By 1880 Chicago's Jewish population was estimated at ten thousand, but it was not homogeneous. As Jews from Russia and Poland increased the numbers, factions within the community became more apparent. The German Jews practiced Reform Judaism while the eastern Europeans remained Orthodox. Class lines separated the Jewish community as well. During the relocation that followed the Chicago fire of 1871, German Jews eventually settled in a northwestern corridor along Milwaukee Avenue and south, close to the native merchants and industrialists. These German Jews adopted many of the values of the native Chicagoans. Although perceived as cerebral rather than athletic, the German Jews even adopted the American game of baseball. However, they maintained their religious identity. In such leisure pursuits as baseball and golf, the German Jews differed markedly from the newer immigrants, who spent their limited free time engaged in religious rituals. For this group, sport seemed frivolous and irrelevant.

The Jewish peasants from Poland and Russia moved into the West Side wards adjacent to the city center, where they carried on a robust street life as sidewalk merchants, peddlers, and craftsmen, replicating the communal lifestyle of the urban ghettos of Europe.

They maintained the cultural practices that set them apart from the German Jews. Yiddish, rather than English or German, remained their language. Daily prayer in the synagogues and yeshivas transmitted an Orthodox heritage, reinforced as eastern European Jews became the majority of Chicago's Jewish population and rabbis emigrated from eastern Europe (Wirth 1928, 8–9, 153–76; Cutler 1995, 122–72; *Reform Advocate* 1891, May 22).

By contrast, the Reform German Jews took significant steps toward adopting the native culture. In 1875 the Sinai Congregation adopted a Sunday Sabbath and stopped wearing hats. As the German Jews adapted they also sought to lessen the differences of their eastern European brethren that set them apart. By 1882 at least four German Jewish clubs were holding charity events to hasten the assimilation of their eastern European brethren. Fundraising efforts were substantial, indicative of the wealth amassed by the German Jewish entrepreneurs in a booming city. Dr. Emil Hirsch of the Reform Sinai Congregation drew a salary of $12,000 by 1887, making him the highest paid rabbi in the world. Yet despite the attempts of the early Jewish settlers to move closer to the mainstream, the growing numbers of immigrants continued to adhere to their conservative ways. The diverging Jewish communities could unite only in the face of nativist anti-Semitism (Wirth 1928, 174–86).

The rising tide of eastern European immigrants became a flood by the turn of the century and threatened assimilation efforts. Anti-Semitism, rampant in late-nineteenth-century Europe, spilled over into the United States. In the 1890s Jews were viewed as part of an international financial conspiracy. Moreover, many of the immigrants, who had been part of the industrial proletariat, brought their socialistic philosophies to America. Eastern European peasants fleeing pogroms and the oppression of serfdom were ripe for conversion to such radicalism, which threatened not only American capitalists but also the businesses of the German Jewish entrepreneurs (Tuchman 1966, 182–84; Wirth 1928 179–89).

Employers, social reformers, and educators allied in the Progressive movement to address such concerns and to homogenize the multitude of divergent cultures into the established American society. While German Jewish capitalists shared the commercial values of other entrepreneurs and assisted in the transition, they faced a dilemma. Americanization programs, conducted largely through the settlement houses, public schools, and social agencies, had a distinctly Christian flavor. Those programs were often spearheaded by the YMCA and Protestant leaders. Jews feared such proselytizing influences and countered with their own. Denied full inclusion in native social organizations and desirous of maintaining their religious differences, the German Jews had already developed parallel cultural institutions. The Hebrew Benevolent Society and a B'nai B'rith lodge operated as early as the 1850s. The Sinai Temple opened a school in 1872, and Jewish benefactors started the Jewish Training School to provide vocational training for immigrants in 1887. Such programs provided self-reliance and the means to sustain the Judaic heritage in Chicago (Flinn 1891, 191, 253; Wirth 1928, 187; Mazur 1977, 264–83; Polacheck 1989, 36–39).

• • •

Playgrounds and settlement houses increasingly attracted Jewish youths. This attraction proved particularly true in the West Side ghetto, where Jane Addams and Ellen Gates Starr opened Hull House in 1889. In New York City, Lillian Wald and other German Jews followed with similar efforts, organizing settlements such as the Educational Alliance to draw children away from the streets to play in its facilities. Progressive reformers felt that supervised play in settlements, parks, playgrounds, and schools addressed such concerns as juvenile delinquency, healthy and wholesome recreation, and the inculcation of such American values as competition, cooperation, discipline, and teamwork. Adult-organized athletic programs could be especially beneficial to the eastern European Jews, who were perceived as weaklings, incapable of contributing their fair share to a country on the brink of world leadership (Riess 1989, 100–101; Lissak 1989, 85–86; Carson 1990, 73–76; Goodman 1979, xiii, 26, 39–40, 49, 65, 112).

In response to such needs and concerns for their welfare, Chicago's German Jews organized the Maxwell Street Settlement in 1893, with a weekly physical culture class. It proved poor competition for the extensive program offered at nearby Hull House. By 1900 as many as eighty thousand Jews lived in Chicago, mostly in the Hull House area. A committee of the fraternal Knights of Zion, headed by lawyer Nathan Kaplan and supported by both Orthodox and

Reform rabbis, organized the Chicago Hebrew Institute (CHI) in 1903 to serve community needs. They soon prevailed upon Julius Rosenwald, chief executive of Sears, Roebuck and a well-known philanthropist, for assistance in securing a better site. With the aid of $75,000 from Rosenwald and the purchase of a former Catholic convent, the CHI moved from 224 Blue Island Avenue to new quarters on Taylor and Lytle Streets in 1908. Like the Educational Alliance in New York, the institute offered a comprehensive program—including Sabbath school, music, art, drama, and lectures in Hebrew, Yiddish, and English—that celebrated Jewish culture as it sought to introduce American values and citizenship (Cutler 1995, 133, 142–43; Lissak 1989, 85–88; Schwartz 1961, n.p.; Wirth 1928, 26; Wagenknecht 1964, 90; Weinberg n.d.; Goodman 1979, 37–40). In so doing, the Jewish American leaders recognized the attraction and importance of sport among youths of all backgrounds (the formal organization of the Playground Association of America, the public parks system, and interscholastic athletic leagues had already been undertaken by the WASPs). The CHI wasted no time in capitalizing on the widespread interest among Jewish youths. Institute officers organized indoor baseball leagues to attract young men and boys in 1908 even before the grounds officially opened on July 4, 1909. The athletic department was formally organized in January 1909 and, consistent with its mission of promoting assimilation and respect for Jews, embarked upon an ambitious athletic program featuring American sports. Jens Jensen, the architect of some of the city's most beautiful parks, landscaped the CHI grounds. The institute covered six acres and included facilities for baseball, track, gymnastics, tennis, and handball. Within a year the weekly attendance of more than eleven thousand surpassed that of nearby Hull House as the Russian and Polish Jews sought greater community with their brethren (*Observer* 1913, Aug.; 1914, Apr.; 1912, Nov.; Dec.; Lissak 1989, 87, 117–18; Collier 1975–76, 225–43).

Aimed primarily at the eastern Europeans, the CHI athletic program was designed to

> improve physical bearing, strength, and courage, the loss of objectionable mannerisms peculiar to our people; and rapid assimilation through contact with other athletes. . . . These results once accomplished much of the prejudice against our people will be removed

and the Jew will then possess those traits and characteristics held in common by the other peoples of the community, and still not lose his inborn Judaism, of which he is so justly proud. (*Observer* 1913, Feb.)

Through sporting activities the Hebrew Institute sought to overcome negative stereotyping and gain acceptance by adopting the middle-class values of the dominant culture. CHI athletes gained the respect of the city's WASP population. Sporting ventures brought greater interactions with Anglos and other ethnic groups, contributing to greater accommodations between divergent groups as they allied in the regulation, administration, and practice of common athletic interests. Crucial to forging such alliances was Harry Berkman, the CHI physical director (*Daily Jewish Courier* 1910, May 10).[1]

Born in Chicago in 1879, a product of its schools and Harvard, the University of Wisconsin, and the Jenner Medical College, Berkman transcended the Jewish American experience. As an early member of Hull House and the German turners, he developed important ties within native and ethnic circles. Berkman demonstrated his administrative abilities by inaugurating a Women's Olympic Track Meet in 1907. Edith Marshak, a CHI competitor, later starred in the annual affair when she won both the shot put and hurdles events. Berkman displayed his athletic abilities as a member of the turner exhibition that toured Europe in 1908, including a demonstration at the London Olympics. His selection as CHI athletic director in 1908 proved fortuitous, and he served for the next fifteen years. Berkman's influence was also enhanced by marriage to Bertha Jerusalimsky, the CHI business manager, in 1916 (Meites 1924, 471–73).

Berkman worked hard to overcome the anti-Semitic stereotype of Jews as bookworms who neglected physical development. Such a perception invited harassment and assault by other ethnic youths of the West Side ghetto, whose self-esteem rested upon their physical prowess. Berkman's athletic program did much to overturn such presumptions of debilitation.

1. For an example of the early merger of Jewish culture and American patriotism, see Chicago Hebrew Institute 1909 and *Lincoln Week Program* Feb. 10–13.

Berkman organized baseball, basketball, and indoor baseball (softball) leagues. Fifteen CHI athletes won individual prizes in open competition in its inaugural year. In 1910 the relay team added its first trophy in a track meet, followed by others in baseball and basketball. The most significant victory, however, was garnered in wrestling, as the CHI team, under coach Ernst Kartje, won the Amateur Athletic Federation (AAF) championship in 1911. A citywide organization, the AAF membership included long-established native clubs, university and YMCA teams, as well as the German turners and Czech *sokols*. The triumph signaled a growing physicality and buttressed Jewish pride among youths who had been long derided for their alleged feebleness (*Observer* 1912, Nov. 7; 1915, June 7).

The CHI wrestlers won individual honors and tied for the team championship the following year in the AAF tournament that featured more than two hundred teams. A newly organized football team went undefeated and tied the Medorah Athletic Club, Chicago's lightweight champs. Thirteen-year-old Otto Baskin won the public schools' high jump championship against two thousand competitors, and the gymnastics team, under the guidance of Harry Berkman, garnered meet trophies that added to the athletic laurels that year. In the spring three CHI baseball teams ventured forth in citywide competition to challenge the Anglos at their own game (*Observer* 1912, Dec. 7).

By 1912 Berkman opened the facilities to Catholics and other ethnic groups; more than seventy-eight thousand enjoyed the facilities that summer, and nearly nineteen thousand patrons used the gym in November alone. Buoyed by the rush of success, the institute moved to expand its athletic program. Fund-raising for a million-dollar gymnasium and swimming pool began in 1913. Golf, tennis, and competition for girls in gymnastics and fencing were added to the extensive program for men and boys. Danny Goodman, a professional boxer with 225 fights, joined the CHI staff, as did Jimmy Lightbody, a three-time Olympian who was hired as the track coach to prepare for competition against the public and Catholic high school teams. The institute's monthly newspaper acknowledged the growing importance of sport in the community as it recognized two Jewish leaders, Julius Rosenwald, one of the wealthiest men in America, and Ben Reuben, five-time Amateur Athletic

Union wrestling champion, as role models for youths. But Rueben, not Rosenwald, was feted with a banquet in his honor (*Daily Jewish Courier* 1912, Aug. 23; *Observer* 1912, Nov., 7, 11–12, 22–23; 1913, Apr., 10–11; 1913, Feb., 5–8, 17; Mar., 12; May, 10; June, 27).

As other ethnic antagonists gained a new respect for Jewish athletic prowess, institute officers solidified bonds with the middle-class establishment of the sport-governing bodies. Berkman served on an AAF committee and chaired the International Gymnastics Union. Harry Berg, a CHI instructor who presided over the institute's baseball leagues, chaired the Mid-City Basketball League. He also worked on the AAF basketball and wrestling committees. H. W. Spurrier, hired as the swimming coach when the new pool opened in 1915, was on the AAU swimming committee. Such services proved beneficial to the institute's public-relations and promotional efforts as it won the right to host numerous tournaments. The athletic spectacles brought entertainment to the masses and revenue to the institute (*Reform Advocate* 1912; 1926; *Observer* 1913, Dec. 12; 1914, Jan., 11; 1915, Nov. 9).

In 1913 the institute hosted more than a dozen major sports events. The Sears Company track meet alone attracted more than twenty thousand spectators. Politicians and commercial interests

5.1. Basketball team, Jewish People's Institute, Chicago, date unknown. Photograph no. ICHi-23305.

offered trophies to promote their causes, and non-Jews soon paid to use the CHI's magnificent facilities. Harry Berg stated that in the five years since its inception, the athletic program had decreased prejudice and dispelled the notion of Jewish cowardice (*Observer* 1913, Feb., 5–6, Mar., 28, June, 27, July, 9–11; Sept., 11, 13; Oct., 11–12; Nov., 9–12; 1914, Apr., 8; 1915, Sept., 11–13).

The institute further expanded its athletic program the following year by hosting major track meets and starting a cross-country team. Perhaps spurred by the achievement of Edith Chaiken, a Jewish student at Northwestern University who captured the women's national championship at 440 yards, it amplified opportunities for women as well by initiating a swimming program that produced champion female athletes.[2] (Meites 1924, 473–75; *Observer* 1914, Apr., 12; Oct., 10; Nov., 10; 1915, Sept., 11–13; *Daily Jewish Courier* 1914; Weinberg n.d., 235).

The United States government ostensibly recognized the prominence of Jewish athletes when it hired four CHI wrestlers—including Ben Reuben, who had recently turned professional—as instructors at the Great Lakes Naval Training Station during World War I. With increasing frequency after the turn of the century, Jewish athletes began to appear in the professional arena (Meites 1924, 473–74). Both the Educational Alliance and the Henry Street settlement houses in New York provided boxing instruction by the 1890s, and a Chicagoan, Harry Harris, became the first modern Jewish champion when he won the bantamweight crown in 1901. Working-class ethnic youths began to perceive sport as a means to greater socioeconomic status, and many Jewish boys received their first formal athletic training at the Jewish settlements. Such a notion conflicted with tradition in the minds of older Jews, who viewed a ballplayer as the "king of the loafers" (Cantor 1928, 50). The situation for boxers even amounted to heresy, for bloodletting was prohibited (Weinberg, folder 4, 119; Blady 1988, 54, 57–58, 201, 230, 245–46).

2. The Emil G. Hirsch Recreation Center at Sinai Temple, founded in 1912, also conducted a comprehensive athletic program that produced many championships, including girls' city titles in basketball and track during World War I. One such champion was Ethel Bilson, a swimming and diving star (*Chicago Tribune* 1920, Dec. 19).

5.2. Boys boxing in front of Chicago Hebrew Institute Gymnasium, ca. 1915. Photograph by Taylor & Lytle, from the Jewish Community Centers of Chicago Collection, G1980.0175.

Self-defense, however, proved a necessity rather than a luxury in the West Side ghetto. Jewish fighters provided protection for the elderly and for scholars on their way to school. Frederick Thrasher, in a study of Chicago's gangs in the 1920s, stated that "the WWW's, a Jewish gang, one-fourth of whose membership was composed of prizefighters, struck terror into the hearts of overaggressive Polish groups" (Thrasher 1963, 150; Cutler 1995, 157).

For other downtrodden families, boxing provided much-needed income, which was the case for the Marovitz family. Born in 1905, the son of an itinerant tailor, Abraham Lincoln Marovitz began earning a few dollars with his boxing skills at an early age. Charlie and Eliot Aaron, local benefactors, provided him with an athletic scholarship to the Chicago Hebrew Institute when he reached adolescence. The CHI and local fight clubs provided Marovitz with a forum to demonstrate his ability. Alfred Austrian, a prominent Chicago lawyer, soon took an interest in the young man. After young Marovitz lost his job over his religious beliefs, Austrian hired him as his office boy, eventually paying his way through law school. Despite initial parental concerns over his boxing, Marovitz parlayed his physical skills into a distinguished legislative and judicial career. Marovitz served as assistant state's attorney, Chicago's first Jewish state senator, and as U.S. district court judge. He became widely known for his (mis)handling of the Chicago Seven trial (Marovitz 1990; Berkow 1977, 141–47, 182–86, 336–46; Ross and Abramson 1957).

Such athletic heroes elicited great pride among Jews, and the advent of national Jewish champions brought an even greater sense of cohesion with mainstream American society. Benny Leonard, the world lightweight champ from New York, wore the Star of David on his trunks and refused to fight on Jewish holidays. He declared that he fought to avenge the bloody noses and mockery suffered by Jewish boys, and even his early pro bouts for $20 earned more than his father's weekly wage. Leonard showed that one could be both a good Jew and a good American. The *Jewish Daily Bulletin* declared that Leonard was even greater than Einstein, for he was not only known by millions but also understood by them as well (Blady 1988, 109–25).

Although Orthodox Jews perceived sport as frivolous, their children took a more favorable attitude. For youths, who faced abject poverty, limited opportunities, and WASP accusations, sport provided a means to greater social mobility and a badge of Americanism. Other young Jews with few choices took an alternative path, engaging in criminal activities to gain a measure of material success. Barney Ross served as an errand boy for Al Capone before he became a boxer, and he continued to enjoy the gangster's support throughout his career. Others, such as Jake Guzik and the Miller brothers, became full-fledged members of the outlaw community. Ross gave up his wayward life to pursue success in the ring after another neighborhood youth, Jackie Fields (Jacob Finkelstein), won a gold medal in the Olympics and a world championship as a professional. Ross later became the darling of Chicago as he went on to win three world championships. By the 1920s Jewish youth found heroes among both athletes and criminals, and the sports program of the CHI meant to limit such choices by demonstrating prowess within the mainstream value structure (Riess 1989, 110–11; Berkow 1977, 141–47; Ross and Abramson 1957, 40–42, 60–

67, 77, 84, 92–97, 105, 125; Landesco 1968, 11, 155–57, 198, 228, 231; Haller 1971–72, 210–34.

In 1921 the directors changed the CHI's name to the Jewish People's Institute (JPI), and its athletes spread the message of Jewish physicality beyond the local community. A Young Men's Hebrew Association formed a traveling baseball team, and the JPI women's basketball team of the 1920s consistently challenged for the city championship. During a decade that produced many outstanding commercially sponsored women's teams, the JPI's women's squad was considered one of the best in the country. By 1923 the JPI had won seventy-six team trophies and twenty-three hundred individual awards (*Sunday Jewish Courier* 1922; Weinberg n.d. 235; *Sports Almanac 1927,* 211; Meites 1924, 473).

Although such athletes won acclaim and respect, they did not fully dispel prejudice. Zionism had always been a part of the CHI program, and such sentiments impressed the native born as parochial and un-American. Nativism reared its ugly head once again in the 1920s. Faced with a resurgent anti-Semitism, Jews sponsored an American tour in 1926 for the Jewish Hakoah soccer team of Vienna, Austria, the European champions. The team manager stated that the players disliked soccer "but played to demonstrate to the world that Jews possessed physical as well as spiritual power and that they would not take a back seat in the sport world" (*Jewish Daily Forward* 1923; 1926). The team's success aroused interest in soccer as youths formed teams and a Jewish Soccer League, which intended "to enter the professional league and produce a national champion" (*Daily Jewish Courier* 1927, July 21, Aug. 13; *Sunday Jewish Courier* 1927).

Such support could have been expected in Chicago, whose 285,000 Jews made it the third largest Jewish city in the world by 1926. By that time many of the Jewish residents had dispersed from the Near West Side to better neighborhoods, many moving northwest to the Lawndale district. In 1927 the JPI followed, opening a new $1.3 million building on Douglas Park Boulevard in the Lawndale area, where young Jewish men and women continued to add athletic laurels to the proud history of the institute. In the next two years the JPI won championships in basketball, swimming, wrestling, and handball, and at least ten Lawndale boys earned athletic scholarships to college (Wirth 1928, 32, 149, 190, 247, 278;

5.3. Boys' and men's swimming tank, Chicago Hebrew Institute, 1915.
Photograph no. ICHi-17318.

Amateur Athletic Federation 1929–30, 24, 28, 29; Weinberg n.d.,
230).

By the time the depression struck, the JPI had accomplished its
goals of earning respect and bringing the eastern Europeans closer
to the mainstream American culture. The athletic program was
pivotal in that process. The JPI, however, had become a victim of
its own success by the late 1930s. The Americanization programs
taught independence, and athletes learned that they could rely on
their physical abilities to make money, even during the hard times
of the depression. Although the JPI still filled a transitional role for
immigrants, Jewish American youths no longer needed its leadership and were reluctant to pay for its services. They preferred to
frequent the public parks or neighborhood basement clubs where
the street culture persisted. Gambling on athletic contests proved
more attractive than the adult-supervised programs at the institute.

The JPI was forced to disband its basketball league when it discovered that the teams had become commercialized. Such occurrences, combined with the financial restraints imposed by the depression, greatly limited the scope of the athletic program (Jewish Welfare Board 1937, 26, 70–71; Seligs n.d.).

For the groups that continued to use the JPI facilities, the depression and American democracy created factionalism based on ideological differences. Free thought allowed radicalism to germinate, culminating in the rise of Communist clubs that opposed the Zionists. The solidarity of the Jewish community faced with anti-Semitism in the 1920s eroded during the 1930s as younger members developed a class rather than an ethnic consciousness. The JPI struggled on for two more decades, changing its name to the Jewish Community Center in 1946, but it lacked the vitality of the past (Jewish Welfare Board 1937, 73–73a; Weinberg n.d., 303–20).

The Jewish Peoples' Institute had, however, already accomplished its goal. In one generation the JPI and its athletic programs had helped forge a new Jewish American culture, in itself a pluralistic phenomenon. It was no longer one but not completely the other. Religion continued to be a conspicuous distinction, but Jewish athletes had adopted American sport forms. Jews were no longer considered un-American; they had won respect yet managed to retain their religious identity. Sport thus served as a ritual process whereby negative stereotypes crumbled and Jews gained a measure of acceptance and recognition as they became more American. All Jews could take pride in their remarkable success. Ironically, such relatively rapid success continues to haunt Jews, for it is just such advancement in all areas of American life that poses a threat to the hegemony of non-Jews, suggesting that the process is not yet complete (Turner 1969; Steinberg 1989; Sollors 1989).

6

"Our Crowd" at Play

The Elite Jewish Country Club in the 1920s

Peter Levine

In 1925 the Progress Club of New York, with its heavily German Jewish membership, bought the 205-acre estate of Mrs. Caroline Read in Purchase, New York, to satisfy "a growing sentiment" among members for a "golf and country club to round out the activities of the club." Surrounded by the impressive Westchester County estates of Oscar Straus and Herbert Lehman and the $1.5 million facilities of the Jewish Century Club, the grounds boasted a white stone mansion of more than forty rooms, "generally regarded as one of the finest homes in the country," overlooking Long Island Sound. Appointed with furnishings from the Italian Renaissance period and remodeled as a clubhouse, it featured a thirty-foot hallway leading into a "distinctive dining hall with tea and breakfast rooms adjoining." The main house also included smoking and billiard rooms, a library and "sumptuous bachelor suites on the upper floors," as well as seven sun parlors overlooking thirty-two acres of flower gardens "bordered by radiant summer flowers, roses, tulips, violets and lilies of the valley." Male members who came by themselves could stay at the clubhouse while they played either of the club's two golf courses, swam in the outdoor pool, fished in the pond, or rode their polo ponies. Five small cottages, available as summer residences for member families, also were available. Whether alone or with spouse and children, members' cars were well protected by a sixty-car stone garage (Hart 1925, 134).

The grand trappings of the Progress Club were far removed from the experience of most Jews living in the United States in 1925. East European Jewish immigrants and their children who came by the millions between 1881 and 1924, far outnumbering their German Jewish brethren, mostly lived in urban ethnic ghettos and engaged in their daily struggle for survival that hardly had room for polo or golf. For both groups, however, definition and control of their leisure worlds contributed to their determinations of what it was to be an American Jew.

Relying primarily on the *American Hebrew,* a weekly magazine published in New York City that catered to America's German Jews, this essay explores one aspect of the leisure world of elite German Jews during the first part of the twentieth century—the country club. Although the country club is hardly the most significant aspect of American Jewish culture, it provides another window into the world of German American Jewry while underlining both the conflict and the possibilities for unity among Jewish Americans of different European backgrounds that marked their struggle for assimilation and acceptance (Levine 1992).[1]

The Progress Club of Purchase, New York, may have been one of the grandest of all of the Jewish country clubs in the United States but it hardly lacked competition. Accompanying the *American Hebrew* photo story about its clubhouse and grounds were similar accounts of the substantial grounds and appointments of the Metropolis Country Club of White Plains, New York, and the Jumping Brook Country Club of Hamilton, New Jersey, "said to be one of the most beautiful and picturesque in the whole state" (Hart

1. In researching *Ellis Island to Ebbets Field,* I collected much material from the *American Hebrew* and other Jewish community newspapers, and from some manuscript collections concerning German Jewish involvement in sport. This essay marks a tentative, incomplete attempt to tell that story. Much of the focus, as the title of the essay suggests, is on the *American Hebrew*, a weekly magazine published in New York, that catered to American German Jews. For the best and most recent study of American German Jews, see Cohen 1984.

1925, 134, 164). One year later, as part of its annual survey of country clubs and sport, the magazine filled out the picture. Dividing the country into "districts," it detailed the location, membership, officers, and origins of fifty-eight country clubs (in twenty states) owned and operated by memberships predominantly Jewish. Not surprisingly, seventeen clubs catered to New York's Jewish elite, including two of the oldest Jewish country clubs in the United States: Inwood, founded in 1901 and the site of the 1923 U.S. Golf Open, and the Century Club, founded in 1898. Clubs in the "New York City District," most begun in the late teens and early 1920s, had a combined membership of 5,816, of which 4,477 were men. Although club names such as Sunningdale, Quaker Ridge, and Fellimore hardly belie the ethnic origins of their members, the names of club officials indicate a totally Jewish clientele, predominantly German with an occasional east European included.

Similar patterns prevailed elsewhere. New York had the most Jewish country clubs, twenty. Illinois was a distant second with seven clubs, all in metropolitan Chicago. Clubs catering to Jewish elites in other Midwestern cities with sizeable Jewish populations—including Cincinnati, Cleveland, St. Louis and Kansas City—accounted for another 3,505 members. Clubs in the Philadelphia area, togther with seven more that dotted the New Jersey shore,

6.1. Metropolis Country Club at White Plains, New York. The club, which comprises more than 105 acres, was planned for about 450 members. The clubhouse was designed in the colonial style. Photograph from *The American Hebrew,* June 5, 1925.

comprised another 3,096 members. The most eminent was the lavish Philmont Club, whose 938 members made it the largest Jewish country club in the United States. Corresponding to contemporary Jewish population-distribution patterns, southern and western states accounted for less of the total but nevertheless demonstrated the existence of wealthy enclaves of Jews throughout the country. The southern district boasted eight clubs, including the Jewish Progressive Club of Atlanta—the only country club to acknowledge in its name any obvious Jewish connection—two clubs in the Baltimore vicinity, and facilities in Miami Beach; Montgomery, Alabama; New Orleans; San Antonio; and Louisville. Western clubs in Omaha, Portland, Oregon, Los Angeles, and San Mateo rounded out the list.

As in the New York area, most Jewish country clubs originated after 1910. Figures for fifty-four of the fifty-eight clubs surveyed by the *American Hebrew* show a total membership of 17,516—13,352 men and 4,164 women. Most women members were either spouses or closely related to male members. And although women made up almost 25 percent of club memberships, twenty-two clubs specifically prohibited women as members ("A Survey of Country Clubs Throughout the United States," 126, 134).

Gentile clubs barred Jews and set fees limiting their clientele by social class and financial place, and Jewish clubs followed similar practices. Club officials placed caps on total membership, established waiting lists for eager social climbers, and charged membership fees beyond the reach of any but the extremely wealthy. Excluded from restricted Seattle golf courses in the early 1920s, wealthy Jews in that city quickly raised most of their initial expenses of $100,000 for building the Glendale Country Club by offering memberships to seventy-eight members who paid between $300 and $2,000 a year for the privilege of joining (Minutes of First Meeting of Glendale Country Club, Jan. 28, 1924, Schwabacher Family Papers, Seattle Jewish Archives Project, Univ. of Washington Library). Although the Golf Park Country Club in Miami, Florida, made clear its intention to be open to people of all religions, this club, established in 1926 "by the Jewish residents of Miami," aimed only at very rich Americans who might choose to live or vacation in a burgeoning vacation and tourist spot. As its promotional literature made clear, its limited membership of one thousand, based on nominations to the Membership Committee, "will be chosen with the utmost discrimination" and "will constitute a social roll of honor" (*AH* 1926, June 4).

Unable to obtain access to local country clubs, prominent German Jews in Columbus, Ohio, incorporated the Winding Hill Country Club in 1921, buying 178 acres of land and constructing a golf course and country club for a cost of $100,000. Although its incorporation papers made no mention of any exclusionary admission policies, calling only for a club that would "provide diversion" and "recreation . . . social and mutual improvement" in "a social club devoted to outdoor sports, rural amusements and country pastimes," the club's membership comprised only wealthy German Jews who could afford its $500 membership fee and annual dues of $200. To insure the purity and social standing of its clientele, prospective newcomers required sponsorship by two members and approval by eight of the nine members of the board of directors for admission (Raphael 1979, 235–36; "American Jews as Sportsmen" 1920, 596, 687; "Among the Country Clubs" 1924, 123, 135–36, 138–39).

A somewhat different but equally impressive display of the wealth and social status connected with Jewish country clubs appeared in an account of the expansion of the Westwood Country Club in St. Louis. Founded in 1907, the club decided to move to new grounds in 1928. Its members pooled their resources and bought three hundred acres of land within nine miles of the city limits. Part of the fund-raising for the new facility included, as the club's president, Louis Rosen, put it, "a small assessment of $600 each on the old membership of 275." Operating with a fund of more than $1 million, the club built three nine-hole golf courses, practice greens and fairways, six tennis courts, a swimming pool, baseball grounds, a small landing strip for airplanes, horse stables, and a four-acre lake with pumping facilities for watering the golf courses. Lots for forty-four homesites were also bought by members. According to Rosen, plans called for regular memberships to close at 350. With a clubhouse alone valued at $425,000 and lavishly decorated in "English Baronial design," it is abundantly clear that only wealthy Jews could apply for membership in Westwood's exclusive circle. Similar stories abound in Portland, Oregon; Los Angeles, Detroit, Milwaukee, and New York City (*AH* 1929, May 3; Toll 1982, 20–37; Lowenstein 1987, 162–63; Vorspan and Gartner 1970, 153; Birmingham 1967; Gabler 1988, 270–75).

Rosters of club members and officials underline the fact that, with few exceptions, club memberships remained limited to successful American Jews of German descent. Chicago's renowned three-hundred-acre Lake Shore Country Club included among its earliest members businessmen Leonard Florsheim, Frederick Mandel, Modie Spiegel, and Julius Rosenwald, president of Sears, Roebuck and the wealthiest man in Chicago. Many of its members were also leaders in the Standard Club, Chicago's preeminent Jewish social organization. Commenting on the formation of the Ravisloe Country Club, one of the first Jewish clubs in the United States, Joe Graffis, publisher of the *Chicago Golfer*, proudly asserted that its "pioneers included a number of men prominent in Chicago's business, civic and social life." Following a roster of German members, Graffis concluded that "the charter membership of the club was a miniature blue book of Chicago's leading Jewish families who figured conspicuously in any movement for the betterment of the community." Although perhaps not in the same Chicago circles as men such as Alfred Austrian, prominent Chicago lawyer and member of Ravisloe, no less important in the *Hebrew*'s eyes were men such as David Litt, president of the Bryn Mawr Country Club of Chicago in 1925, a Mason and an Elk, and for forty years chief buyer for the rug and carpet department of Carson Pirie, Scott, wholesalers. Such brief biographic descriptions scarcely were necessary in describing the country club doings of the Guggenheims, Lehmans, Schiffs, Seligmans, and others who made up New York's "our crowd" as they milled about on the playing fields of their clubs on Long Island and in Westchester (Graffis 1925, 137; Ebner 1988, 223; Birmingham 1967).

Jews built their palatial clubs, took up golf, polo, and yachting, and set fees that limited their clientele by social class and financial place. The goals were undeniably clear—to demonstrate their credentials for acceptance by a dominant upper-class, white, Anglo-Saxon, Protestant elite and to distance themselves from the waves of east European Jewish immigrants living and toiling in urban ghettos who seemingly threatened to overrun America and their place in it (Mrozek 1983, 103–36).

Jewish country clubs, at least in their formal announcements and in corporation papers, did not admit they were using elite sport and its trappings to separate American Jews of German and east European ancestry. Indeed, begun in many instances because anti-Semitism prohibited wealthy German Jews from joining elite Protestant clubs, Jewish clubs often indicated that membership was open to people of all religious faiths (*AH* 1925, Oct. 16). Nevertheless, the pages of the *American Hebrew* implicitly brought the message of social exclusion home in its continual coverage of country club doings, the advertisements it carried, and occasionally in its editorials about the progress of Jewish assimilation.

Aside from its country club and sport issue, which became an annual feature of the magazine, the New York-based periodical carried constant news of the social doings of prominent German Jews everywhere. The summer vacations of people such as Adolph S. Ochs, publisher of the *New York Times,* at his summer estate, Abenia, on Lake George, along with the crowd of prominent Jews including Rabbi Stephen Wise and his family and also Mr. Solon Frank, an "international authority on polo," who vacationed at "Lake Placid's big summer colony," were reported regularly. A far cry from the farmhouses of the Catskills that catered to east European Jews who managed to escape the New York City heat for a week, these elite vacation spots, like the country clubs closer to their homes, were clearly off-limits to all but Jewish society's finest (Kanfer 1989).[2]

Covered in its pages as well were the splendid estates of exceptionally wealthy and prominent Jews, such as Albert D. Lasker, an influential Chicago lawyer who was instrumental in resurrecting major league baseball from the abyss of the 1919 Black Sox scandal. Lasker's Mill Road farm in Everett, Illinois, featured its own golf course, a seven thousand-yard layout rated among the best in the country. The $1,000,000 course was known not only for its design but also because of the notable guests that had enjoyed the privilege of playing it (Gunther 1960, 175-77).[3]

2. Stories such as these appeared in the *American Hebrew* column "Society and Its Doings" and in special articles such as "Where the Billow Breaks," an article on New Jersey shore summer retreats (1917, July 13; 1924, Aug. 1).

3. Occasionally included were descriptions of the estates of wealthy east European Jews, such as Adolph Zukor's Rockland County, New York, Mountain View Farm, described in a May 3, 1929, issue as a mark of "the grand achievements of Jewish men." Even Zukor's wealth, however, was not enough at first to buy him admission to Los Angeles's German Jewish Hillcrest Club.

Advertisements featuring the latest and most expensive sporting clothes and equipment from New York's most exclusive stores merely underlined the connection between German wealth and elite sport. Bonwit Teller's pure silk tricot jumpers with turtlenecks at only $49.00, de riguer for the woman golfer, featured in a June 5, 1925, *American Hebrew* advertisement, clearly were out of reach of all but the very wealthy. Women who preferred Fifth Avenue's B. Altman's store for "correct sports clothes" could look to the magazine for full-page advertisements depicting the latest female fashions for golf, swimming, tennis, and horseback riding. No less exclusive were the golfing outfits sported in a promotion by James W. Bell and Sons, "Gentlemen's Tailors," who offered "Smart Dress for Men who Desire Unusual Clothes to Measure of Most Exceptional Character, Genuine Comfort, Exclusive Quality, and Unmistakable Distinction" (1919, May 16; Dec. 5; 1920, July 2; 1923, May 4).

Even a 1925 editorial that attacked the "cheap exclusiveness" of the New London Country Club for barring Jews became less an attack on anti-Semitism than an opportunity for distinguishing one kind of Jew from another. Granting that "people have the right to choose those whom they regard as congenial," the *Hebrew* noted that its "main objection" to the exclusion of Jews from the Connecticut club and "other groups of a similar kind who bar Jews" is that "generally their action is motivated by moral obtuseness and mob stupidity" because "they include at one swoop all Jews, those socially desirable and those who in any gathering of the refined might be *de trop*." Hopeful for a world in which individual worth rather than "the accidentals of faith, nationality or color" determined a person's opportunity, the *Hebrew,* speaking for its wealthy German subscribers, "resent[ed] being placed in a category, 'Jew,' which to many minds is synonymous with *persona non grata.* Fortunately," it concluded, "refined Jews pay no attention to slurs of this nature and are never driven to retaliate in kind" by barring non-Jews from clubs predominantly of Jewish membership (1925, Oct. 16)

Separating themselves from east European Jews and opening their golf courses and polo fields to wealthy Gentiles who denied them entry into their clubs and social circles seems to have held no irony for *American Hebrew* editorialists or for the Jewish country club set. Indeed, virtually every argument they offered for the promotion of elite sport—even the idea itself of participation in elite sport for social distancing—aped the beliefs and actions of the wealthy Protestant world they hoped to join.

From as early as the mid-seventeenth century, American upper classes concerned with wealth and social status defined their exclusiveness, in part, by the sporting activities they avoided as much as by those they enjoyed. Baseball, for example, began as a sport for respectable and prosperous middle and upper middle-class gentlemen in the 1850s but the game became most popular with middle- and working-class men and boys. Although a bicycling craze swept the country in the 1890s, its appeal to a middle-class audience made it unattractive to the wealthy, who sought instead the country club, golf, tennis, polo, and yachting for combining athletic enjoyment with visibly large outlays of capital that distinguished these activities as off-limits to any but the rich (Mrozek 1983, 105–7; Adelman 1986, 123).

If wealthy German Jews eager for assimilation and acceptance found in the country club movement an opportunity to distinguish themselves from "de trop" Jews, they also hoped it would ease their admission into an elite Protestant culture familiar with its utility for social distancing and for social acceptance. Time and again, those who wrote about the importance of Jewish involvement in elite sport alluded to this possibility. Next to a full-page advertisement promoting the golf and tennis equipment available at the sporting goods department of New York's exclusive B. Altman's, the *Hebrew*'s editorial page of May 4, 1923, explained its decision to devote an entire issue to "Country Clubs and Sports." A column titled "The New Art of Recreation" began with the response of a "well-known New York sportswriter" to this planned special issue.

> What you say amazes me, [he] exclaimed . . . after he had heard the story of our projected sports issue. He knew there were many Jews who were outdoor enthusiasts. He had heard that there were in the vicinity of New York City several golf clubs in which the predominant membership was Jewish. . . . He had even heard that out in Chicago there is a young Jew who is a top notch polo player. . . . When, however, he heard that sports clubs in which the membership is predominantly Jewish, possessing golf links of a high order, tennis courts, outdoor and indoor swimming pools dotted the country from New York to the coast in the vicinity of large cities, he was, as he said amazed.

Determined to do away with such amazement once and for all and to "brush away [the] moth-eaten fiction" of "Jews being immersed in commercial pursuits to the exclusion of all things," the magazine proposed to offer its readers the story of new golf clubs catering to Jewish business and professional men to demonstrate full Jewish involvement in "the new art of outdoor recreation" so popular in the United States. According to the editorial, Jews, who easily adapted to the American environment, found that "American love for sports, no less than ardor for democracy, fair play, and the square deal, enters the Jew's soul." Although excluded for "social reasons" from joining established country clubs, they have built their own, "developing them with the same avidity that they pursue their businesses, follow their professions, and support their philanthropies." Not surprisingly, the *Hebrew* concluded, "the last decade . . . witnesses a forward movement toward golf and athletics among the Jews of America," which is teaching Americans that "given half a chance and shown the way, the Jew proves himself as human and out of doors as other Americans . . . and that only repressions have kept him from participation in every field activity, from banking to billiards, from science to sports" (779).

Although the editorial's demand for Jewish inclusion in an American gentile world did not deny that anti-Semitism was at the heart of a pattern of exclusion, its tone is generally optimistic about future possibilities for the lessening of prejudice and for social acceptance. Essential to this belief was the hope that the participation of wealthy German Jews in elite sport would demonstrate that they were no different from their gentile counterparts, either as Americans or as elites, thus doing away with any logical reason for their exclusion. Not only by their participation but also by the reasons they gave for doing so, Jews attempted to make their case. Like the Protestant wealthy who applauded their own involvement in the country club movement as activity that would reinvigorate American virility for battle in the boardrooms or on San Juan Hill, Jews, as one writer put it, noted their own participation as evidence of their "love of the outdoors," itself "one of the great manifestations of the American spirit" (Mrozek 1983, 105–7; Levine 1989b, 62–68).

Whenever the *American Hebrew* chose to write about the sporting accomplishments of its most privileged subscribers throughout the late teens and 1920s, it repeated this message. Whether reporting on the plans of the City Athletic Club of New York, a club for wealthy German Jewish businessmen, to erect a new building with better athletic facilities to promote the "virility" and "alertness" of its members, noting the importance of golf as a reinvigorating sport for the "tired business man," or promoting the country club as a source of social enjoyment as well as an opportunity to display Jewish physical aptitude, the magazine continually made the case that Jews, if given the chance, were normal human beings who did not deserve to be excluded from any social, economic, or cultural circle ("City Athletic Club to Build" 1920; "From Marbles to Polo" 1924). Even in its very first article devoted to Jewish participation in elite sport, which appeared in 1920, the *Hebrew* made clear that it had no "desire to exploit or extol Jewish country clubs." Rather, it offered the country club as part of the "chronicle of the tremendous advance of Jews in America," hopeful "for the advent of the day when men and women will be welcomed in a country club by virtue of their sportsmanship and not their religious affiliations." A decade later, still in search of this fulfillment, the magazine reiterated its appeal in ways consistent with the message of a whole range of Jewish reformers who argued that Jewish prowess in sport would do away with stereotypes depicting Jews as abnormal. Noting the opening of six new country clubs and of the thousands of Jews who played golf and tennis, the *Hebrew* emphasized how enthusiastically "Jewish folk heed the call of the open. The physically bent hack, the puny muscles, the dimmed eye are vague memories of an era which the average American Jew of today knows nothing about" ("American Jews as Sportsmen" 1920, 596, 598, 687; *AH* 1929; Levine 1992, 11–25).

Arguments of the utility of Jewish country clubs in promoting the reconciliation of Jewish and gentile elites emphasized more than this theme of normalcy and acceptance. In a long account of new, predominantly Jewish country clubs, one writer noted that there "Jews and Gentiles meet on a ground of sportsmanlike equality" and exhibit "a heartening absence of social or religious discrimination." If familiarity bred something other than contempt, even more heartening to the Jewish readers who yearned for social acceptance were the comments of Gene Sarazen, U.S. Open champion of 1922 and then golf professional at the Jewish Fresh Meadow

Country Club. In an article entitled "The Common Ground of Golf," this gentile spokesman for the sport labeled it "one of the most potent forces in breaking down the age-old prejudices of race between the Jew and the non-Jew." Blaming past antagonisms on a lack of mutual understanding, Sarazen credited "18 holes of leisurely pleasant sporting rivalry" and "the in between chats that develop as they wander over the fairways" as appropriate cure for religious prejudice. Although omitting any reference to the fact that such friendly wandering could take place only on club grounds built by Jews, Sarazen praised their courses as among the best in the country. Noting that of the estimated five hundred thousand golfers in the United States, more than thirty thousand were Jewish, he argued that this number, "entirely out of proportion with the Jewish proportion of the population," demonstrates the popularity of the sport among Jews and ultimately its force promoting "interracial relationships." Although neither a sociologist nor a demographer, Sarazen also noted that contact between Jew and Gentile on the links positively contributed to Jewish acculturation in ways that might disarm even the most prejudiced anti-Semite. Out on the links and in the clubhouse, he concluded, the Jew "has absorbed many of the habits, customs, and social amenities of the American non-Jews [including] the secret of relaxation" (Sarazen 1925, 135).

Learning that "secret," however, could be hard work. Describing the avidity with which members of the Inwood Country club in 1920 made use of the club's tennis courts, shooting range, and golf courses, one report noted that "members take full advantage of the possibilities for sport to such an extent that on Saturday afternoons . . . the players must leave the tee on a three minute schedule or miss the opportunity to play." Nowhere in this *Hebrew* piece entitled "American Jews as Sportsmen" did the author suggest any inconsistency between playing on the Sabbath and being Jewish— a view that became increasingly acceptable not only to a German Jewish elite but also to second-generation children of east European immigrants who made their mark in sports far removed from the world of the country club ("American Jews as Sportsmen" 1920, 596).

Motivated by a desire for acceptance denied them by anti-Semitism, German Jews created a parallel leisure world of sport in the hope that its existence would negate its very reason for being. They remained mostly disappointed. Only after World War II did policies against Jews, at country clubs, colleges, or in the business, political, and professional worlds, begin to come down. Nevertheless, the social world they created, full of elite sport and attendant social activities from debutante balls to charity sporting contests, provided rewards while offering wealthy Jewish women a prominence denied most other American females.

Although golf was clearly the centerpiece of country club sport, most facilities also provided opportunities for tennis and skeet shooting. No doubt Bernard Baruch's daughter, Renee, and the great financier himself, both featured in a pictorial, "Outstanding Sport Devotees," displaying their marksmanship hunting grouse in Scotland in the 1930 country club issue (July 4) of the *American Hebrew,* learned how to shoot at American Jewish country clubs. Accompanying pictures of the Baruchs was one of Robert Lehman, son of Herbert, New York's lieutenant governor and soon to be governor—mallet in hand atop his polo pony and described as a "crack member of the Westchester Country Club." Also included was a photo of Mrs. Bernard Gimbel and her two daughters, members of the family that owned New York's Gimbel's department store. Decked out in top hats and riding outfits atop their trusted mounts groomed at their Port Chester estate, the Gimbels, as the caption pointed out, posed as they readied for yet another riding competition.

By the mid-1920s several Jewish clubs promoted polo as well as horsemanship. According to one account, so popular was polo among Philadelphia's gentile elite that the predominantly Jewish Philmont Club organized its own team in 1924. Led by the Gimbels, two quartets representing the club not only engaged each other at Philmont's "splendid oval" but also won six of their eight matches against outside competition in their first year, even giving the crack team of the Pennsylvania Military College a tough contest. Noting that the sport is one not yet popular "with the masses" (perhaps in part because each player required three to four ponies for each match), one Philmont supporter predicted that the team would soon be strong enough to "hold its own among such well known fours as Bryn Mawr and the Philadelphia Country Club" (Stern 1926, 114).

So popular was the sport among some members of the Norwood Golf Club in West Long Branch, New Jersey, that interested members formed their own polo club in 1922. Although the Monmouth Polo Club remained a separate organization with its own officers, to be a member also required membership in Norwood. The polo club leased its large 900' × 450' playing field and practice grounds from the country club, whose facilities were fully available to those who preferred clubbing balls from atop horses rather than with their feet planted firmly on the ground. Complete with a clubhouse for polo club members as well as the private stables of its most prominent players, Monmouth scheduled intramural matches every Wednesday at five o'clock and every Sunday at four o'clock from spring through late October. As a member of the United States Polo Association, the club also played local competitors, including the restricted Rumson Country Club and an army team from Monmouth. Members also participated in and helped run the county's annual horse show (Stern 1926, 114; "Highlights on Links and Polo Fields" 1928).

Although he usually played alongside Gentiles rather than Jews, Eugene Byfield of Chicago's Sherman Hotel—captain of the Grasmere Farm polo team that were "Midwest champions" in 1922—suggested that the sport is "peculiarly suited for the quick thinking, high strung Semitic temperament." More often, however, those who wrote about Jewish participation in this "fascinating . . . albeit costly" sport chose to emphasize less ethnic strains. Commenting on the success of the Norwood and Philmont teams in 1926, one writer made clear the utility it had for Jewish elite aspirations. By referring to it as a "royal" and "ancient" sport, he connected Jewish participation to the tradition and class that elite German Jews aspired to. Moreover, by emphasizing that polo players "above all" required "courage in power, and quick thinking," he saw Jewish success in the sport as evidence that Jews "were not lacking" in any of the "attributes" considered normal and essential for social advancement (Gordon 1925, 162; Stern 1926, 114, 151).

For those who preferred sea to land, yachting—whether by sail or motor—offered still other opportunities for leisure defined by prominence and exclusion. Although yachting was hardly catalogued as frequently as the activities of polo players or golfers, the *American Hebrew* occasionally took note of the extravagant boats and outings of its Jewish constituents. Much as it did in its descriptions of golf courses and clubhouses, the magazine often gave meticulous detail of boats and outings—still another way of demonstrating both the good taste and wealth of those involved. Most notable was "Commodore" Julius Heilner's ninety-nine-foot *Irwin*. Anchored at the Colonial Yacht Club on the Hudson River in Hudson River, New York, the boat, driven by two six-cylinder engines with a cruising speed of thirteen miles per hour, came "completely equipped with luxurious conveniences," five large staterooms, three bathrooms, a music room, and dining room. Although Felix Warburg's *Carol* may not have been as elaborately fitted, he found the time in the summer of 1926 to sail up the Atlantic coast to Maine. Louis Strouse plied his *Bedouin III* in and out of Long Island Sound and along the eastern shores of the Maryland coast in search of grouse as well as invigorating sailing (Gordon 1926, 104, 151).

Perhaps because they were too few and because the expenses involved permitted the participation of only the very wealthiest, these Jewish boatmen generally did not start their own clubs. Warburg belonged to the Eastern Yacht Club of Boston and Strouse to the Knickerbocker Yacht Club of Port Washington, Long Island. The exception was the Rockaway Park Yacht Club on Long Island. Founded in 1916, ten years later the club boasted a membership of seventy-five. Catering to both sail- and motorboat enthusiasts, it sponsored an annual speedboat regatta, but more important, with its clubhouse, dance floor, and kitchen, served, if the *Hebrew* was correct, as "the recognized center of all yachting and social activities of the community" (Gordon 1926, 151; "Cruising on Summer Seas" 1925).[4]

Especially in spring and summer months, the same could be said for the *American Hebrew* country club set. Be it dances, dinner, debutante balls, or participation in sport, the clubs provided opportunities for small talk, social climbing, and business in extravagant setting. Often extensions of city clubs, their growth, according to one commentator, not only served as a sign of prestige but also provided opportunities for "social intercourse" not always possible in day-to-day urban life. Whether in Chicago's suburbs or the rolling hills of Westchester County, those who could afford it even built summer homes near their clubs, which served as community

---

4. Jewish men who enjoyed rowing also found it necessary to form their own club, the Lone Star Boat Club, near Dyckman Street (*AH* 1928, June 1).

centers for their busy social life. As Louis Robertson, president of the Woodmere Country Club of Long Island put it, golf clubs evolved from places to play the game to elaborate facilities "surrounded by comfort and luxury" that catered to the social and athletic needs of the entire family (Robertson 1926, 120).[5]

Although he did not mention them specifically, wealthy Jewish women were certainly part of Robertson's equation. On country club tennis courts, golf courses, shooting ranges, and horse stables, participating as individuals and occasionally as members of Jewish women's organizations, the wives and daughters of wealthy Jews took up games and sport denied most American women by sexual and class distinctions. Pictures of women showing horses, shooting skeet, and playing golf and tennis adorned the pages of the *American Hebrew* and the society columns of newspapers such as the *Detroit Jewish Chronicle*. Also prominent were accounts of events that combined sport and other social activities. As the publicity chair of the charitable Junior Auxiliary of the New York section of the National Council of Jewish Women reported in November 1924, a golf tournament at the Fenimore Country Club in White Plains, New York, combined with a tennis tournament at courts on Manhattan's Upper West Side rather than "a bridge or a tea or something equally feminine," became the accepted way of the group's winter activities (Blitzer 1924, 853; *AH* 1925, Sept. 4, Nov. 6).

More than any other sport in which these women engaged, golf clearly was the favorite. Articles and pictorials on "Personalities in Sports"—regular features of the *American Hebrew* in the 1920s—gave as much attention to the exploits of female golfers as of males. Complementing its yearly listing of men and women golf champions of country clubs, for example, a May 3, 1929, pictorial, "A Brilliant Galaxy in Golfdom's Sky," featured the pictures of eight women and four men highlighting the athletic achievements of the nation's Jewish elite. The same issue also reported the names of 150 Jewish women ranked among the top 1,237 female players by the handicap committee of New York's Women's Metropolitan Golf Association of New York. Included in the list was Mrs. Leo G.

5. Virtually any annual country club issue makes this point as does seasonal coverage of similar activities in local Jewish community newspapers, such as the *Detroit Jewish Chronicle*.

Federman, a two-handicapper of such note that she was also featured, along with Mrs. Harry Grossman and Mrs. S. L. Reinhardt, in an article highlighting the most outstanding Jewish golf and tennis players in the country.

For Mrs. Reinhardt, the former Elaine Rosenthal of Chicago, such attention was hardly new. In 1925, celebrating her third women's Western Open golf championship, the *Hebrew* (1925, Nov. 6) featured her accomplishments in a full-length article. Then living in Texas with her husband, Reinhardt, who played golf as a married woman under her maiden name, learned the game at the Jewish Ravisloe course in Chicago. Although the magazine was not sure how often she had made her husband "a golf widower," her successes in the Western Open, coupled with her past performances in the Women's National championship, put her "in the front rank of women players in the country."

Much like their husbands, elite Jewish women in choosing their sports made sure to select those that sharply distinguished them from women in less fortunate economic circumstances. A few young Jewish working-class women as well as those who attended college engaged in a wide range of recreational and organized sport in the 1920s and 1930s. Whether they played in industrial league basketball games or intercollegiate contests, earned honors in sports such as track or swimming, participated in athletic competition at Chicago's Jewish People's Institute, or confined themselves to the elite sport of their country club set, Jewish women regardless of class, shared one thing in common: rarely was their ethnic or religious background cause for commentary. Although male and female physical educators and social activists debated the meaning of women's participation in sport as early as the late nineteenth century, they mostly ignored any discussion of its significance for understanding questions of the assimilation of immigrants, discrimination based on religious difference, or challenges to ethnic stereotypes—all matters that engrossed those who took note of Jewish male participation in sport. Instead, arguments for or against women's involvement in sport or discussion of its social significance remained bound by the politics of gender. Whether female participation damaged socially prescribed feminine roles as mother and homekeeper or posed a threat to male control of a patriarchal America bound the debate (Levine 1992, 8).

In coverage of elite Jewish women's sport, even these matters were rarely engaged directly. A 1928 *American Hebrew* piece highlighting the achievements of Mrs. Louis Lengfeld of San Francisco is illustrative. As in most articles that described the athleticism of married women, her status as wife and mother balances accounts of her prowess on the links. In the account of her triumph in the Northern California Women's golf championship as well as her golfing prominence at the Beresford Country Club at San Mateo, "one of the most exclusive country clubs in the West," she is consistently referred to as Mrs. Louis Lengfeld. Only in passing do we learn that before she married her name was Helen Foorman. Although descriptions of her "aggressive play" and her ability to "bang at the ball with man-like determination" suggest language often used by those who feared that women's participation in sport was unnatural and damaging to proscribed male and female roles, at least in Lengfeld's case, her management of a "lovely country home" and her role as the mother of three children guaranteed her feminine credentials ("Highlights on Links and Polo Fields" 1928, 94–95).

Four years earlier, in a sidebar to a feature story that described the accomplishments of male and female Jewish golfers, the *Hebrew* addressed itself tongue in cheek to its female readers on golf in ways that are suggestive of the ambivalent feelings about sexual roles their own participation in sport might have provoked. Entitled "Improving Your Husband's Game," it summarized suggestions first offered in *The American Golfer* designed to help a wife concerned with lowering her husband's golf score. "To be a real champion and a helpmate . . . a wife should insist that she play golf with her husband" in ways that would inspire his own confidence. The first way to accomplish this is for the woman to display total ignorance of the game by "using a midiron in the first bunker, thus giving him a legitimate excuse to display the finer points of the game by demonstrating how impracticable this would be." No doubt, the magazine opined, he will be "delighted" to do this while two foursomes play through his game. Having given him the opportunity to show his superiority, the *Hebrew* provided several ways for wives to offer encouragement and solutions for any problems in their husbands' games. Predicting that the husband, upset about having to let other golfers play through, would swing too hard at his next shot, it told women what to say if he misplayed it or missed the ball altogether. Noting that "a snicker or suppressed laughter . . . would be out of place," it suggested instead "some encouraging little proverb . . . like 'Better luck next time,' or 'Practice makes perfect,'" remarks calculated to "assist him immeasurably in his game." After providing some additional "consoling remarks" for other misadventures on the fairway that "will be of great comfort to his harassed soul," the *Hebrew* suggested the possibility of engaging the husband in conversation that might "smooth his troubled brow . . . and calm him." Talk of "new gowns" or of the "new marquisette draperies for the library . . . will help greatly." In closing, this advice column suggestively offered one last chance for wives to serve as helpmates to fragile males concerned with getting the ball into the hole.

> The last chance to help will come on the putting green. The husband's third putt will be short of the cup by about two inches. The helpful wife will then say: "Tush, tush, Clarence. Never up, never in." It will be a new one on the hubby. It is a trite saying but true. The wife, now knowing the course very well, will ask where to go next—and the husband will tell her. ("Improving Your Husband's Game" 1924)

There is no way of knowing how an Elaine Reinhardt or Helen Lengfeld, or for that matter, how other women who read the *American Hebrew* but never dared venture out on a golf course responded to depictions of women as ignorant helpmates concerned with dresses and drapes who managed to enrage and emasculate their mates on the links. Nor would it be wise to read too much into a column clearly intended to amuse its audience. Nevertheless, in the context of the early 1920s, when many wondered if the Nineteenth Amendment to the United States Constitution, the flapper, and the automobile might free women from sexually prescribed roles in ways that threatened to endanger the social balance, the column did offer a message that even women's frivolous participation in the masculine world of sport posed a danger to male prowess and power.

Especially in the past twenty-five years, as women's increased involvement in athletics coincided with a reinvigorated feminist movement, debate over such issues has become commonplace. For wealthy Jewish women who participated in elite sports in the

1920s, however, it was largely muted. Women in the 1920s engaged in sport in a circumscribed and limited world of female activity, in which their primary public identity was defined by whom they married and to which country club they belonged. Nevertheless, playing golf in extravagant settings, either among themselves or in state, regional, or national tournaments, gave them opportunities to enjoy competition, companionship, and physical pleasure. It also demonstrated that by playing the "right" games, they deserved to belong to an American aristocracy defined by wealth and place.

As with their husbands, however, their claims for respectability and acceptance were not necessarily well received. Although golfers such as Reinhardt and Lengfeld copped regional and state titles and competed effectively even in national competition, at least on one occasion Jewish women golfers confronted anti-Semitism and exclusion from elite circles much the way their husbands did. Although hardly devoted to covering elite sport for its Chicago working-class east European audience, in 1923 that city's Yiddish *Jewish Daily Forward* recounted a story originally reported in the *Chicago Tribune* concerning the exclusion of Jewish women golfers from a city tournament sponsored by the Women's Western Golf Association. Under the headline "Anti-Semitism in Women's Western Golf Association," it reported that not one of the ninety-one women invited to play in the organization's Chicago tournament was Jewish even though there were many Jewish golf clubs in the city. This news hardly surprised the *Forward,* which noted that this openly anti-Semitic organization two years earlier had denied full membership to Jewish country clubs, prompting them to withdraw from the association. It was "well-known that the anti-Semitic serpent ha[d] injected its poisonous fangs into . . . American colleges and universities," and the paper deplored that it had not "infected the sports world—that phase of American life wherein Americans have always maintained that racial intolerance is not to be found" (*Jewish Daily Forward* 1923).

Apparently, even Chicago's Jewish country clubs that turned out fine women golfers such as Helen Reinhardt and whose members consciously mimicked the style, extravagance, and play of the gentile elite they hoped to join could not count on success. Nor, in this instance, did they ignore the discrimination directed toward them.

Instead, they severed all connections with the Women's Western Golf Association to underscore their displeasure. Reporting the news, the *Forward* applauded the golf clubs' action, making no mention that these very clubs were now experiencing discrimination and exclusion in much the same way that members of such clubs excluded east European Jewish immigrants. In short, when push came to shove and anti-Semitism threatened life or opportunity, as far as the *Forward* was concerned, a Jew was a Jew, whatever the differences in European religiosity or class.

No matter how much wealthy German Jews or select east European brethren who made their mark in industries as diverse as textiles and the movies sought to deny aspects of their Jewish heritage to win acceptance and full assimilation, they still were identified as Jews by the larger culture. Consciously or not, as much as they tried to deny this fact, they also carved out their American-Jewish identity. Whether that identity was anathema to contemporary coreligionists who abhorred the diminishment of religious observance and orthodoxy or to present-day naysayers concerned with the collapse of American Jewry, these people nevertheless created their own meaningful American Jewish world.

This world included involvement in elite sport in extravagant settings designed to separate themselves from lower-class east Europeans and the Jewish stereotypes surrounding them. Often this involvement meant an absence of traditional Sabbath observance and even, at some clubs, celebration of Christmas as an opportunity for gala balls and parties (Gabler 1988, 271; Vorspan and Gartner 1970, 153). However, it also included matters that defined obviously Jewish concerns. Whether raising money for the relief of destitute Jews in eastern Europe, to resettle east European immigrants in Texas, or to encourage their Americanization through such agencies as the Educational Alliance or the YMHA, philanthropy aimed at improving the lot of Jewish people was a major component of their Jewish sensibility. Although some have argued that this activity was self-serving—little more than a material measure of respectability and status aimed at dragging distasteful east Europeans into the American mainstream whether they liked it or not—there is no denying that those who gave money through the Jewish Federation or the B'nai B'rith understood their actions as positive expressions of their Jewishness that otherwise limited their rise in society.[6]

These people's religious beliefs are less clear. But if we can extrapolate anything from descriptions of New York's "our crowd" or accounts of Portland, Oregon's German Jewish community, who hooked and sliced at their Tualatin Country Club, it appears that Reform Judaism in one variation or another served the formal religious needs of these people. Nor, if advertisements in the *American Hebrew* for Goodman's Passover egg matzohs or Horowitz-Margareten egg noodles are any indication, did the desire for absorption into the gentile mainstream fully crush impulses reminiscent of other times and places.[7]

Full of internal conflicts and anxieties and off-limits to all but America's wealthiest Jews, this American Jewish world represented one choice in the spectrum of assimilation. In a particular historical context, as evidenced by the story of the Hillcrest Country Club of Los Angeles, it even encouraged unity between east Europeans and German Jews that contributed to the shaping of an American Jewish identity still relevant today.[8]

Hillcrest began in typical fashion, a response to the intrusion of east European Jews into Los Angeles's predominantly German Jewish community and to open anti-Semitism in the 1920s that closed social and business opportunities previously accessible to wealthy German Jews. By all accounts, before World War I an established German Jewish elite eager for acceptance by their gentile counterparts met much success in entering their exclusive social and economic world. Led by Edgar Magnin, they fashioned a kind of Reform

---

6. Sometimes German Jewish philanthropy took on interesting sportive forms. The *Chicago Jewish Advocate* (1891, June 12) reported a charity baseball game between the Standard and Lakeside Clubs, and the *American Hebrew* (1924, Aug. 29) noted a golf match to raise money for the Jewish Federation at the Norwood Country Club in West Branch, Long Island.

7. Others are far more qualified to discuss the meaning and significance of Reformed Judaism to German Jews. My assumption is that no matter how much some Orthodox Jews might have ridiculed their beliefs, German Jews found them a meaningful part of their own sense of being Jewish.

8. Unless otherwise noted, the following account of Hillcrest and the so-called Hollywood Jews comes from Gabler 1988.

Judaism with the bare bones of Jewish observance aimed at showing Gentiles that they had nothing to fear. Nevertheless, rising
anti-Semitism after the war marked by the public rantings of Henry
Ford and Father Coughlin, "the radio priest," restrictive immigration laws, and the influx of many east European Jews to Los Angeles changed things. The most visible forms of discrimination
included quota systems for Jewish college students and exclusion of
Jews from country clubs that had formerly admitted Jewish
members—the latter development, according to one account, was
in response to fears of being invaded by the Hollywood Jews, a
sobriquet reserved for east European Jews who made their fortune
by creating the motion picture industry.

Scorned by a gentile elite that they admired and no less disdain-
ful themselves of newly arriving east European Jews of any social
class, Los Angeles's wealthy German Jews launched Hillcrest in
1920. With its golf course, tennis courts, palatial clubhouse, and
immaculate grounds, this 142-acre enclave just south of Beverly
Hills became, in Magnin's words, the place of choice for "the aris-
tocrats and the Jewish big shots of the time." Hoping to establish
"a Jewish country club, the membership of which should be both
cosmopolitan and select," Hill purposely excluded persons such as
Louis B. Mayer, the Warner brothers, Adolph Zukor, and the other
remarkable east European Jewish immigrants who owned Hollywood motion picture studios but were considered too tainted by
their European roots for membership despite their obvious wealth
and desire to belong (*B'nai B'rith Messenger,* quoted in Vorspan and
Gartner 1970, 144; Gabler 1988, 270–75).

Ironically, no group of Jewish immigrants to America was more
eager to discard all connections with their European Jewish roots
and embrace American ways than these Hollywood Jews. Described
as men who hungered for assimilation and acceptance in a genteel
and gentile American world, they created a way of life totally di-
vorced from the beginnings they longed to forget—a world of
conspicuous consumption complete with lavish estates, servants,
luxury automobiles, polo ponies, and similar retreats, emulating
the "rich Gentiles in hopes of becoming them." In their movies
they espoused values and depicted a glorified American world that
bore no relation to their own boast, a world that was about as
unethnic and un-Jewish as could possibly be created (Gabler 1988,
240).

Although the Hollywood Jews were never admitted into the gentile sanctuaries such as the Lakeside or Santa Monica County Clubs, the depression opened Hillcrest's doors to them. Forced to file for bankruptcy, its membership cut in half, Hillcrest in the early 1930s sought new members from the moviemaking industry. Zukor, the Warners, Harry Cohn, Louis B. Mayer—virtually all of the industry's elite—became members. Others of east European background with less money were even offered inducements to join. As Neal Gabler delightfully reconstructs the story, Milton Sperling, then a young writer working at the Fox studios, recalled a man knocking on his office door. After making sure that Sperling was Jewish and from New York, he asked, "When was the last time you had a bowl of chicken soup and a little chopped chicken liver and some marinated herring? When you left New York, hah?" When Sperling nodded yes, the man took him across the street to Hillcrest for a Jewish lunch, during which he said to him: "Do you see this place? This is the only place in Los Angeles where a Jew can play golf." When Sperling replied that he did not play the game, the man replied, "But you're going to play golf. You're a nice Jewish boy. You have to support this club. We'll have to close down if people like you don't give money." We do not know if Milton learned the game, but he did join the club, receiving a $100 membership on credit and a month's worth of free lunches in the bargain (Gabler 1988, 274–75).

According to Gabler (276), the Hollywood Jews transformed Hillcrest from a replica of WASP gentility to a place where people could drop their guard and revert, at least in food and convivial style, to their east European Jewish roots. As he puts it, "If the German Jews had founded their club as the genteel seat of the Jewish community, the Hollywood Jews used Hillcrest differently. Regardless of why they applied and regardless of the formality of the setting Hillcrest became a sanctuary for their Jewishness." Although he offers no precise definition of what he means by "Jewishness," Gabler suggests one heavily emphasizing a certain social style—an opportunity for shirtsleeve interaction and relaxation, a chance to share stories and jokes from the old country and to transact their business in informal manner. It was at Hillcrest— of which Groucho Marx once said, "I wouldn't be a member of any club that would have me"—that the Hollywood Jews held their annual golf outing. Dressed in costumes, they toured the links

while avoiding obstacles such as "gunshots, animals crossing fairways, and Harpo Marx charging around the course in a gorilla
suit." The admission of the Hollywood Jews to Hillcrest symbol-
ized an accord driven by economic circumstances among the various strands of the Los Angeles Jewish community that, in the
context of World War II and the Holocaust, became even stronger.
Confronted by the America First Committee and the Los Angeles
Bund, which attacked the Hollywood Jews and the movie industry
they controlled, they banded together to launch a counterpropaganda
through the Community Relations Committee, which was organized and held its meetings at Hillcrest. Later, faced with the
Holocaust, they worked together, as did Jews across the nation to
raise money for the establishment of a Jewish homeland in Israel
and for the relief of European Jews (Gabler 1988, 276, 338–47).

In the end, common enemies at home and abroad who indis-
criminately identified people as Jewish regardless of their ethnic
origins, social customs, or religious beliefs united these wealthy
German and east European American Jews in a common struggle
for survival. However much in their American choices they had
discarded trappings of their Jewish pasts and did battle with each
other for full acceptance by a gentile world, this connection to a
larger Jewish concern for survival became critical to their Jewish
identity. Whether forced upon them by direct anti-Semitic challenges to their personal well-being that underlined the precarious
security of their American existence, by continuing news of Hitler's
atrocities, by guilty consciences, by a basic human sensibility for
the suffering of others, or more likely by some combination of all
of these factors, concern for Jewish survival became part of their
consciousness. It also became part of the legacy this generation left
to their children and grandchildren compelled to come to terms
with being Jewish in a different American landscape.

7

Hank Greenberg

The Jewish American Sports Hero

William M. Simons

Throughout the first half of the twentieth century, baseball reigned as the undisputed "national game" (Mead 1978, 7; Murphy 1934, 33). At times it evoked a depth of concern that suggested a secular religion as the following paean by a sporting enthusiast suggests: "[Baseball had] all the attributes of American origin [and] character. . . . [It was] the exponent of American Courage, Confidence, Combativeness; American Dash, Discipline, Determination; American Energy, Eagerness, Enthusiasm" (Voigt 1966, 12–13). Also, during World War II *The Sporting News,* which unabashedly referred to itself as the "Bible," pontificated that "Japan never was converted to baseball. . . . No nation . . . could have committed the vicious, infamous deed of . . . December 7, 1941, if the spirit of the game ever had penetrated their yellow hides" ("It's Not the Same Game in Japan" 1941). As a microcosm of the American mind, baseball thus provides one means of evaluating attitudes toward important societal phenomena, including ethnicity.

This essay analyzes media depictions of baseball's premier Jewish standard-bearer, Hank Greenberg, during the 1930s. After surveying the general status of ethnicity in press coverage of 1930s baseball,

7.1. Hank Greenberg, three-time American League home run champion, twice Most Valuable Player, and member of two Detroit Tigers world champion teams. *Courtesy of the National Baseball Hall of Fame Library, Cooperstown, New York.*

recurrent images of Greenberg are identified. Then the focus shifts to the journalistic controversy surrounding Greenberg's decision to play baseball on the Jewish New Year in 1934. Finally, the assimilative connotations of Greenberg's image for fellow ethnics receives attention. Detailed examination of 1930s' print media, including the Anglo-Jewish press, sporting publications, national magazines, contemporary books, and general circulation newspapers from all cities with major league baseball teams, provides the empirical base for the content analysis that follows.

The 1930s furnish particularly fertile ground for probing perceptions of ethnicity in the "national pastime." Although Anglo-Saxon Protestants from small towns constituted baseball's largest contingent, the major leagues possessed a significant ethnic dimension. During the 1930s, however, baseball's ethnic composition changed substantially, and this highly visible transformation attracted extensive contemporary comment. While "the English, Irish and the German," noted a depression-era sportswriter, "were well grounded in the fundamentals and spirit of the game before the other lads from the continent," the German and Irish presence waned somewhat by the 1930s (Bryson 1938, 365–66). Another 1934 article noted that "in recent years there had been a grand invasion of other nationalities," prominently featuring players with southern and eastern European antecedents (Lane 1935).

Jews, sons of immigrants who fled eastern European *shtetls* between the assassination of Tsar Alexander II and the outbreak of World War I, contributed, albeit in a limited form, to the ethnic recasting of baseball during the 1930s. As with their counterparts from other ethnic groups, Jewish major leaguers confronted the universal dilemma of the second generation, resolving the conflict between the Old World values of their immigrant parents and those of the large society, embodied in the "national pastime" (Herberg 1960, 16–23; Hansen 1940, 93). Beyond the shared "marginal man" phenomena, however, Jewish major leaguers of the 1930s faced additional anxieties often not encountered by gentile athletes. American anti-Semitism, fueled by the social and economic abrasions of the depression, peaked during the 1930s (Dinnerstein and Reimers 1975, 76). Thus, given the ambiance of the 1930s, the second generation's struggled to resolve the tension between ethnic and host society expectations assumed a special dimension for Jewish athletes.

Depression-era commentators frequently asserted that "one race . . . that was always weakly represented" in baseball "was the ancient Jewish stock" (Lane 1935, 483). Although they depicted the presence of Jews in baseball as on the rise, depression-era journalists devoted considerable print to the reasons for the supposed paucity of Jewish major leaguers. *The Sporting News*'s Fred Lieb, one of the most influential sportswriters of his time, claimed that "Jewish boys are smaller than kids who spring from other races. The Jewish boy was pushed aside on the playground diamond by the bigger youth with an Irish, German or Scandinavian name. Also the Jews did not possess the background of sport" (Lieb 1935, 3). In a 1934 article that appeared in the New York *Evening Post* and in *The Jewish Advocate*, Phil Weintraub, a Jewish outfielder on the New

York Giants, blamed Jewish parents for opposing the athletic ambitions of their sons: "Jewish mothers don't want their sons to be ballplayers. They dream of them becoming professional men, successful in business. But first of all they want them to become educated." Several articles also claimed that boxing reflected the Jewish temperament more fully than did the "national pastime."

> For centuries, the Jew in his individual business had to fight against heavy odds for his success. It sharpened his wit and made him quick with his hands. Therefore, he became an individualist in sport, a skillful boxer and ring strategist, but he did not have the background to stand out in a sport which is so essentially a team game as baseball. (Lieb 1935, 3)

Although several coreligionists preceded Hank Greenberg, baseball's original "Hammerin" Hank, in the big leagues, scribes hailed him as the first "really great Jewish player." Greenberg became "that long-sought Hebrew star" (Lieb 1935, 3). Except for Sandy Koufax, the pitching sensation of the 1960s, no rivals challenge this Hall of Famer's status as baseball's premier Jewish player. Born in 1911, the New York City native's major league tenure spanned the years 1933 to 1947, with four and one-half years lost to military service during World War II. Aside from his final season with the Pittsburgh Pirates, he spent his entire major league career with the Detroit Tigers (Hollander and Fox 1966, 89–91).

Greenberg, a first baseman–outfielder, ranks with the most powerful sluggers who ever played the game. Four times Greenberg led the American League in home runs, and no right-handed batter has ever surpassed his 1938 total of fifty-eight (*Baseball Encyclopedia* 1969, 152; Broeg 1971, 107–14; Drees and Mullen 1973, 36–41; Litsky 1975, 13; Daley 1962, 179–86; Graham 1969, 65–77). Although much evidence exists to support Greenberg's position as the game's greatest Jewish player, a middle-aged man, writing during the 1970s, summed it up best: "Imagine a boy of today, growing old in 2018. When he looks back at the seventies, which sports hero will he remember? If there is one whose specific individual feats he can recall as clearly as I recall so many of Hank's he will have something special to think about (Hill 1978, 31).

Sportswriters in the 1930s frequently noted Greenberg's ethnic identity even in accounts of mundane interests. Numerous ethnic sobriquets attached to Greenberg, including "Hebrew star," "the Tigers' Great Jewish first baseman," "the Jewish slugger," and even "a conscientious orthodox Jew" (Lewis 1934, 7; *Boston Globe* 1934, Sept. 12; *New York World-Telegram* 1934, Sept. 11; *NYHT* 1934, Sept. 11). At times the press demonstrated imagination in its allusions to Greenberg's ethnicity as with *The Sporting News's* explanation that he "does everything in orthodox fashion" (1934, Oct. 4). Too, a New York *Evening Journal* article (1934, Sept. 19) repeatedly referred to Greenberg as "Henry David," the connotation of "David" being more obvious than that of "Benjamin," Greenberg's actual middle name. The press of the 1930s also did not neglect the antecedents of other Jewish players. Journalists described outfielder Morrie Arnovich of the Philadelphia Phillies, for example, as a "Jewish athlete," "the chunky Hebrew lad," and "the little Hebrew" (Feldman 1937, 3; Kirksey 1940, 408).

In identifying the ethnicity of Jewish players and designating that background as a race, reporters were not treating Jewish big leaguers differently from their gentile counterparts. Much evidence, including such press descriptions as "an Italian Baseball Guide," "the fiery Frenchman," "the even-tempered Bohemian," "McCarthy . . . the Buffalo Irishman," "Urbanski . . . hard-working, likable Polish recruit," and "Lou Novikoff . . . the mad Russian," illustrates the pervasiveness of ethnicity in baseball literature of the depression (Merin 1934, 464; McAuley 1940, 3; *TSN* 1945, Nov. 1; Ward 1935, 368; *DFP* 1934, Sept. 21). Sportswriters repeatedly portrayed baseball as the "great American melting pot," which facilitated the assimilation of its heterogeneous participants (*TSN* 1937, Mar. 25; *New York Evening Journal* 1934, Sept. 19). *The Sporting News* preached that "baseball . . . [provides] the world an example of how nations may be brought together through the universal brotherhood of sport" (1942, Mar. 19). The *New York Evening Journal* depicted the Detroit Tigers as a veritable League of Nations: "Greenberg is a Jew and his boss, Cochrane, is a Catholic, and there are other Catholics and Protestants and nonbelievers on the Club. Yet it functions like a well oiled machine. . . . The Players have been fused into a unit. . . . They are willing to make any sacrifice for the sake of the club" (1934, Sept. 19).

The press portrayed players with ethnic antecedents as symbols of assimilation at work. Although scribes thus viewed these players as transitional figures, leading their co-ethnic to the figurative melting pot, writers enthusiastically approved of publicizing ethnic standard-bearers to attract fans and increase game profits. *The Sporting News*, for example, endorsed the Cincinnati Reds' exploitation of Alex Kampouris, "the only Greek in the big show," as a useful device for luring other Greeks to the game: "[F]or the last three seasons, a delegation of swarthy citizens would march to the home plate. . . . The swarthy citizens always are Greeks. And when the Greeks come bearing gifts where the Reds are playing, it is Alex Kampouris, dashing second baseman of Cincinnati's team who gets them" (Swope 1937, 3).

Even without the ethnic dimension, sheer size made the six-foot-four-inch Greenberg conspicuous in an era when the average players stood about five-feet-eleven. Sportswriters incessantly attached the adjectives "big," "giant," "huge," and "tall" to Greenberg's name (*Cincinnati Enquirer* 1934, Sept. 11; *Cleveland Plain Dealer* 1934, Sept. 23; Lewis 1934, 8; *Philadelphia Inquirer* 1934, Sept. 1; *Chicago Tribune* 1934, Sept. 11). More significant, however, a constellation of related media images orbited Greenberg's Jewishness. With phrases such as "late of Bronx" and "slugging first baseman from the Bronx," scribes highlighted Greenberg's association with New York City, "the hub of the Hebrew population of the United States" (Hunt 1934, 39; *Washington Post* 1934, Sept. 19; Bloodgood 1934, 407). The *Saturday Evening Post* portrayed Greenberg as more attached to urban life with its "theater, nightclubs and bright lights" than "most ballplayers" (Frank 1941, 37). With repeated assertions that "Hank was born with a silver spoon in his mouth," the press exaggerated the economic situation of Greenberg's parents, thus paralleling prevailing, and erroneous, stereotypes about Jewish wealth (Spink 1940, 4; Appel and Goldblatt 1974, 184). Although Hank's father, a Romanian immigrant, did own a cloth-shrinking plant, the Greenbergs were not wealthy.

Greenberg, according to 1930s' writers, also differed from most gentile contemporaries owing to the aspirations of his parents. Journalists emphasized that his parents "wanted him to go to college, then into business" (Spink 1934, 4; Farrington 1934, 3; Broeg 1970, 18). Moreover, sportswriters depicted Greenberg as the quintessence of traditional Jewish respect for learning, which America transformed into a passion for secular knowledge. Commentators lingered over his cerebral qualities. Some of the descriptions of Greenberg's intellect conjure up a talmudic scholar more readily than an athlete: "put more thought . . . into his work than any other player"; "has demonstrated . . . intelligence and imagination"; "the most energetic . . . researcher"; and "he studies the best methods and practices as earnestly as a young physician" (*TSN* 1934, Oct. 3; Murphy 1934, 33; Anderson 1938, 45; Wood 1941, 437; Otis 1934, 9). Besides intellect, the press suggested that Greenberg shared another trait commonly associated with his coreligionists, an oversensitivity to criticism. Numerous journalists declared Greenberg "inordinately sensitive to public opinion" (Frank 1941, 40; Graham 1969, 68; Ward 1934c, 1–2; clippings, Hank Greenberg file, BBHFL) Yet not one 1930s' article ever acknowledged the anti-Semitic taunts fans and opponents showered on Greenberg.

In distinguishing Greenberg from his gentile peers, most of whom were considered more athletically gifted, sportswriters repeatedly depicted the Detroit slugger as a self-made ballplayer. Numerous articles portrayed the young Tiger as "clumsy," "naturally slow," "awkward," and "[possessing] little natural ability" (Wood 1941, 437; Frank 1941, 40; *Current Biography 1947*). With near unanimity, however, pundits cast Greenberg as a Jewish Horatio Alger hero, who "overcame . . . [his] glaring weakness" by "hard work and determination" (*EJS*, 61). A *Saturday Evening Post* article entitled "Hank Made Greenberg" contended that "Greenberg is purely a self-made star. . . . His enormous capacity for work staggers everyone. . . . He has spent so much time in Tiger Stadium that the groundskeeper once suspected he had set up light house keeping there to save rent" (Frank 1941, 35). The *Detroit Times* lovingly reported that "Greenberg is a good first baseman because he works at the job. . . . He works at it 24 hours a day" (Shaver 1934, 18). Although the press gave significant attention to several financial controversies involving Greenberg, most scribes believed that Greenberg, through hard work and tenacity, merited his success. "No one will begrudge Greenberg honors," declared the *Detroit News,* because "he has earned them." Many writers repeated the refrain that "no ballplayer probably worked harder to prepare himself for success" than Greenberg (Salsinger 1934a, 21). In the 1930s' press the Jewish Greenberg appeared as a symbol of the rewards that hard work could bring to even the awkward son of an immigrant in baseball's melting pot.

Media portrayals of Greenberg as a Jewish standard-bearer bur-
geoned during September 1934 owing to controversy over whether
the Detroit slugger should play on the Jewish High Holidays.
Although rookie Greenberg's decision not to play on the 1933
High Holidays attracted little attention, the improved play of the
twenty-three-year-old Greenberg and of his team during the 1934
season created new pressures. Not since 1909 had the Tigers won
the American League pennant, and the Bengals' 1934 surge, which
culminated in a first-place finish, created a "frenzied public" (*TSN*
1946, Feb 28). The *Dearborn Independent* claimed that one overzeal-
ous fan succumbed to a coronary while listening to a radio broad-
cast of a Tiger game (*St. Louis Post-Dispatch* 1934). And the *New
York Times* reported, "The old Tiger town has gone baseball crazy"
(*Dearborn Independent* 1934, Sept. 21). Apart from loyalty to the
Tigers, social bonds between Detroiters, residents of a "tough town"
hard hit by the depression, were "frail" (Green 1957, 214; Falls
1975, 11).

Historian Ralph Jones asserts that "Detroit's . . . susceptibility to
economic, ethnic, racial, and territorial outbreaks is impressive and
persistent" (Janis 1978, 1). Also, Greenberg's High Holiday dilemma hardly occurred during a golden age in Detroit's ethnic
dynamic. Greenberg's Detroit has a propensity for lifting bigots,
such as Henry Ford and Father Charles Coughlin, to the status of
folk hero. Neither the city of Detroit, which had a Jewish population of only 5 percent, nor Greenberg's Tiger teammates, more than
80 percent of whom hailed from parochial areas of the South and
Southwest, entered September 1934 with much understanding of
the reasons for observing the Jewish High Holidays (Weiner 1934a,
7; *NYT* 1934, Sept. 19). According to the press, however, Tiger
players and fans clearly understood the importance of Greenberg to
their feverish dreams of a pennant.

Publications varied markedly in the extent of coverage they
granted Greenberg's High Holiday conflict. Most journalistic descriptions of the episode, however, shared a core of common assumptions. Some minor differences in nuance did occur. Nevertheless,
a widespread consensus of interpretation dominated press portrayals
of Greenberg's behavior during the 1934 High Holidays.

When Greenberg casually mentioned he might not play in the
September 10 home game against the Boston Red Sox because the

contest fell on Rosh Hashanah, the Jewish New Year, the media promptly recited Greenberg's secular responsibilities. Although the Tigers led the second-place New York Yankees by four games on the eve of the Jewish New Year, the press still referred to a "nick-and-neck pennant race" (Bell 1934, 36). Scribes also noted the Tigers suffered from flagging momentum. The *Philadelphia Evening Bulletin* (1934) stated, "The Tigers look pretty sad at this moment." Alone of "the Tiger mainstays," Greenberg continued to hit well despite the general team slump (Veyoveh 1934, 1, 4; *Detroit News* 1934, Sept. 11, 18). Thus, the Tigers needed Greenberg's presence more than ever during this crucial phase of the season.

Given the tight pennant race, journalists stressed Greenberg's obligation to the city of Detroit. People wrote letters to Detroit newspapers pointing out that whereas Rosh Hashanah came every year, Detroit had not won a pennant since 1909. Sportswriters also emphasized Greenberg's special "duties toward his teammates" (S. Frank 1941, 45; *Detroit News* 1934, Sept. 11, 1; Green 1934, 1; *TSN* 1934, Sept. 20).

The *New York Evening Journal* stated that Greenberg's Rosh Hashanah absence from the lineup would have constituted a massive "loss to his companions" (1934, Sept. 19) Moreover, every member of the Tiger infield had thus far played "every inning of every game," a record that Greenberg's observance of the Jewish New Year would snap (Salsinger 1934b, 21; Isaminger 1934, 6). Finally, and least important of the secular responsibilities cited by the press, Greenberg needed, on the eve of Rosh Hashanah, "only 11 more [doubles] to equal the American League record of 67" (*DFP* 1934, Sept. 8, 12; *Cleveland Plain Dealer* 1934, Sept. 8, 17).

During September 1934 the media also gave prominent attention to Greenberg's religious responsibilities, although journalists ultimately found them less imperative than his secular obligations. The Anglo-Jewish press and several general circulation journals described the Jewish New Year as Rosh Hashanah approached. The *Detroit Times,* for example, stated: "Essentially, Rosh Hashanah is not a joyful but a thoughtful day. Unlike the celebrations of the New Year among other nations that New Year of the Jew is devoted to supplications and to the searching of one's self" (Parker 1934, 10). Some newspapers, including the *Detroit Free Press,* noted that Orthodox Jews, such as Greenberg, "did not work . . . [or] play" on

Rosh Hashanah (Ward 1934a, 19). Nevertheless, references to the Jewish temple or synagogue as a "church" in a number of papers suggest a muted understanding of the High Holidays by the media (Iffy the Dopester 1934; *Chicago Tribune* 1934, Sept. 11). Furthermore, whereas the press related Greenberg's secular responsibilities to loyalty due community and teammates, it tended to depict religious obligations as largely individual conscience or preference.

Several newspapers reported and analyzed the formal statement of Dr. Leo M. Franklin, chief rabbi of Detroit, concerning Greenberg's problem. Rabbi Franklin's comments, issued just before the Rosh Hashanah game, appeared in a number of journals.

> In the Jewish faith there is no power granted to the rabbi to give dispensation to anyone for doing anything which reads contrary to this own conscientious convictions—indeed we insist upon the doctrine of personal responsibility.
>
> In such a case as this, Mr. Greenberg, who is conscientious Jew, must decide for himself whether he ought to play or not.
>
> From the standpoint of Orthodox Judaism the fact that ballplaying is his means of livelihood would argue against his participation in the Monday game. On the other hand, it might be argued quite consistently, that his taking part in the game would mean something not only to himself but to his fellow players, and in fact at this time, to the community of Detroit.
>
> But in the last analysis, no rabbi is authorized to give or withhold permission for him to do so. (Shaver 1934, 18; Salsinger 1934b, 21; *Detroit Times* 1934, Sept. 10; *Boston Herald* 1934, Sept. 11; *Boston Post* 1934, Sept 11).

Despite the ambiguous tenor of Dr. Franklin's remarks, writers, while conceding the impossibility of a dispensation, eagerly noted that the rabbi's comments constitute no fiat against Greenberg's participation in the Rosh Hashanah game. *The Sporting News*, for example, interpreted Rabbi Franklin's proclamation to mean "that the question lay strictly between Greenberg and his conscience and that the Church had no right to . . . criticize him if he played" (Greene 1934b). Thus the terse headline of a *Detroit Times* story on Dr. Franklin's statement read "Greenberg Decision Own" (1934, Sept. 10).

Some journals also reported and examined another Detroit rabbi's position on Greenberg's conflict, that of Joseph Thumim. Rabbi

Thumim's declaration, which was even more delphic than that of Dr. Franklin, implied that "Greenberg . . . can play ball today" subject to "three stipulations": "no tickets could be bought by the Orthodox on the day of the match; that there should be no smoking; and that the refreshments distributed should be kosher." Oblivious to the three restrictions Rabbi Thumim cited, a *Detroit News* article proclaimed, "Henry Greenberg need have no pangs of conscience because he plays baseball during the Jewish holidays" (*Detroit News* 1934, Sept 11). The *Detroit Jewish Chronicle,* the only Anglo-Jewish newspaper published in Michigan, agreed with the *News's* interpretation of Rabbi Thumim's statement (Veyoveh 1934, 6). No paper consulted gave detailed attention to strong rabbinical pleas that Greenberg not play on Rosh Hashanah, although *The Sporting News* reported that Greenberg received "telegrams from rabbis and Jewish advisors from all over the country. Some told [him] . . . of the mistake [he] . . . would make if [he] . . . did not observe the day properly" (Farrington 1934, 3).

While the media assessed Greenberg's secular responsibilities from its impact on other people, which it largely eschewed in its examination of his religious responsibilities, the press portrayed the intense pressures converging on Greenberg as emanating largely from two competing value systems rather than from the articulated demands of specific individuals or groups or the press itself. Thus, journalists to a significant degree abstracted the struggle between the divergent forces contending for Greenberg's conscience. Nevertheless, some scribes noted pressure from specific individuals and groups. Not surprisingly, Anglo-Jewish newspapers levied the strongest claims that Greenberg was hectored to play. The *Detroit Jewish Chronicle* and the *Jewish Daily Bulletin* asserted that "a flood of telephone calls came to him [Greenberg] from Manager Mickey Cochrane, from Frank and Charles Navin, the owners of the ball team, from teammates and leading citizens. 'This is a civic duty,' they told him. 'If Detroit is to win the pennant, you must play'" (Veyoveh 1934, 6; *Jewish Daily Bulletin* 1934, Sept. 14). Conversely, the *Boston Post* reported, "A large number of Detroit Jews tried to keep Henry Greenberg out of today's game in observance of Rosh Hashanah" (1934). More characteristically, however, *The Sporting News* and the *Detroit Free Press* quoted Greenberg's comment that Tiger manager "Mickey Cochrane told me it was a personal matter that I must handle myself" (Farrington 1934, 3; Carvath 1934, 19). By juxtaposition the *New York World Telegram* linked the decisions of Mickey Cochrane, the symbol of secular authority, and Rabbi Franklin, the symbol of religious authority, to "let Greenberg decide the question for himself" (*TSN* 1934, Sept. 20).

Most journalists emphasized that the real conflict was within Greenberg's conscience. Moreover, media images of Greenberg's problem assumed titanic proportions as the Detroit slugger "waged a terrific battle with himself" over "conflicting duties to his religion and to his team" (*NYHT* 1934, Apr. 20, 20; Carlisle 1934, 1). The press generally treated Greenberg's ordeal and consequent suffering with utter seriousness and dignity. In the pages of the *Detroit Free Press* the beleaguered Greenberg almost assumed the dimensions of a tragic hero.

> He is an orthodox Jew and practices his religion faithfully. . . . Hank started his day by attending services in the congregation Sharrey Zedek. . . . But he was worried about the ball game. Should he play? or should he take the day off and risk depriving the Tigers of a chance in the World Series? Hank did not know.
>
> All Sunday he had debated that question with himself. Like Jacob of old, he spent the night wrestling with the angels. He sat up late wondering, wondering. And when he went to bed he tossed uneasily as he tried to make up his mind.
>
> Greenberg had reached no decision as to playing when he arrived at the ball park yesterday. (Ward 1934a, 19)

Several writers stressed that Greenberg remained "conscience stricken" even after making a reluctant decision to play (Carvath 1934, 19; *Chicago Tribune* 1934, Sept. 11; *TSN* 1934, Sept. 20). Indeed, Greenberg half expected some sort of divine retribution: " 'I'll probably get my brains knocked out by a fly ball'," Greenberg, according to the *Detroit Free Press*, said gloomily as he left the dugout. "But I'm going to play'" (Ward 1934a, 25).

Both the Anglo-Jewish and the general circulation press approved of Greenberg's decision to play for "the welfare of the Tigers and the interests of the community," as he "subordinated his own inclinations for the good of the whole" (*New York Evening Journal* 1934, Sept. 19). A *Detroit News* headline read, "Playing for Community . . . Tiger First Baseman Serves His Fellows on Jewish Holy Day"

(Salsinger 1934b, 21). The *Detroit Jewish Chronicle* and the *Jewish Daily Bulletin* both recorded sportswriter Ty Tyson's tribute to Greenberg's "sacrifice" (Veyoveh 1934, 6; *Jewish Daily Bulletin* 1934, Sept. 9). The media stressed the positive consequences of Greenberg's decision.

The Tigers triumphed 2 to 1 over the Boston Red Sox in the crucial Rosh Hashanah game, extending their American League lead to four and one-half games. Moreover, emphasized the press, Greenberg "almost single-handed[ly] won . . . the ball game with two home runs." The *Detroit Free Press* exclaimed, "Greenberg . . . had enjoyed the best day of his career. . . . Ruth at his best never hit a baseball to more effect or never won a ball game more dramatically" (Carvath 1934, 19). Given the heroic victory of Greenberg's Tigers, some sportswriters interpreted the triumph as heavenly approval of his Rosh Hashanah activities. According to *The Sporting News*, for example, Greenberg concluded, "Some divine influence must have caught hold of me that day" (Farrington 1934, 3). Moreover, not only did God bless Greenberg's nontraditional observance of Rosh Hashanah but the Tiger manager also did: "What he did at the plate led Mickey Cochrane the next day to elevate him to the clean-up position" (Greene 1934b).

According to the press, Greenberg read Rabbi Franklin's statement for the first time after the Rosh Hashanah game, "which caused him to brighten visibly," for he construed it to mean that "I didn't do the wrong thing after all" (Ward 1934a, 19, 25). Also, several newspapers noted Greenberg still had time to go "back to the synagogue" after the game (*New York Evening Journal* 1934; *Jewish Daily Bulletin* 1934, Sept. 14; Carvath 1934, 19). Moreover, the *Detroit Jewish Chronicle,* emulating locker-room jargon, showed enthusiasm that Greenberg was "acclaimed by boys in the synagogue" (Veyoveh 1934, 1). Indeed, no less an authority than Tiger third baseman Marv Owen advised Greenberg that all he had on his "conscience" was "a couple of home runs" (Carlisle 1934, 2). Apparently, once Greenberg had recognized the primacy of community needs over ethnic considerations, the painful crisis yielded to glorious success.

The postgame trivialization of Rosh Hashanah markedly differed from the tone of respect accorded this solemn holiday in pregame commentary. The *Detroit Free Press* saluted Greenberg's hitting with the refrain, "A Happy New Year for Everybody" (1934, Sept. 11). A woman reporter for the *Detroit News* coquettishly wished that "every day were Rosh Hashanah, [so] our [baseball] worries would be over" as Detroit fans, "grinning broadly," yelled "Happy New Year" (Stark 1934, 23). "Iffy the Dopester," (Malcolm W. Bingay) august commentator for the *Detroit Free Press,* magnanimously declared (1934), "I'm here to testify to the world as a baseball expert that the two hits he [Greenberg] made in the ball game were strictly kosher." Stuart Bell (1934b) of the *Cleveland Press* demonstrated a dubious sensitivity: "Only one fellow blew the shofar yesterday so you could hear it. He was Hank Greenberg. He blew the shofar twice, and the ears of the Boston Red Sox are still ringing. Blast No. 1 from his shofar was a homer. . . . Blast No. 2 from Hank's shofar was a home run . . . will you please take me home shofar?" Amid the postgame euphoria, the press depicted the solemn Rosh Hashanah as a near twin of the larger society's raucous first of January.

Although Greenberg still faced a conflict over whether to play on Yom Kippur, this episode generated much less media attention than his New Year's ordeal, because the Tigers had the pennant "in the bag" by Yom Kippur. Nevertheless, several articles claimed that Greenberg's observance of Yom Kippur entailed some sacrifice from his fans and teammates (*Detroit News* 1934b; Poznanski 1935; *Cleveland Plain-Dealer* 1934b; *Philadelphia Inquirer* 1934b; Meany 1934; Segar 1934; Rennie 1934). Several newspapers, for example, noted that Greenberg's absence would end the Detroit infield's streak of starting the same four regulars at 143 consecutive games. Although when questioned and interviewed (1978, 1979), Greenberg, second baseman Charles Gehringer, and sportswriter Fred Lieb all characterized the consecutive game mark as a "trick record." The media at the time termed it "one of the most amazing streaks in history" when Greenberg missed the Yom Kippur contest (Greene 1934a). Nevertheless, despite the infield record and the defeat of the Tigers by the Yankees on the Day of Atonement, the press generally felt Greenberg, after having contributed to the pennant's inevitability by his Rosh Hashanah heroics, merited Yom Kippur off (*Philadelphia Inquirer* 1934c; Iffy the Dopester 1934b). Overall, however, the press commented on the Yom Kippur incident as it had during the Rosh Hashanah controversy, to wit, the assumption that responsibilities to the secular community transcended those to the ethnic group. By its application of baseball criteria, the press implied that if the Tigers still had to fight for the pennant and if Greenberg's past performance had fallen within the mediocre range, he could not justify missing the Day of Atonement game. Even the tribute to Greenberg by the syndicated folk poet Edgar Guest defended Greenberg's Yom Kippur observance by reference to secular achievements.

> In July the Irish wondered where he's ever learned to play . . .
> But upon the Jewish New Year when Hank Greenberg came to bat
> And made two home runs off pitcher Rhodes—
>   They cheered like mad for that. (Guest 1934, 6)

Scribes acknowledged that Greenberg might serve as a symbol "that hard work, determination and perseverance, can take a man to the top" to all "the youth of America" (Daley 1962, 186), but the press emphasized Greenberg's position as an ethnic standard-bearer. Many nonsectarian journals noted the honors, awards, and adulation Greenberg received from his coreligionists (*NYT* 1946, Apr. 16; *Detroit Jewish Chronicle* 1934, Sept. 28; Frank 1941). A few days before Rosh Hashanah 1934, for example, the *Detroit Free Press* described how nine-year-old Sammy Kaufman attempted to carry the 215-pound first baseman's heavy traveling bag for him (Sept. 1). The *Detroit Jewish Chronicle* reported that when he attended synagogue services during the 1934 High Holidays, a "youngster pleaded to be permitted to sit in Greenberg's seat," which the paper likened to a "'chassi' and 'Rebbe' fad" (Salsinger 1934c). Moreover, the Anglo-Jewish press heralded Greenberg's 1934 selection by "Jewish admirers" in a poll conducted by the Jewish Telegraph Agency as the "greatest Jewish Baseball Player of All Time" (Weiner 1934c).

Both the Anglo-Jewish and general circulation press perceived a lesson for Greenberg's coreligionists in the slugger's September 1934 behavior: the appropriateness of an ethnic standard-bearer and by implication his followers giving priority to the demands of the secular community over those of the ethnic group. Pundits claimed even "the most orthodox Jews" "respected" Greenberg for subordinating his religious preferences "for the good of the whole" on Rosh

Hashanah (*New York Evening Journal* 1934, Sept. 19). According to the media, "the public judges people by the idols they produce," and the Jews ought then to take pride in Greenberg, "a credit to . . . Jewry" (Ribalow 1948, 46). "The Jewish people are to be congratulated," editorialized the *Detroit Jewish Chronicle,* "that Greenberg is such a splendid type of their people. He is in a position to do untold good in breaking down the mean and vicious prejudices against an ancient and honorable people" (Bingay 1934). For the most part, the press portrayed Jewish standard-bearer Greenberg as a symbol of assimilation, leading the way toward the melting pot. Greenberg's baseball heroics, suggested most 1930s' commentators, facilitated the Americanization of his fellow Jews. *Baseball Magazine,* for example, cast Greenberg as a latter-day Moses.

> He had led his ancestral race into a new promised land, the field of major league baseball, a field where they have been comparative strangers.
>
> Since America is the melting pot of all nations, it is quite fitting and appropriate that baseball should be represented by players of all racial strands and stocks. (Bryson 1938)

By taking pride in a coreligionist's accomplishments in the "national pastime," Jews hastened their collective entry into the main currents of American life. The Anglo-Jewish press, sensitive to "what do the Gentiles say?" acknowledged that their standard-bearer was the "only . . . Jewish lad [who] mattered" to the larger community on Rosh Hashanah 1934, and praised Greenberg for fulfilling his secular responsibilities, thus combating anti-Semitism by winning "the admiration and affection of the [gentile] fans (Veyoveh 1934, 1; Bingay 1934).

From the vantage point of Greenberg commentators, then, individual standard-bearers rather than Jewish values constituted the appropriate contribution of Jews to America. A few highly atypical articles, however, depicted Greenberg as an instrument through which Jewish principles enriched American society. The *Detroit Free Press,* for example, related his honest refusal to settle for a two-base hit on a triple, which would have facilitated his assault on the American League record for doubles, to his ethnicity: "Hank Greenberg, being Jewish, has an innate sense of values" (Ward

1934b, 13). Nevertheless, typical 1930s analysis depicted notable individuals, not Jewish principle, as the Jewish contribution to the "national pastime." During the 1930s both Anglo-Jewish and general circulation publications invariably depicted ethnicity in a fashion like that used by many depression-era historians of immigration. In *We Who Built America* (1939), for example, the influential scholar Carl Wittke, by listing many of specific immigrants and their progeny who contributed to American advancement in various ways, suggested that individuals with "old world" antecedents, not ethnic groups as a whole, "built America." Wittke believed pride in ethnic heroes instilled a sense of potential and security in the foreign born and their children, thus fostering Americanization. Hence, eponymic standard-bearers, not the immigrant groups that nurtured them, constituted the appropriate ethnic contribution to America.

Anglo-Jewish journals, like the general circulation press, almost invariably adopted a Wittke-type approach to Greenberg and other Jewish athletes. English-language Jewish papers noted scores and scores of Jewish athletes, often either of limited ability or in esoteric sports, without usually demonstrating anything distinctively Jewish about the individuals cited for their achievements, save, as Wittke believed in *We Who Built America,* "old world" antecedents. The *Chicago Jewish Chronicle,* for example, did not usually probe for a Hebraic legacy in the character, training, or ring style of those it designated "Jewish boxers" (1934, Sept. 14). The *Detroit Jewish Chronicle* exulted, without identifying the Jewish mores typified by the many individuals listed, "We as Jews can be proud of the fact that we have a champion in almost every field of sport" (Weiner 1934b, 7). It almost appeared at times as though Wittke freelanced for the *Jewish Advocate.*

> In the long and arduous climb of Jewish athletes to fame and success the year 5694 [1934] will rate as a landmark, for during the past twelve months more Jews reached the top rung of athletic achievement than in any other similar period within memory. . . . If the sensational playing of a number of Jews in the minor leagues means anything the National and American Leagues will have a dozen Jewish players next year. . . . The American Association also swarms with Jewish talent: Milt Galatzer of Toledo . . . Andy Cohen of Minneapolis, Si Rosenthal of St. Paul.

No year in the last decade has passed without the inclusion of at least one Jew on the mythical All-American eleven. This past season developed two Jewish All-Americans, Aaron Rosenberg of Southern California and Paul Geisler of Centenary. . . . Other outstanding Jewish gridiron heroes of the past season were Chick and Leo Kaufman of Princeton. (Cohen 1934)

The *Jewish Advocate* concluded with a copious list of Jewish boxers, basketball players, golfers, tennis stars, auto racers, bicyclists, horse trainers, swimmers, wrestlers, fencers, rugby enthusiasts, track and field participants, softball standouts, and Ping-Pong athletes (ibid.). Greenberg, however, "the outstanding Jewish figure" (Weiner 1934c, 7) in the "national pastime," reigned as the premier standard-bearer.

Both the Anglo-Jewish and general circulation press applauded Greenberg for demonstrating to his coreligionists the American way. The *Detroit Free Press,* for example, approvingly reported Greenberg's participation in Detroit's 1934 Community Fund Drive (1934, Sept. 28). Contemporaneously, several newspapers lauded Greenberg for declining a tribute the Jews of Detroit planned for him.

> While the Tigers were on the road the biggest and wealthiest members of Detroit Jewish life made arrangements for a big testimonial banquet to the Hebrew star. . . . They arranged for a sumptuous feast . . . and . . . were going to buy him a valuable present. Hank had no inkling of the affair until his return to Detroit. . . . "Nothing doing," replied Hank after offering his heartfelt thanks for the honor. . . . Members of the committee, at first aghast and deeply disappointed finally saw the point. Now they are prouder of the first baseman than ever before. (*Philadelphia Inquirer* 1934c).

The *Detroit Jewish Chronicle,* fearful that the proposed Greenberg tribute would have alienated Detroit's gentiles, vigorously applauded Greenberg's decision.

> Hank vetoed the idea. He displayed good sense in doing so and his arguments were sound. There are K.C. members on the Tiger team, are there not he asked. How come that Catholics do not offer to sponsor testimonials in their honor? It is simple, he concluded, that the triumph of the Tigers is not the concern of any one group or of several groups. It is a community affair. (Sept. 21).

According to the *Detroit Jewish Chronicle,* "outstanding Jewish leaders" fully endorsed Greenberg's decision to place community over ethnic considerations. The *Jewish Chronicle* deemed the canceled Greenberg dinner particularly offensive because it would have taken place "in advance of the event planned in honor of the Tigers by the Detroit Board of Commerce at the end of this month" (ibid.). As with the contemporaneous High Holiday controversy, the press felt Greenberg deserved to participate in ethnically based events, such as being guest of honor at a B'nai B'rith dinner sometime after he canceled the earlier testimonial, provided it did not detract from community interests, such as the Detroit Board of Commerce's salute to the Tigers or an important baseball game.

Essentially, the media depicted the Jewish standard-bearer as a transitional phenomenon. Because parochial attachments continued, Americanizers paradoxically used those ethnic attachments for assimilationist ends. Although Jews, not far removed from the world of the *shtetl,* still deviated somewhat from the mainstream, Greenberg's success in the "national pastime," a microcosm of United States society, would inspire coreligionists to follow his "all-American" example. Thus, ethnic groups and the standard-bearers they spawned, implied the press, would become an anachronism. Ironically, the press emphasized Greenberg's position as an ethnic standard-bearer to illustrate assimilation in baseball's melting pot.

The assimilationist implications of Greenberg's press image coincided with aspirations harbored by many Jewish Americans during the depression era. As progeny of immigrant parents, many Jews of this period belonged to the second generation. The second generation, ambivalent about its religious heritage, eager to acquire middle-class respectability, and anxious about the opinion of the gentile community, found Greenberg an appropriate standard-bearer. Unlike the often flamboyant, braggadocio, poorly educated, financially imprudent Jewish boxers, who flaunted their ethnicity with the Star of David emblazoned on their trunks, engaged in nocturnal adventures with *shiksas,* and carried the ambience of ghetto pugnacity with them, "modest," "retiring," "clean-living" Hank Greenberg, as portrayed by the press, was an Americanized *mensch* (*Chicago Daily Tribune* 1934 Sept. 12; Anderson 1938; Ribalow 1948, 37, 46; S. Frank 1941, 37; Philadelphia *Inquirer* 1934, Sept. 9). The Greenberg of the media, who eschewed calling attention to his private religious beliefs, offered fellow Jews an example of an upwardly mobile lifestyle that attracted relatively little animosity from gentile neighbors. The *New York Evening Post* in 1934, for example, linked Greenberg's personal success with the movement of Jews from the Lower East Side ghetto: "The last time Detroit got into the October set of games there were not nearly as many Greenbergs in the Bronx as there are now" (Burr 1934). Newspaper photographs of the articulate Greenberg, who had attended New York University for a year, often displayed a neat, immaculate gentleman, dressed in tie and jacket with a newspaper in hand and resembling a young professional or businessman more than he did a baseball player.

Both the Anglo-Jewish and general circulation press perceived Greenberg as the most exemplary of the Jewish athletes and commented critically on world welterweight boxing champion Barney Ross's decision not to fight on Rosh Hashanah 1934. When rain canceled his match with "Irish Jimmy McLarnin," Ross refused to have it rescheduled on Rosh Hashanah. Instead, the pugilistic champion suspended training and attended synagogue services on the Jewish New Year (*Chicago Jewish Chronicle* 1934, Sept. 14; *New York Daily News* 1934, Sept. 11). Rather than emphasizing Ross's piety, however, several newspapers related Ross's Rosh Hashanah observance to financial calculations. According to the *Chicago Tribune*, "The promoters know that New York's Orthodox Jews also would decline to attend" (Smith 1934). Too, the Boston *Post* cynically asserted, "the ordinary two-day postponement would have resulted in a financial flop" (Cunningham 1934). The Anglo-Jewish press also did not note Ross's High Holiday observance sans caveat. The *Jewish Daily Bulletin*, for example, although conceding the pugilist's sincerity, argued that Ross's example of refusing to participate in an athletic contest on Rosh Hashanah had not, and ought not to have, unduly impressed Hank Greenberg.

> The controversy hinged on whether Hank Greenberg was "Right" in playing ball on Rosh Hashanah. It was pointed out that Barney Ross refused to fight on this holiday and that Greenberg could have done likewise . . . [but] neither Ross nor McLarnin could have put up a decent show if the fight . . . would have been held, after being postponed three nights, on Monday. . . . The fighters would not have

been able to give the same top-notch performance after such a lay-
off . . . the fighters needed plenty of time to whip themselves back
into the pink after a three day lay-off. (Weiner 1934)

Thus, implied the Anglo-Jewish press, Ross's observance of the
Jewish New Year furthered his boxing interests, while Greenberg's
violation of normative Rosh Hashanah practices constituted "a civic
duty" (*Jewish Daily Bulletin* 1934, Sept. 14).

Throughout the 1930s the press continued to emphasize
Greenberg's ethnic identity. After 1934, however, the press never
again depicted Greenberg as engaged in a soul-searching choice
between his personal religious beliefs and community interests.
Precedent and circumstance served as a prophylactic against the
intense pressures that peaked in September 1934. In 1935, for
example, as a 1979 Greenberg letter notes, "I did not play on Yom
Kippur in the World Series of 1935 against Chicago, as I was
injured at the time, no decision was necessary." More important,
from the viewpoint of media image, the premier Jewish standard-
bearer had already made his irrevocable choice between community
and ethnic interests in 1934.

Although 1930s' newspapers printed many articles about anti-
Semitism, neither the Anglo-Jewish nor general circulation press
acknowledged its existence in baseball. Interviews reveal that
Greenberg was the target of many anti-Semitic taunts (Morgan conversation; Greenberg questionnaire; Lieb interview), but contemporary writers refrained from any mention of the phenomenon. During
the 1934 World Series, for example, the St. Louis Cardinals, a raucous ensemble embodying the small-town provincialism cherished by
Henry Ford, continually referred to Greenberg as "Moses" and reviled
him with anti-Semitic epithets (Broeg 1970; Falls 1975, 155; Lieb
interview). Although the press noted Henry Ford's fondness for Dizzy
Dean's "Gashouse Gang," sportswriters attributed the tenseness
Greenberg displayed to the pressures of playing in his first World
Series and indicated the taunts he received from the Cardinals related
to some errors on the playing field (Ward 1934c; Vaughn 1934; *TSN*
1934, Oct. 11). Perhaps sportswriters felt impelled to protect the
pristine image of the "national pastime," an idealized reflection of
American society at large. Moreover, acknowledging anti-Semitism
would have questioned the efficacy of baseball's melting pot.

Media references to Greenberg as a Jewish standard-bearer declined during World War II. Greenberg, the only baseball superstar ensnared by the pre–Pearl Harbor draft, received his army discharge on December 5, 1941, but reenlisted immediately after Pearl Harbor. Unlike many baseball players who served as athletic directors, Greenberg, the press noted, volunteered for combat, serving "in the China-Burma-India Theater with the Twentieth Bomber command, the first B-29 unit to go overseas" (*NYT* 1946, Feb 19). Comments germane to Greenberg's ethnicity became infrequent. The media now portrayed the big slugger not as a Jewish standard-bearer, but as the embodiment of the "national pastime," and thus "the American way of life" (Mead 1978; *TSN* 1941, Dec. 25). A *Sporting News* cartoon, for example, depicted Greenberg trading a bat for a rifle (B. Jenkins 1941). Ethnic depictions of Greenberg did not resurge or again become common after the war. When Greenberg returned to baseball, the media viewed him as a heroic symbol of veterans seeking to regain their civilian skills. The "Jewish first baseman" of the 1930s had become "Captain Henry," a designation repeatedly used by scribes during Greenberg's post–World War II career.

The decline of press references to a Jewish standard-bearer paralleled the general decline of media attention to ethnicity. The chronological distance from the era of mass immigration, the appearance of the third generation, the consensus created by World War II and sustained by the cold war, and the growing mass culture, soon to be buttressed by the "new suburbs," interstate highways, franchises, and television, reduced the need for ethnic standard-bearers. After Branch Rickey signed the incomparable Jackie Robinson to a contract in the Brooklyn Dodger's farm system during late 1945, race filled the vacuum left by ethnicity. As *The Sporting News* realized (Nov. 1), the age of the racial standard-bearer had arrived.

Jackie . . . will be haunted by the expectations of his race. To 15,000,000 Negroes he will symbolize not only their prowess in baseball, but their ability to rise to an opportunity. Unlike white players, he can never afford an off-day or an off-night. His private life will be watched, too, because white America will judge the Negro race by everything he does. And Lord help him with his fellow Negroes if he should fail them.

A journalist might have written similarly about Greenberg a decade before.

The press no longer sought a Jewish standard-bearer because assimilation and time had largely dissipated the constituency for one. Greenberg and other second-generation Jews had significantly ameliorated the secular community–ethnic group dichotomy by the end of World War II. As Hank's father, David, recognized, the second generation resolved their conflict in ways that often deviated from the traditions of their immigrant fathers. "I take keen pride in my son, in his work, in his accomplishment. . . . I have seen him in every game he played in the Yankee Stadium. I did not see him in the World Series this year because of the Jewish holidays. I believe in religion—in every man's religion for himself" (Spink 1940a). The third generation, scions of the "marginal men," needed no Jewish standard-bearer to symbolically resolve their conflicts, facilitate their Americanization, or attract them to ballparks. When Greenberg's son, Steve, captain of the Yale baseball team, agonized over whether to take the field during the spring 1970 campus strike, humanistic concerns about war and justice, devoid of overt Jewish imperatives, formed the criteria for decision making (Reel 1970). The differences between Hank Greenberg's 1934 conflict and that of his son thirty-six years later largely define the distance between the second and third generations. During the 1930s Hank Greenberg served as a potent media symbol for second-generation Jews, who applauded the success of a coreligionist in the "national pastime" because it provided reassurance of their ability to resolve the strain of assimilationist ethnic polarities and to succeed within the American mainstream. In 1979 a Jewish writer recalled Greenberg's meaning for the second generation.

> I found the heroes of my time: Hank Greenberg and Bess Myerson. I can think of no public personages in all the succeeding years whom I've followed with such feeling. . . . Hank and Bess were winners, like DiMaggio and Grable—only smarter. They were as American as apple pie and the Fourth of July—and as Jewish as *Knishes* and Yom Kippur. They belonged to a race of victors, not victims. They transcended the categories which trapped other Jewish luminaries of that era. . . . [F]or the first time, Jews had successfully crossed over from ethnic favorites to national heroes . . . they had arrived. (Kopkind 1979)

8

Lester Harrison and the Rochester Royals, 1945–1957

A Jewish Entrepreneur in the NBA

Donald M. Fisher

American professional basketball underwent a dramatic transformation in the decade after World War II. The history of the Rochester, New York, Royals club illustrates many of the sport's peculiarities, including its business structure and relationship to society and individual communities. As with other modern professional team sports, basketball's maturation was marked by the creation of a centralized monopolistic organization, a commitment to commercialism and the marketplace, and a migration of many franchises to larger cities. Indeed, the Rochester Royals were part of this transformation. The team's migration to Cincinnati in 1957 demonstrated changes taking place in the sports world of postwar America and particularly why small cities were not suitable to the new system that emerged. This essay seeks to show how and why the sport changed after World War II by scrutinizing one team and the challenges it faced as a business franchise, as a social unit, and as a community institution. Besides the Royals being representative of the great changes taking place during this period, the franchise itself was somewhat pivotal in the sport's transformation.

Unlike most modern professional sports franchises in the United States, the Rochester Royals evolved from a neighborhood semiprofessional team rather than originating as a business franchise in an organized league. After graduating in 1923, former Rochester high school basketball star Lester "Lucky Les" Harrison organized and played for teams sponsored by the Ebers Brothers and Seagrams liquor companies. The Jewish son of Russian and Polish immigrants, Harrison continued to play through the Great Depression, while also operating a local fruit and vegetable business to earn a living and to support his brother, Jack, at the University of Rochester. His teams dominated local competition for years, and eventually played the nation's top independent clubs and industrial league teams, such as the Akron Firestone Non-Skids. As a semiprofessional team always trying to improve in stature, the club shifted its home court several times, playing at St. Stanislaus Hall, the Columbus Civic Center, and the East Main Street Armory. Harrison paid his players on a per-game basis and even enticed other teams' players to switch teams in midseason, following practices common among semiprofessional teams operating outside formally regulated competitive structures. Harrison was able to get Al Cervi, a noncollegiate player from Buffalo, to join his team in 1939, and he persuaded black "hindu" star Wilmeth Sidat-Singh of the Syracuse Reds to jump to the Rochester Seagrams in 1940 (Angevine 1951, 39, 57–62; Peterson 1990, 137–38; *BDAS* 1989 under "Harrison, Lester"; Rochester Royals 1946–47 Official Program; Harrison interview; Cervi interview; Chalk 1975, 99–101; *Chicago Herald-American* 1940, Mar. 13).

Unlike major league baseball and football, the world of professional basketball in which Les Harrison's team operated lacked a central, major market organization before 1946. Whereas the highest level of baseball included the eight-team National and American Leagues, professional basketball consisted of several regional leagues, the most prominent being the National Basketball League (NBL) in the Midwest; postseason invitations such as the Chicago *Herald-American*–sponsored World Professional Basketball Tournament; independent and barnstorming clubs, such as the all-black New York Renaissance; and quasi-professional Amateur Athletic Union teams. Most professional clubs were owned by local civic-minded businessmen and former players such as Harrison, performed

8.1. Lester Harrison, owner of the Rochester Royals, 1945–57. Courtesy of the Naismith Basketball Hall of Fame, Springfield, Massachusetts.

in small arenas and armories in small cities, and were usually not overtly commercial enterprises. The American public regarded college basketball as superior to the more physical professional game, and hence the latter was oftentimes absent from major metropolitan cities that supported the college game (Applin 1982, 231–34; Riess 1989, 232; Vincent 1991, 279–84, 291).

The Rochester Seagrams competed in the Chicago championship tournament in 1940 and 1941, bowing out in the first round both times. Because of pressure from local liquor stores on Rochester's dry Gannett newspapers, Harrison dropped the club's liquor-inspired nickname and renamed the team the Rochester Pros for the 1944–45 season. Desiring to go "big time" with brother Jack, he bought an NBL expansion franchise for $25,000 in 1945, and "put everything he had into the venture," thus transforming the team from a semiprofessional independent club with neighborhood roots into a professional franchise in an intercity league. Their playing careers ended, Les Harrison became the team's president, manager, and co-coach, while longtime playing partner Eddie Malanowicz of Buffalo served as nominal head coach. A local fifteen-year-old schoolboy chose the new NBL franchise's nickname in a contest: "Webster defines Royals as 'pertaining to a king or crown; befitting or like a king; majestic.'" "What could be more fitting than this as a name for the team Les Harrison is going to send out to bring the crown to Rochester?" In joining a formal organized league, Harrison became obliged to sign players to standardized contracts, and quickly put together a new team at the end of the war. He recruited former star college players, including a few recently discharged from military service. With this nucleus the Royals won two championships (1945–46 and 1946–47) in their three years of NBL competition (*D&C* 1940, Mar. 18; 1945, Nov. 9; *T-U* 1941, Mar. 17; Cervi interview; "Rise of Les Harrison"; Peterson 1990, 128, 138, 205; Harrison interview).

With the establishment of the Basketball Association of America (BAA) in 1946, the decentralized and civic-minded system of basketball that the NBL represented was joined by a more centralized and commercial organization with a concern for the marketplace. The BAA consisted of franchises managed by eleven major arena proprietors—ten of whom owned major or minor league hockey franchises—who sought to fill their eastern and midwestern arenas on nights not occupied by professional hockey games, ice shows, circuses, or boxing matches. Despite being inexperienced in basketball management, these owners were skilled commercial sports promoters and had well-established links with the national media. According to the basketball director of Madison Square Garden, Ned Irish, "It is our belief . . . that our [the BAA] efforts to introduce a fourth major sport will be stamped with success. In the past this truly American game has not been properly presented professionally, but we feel that we are ready to do the job correctly, backed by the major arena owners in eleven cities." The BAA also restricted franchise placement mainly to large metropolitan markets, and furthermore enforced an exclusive scheduling system, unlike the NBL, which needed nonleague exhibition competition to remain financially viable (Koppett 1968, 15–43; Applin 1982, 235–

37; Vincent 1991, 289–90, 300; Riess 1989, 232; *NYT* 1946, Oct. 24).

The BAA quickly challenged the primarily midwestern NBL and the strengths and weaknesses of the two leagues became apparent. The BAA had the major arenas in large markets with few celebrity athletes, while the NBL possessed the top star players in the country, but was based in small cities. During the 1947–48 season, the BAA had an average city size advantage of nearly 10:1 (U.S. Dept. of Commerce, Bureau of the Census 1952).[1] Realizing that it needed NBL gate attractions, such as George Mikan and Jim Pollard of the Minneapolis Lakers and Bob Davies and Arnie Risen of the Rochester Royals, to help fill its spacious arenas, the BAA lured four prominent NBL franchises, including the Royals, to its circuit for the 1948–49 season (Koppett 1968, 34–36; Applin 1982, 238; Rader 1983, 295).[2]

After a three-year interleague war, a merger between the leagues resulted in the formation of the National Basketball Association (NBA) on August 3, 1949. The new NBA's constitution was a revised version of the BAA's charter, reflecting the influence of the former BAA owners in the new league's power structure. These men stuck to their principle of being a big-city operation by constructing a playing schedule and a divisional alignment that ensured a minimal number of games between former BAA and NBL teams, denying some of the small-market franchises big-city exposure. Furthermore, restricted scheduling eliminated nonleague exhibition games, on which the former NBL teams had depended for supplementary income (*NYT* 1949, Aug. 4; NBA, Bulletin No. 2; Koppett 1968, 44–45; Vincent 1991, 304).

1. BAA cities (2,155,416 average population) included Baltimore, Boston, Chicago, New York, Philadelphia, Providence, St. Louis, and Washington, D.C., while NBL cities (217,568) included Anderson, Ind., Fort Wayne, Indianapolis, Flint, Minneapolis, Oshkosh, Sheboygan, Rochester, Syracuse, Toledo, and the Tri-Cities (Moline, Rock Island, and Davenport).

2. The Royals' Davies was indeed one of professional basketball's top stars during the 1940s and 1950s because of his athletic talent and "all-American" image. In fact, Clair Bee, the longtime Long Island University coach, administrator, and author, used Davies as a model for his Chip Hilton sports novels. Bee's series included such basketball stories as *Championship Ball* (1948), *Hoop Crazy* (1950), and *Backboard Fever* (1953) (*BDAS* under "Bee, Clair"; Roeder 1948, 50–53, 87).

After its first season, the NBA shrank from seventeen to eleven teams in a survival-of-the-fittest test shakeout as small-market teams such as the Sheboygan, Wisconsin, Redskins dropped out. This new basketball cartel underwent several more changes to solidify itself as a business and its remaining small-market franchises faced two choices: relocate or fold. Although reduced to eight teams by 1954, the NBA secured partial major league legitimacy with its first national television contract with the Dumont Television Network in 1952, and the beginning of permanent racial integration in 1950. Furthermore, the introduction of the twenty-four-second shot clock in 1954 made the game more appealing to spectators, reflecting the owners' commitment to product marketability (Koppett 1968, 44–89; Applin 1982, 239–41; Vincent 1991, 304–7; Riess 1989, 232–33; Rader 1983, 295–96; Rader 1984, 145–46; Chalk 1975, 110).

At this point basketball became a bona fide "major league" sport, as defined by interregional coverage of recognizably large markets, a widely held acknowledgment of high athletic quality, and outright professionalism and commercialism. The NBL had possessed only one of these characteristics, as it was indeed recognized as having the best ballplayers in the country. Despite this, the NBL was primarily a regional league in the Midwest, with few franchises outside the area, and was not fully committed to the principles of modern sports commercialism. On the other hand, whereas the BAA was firmly rooted in major cities in both the Northeast and Midwest, and was fully devoted to professionalism and commercialism, it did not possess the best athletic talent. In fact, the 1947–48 Baltimore Bullets earned the nickname "a dull and nameless champion" (Vincent 1991, 299; Neft and Cohen 1990, 71). With the merger, the two leagues combined their strengths, and developed to become another major league on America's sporting landscape.

The NBA survived and became more popular partly because of the stars imported from the old NBL. The old NBL clubs boasted enough top-quality players that the first six NBA champions were all former NBL teams, including the Minneapolis Lakers with four titles and the Royals and Syracuse Nationals with one each. Although these former NBL teams dominated the league on the court, large-market BAA teams—namely, the New York Knickerbockers and the Philadelphia Warriors—developed an edge at the box office, owing in part to a league rule stipulating that all gate receipts went to the home team. These clubs also had fiscal stability because their owners had other business interests to offset their losses in basketball; for most former NBL owners, basketball was their sole business. The NBA grew in popularity during the 1950s, but the constraints of small markets forced several franchises, including the Royals, to move. By 1963, when the Syracuse Nationals became the Philadelphia 76ers, all of the NBA's clubs were based in large metropolitan markets (U.S. Senate, Committee on the Judiciary 1958, 576, 578; Koppett 1968, 112; Vincent 1991, 305–7; Riess 1989, 232–33).

The Rochester Royals, as a business, was trying to succeed in two distinct marketplaces. First, the team had to contend with other leisure activities in Rochester. More directly, it was in competition with the rest of the league's franchises. For Les Harrison the team was his livelihood and he focused all of his energies and resources into its operation. The success of the Royals, as with other sporting businesses, depended on ownership entrepreneurialism, competitive marketing and athletic performance, a strong base of community support, and answering challenges in the marketplace. For the Royals all of these factors proved crucial to the success or failure of the franchise. Despite changes Harrison made to meet the demands of the marketplace, the Royals lost their competitive edge at the box office by the early 1950s. They suffered a decline in attendance and could not compete financially either in the Rochester marketplace or with the rest of the NBA.

Harrison tried to improve his franchise's financial position during its twelve-year stay in Rochester. Before joining the NBL in 1945, he had for two decades operated his team in a world somewhat removed from formalized professional major league team sports. Though the team was his livelihood after 1945, its operation was not geared exclusively to profit; it was a civic as well as a commercial venture. Harrison carried this double-edged view toward community and business with him after joining the ranks of the big-city BAA teams in 1948, which may have undermined his ability to compete with large-market operations over the long run.

Commercial sports owners and promoters often undertake specific entrepreneurial activities to ensure their survival in the marketplace and to improve their position relative to competitors. Such actions include signing new players, improving or changing playing facilities, staging promotional events, reducing operating expenses, modifying the membership within the competitive organizational structure, and transferring to a new metropolitan market (Hardy 1986, 14–33). As entrepreneurs in a relatively new commercial sport, the various NBL, BAA, and later NBA owners made several changes out of economic necessity. Trying to make each game as much a social event as an athletic contest, the civic-oriented NBL owners often encouraged spectator participation through halftime free throw contests, free roses on ladies' nights, and other gimmicks to maintain or boost their modest attendance figures. Meanwhile, the BAA emulated other major league team sports by staging the games as consumer entertainment commodities to supplement the arena's other offerings. After 1949 the NBA adhered to the BAA marketing model by concentrating on improving its quality of play. This effort eventually paid dividends in the late 1950s, when the league began to outdraw collegiate basketball (Vincent 1991, 290–93).

Perhaps Harrison's most important entrepreneurial effort was his decision to abandon the NBL for the BAA in 1948, a move dictated mainly by economic factors. Harrison bolted the NBL for the BAA after three seasons of NBL competition, and there had even been rumors of a defection earlier, in the spring of 1947. Informal discussion between NBL owners with high aspirations and BAA leaders began after a bidding war for players, and rumors of a possible defection by a few NBL teams surfaced in February 1948. Realizing that the more-established NBL possessed better talent, the arena owners of the BAA sought to resolve their business conflict with the NBL and proposed a merger of the two leagues in April 1948 ("Les Harrison on Fence Regarding Shift of Royals to BAA"; *D&C* 1947, Apr. 12; *NYT* 1948, Feb. 10; Apr. 8).

The NBL rejected the BAA's proposition and the BBA responded by trying to persuade the recently crowned NBL champion Minneapolis Lakers to switch leagues. Citing their own dominance of the NBL, the Lakers declined the offer; the BAA then turned to the Indianapolis Kautskys and the Fort Wayne Zollner Pistons, both operated as advertising vehicles for their respective owners' business interests. The Indianapolis franchise was owned by Fred Kautsky, a florist who also owned a grocery store chain, and the Pistons were run by Fred Zollner, owner of the largest piston company in the country. The two teams saw the opportunities for advertising in large cities such as New York, Chicago, and Boston, and thus joined the new league, finally bearing out speculation that NBL teams would defect to the BAA. According to a Kautskys' spokesman, the NBL clubs regarded the BAA as "a 'tougher league' with 'bigger crowd potentials'." Not wanting to be left out of the exodus to a league perceived to possess greater economic potential, the Lakers reversed their decision and also joined the BAA. The Royals completed the defection when Les Harrison persuaded the BAA to adopt his star-laden squad as well. With the Royals' jump to the BAA, they were not only bringing new big-city opponents into Rochester but were also joining a more commercialized business association (*Chicago Herald-American* 1948, May 9; May 10; May 11; *NYT* 1948, May 9; May 11; Koppett 1968, 34–36; Peterson 1990, 163–65; Vincent 1991, 292–302).

Harrison's decision to join the BAA linked the small-city traditions of the past with the big-market commercial opportunities of the present. His various teams from the 1920s to the late 1940s had gradually generated heightened fan interest in Rochester, so that by the time the NBL enfranchised the Royals in 1945, they were the talk of the town. Their home court, Edgerton Park Sports Arena, held between thirty-eight hundred and forty-two hundred spectators and always sold out during the seasons after the end of World War II. Royals tickets were highly coveted and Harrison had few worries about filling seats. In contrast, most BAA franchises could not fill their more spacious arenas and had to spend more time and energy on generating spectator interest. Harrison had no immediate need to focus on promoting the team in ways like those exhibited by larger-market franchises. His arena consistently sold out.

With little need for entrepreneurial marketing innovations, the Royals' mode of promotion stagnated. The team was filled with stars, won a high percentage of its games, and most important, unfailingly filled Edgerton Park. Royals fans bought their tickets at Sibley's department and Edwards clothing stores, read about their heroes in the local newspapers, and were secure in knowing that their team was one of the country's best. Therefore, Royals management saw no need to plan for an innovative marketing program using modern public-relations techniques. One early NBA critic wrote that former NBL teams such as the Royals, which did not have "a drawing to depict their nicknames," should "run a home town contest to have some fan suggest or draw a figure that could be exploited by the cartoonists in all the papers, the same as baseball does" (NBA, Bulletin No. 308A). Though a seemingly minor point, it illustrates an indifference by the Royals to maximize their ability to publicize the franchise.

Other NBA franchises continually sought to promote themselves in different ways. The Minneapolis Lakers had an extensive marketing program in 1951 that included public appearances by players, cultivation of the media, and sales of discount tickets at local firms and high schools. These promotions were designed to "fill the many empty seats which otherwise would be unoccupied" and to "introduce basketball to many people who have never seen professional basketball." The franchise also generated fan interest by making a comic book on star George Mikan's life, producing yearly highlight movies, mailing calendars and brochures, and conducting clinics and attending luncheons on a preseason tour of twenty-five Minnesota cities. Lakers' management also chartered bus trips into Minneapolis for games, and increased program sales as it tried "to make our basketball program a basketball magazine instead of just a book of advertising" (NBA, Bulletin No. 308A; Bulletin No. 138). Unlike the Royals, two factors unique to the Lakers' situation stimulated this extensive marketing program: a much larger market to draw from and a larger arena to fill. Overall, the promotional campaign of the Royals was less extensive than that undertaken by the Lakers.

Although individual franchises initiated promotions to improve their economic well-being, the NBA also attempted to make itself more marketable. Essential to this attempt was the direction given by the league's president, Maurice Podoloff, and its board of governors. Podoloff was a Russian-born graduate of Yale University with experience as a lawyer, banker, and real estate entrepreneur, but with little background in basketball. A skilled executive, he was president of the American Hockey League and also operated the New Haven Arena. Under his leadership, the NBA attained a more positive image among spectators and greater rapport with the media. One step included the league's removal of angry and embarrassing team owners from the arenas' bench areas in November 1949. The league also responded to charges of boring games by passing Danny Biasone's twenty-four-second shot rule in 1954.

Podoloff showed his promotion skills when he urged teams to supply player photos to the media, and told owners that releasing low gate-receipt figures was bad publicity for the league (Koppett 1968, 17–18, 83–86; Peterson 1990, 151–52; NBA, Bulletin No. 41; No. 47; No. 63). Testifying before Congress in 1957, Podoloff stated,

> The people who have chosen me to be president of the organization have chosen me not to have an eye single to the players, and not to have an eye single to the governors. They want a proper production of basketball. In the proper production of basketball, there are three ingredients, sir—players, without whom you cannot play; governors, who have got to be entrepreneurs who are prepared to put their money into the promotion of the basketball—without them you can't play. The third, and most important of the three factors, are the spectators who make the entire proposition worthwhile. (U.S. House Committee on the Judiciary 1958, 2864)

So great was the NBA's concern for its image and marketability that it attempted to encourage clubs to capitalize on local stars. To benefit from the interest in prominent local college players, the NBA continued an old BAA rule in which each franchise was allocated one territorial draft pick each year. Before teams began their reverse order multiround collegiate draft, the league allowed each team to select a player who played collegiately for a school "within a radius of 50 miles of the corporate limits of the city" (U.S. House Committee on the Judiciary 1958, 2857). If teams took a territorial choice, they forfeited their first-round draft choice.

Throughout the NBA's third campaign—the 1951–52 season—several franchises, including the Rochester Royals, suffered a drop in attendance and gate receipts. Podoloff attributed the problem to competition from college and professional football, television, and a public distrust of basketball caused by the college point-shaving scandal of 1951. He also pointed to "inadequate promotion" and "few [leisure] dollars available for professional sports and other amusements and therefore more discrimination in spending them." To increase public interest in the NBA, Podoloff advocated rule changes to make games more exciting. Expressing concern over the common tactic of repeated fouling at the end of a game he had just witnessed, he believed "the game which the spectators and I saw was not an attraction and if the paying customers stayed away in crowds they could hardly be blamed" (NBA, Bulletin No. 242; Figone 1989).

Despite any attempts by Harrison to improve the Royals, both on and off the court the team suffered a decline in attendance. During the late 1940s the Royals consistently sold out their games— more than 100,000 in total nonexhibition attendance per season— and during the 1946–47 season the team produced a $40,000 profit. However, according to official business records, they attracted only 81,872 spectators during their championship season of 1950–51. George Beahon, who covered Harrison's teams in 1940–41 and 1945–57 for the *Rochester Democrat and Chronicle*, disputes this official figure and maintains that most Royals games were sold out that season. By the 1951–52 season, the Royals' total paid attendance fell to 79,212. It further declined over the following two seasons to 65,535 and 45,150 respectively, before rising after a 1955 move into the new Rochester Community War Memorial. In the three years before moving into the 8,000-seat War Memorial, the Royals had lost $55,563. Attendance rose during the Royals final three seasons in Rochester from 58,800 to 74,550, and finally in the 1956–57 season to 83,330 (Roeder 1948, 52; Vincent 1991, 298; NBA, Bulletin No. 187B; Beahon telephone conversation; U.S. House Committee on the Judiciary 1958, 2928, 2931, 2934-c).

A decline in any team's attendance is usually attributable to more than poor team attendance or a lack of gate attractions. In fact, the Royals' attendance declined when the team was still winning. The small arena size of Edgerton Park apparently had a negative effect on this popular team, because it inadvertently reduced the pool of potential spectators in Rochester. Bobby Wanzer, signed as a Royal in December 1947 and a resident of Rochester since 1950, offered the following analysis of what happened to Royal fans.

I think what happened was that in the beginning, we were in demand. . . . And I guess we had a lot of season ticket holders. And this is—maybe I'm wrong—but we couldn't build any new fans because we were sold out in the beginning, so I think what happened is that after a while people stopped trying to get tickets. There comes a time when they are available, people don't have the incentive to try and get them. (Wanzer interview)

Most Royals spectators during the immediate postwar years were season-ticket holders. General admissions were eliminated "in order to discontinue the long waiting lines of fans who shivered in the cold waiting for the ducats to go on sale only to have the tail enders find out that they were all gone before they reached the box office" ("Rochester Royals Probably Best Team in Country").

The shortage of tickets, the long lines during the winter, and the decision to end general admission alienated a significant portion of the Rochester sports community. Dave Ocorr, having gone to Royals games as a teenager in the late 1940s, covered the Royals for the *Rochester Times-Union* during the team's final two campaigns in Rochester. He saw the Royals' problems resulting from turn-away crowds who got upset when they could not be accommodated. A *Times-Union* writer noted in February 1933 that "perhaps the team won so often that mere victory no longer satisfies the fans. Perhaps the fans of the early lush years have had their fill of basketball and the younger element has not yet taken to it. Perhaps people are fed up with the inadequate Edgerton Sports Arena." To compound the problem of scarce tickets and shut-out or complacent fans, there were also rumors that the Harrison brothers were scalping their own tickets (Ocorr to author, Mar. 23, 1992; *T-U* 1953, Feb. 27; Massino interview).

Besides the problem of disgruntled fans, by the early 1950s the Royals also encountered outside competition in the local leisure and entertainment spheres of Rochester social life. Like Americans in general, Rochesterians became infatuated with television during this period, and spectator sports often suffered. Looking back, Less Harrison said, "When TV itself came in, we operated on Tuesday and Saturday nights. Milton Berle put us out of business on Tuesday. And then on Saturday with Sid Caesar and Imogene Coca—they put us out of business. That's why we didn't draw. The people stayed home and watched—had beer parties and watched the games there" (Harrison interview). Television not only offered competition in the form of comedy and drama but it also gave people another reason to remain home by telecasting sporting contests, including NBA games. For example, the Royals opened the 1951–52 season in defense of their NBA crown by attracting only 2,316 spectators because "many watched the game on television sets as the Royals were picked up by the TV camera for the first time ever at home."

By 1956 Rochester sports fans also had another major choice on the local winter sports menu: minor league hockey. The newly enfranchised Rochester Americans of the American Hockey League also played in the War Memorial and almost always outdrew their basketball cotenants (Rader 1984, 33, 51–55, 58–59, 67; Harrison interview; *D&C* 1950, Nov. 2; *T-U* 1956, July 3; McKelvey 1961, 258, 342–43).

Yet another reason for the general falloff in attendance between the late 1940s and the mid-1950s was that the team was getting old. The stars of the late 1940s gradually disappeared and the team declined in the standings. Al Cervi departed for the Syracuse Nationals as a player-coach after a falling-out with Harrison; Andrew "Fuzzy" Levane followed Cervi to Syracuse a year later; William "Red" Holzman retired in 1953; and in 1955 Harrison traded Arnie Risen to the Boston Celtics, and all-pro Bob Davies retired. These gate attractions of the championship years were replaced in 1955 by collegians Jack Twyman, Ed Fleming, and the 1956 rookie of the year, Maurice Stokes. Together these new Royals and a new home court helped boost attendance slightly, but other forces were at work that made the Royals' days in Rochester numbered.

While the Royals were suffering a decline of support in Rochester, the team was also slipping relative to the rest of the league, both on and off the court. Harrison decided to shift to a youth movement beginning in the 1955–56 season and signed seven new ballplayers. However, the team sank in the standings to a last place 29–43 finish in the NBA's four-team Western Division, a position quite unfamiliar to the Royals. This deterioration in the quality of the team surely contributed to the lessening of spectator support in Rochester that had already begun years earlier. As early as the 1950–51 season—the season the Royals won their only NBA title—Rochester's paid attendance and gate receipts were near the league's cellar. In fact, its average of 2,408 spectators per game was ninth among the circuit's eleven franchises. There was a high—but not absolute—correlation between winning percentage and gate receipts; four of the five top gate winners were winning ball clubs. Also, the old BAA teams' large arenas and metropolitan markets did not guarantee higher attendance than former NBL clubs, for the Syracuse Nationals led the league in attendance despite having a losing record. Although the original eleven BAA owners joined together

in 1946 because they had large arenas, markets, and financial backing, only three of these clubs (New York, Boston, and Philadelphia)
survived to see the NBA's 1954–55 season. Ironically, the older
small-city NBL teams managed to survive in the short run by
winning on the court, and in the long run by relocating to larger
cities (table 8.1). There was a further sharp distinction in net profits
and losses from 1951 to 1957, as the league's three former BAA
teams turned out to be the most economically viable business operations (table 8.2).

Another indication of how the Royals lost their competitive edge
was Harrison's inability to keep up with increases in salaries, and
this surely hurt the club's attractiveness to new players. Three of
the former NBL teams (Rochester, Minneapolis, and Syracuse) all
had an extremely modest team payroll growth between 1952 and
1957, while the league's other five franchises had increases between

Table 8.1
Economics of the NBA, 1950–51

Franchise	Home Games	Gate Receipts	Average Attendance	Per Game	Winning Percent	Prior Affiliation
Minneapolis	34	$234,276.89	172,410	5,071	.647	NBL-BAA
Syracuse	33	223,856.89	174,094	5,276	.485	NBL
Boston	34	196,023.70	158,748	4,669	.565	BAA
New York	27	175,893.03	146,347	5,420	.545	BAA
Philadelphia	33	146,699.11	107,565	3,260	.606	BAA
Fort Wayne	34	131,629.95	107,019	3,148	.471	NBL-BAA
Rochester	34	118,545.80	81,872	2,408	.603	NBL-BAA
Tri-Cities	35	114,014.37	101,331	2,895	.368	NBL
Indianapolis	34	110,014.16	119,536	3,516	.456	NBA
Baltimore	33	85,919.24	55,374	1,678	.364	BAA
Washington*	18	28,601.85	35,654	1,981	.286	BAA

Source: NBA, Bulletin No. 187B; Neft and Cohen 1990, 95

*folded during season

Table 8.2

Net NBA Profits/Losses, 1951–57

Franchise[a]	1951–52	1952–53	1953–54	1951–55	1955–56	1956–57	Total	Average
New York	$46,042	$91,623	$77,548	$113,788	$120,106	$86,978	$536,085	$89,348
Philadelphia	n/a	–33,389	–19,463	–7,183	56,408	26,072	22,445	4,489
Boston	44,031	–5,127	–53,385	33,852	35,352	46,997	4,342	–1,057
Syracuse	–2,215	–12,337	940	–12,552	–16,896	4,817	–38,243	4,374
St. Louis[b]	–10,930	229	–15,876	–30,482	6,639	2,536	–52,956	–8,826
Rochester	–10,663	–30,400	–14,500	–34,600	–23,600	–17,500	–131,263	–21,877
Minneapolis	–11,093	5,562	–17,781	–35,740	–35,346	45,524	–159,922	–26,654
Fort Wayne	46,000	–71,068	–59,302	–25,360	–19,711	–24,632	–246,073	41,012

Source: House Committee, 2928, 2931, 2935.
Notes: All figures rounded to nearest dollar.
[a]Teams that folded between 1951 and 1957 are not included.
[b]This franchise played in the Tri-Cities from 1947 to 1951 and in Milwaukee from 1951 to 1955 before moving to St. Louis.

31.24 and 62.81 percent. In fact, the Royals' payroll of $71,000 in 1952–53 grew to only $75,000 by the 1956–57 season, while the Milwaukee (and later St. Louis) Hawks jumped from $56,826 to $92,518.

One incident at the end of the 1955–56 season illustrates Harrison's dire economic straits. Finishing with the league's worst record, the Royals had the top draft choice in the 1956 college draft, and University of San Francisco star Bill Russell was the most coveted player available. Russell made it known that he would not play for a small-city team such as the Royals and declared that if Rochester drafted him he would sign with the Harlem Globetrotters, who were supposedly offering more money than Harrison. Russell would not be available until December because of his commitment to the U.S. national team competing at the Melbourne summer Olympics in November, and the Boston Celtics knew Rochester's chances of drafting him were low. The Celtics traded Ed Macauley and Cliff Hagan to the St. Louis Hawks for the second pick in the draft. To ensure that Rochester would not draft Russell, Boston made a deal with Harrison: the Royals would pledge not to pick Russell and in return Harrison would get Celtics owner Walter Brown's ice show in Rochester for two weeks a year (Koppett 1968, 100; Auerbach 1991, 20, 60; *NYT* 1956, May 1).[3] Russell became a Celtic and helped Boston win eleven NBA titles.

With a metropolitan population base, television market, and arena that were all modest in size, the Royals began to lose their financial ground to larger-market teams at the century's midpoint. To compound the problem, Harrison's sole commercial interest was basketball, unlike most of the big-city owners who had other businesses to offset their basketball team's financial problems. Playing in tiny Edgerton Park during the 1940s had the negative effect of alienating many Rochesterians and with the retirement of star players such as Bob Davies and competition from television and minor league hockey, it was almost inevitable that the Royals would eventually have to relocate.

The Rochester Royals franchise was more than a business operation. To Harrison and the players, the team was both a family and

3. In his interview Harrison declined to comment on Russell and the 1956 college draft.

a livelihood. For the people of Rochester the Royals were a source of civic pride, entertainment, and an institution around which the city's affluent population could gather. This feeling predominated during the "glory years" and "heyday" of Harrison's team—roughly from 1944 to 1945 through their NBA title in 1951—but eventually changed as support for the franchise began to evaporate. The experience of the Royals also illustrated the changes in attitudes toward the role of community in people's lives, race and ethnicity in athletics, sports consumption patterns, and the peculiarities of the city of Rochester in the context of the postwar professional sports scene (Riess 1989, 231–51).

During the 1930s, Harrison operated his team on a semiprofessional level and was able to assert influence both as a player and organizer. With the formation of the Royals, the team was already a virtual extension of Harrison, and his office staff included only his brother. Jack. and a secretary. Possessing a high degree of control both on and off the court, he developed specific values that he retained through the 1950s, including his sense of community. In fact, Harrison was an organizer for a local Police Athletic League, a nonprofit organization that gave children an alternative to delinquent activities during the summer.[4] Still, Harrison's ambition was in many ways circumscribed and even restricted by Rochester's market size. His otherwise boundless work ethic and commitment to the team was limited by the size of the local population. After the team's 1951 NBA championship, a newspaper noted:

> No guy ever worked harder, no guy ever took more of a gamble, no guy ever more deservedly earned the pro basketball success which has come the way of Harrison since he became the boss of the Royals. . . . It's been quite an experience for a guy playing around with his own bankroll, stymied by a town which hasn't an adequate sized arena in which to parade his high-priced and talented performers. A peek at the record bears out the fact that he has done okay. (*T-U* 1951, Apr. 23)

---

4. According to the *New York Times* of May 25, 1944, Harrison also served as New York City mayor Fiorello LaGuardia's PAL membership campaign chairman, but Harrison denied his association with LaGuardia (*BDAS* 1989 under "Harrison, Lester").

Perhaps the most important of Harrison's values was the sense of family that he instilled in his players. According to Bobby Wanzer, a longtime Royal, "Les was smart. He was like a bit of a psychologist in a way. He knew how to get the fellas up for the game and how not to let them become complacent. Then when they were down, he knew how to pep 'em up." While maintaining control over his players, he also respected their knowledge of the game by allowing them coaching input. During Eddie Malanowicz's term as head coach (1945–49), Harrison sat on the bench, and they, together with the experienced players, made decisions collectively (Wanzer interview; Beahon conversation; Roeder 1948, 53; Cervi interview; Auerbach 1977, 232; Auerbach 1991, 75). According to Al Massino, a native Rochesterian who was a Royals spectator before and after his short playing career as a Royal in 1954,

> I think everybody knew their role and I think Les Harrison knew his role. Even though he was the owner-coach, he accepted the suggestions of some of the players on the team. It was a team that didn't need a coach and yet they were all coaches. How much influence did Les have when he sat on the bench? As much influence as he wanted because he was the owner. But it wasn't difficult to coach the Royals before they were in the NBA because they were all knowledgeable players. (Wanzer interview)

Harrison was successful in integrating his players into a cohesive unit in the early years of the Royals for several reasons. Most basketball players were happy to earn a living performing the game they had played since their youth. Harrison's paternalistic attitude toward his players also assured cohesiveness; as he said, "I made sure that we were close. I made sure that nobody was snubbed or anything like that. I controlled the team." Red Holzman wrote that "we had a built-in togetherness, but Les had his own little way of helping." The extent to which the Royals were a familylike organization can also be seen in Harrison's decision to name who would succeed him as coach from within the organization, choosing Wanzer in April 1955 (Harrison interview; Holzman 1971, 34; *NYT* 1955, Apr. 29).

Train travel had the positive effect of contributing to a sense of camaraderie for the Royals. Both Wanzer and Cervi said that long train rides to the league's other cities kept the team "close knit," as the Royals spent hours together talking and playing cards. Besides time spent together on trains, the players also socialized away from the court, going to bars, restaurants, and movie theaters. There was relatively little jealously between players, because most of the Royals were unaware or disinterested in what their teammates' salaries were. As Cervi put it, "It was a very hidden secret and we wouldn't talk salary; it was more or less taboo." A relative lack of resentment by players of each other's salaries, and a lack of commercial endorsement incentives—owing to Rochester's market size—helped eliminate points of contention between players. According to Massino, "The pressures that pull people together—being with each other on a train for a long time, playing cards, together and trying to entertain ourselves—were there. We had so few distractions that we relied upon ourselves" (Cervi interview; Wanzer interview; Massino interview; Roeder 1948, 52).

Despite claims of harmony from Royals players, there was room for conflict. Some Royals did dislike one another, but the suppression of conflict for the sake of the team created a sense of group cohesiveness and what some former Royal players described as a "family atmosphere." Writing more than thirty years later, Bob Davies declared that "it was a celebration time for the years of 1946, '47, and '48. Later on, it became more of a business. But in those days there was an athletic camaraderie. Today everyone seems to go his own way" (Cervi interview; Massino interview; Salzberg 1987, 59–60).

During the "heyday" of the Royals, when the team was winning championships and attracting standing room–only crowds, Harrison was generous with his players in the salaries he paid and the way he treated them. To keep his star-laden and winning team happy, Harrison often bought his players whatever food they wanted on road trips. But as money became tight with the Royals by the early 1950s, Harrison had to curb his generous spending. In Minneapolis he made his players walk to the hotel from the train station: " 'C'mon fellas,' he'd say, 'it's only a ten-block walk to the hotel. We don't need cabs. The walk will invigorate you. It's cold but it's a dry cold. You'll never feel it.' Les had come a long way from the days of offering all we could eat" (Holzman 1987, 18, 28). Ethnicity and race apparently were important in Harrison's selection of players.

He attempted to sign players because of their nationality, hoping to capitalize on their potential ability to attract specific segments of the Rochester community. A lifelong resident of Rochester, Massino said the Royals had significant numbers of Italian and Jewish spectators (Massino interview; Golenbock 1984, 155–59). Harrison signed Levane to a contract in 1945 because he thought Levane was Jewish and would appeal to the team's relatively prominent Jewish spectators. Learning that Levane was Italian, Harrison said to him, "Get me a Jewish player. I don't care if he can play or not. Just make sure he's Jewish." Levane recommended William "Red" Holzman of CCNY, whom Harrison signed and put on the bench for spectator appeal. A fine performance in a game against the Sheboygan Redskins moved Holzman into the team's starting lineup. According to Holzman, "Back in those days team had what they called 'sticks,' players hired for ethnic or local appeal who spent the game mainly on the bench. I always look back on that game as the one that saved me from a budding career as a 'Jewish' stick" (Holzman 1987, 15, 16).[5] Al Cervi said many Rochester Royals spectators "would come out because they liked a certain player," partly because of his ethnicity (Cervi interview). Massino also stated,

> I think Al Cervi was attractive to the Italian community and Red Holzman was attractive to the Jewish community. In my judgment it was a game that was played by the Italians and the Jewish people and they're the ones that attended the games. You come up through poverty and you have nothing else to do but play basketball on the playground so that's what you do and so that group becomes good at that game. (Massino interview)

Although urban basketball had already been a "melting pot" for ethnic Americans before World War II, the racial integration of professional team sports began soon after the end of the war. Les Harrison played a somewhat forgotten role in that process when he signed black star William "Dolly" King to a contract in October 1946. About King, Harrison's "motto was 'If he can play, he can

5. For examples of baseball franchises signing ethnic players for box office appeal during the postwar era, see Golenbock 1984, 155–59, 260–67.

play'." Harrison had signed both King and a second black, William "Pop" Gates, in August, but Harrison let Gates go to the Buffalo Bisons instead (*D&C* 1946, Oct. 16; *T-U* 1946, Oct. 16; Holzman 1991, 35; Copy of Player Contract of William P. Gates; *Pittsburgh Courier* 1946, Nov. 2). Whereas Organized Baseball and the National Football League excluded blacks before and during the war, professional basketball practiced limited integration, possible because of the decentralized nature of the game at the time. There were integrated defense plant teams, such as the Chicago Studebakers, during the war, and the all-black Harlem Globetrotters and New York Renaissance played in and won several Chicago *Herald-American* championship tournaments (Peterson 1990, 11–13, 130–31, 161, 204–9; Chalk 1975, 3–80, 83–118, 211–54; Smith 1988, 255–81; Simons 1985, 39–64; Wiggins 1983, 5–29; Tygiel 1983).

Harrison chose to sign King for several reasons, including the fact that he wanted a veteran to come off the bench and spell starters. As a reserve, the pressure for King to perform well was not great. King played for Long Island University from 1938 to 1940 and was captain of the New York Renaissance before signing with the Royals. The team introduced King to its spectators in its 1946–47 game program by stressing his experience and positive qualities: "His presence in the lineup gave the Rens poise and steadiness." Though the Royals signed King at age thirty for their second campaign in the NBL, King was not unfamiliar to Harrison. In the semipro years of Harrison's team, King played briefly for the Rochester Seagrams (Rochester Royals 1946–47 Official Program; *T-U* 1946, Oct. 16; *D&C* 1984, Feb. 7).

King's signing may also have been Harrison's attempt to generate national public interest in the Royals. About one year before, Brooklyn Dodgers general manager Branch Rickey signed Jackie Robinson to a contract, a feat that had generated much public discussion and comment. Just as Rickey warned Robinson, Harrison told King that "if you're gonna play, you're gonna have to accept the abuse; if you'll take a chance, so will we" (Harrison telephone conversation; Tygiel 1983, 65–67). Wendell Smith, sports editor of the all-black *Pittsburgh Courier,* congratulated Harrison for signing King: "I wish to take this opportunity to congratulate the officers of your famous team for signing a player without regard to race, creed or color. It is another democratic step in the field of sports, and I am sure your liberal attitude will be appreciated by thousands of basketball fans throughout the country" (Smith to Harrison).[6]

During King's one campaign in Rochester, he had few problems with his teammates or Rochester fans, but incidents did occur while on the road. King's character and personality, not unlike Jackie Robinson's, made acceptance by his teammates and hometown fans relatively easy. King was perceived by his teammates and the media as "a class guy" and an intelligent "gentleman" who avoided talking about racial issues. King's Rochester teammates often defended him. Generally, the Royals had few problems while on the road with King, except in Fort Wayne and Indianapolis. According to Red Holzman, "On the road bigots shouted racial slurs at Dolly. In Indianapolis at the Claypool Hotel the whole team wound up eating in the utility room of the kitchen when service was refused to Dolly in the restaurant. After that Fuzzy [Levane] and I made up our minds to eat in the hotel room with Dolly." Levane recalled in February 1986 that "for some reason, it only happened in Indiana. . . . We went into a restaurant and they wouldn't serve us. We said, 'Holy cow, what's this?' And we all walked out." During the 1946–47 play-offs against the Zollner Pistons, King heard racial slurs from the Fort Wayne bench. When the series shifted to Rochester and the Royals won, 76–47, the *Democrat and Chronicle* reported that the win vindicated the team's "great Negro star and gentleman athlete" and that the Pistons' conduct was "a disgrace in democratic America." King played only one season with Rochester, then returned to New York City and obtained a city recreation job. According to a telephone conversation between Pop Gate and former tennis star Arthur Ashe in April 1985, Gates and King both played only one season in the NBL because of a racially motivated on-the-court fight between Gates and Chuck Meehan of the Syracuse Nationals (Tygiel 1983, 64, 190; Holzman 1991, 33–34; Holzman 1987, 20; Cervi interview; Occor correspondence; *D&C* 1986, Feb.

---

6. The sports pages of the *Pittsburgh Courier* of November 30, 1946, highlighted the feats of American black athletes and teams. It reported that in a recent exhibition game, King played "a brilliant game in the pivot" in front of a Rochester "crowd of approximately ten thousand," although he scored only one point and Edgerton Park could not possibly hold that many people. For more on Smith, see Wiggins 1983, 5–29 and Tygiel 1983, 33, 35–36, 63–64.

1; 1947, Apr. 2; 1986, Feb. 2; Ashe 1988, 3, 50, 80). Apparently, the league's owners may have feared future racial incidents. Harrison did not sign another black player until 1955, when he drafted Maurice Stokes and Ed Fleming, and obtained Dick Ricketts in a trade.

The sense of camaraderie among the players went beyond the relationships between Harrison and the various players, extending to the city of Rochester. Because of the support given the team during the immediate postwar years, the Royals of the late 1940s took pride in playing for their city of employment. According to Wanzer,

> At the time, I don't think you figured you were playing for Rochester. When I first came. Because I knew the Royals—that they were a hell of a basketball team. And I was going to one of the best teams. Then when I got to know it, I felt pretty good about playing for Rochester because I think it's a great city. When you're from New York City, Rochester is like "Oh yeah, that's the salt city" [referring to nearby Syracuse's nickname]. . . . I think I played for the team, I didn't play for the fans. My idea was always just to win. . . . But did we want to win for the people of Rochester? Yes. We wanted to win for the people of Rochester because they supported us. They supported us very well the first few years and then we wanted to win for them. (Wanzer interview)

Many Royals players—including Cervi, Wanzer, Arnie Johnson, Arnie Risen, and Dick Ricketts to name a few—became permanent residents of the city, an indication of their admiration for Rochester and their realization of employment opportunities.

Not only did some of the Royals feel an attachment to the city but the team itself was integral to the Rochester middle-class social scene after the war, as the Royals attended luncheons and banquets in their honor during the mid- to late-1940s. For example, the Royals were given a dinner in April 1947, hailed as "the biggest sports dinner ever held in Rochester" (RRS, 1946–47). Harrison made player appearances mandatory. As Cervi said, "We did it because we had to do it; we couldn't say 'no'. It was to perpetuate the game and sell the franchise." Harrison took these events very seriously, so much that when rookies Bobby Wanzer and Bill Calhoun missed a formal dinner during the 1947–48 season, Harrison fined and suspended both men, but later rescinded on his pronouncement. Wanzer recalled, "I guess at the time we didn't realize that it was mandatory to go to the function. . . . It was some sort of dinner—maybe Kiwanis." Harrison's sense of community went beyond mere promotion. He believed community service was important, and he sometimes had players visit patients in local hospitals. The relationship was reciprocal during the 1940s, as the city honored Al Cervi with a dinner in April 1946 at the Powers Hotel ballroom (Cervi interview; Wanzer interview; Holzman 1987, 12; Rochester Royals Souvenir Program of Testimonial Dinner Honoring Al Cervi).

Royals spectators in the years after World War II were relatively affluent businessmen, professionals, and white-collar workers—in other words, upper-middle-class men and women. Five players—Davies, Levane, Wanzer, Cervi, and Holzman—all support this claim in their descriptions of fans from those years. Bob Davies said Rochester Royals fans were "really high class" people who wore fur coats and that "the whole first ten rows were very affluent people," and Wanzer described Royals fans as "pretty well-to-do." Fuzzy Levane, a Royal from 1945 to 1949, wrote that "most spectators in that era were white collar workers—middle class—some upper class as we were the *Team* in Rochester. Sell out every game. It was the place to go for every Rochester family." According to Cervi, attending a Royals game "was like going to the opera." Red Holzman, with Rochester from 1945 to 1953, believed that "anyone who was anyone came to our games. It was go to the game and dinner afterward—a Rochester Saturday night ritual, a dress-up night. Men wore good suits and women put on their best dresses. Families came to the game and young marrieds, and political types came to be seen" (Salzberg 1987, 60; Wanzer interview; Andrew Leane, correspondence; Cervi interview; Holzman 1991, 18).

Besides these player testimonies, Jerry Flynn, who did radio play-by-play for the Royals' 1951 championship series, told a newspaper reporter in 1990 that "in those days, everybody who was anybody would show up for the Royals games, especially on Saturday nights. It was a big social event." Though Flynn and most of the former Royals testified that Royals fans were affluent, holders of the more expensive tickes were inevitably closer to the court where the players would have seen them. Both Cervi and Massino asserted that there was indeed a mixture of white- and blue-collar workers in the stands, usually divided by ticket price (*D&C* 1990, Feb. 4; Cervi interview; Massino interview).

The decline in attendance during the early 1950s indicates that some of the white-collar spectators of the late 1940s apparently began to spend their disposable income elsewhere. A solid core of fans did remain loyal to the Royals from 1945 to 1957, though their number probably varied from one to two thousand. According to Dave Ocorr, "The nucleus that was at Edgerton Park remained the nucleus at the War Memorial. But again [with] the increase in the size of the arena they didn't grab new fans, and at that time they started to lose and therefore did not have the excitement of right after the war." George Beahon concurred, stating the Royals retained a small core of upper-middle-class spectators throughout the team's stay in Rochester. Richie Regan, who started for the Royals during their final season in Rochester, recalled Royals spectators as "middle to upper middle class" and "blue-collar fans" (Ocorr correspondence; Beahon telephone conversation; Regan telephone conversation). Little primary evidence exists that can either confirm or deny the perceptions of crowd composition as reflected in the testimonies of the men who played for or covered the Royals. However, game programs shed some light on spectator change at Royals games over the years. The programs, like all advertising, were oriented toward a specific element of the population. It is possible to make quantitative and qualitative examinations of the advertisements in three Royals game programs (1946–47, 1950–51, and 1953–54) and see how they changed over time.

Quantitatively, the most noticeable changes in the programs are the reduction in both the length of the program and the number of advertisements. This obviously indicates that local businessmen gradually lost confidence in the Royals as a viable product to sponsor. The 1946–47 season program with its fifty-four pages and ninety-one advertisements stands in great contrast to the 1953–54 program with its twenty-four pages and forty-eight advertisements (table 8.3).

Many of the advertisements aimed at the "well-to-do" declined. During the late 1940s, Royals patrons often went to restaurants before games or to bars and nightclubs afterward (Wanzer interview; Cervi interview; Massino interview). Whereas the 1946–47

Table 8.3
Rochester Royals Game Programs, 1946–54

	1946–47	1950–51	1953–54
Total Pages	54	32	24
Ad Pages	38.25	27.4	19.52
Ad Percentage	70.83	85.62	81.33
No. of Ads	91	81	48
Non-Ad Pages	15.75	4.6	4.48
Non-Ad Percentage	29.17	14.38	18.67

Sources: Rochester Royals Official Programs 1946–47, 1950–51, 1953–54

program shows that 13.07 percent of advertising was from these nightspots, the figures for the successive two programs show that these advertisements sank to 7.84 and 3.94 percent respectively. Other significant quantitative declines included advertisements for printing, photography, and office equipment; home improvement products, airlines, and luggage. Naturally, these advertisements were directed at businessmen and members of the professional class (table 8.4).

Major relative increases in advertisements were for home appliances, alcohol and tobacco, the media, and sports recreation. Advertisements that remained relatively prominent and stable throughout all three programs included automobile dealers and service, clothing, and food.

There were also qualitative changes in advertisements in the three programs. Whereas the most common clothing advertisements were for affluent men's and women's apparel and shoes in the first program, cheaper sportswear and sneakers made significant appearances in the second and third programs. Perhaps the most revealing qualitative shift was the decline of advertisements for Rochester's nightspots for liquor and beer advertisements. Thus, the change in advertisements illustrates that the link between the Royals and elite Rochester community social life was damaged as it became more common in the early 1950s for Rochesterians to

Table 8.4

Rochester Royals Game Program Advertising, 1946–54

Advertisement Categories	1946–47		1950–51		1953–54	
	Pages	%	Pages	%	Pages	%
restaurants/hotels/bars/ nightclubs	5.00	13.07	2.15	7.85	0.77	3.94
auto dealers/service	5.50	14.38	3.35	12.23	1.99	10.19
clothing/sportswear/ footwear	6.00	15.69	2.59	9.45	2.64	13.52
printing/photography/ office equipment	1.75	4.58	0.72	2.63	0.33	1.69
music/home appliances/ radios/TVs	2.00	5.23	2.00	7.30	1.66	8.50
beer/liquor/tobacco	1.65	4.31	5.01	18.28	2.78	14.24
food/beverage	3.00	7.84	2.89	10.55	1.85	9.48
professional service[a]	1.50	3.92	0.38	1.39	0.33	1.69
personal service[b]	2.25	5.88	2.21	8.07	1.52	7.79
home improvement/ furniture	1.75	4.58	0.11	0.40	0.11	0.56
media	1.50	3.92	1.66	6.06	1.44	7.38
airlines/luggage	1.75	4.58	0.11	0.40	0.11	0.56
sport recreation/ horse racing	1.25	3.27	1.00	3.65	2.33	11.94
transportation	0.35	0.92	0.11	0.40	0.22	1.33
jewelry/watches	1.25	3.27	1.00	3.65	0.33	1.69
delicatessens	0.50	1.31	0.00	0.00	0.00	0.00
gasoline	0.50	1.31	1.00	3.65	0.67	3.43
flowers	0.50	1.31	0.33	1.20	0.33	1.69
other[c]	0.25	0.65	0.78	2.85	0.11	0.56
Totals	38.25	100.02	27.40	100.01	19.52	99.98

Sources: Rochester Royals Official Programs 1946–47, 1950–51, and 1953–54
Notes: [a] Includes life insurance, financing, real estate, stocks, banking.
    [b] Includes dry cleaning, drug sores, department stores, modern stores, eye care, furnace cleaner.
    [c] Includes sports goods/toys, school, metal works, vending machines, utility, government.
    Errors in totals due to rounding.

stay home to drink alcohol and socialize. The shift also indicates a move by Royals sponsors away from the products associated with postwar white-collar America. A middle-class migration to Rochester's suburban areas was partly responsible for the dissociation between the Royals and professional and white-collar Rochesterians, as those with greater affluence focused on domestic life and abandoned the central city to less-affluent newcomers, namely blacks and Hispanics. In fact, Rochester's growth rate between 1940 and 1950 was only 2.3 percent, while the rest of Monroe County grew by 36.7 percent (McKelvey 1961, 262, 282–83, 308–10; Rader 1984, 34–35; Jackson 1985, 272–82; U.S. Bureau of the Census 1952, 15–32).[7] For many Royals fans of the late 1940s, the drive to Edgerton Park on the city's west side may have simply become an inconvenience.

The decline in fan support was evident as early as the 1950–51 NBA championship season. The local newspapers publicized the Royals' victory over the New York Knickerbockers and recognized the achievement, but the city was not excited about the victory. Both Rochester newspapers congratulated the Royals with brief editorials for their world title, the *Democrat and Chronicle* admitting that the championship was "a valuable shot-in-the-arm for local sports." Referring to the title, Harrison said, "I left the next day for Florida. [The people of Rochester] didn't do anything. They didn't have any cheers. They didn't give us any dinners. They didn't have any luncheons." At a team reunion in May 1984, Bob Davies said, "A lot of people just took it for granted when we won it in '51. They didn't do things like have parades back then" (*D&C* 1951, Apr. 23; 1984, May 13; *T-U* 1957, Apr. 23; Harrison interview). The statements by Harrison and Davies indicate the complacency of Royals fans by 1951, and suggest problems with community support that worsened in the season to come.

The Rochester Royals franchise was a central community institution of middle-class Rochesterians after World War II, and Les

7. From 1940 to 1950 Rochester's population rose from 324,975 and the rest of the county rose from 113,255 to 154,874. By 1960 the city's growth rate was −4.2 percent, as its population fell to 318,611, while the rest of the county's grew by 72.9 percent to 267,776 (U.S. Dept. of Commerce 1961, 16–34).

Harrison's control over his team ensured a familylike atmosphere that corresponded well with the values of its fans. Though ethnicity and race were important in the selection of players, the men who played the game associated themselves with the team, and not by ethnic heritage. Finally, the crowd composition of the Royals changed as attendance declined and Rochester's upper-middle-class population abandoned the city's only major league franchise for other interests.

It was evident by the mid-1950s that Harrison and the Royals were having a difficult time accepting the fact that the team's performance level and attendance were poor. Harrison symbolically vented his frustration when he and his players intimidated a referee in March 1954 after a loss to their rivals, the Minneapolis Lakers. For the Royals' actions, Podoloff levied a $500 fine (then an NBA record) on Harrison. After twelve seasons in league play, a 456–302 regular season record, countless exhibition wins, four division titles, and three championships, Harrison decided to transfer the Royals to Cincinnati in April 1957. This decision followed a trend, common in the 1950s, for professional franchises to shift to larger and vacant markets. A few months earlier, the Fort Wayne Pistons announced that they would move to Detroit. The Royals averaged about twenty-three hundred people per game for the 1956–57 season, and according to Harrison, the team needed to average thirty-five hundred to offset operating expenses. He cited escalating operational costs and Rochester's relatively small metropolitan population as the main reasons for the move (*NYT* 1954, Mar. 30; 1957, Feb. 15; *D&C* 1957, Apr. 4).

Though Cincinnati was 36.6 percent larger than Rochester in city population and 50.3 percent larger in total metropolitan population, other factors that helped Harrison choose Cincinnati were the presence of a fourteen thousand-seat arena, the eventual availability of local collegian Oscar Robertson (University of Cincinnati) through the territorial draft, and the area's general interest in basketball. The new Cincinnati Royals finished the 1957–58 season with a record of 33–39 and averaged only thirty-seven hundred in attendance. The poor season, low attendance, and the contraction of encephalitis by star Maurice Stokes all pushed the Harrisons to sell the franchise and get out of the professional basketball business after more than twenty-five years (U.S. Bureau of the Census 1962; *D&C* 1957, Apr. 3; Apr. 7; *NYT* 1957, Apr. 4; Harrison interview).

The first potential buyer of the Royals was Norman Shapiro of Rochester, who sought to return the team to its birthplace. The Harrisons agreed to sell the Cincinnati Royals to Shapiro for $200,000, with the stipulation that Les Harrison be retained as a consultant and scout for five years at $10,000 per year. Petitions were circulated in the city in an attempt to convince the NBA owners of the sincerity of the proposed franchise transfer, but the league did not approve it (*D&C* 1958, Mar. 19; Mar. 27; Mar. 28; Apr. 1; Apr 3; Apr. 5; Apr. 8; *NYT* 1958, Mar. 27; *T-U* 1958, Apr. 8). The league's owners refused to approve the transfer out of fear that a major television contract, then in the negotiating stages, would be dropped, as the "sponsors supposedly want the games coming from "major league cities" and they do not rate Rochester a 'major' "(*D&C* 1958, Mar. 29). The only owner who publicly supported the Royals' move to Rochester was Danny Biasone of the Syracuse Nationals (*D&C* 1958, Mar. 25). This sentiment was an early indication of the growing importance of television market size to the location of professional sports franchises. After the NBA voided the Harrison-Shapiro sale, a local Cincinnati group headed by Frank E. Wood Jr. bought the Royals for $225,000 at the same meeting. Wood was a major stockholder in the Royals' home court, the Cincinnati Garden (*D&C* 1958, Apr. 8; *NYT* 1958, Apr. 8; Koppett 1968, 114–15).

The decision to move the Royals from Rochester to Cincinnati and the resolution to sell the team a year later were no doubt difficult for Harrison because of his attachment to his lifelong home and his lifelong love.

I didn't want to leave my—I didn't want to leave Rochester born and brought up here and I didn't want to take them [the Royals] out of here. We didn't have money. We figured we'd move to another city, maybe we could do better. . . . This is a minor league city. If they are supporting a minor league hockey team and don't want an NBA basketball [team] they should have their head examined. . . . They didn't realize what a good thing they had here. That's all. They didn't realize it. That was something special. . . . Here we had a product—one of the nicest products this town'll ever have—they'll never be major league I liked to give my town here and they didn't support it. And a lot of 'em are ashamed of themselves now. They'll see me today and they'll say, "Geez, Les, we should have supported you." What are you gonna do? (Harrison interview)

In retrospect, the fate of the Rochester Royals carried the air of inevitability. Given the major trends in professional team sports during the postwar era, relocation or dissolution were the only likely outcomes. Major league baseball and football franchises usually moved to other cities during the postwar era because they already occupied a multiteam market in which one team gained supremacy in popularity and attendance, their stadium or the neighborhood or both surrounding the stadium were deteriorating, or they wanted to exploit an open market (Lowenfish 1978, 71–82; Sullivan 1987; Riess 1989, 231–37; Rader 1984, 58–67; Golenbock 1984, 428–49). The reasons for basketball shifts are similar, and the Rochester Royals moved mainly because of insufficient support and to capitalize on open territory in Cincinnati.

Modern professional sports franchises have often had the dual identity of being a profit-oriented business and an emotionally charged community institution. Promoters, owners, and politicians have often blurred the two or emphasized the passion and psychology of sports at the expense of its role as a business in attempts to show the special role of sports teams in American society and even to warrant special consideration. The United States federal government investigated the four major sports leagues in 1957, trying to determine whether or not they were in violation of antitrust laws, and the NBA stressed the passionate side of sports. Realizing the economic difficulties of his league's owners, NBA president Maurice Podoloff testified before a House committee that

Professional sports is not a business: professional sports is not a business because if you look at these—if you look at these gate receipt reports and see the money they have lost, you must be an addict and a bit of a lunatic to stay in professional sports. It is something unusual. I think the man who promotes professional sports is a frustrated athlete who vicariously tries to do what he cannot because . . . I have seen more than one team owner and manager come off the floor on the verge of tears. He didn't moan and groan because he had lost money. He moaned and groaned because he had lost the game. (U.S. House Committee on the Judiciary 1958, 2896)

Podoloff's statements contain elements of perceived myth and economic truth and in sum they indicate the identity crisis this youthful commercial enterprise experienced during its transformation in the postwar era. Though he was surely talking about basketball when he generically referred to "professional sports," he probably also had Les Harrison in mind in his vague description of NBA owners of the 1950s. This duality engendered problems for Harrison, all culminating in his decision to sell the franchise in 1958. What began as one man's dream to play and organize basketball ended in the sad ordeal of having to sell what had become dear to his life.

The Royals had a 555–634 record in their fifteen-year stay in Cincinnati before moving to Kansas City in 1972. The team was renamed the Kings because it did not want to confuse the franchise with the Royals of baseball's American League. From there, the franchise shifted once again to Sacramento in 1985 where a championship banner from the 1950–51 season—the franchise's sole NBA title—still hangs, linking the past with the present. The feats of the old Rochester Royals were not forgotten as Bob Davies (1969), Les Harrison (1979), Al Cervi (1984), Red Holzman (1985), and Bobby Wanzer (1986) were elected to the Naismith Memorial Basketball Hall of Fame in Springfield, Massachusetts. "In recognition of his community service and as a major league sports pioneer," Nazareth College of Rochester awarded Harrison an honorary doctor of humanities degree in May 1985. And finally, after a thirty-three-year wait, the NBA presented a championship trophy to the members of the 1950–51 Royals in May 1984 in Rochester (*T-U* 1988, Mar. 30; Rochester Basketball Classic Program 1991; *D&C* 1984, May 13).

9

Becoming American

Jewish Writers on the Sporting Life

Allen Guttmann

A commonplace of literary criticisms is that Jewish writers emerged in the 1940s and 1950s as a major force in American letters. Less widely realized is that Jewish writers have also contributed disproportionately to the development of sport as a theme for novels, plays, poems, and stories. The explanation for both phenomena lies in the complex processes by which immigrants to the United States have become Americans. To understand why Jews seemed in the postwar period to almost dominate American literature and why Jewish writers seemed especially fascinated by baseball and other sports, we must be students of history and sociology before we can be psychologists or textual analysts. To say this is not to denigrate psychological or linguistic approaches to literature; it is merely to insist that such themes as "the son's search for the father" are best understood when one realizes who these fathers and sons were and what kind of world they inhabited. (For the fathers-and-sons approach, see Malin 1965.)

I have argued elsewhere, at some length, that Jewish writers seemed to dominate the postwar literary scene because they were obsessed with the theme of Americanization. As they became fully assimilated into American society, they began to ask themselves, often with searing intensity, how is it possible to be simultaneously a Jew and an American? (Guttmann 1971)—not *is* it possible, which might have seemed a reasonable question before assimilation had begun, but *how* is it possible. In other words, assimilation and the resultant crisis of identity fueled the fires of literary ambition. From the need to understand the self came the ability to show others the complexity of modern identity. Jews were not the only people to arrive at Ellis Island and experience culture shock, but Jewish immigrants from the ghettos and *shtetlach* of eastern Europe can be distinguished by two facts: first, their journey to America was a more nearly total cultural transformation than was, for example, the immigration of Protestants arriving from the British Isles; second, they already possessed a highly developed literary tradition. Although Catholic immigrants who had been driven from the peasant villages of Ireland or Italy and Africans uprooted from the tribal societies and sold into slavery also suffered intense dislocation and cultural disorientation, they did not very often, at least not until rather recently, turn their anguished experiences into literature. The *Ostjuden* did. (It is significant that German Jews arriving in the United States during the nineteenth century were seldom moved to dramatize the experience of assimilation in fiction or poetry. They had the requisite verbal skills but not the psychological need.)

The Americanization of east European Jews was characterized by another important factor. While most immigrants, even the Afro-Americans who were scarcely "immigrants" in the ordinary sense, tended to linger at least a generation in a cultural twilight zone between the old homeland and the New World, first-generation Jews frequently rejected the rich but burdensome traditions of their Orthodox ancestors to survive and succeed in America. The dilemma of the Orthodox Jew was poignantly described by the hero of Abraham Cahan's novel (1917), *The Rise of David Levinsky*:

> If you are a Jew of the type to which I belonged when I came to New York and you attempt to bend your religion to the spirit of your new surroundings, it breaks. It falls to pieces. The very clothes I wore and the very food I ate had a fatal effect on my religious habits. A whole book could be written on the influence of a starched collar and a necktie on a man who was brought up as I was. It was

inevitable that, sooner or later, I should let a barber shave my sprouting beard. (110)

For Russian or Polish Jews like Levinsky, the culture shock was intense, and the literary response was equally intense. But what does this have to do with sport? A great deal. Sport, an increasingly important modern institution, became a central metaphor for Americanization, of which it was a small but vital part. Because sport had never been a significant aspect of Orthodox tradition, it was an especially powerful metaphor of contrast.

For Jews as for others, the relative freedom of modern sport from the ascriptive limitations of race, religion, nationality, gender, and social class made it an especially attractive embodiment of democratic ideals. Jews, like other disadvantaged groups, were aware of the all too numerous betrayals of the ideal, in sport as elsewhere, but sport seemed nonetheless the domain where the ideal was most closely approached. Because sport also provided opportunities for what Johan Huizinga, following Friedrich Schiller, called "the play-instinct," its appeals were all but irresistible.

These generalizations, inevitably simplified, can be exemplified by a scene from Cahan's first novel, *Yekl: A Tale of the New York Ghetto* (1896). The novel opens in a sweatshop in which Yekl, now renamed Jake, boasts to his fellow immigrants that he is a real American because he understands the mysteries of sport. He tells the others all about John L. Sullivan. Indicating that Yekl communicates mainly in Yiddish, Cahan uses italics for interspersed English terms, many of which refer to sport. "Jimmie Corbett *leaked* him and Jimmie *leaked* Cholly Meetchel, too. *You can betch you' bootsh!* Johnnie could not leak Chollie, *becaush* he is a big *bluffer*, Chollie is . . . But Jimmie *pundished* him. *Oh, didn't he him out of shight!*" (4) When the other workers, simultaneously impressed and appalled, point out that boxing is a brutal and brutalizing activity, unsuited for an educated and civilized person, Yekl has a ready answer: "*Alla right*, let it be as you say; the *fighters* are not *ejecate*. No, not a bit! But what will You say to *baseball*? All *college boys* and *tony peoplesh* play it" (10). The others admit to the truth of these assertions. That "college boys" were more likely to play football than baseball is irrelevant. Baseball was the national game. To know baseball was to be a real American.

Cahan never did write an entire novel in which sport was a central theme, but one should note that the protagonist of his longest and best work, David Levinsky, falls in love with a Russian-born girl whose Americanization has reached the point where she, like Philip Roth's Brenda Patimkin, plays a mean game of tennis.

The two sports that attract Yekl, baseball and boxing, were the first sports to fascinate American writers, Jews and non-Jews alike. Jewish writers possibly turned to these sports because they seemed to represent the attractive and the unattractive aspects of Americanization. If baseball, despite its urban origins and popularity, carried with it pastoral connotations (hence the myth of Abner Doubleday and the cow pasture), boxing was unmistakably associated with the rough and tumble of city streets. Baseball was the fair promise of a place in the sun; boxing was the grim reality of survival of the fittest. Jewish writers tended to ignore the fact well recognized by Robert Coover in *The Universal Baseball Association* that baseball was also a very modern game characterized by a myth of "scientific play" and an obsession for quantified, measurable achievement (Guttmann 1978, 92–114).

In the generation of Jewish writers that followed Cahan, sport remained a minor metaphor. Ludwig Lewisohn's fictionalized auto-biography, *The Island Within* (1928), is a passionate polemic against assimilation and for the concept of Jewish peoplehood. Lewisohn's reference to the national game is part of his Menckenesque dismissal of American society as a mob of half-wits: "The state is an image—brazen, remote, implacable except by stealthy magnates, the augurs, fat-paunched, bellow at each other on the public roads, the gates of the land are sealed; the duped and stupefied populace . . . dances about fundamentalist preachers, baseball pitchers and a Rumanian queen" (5). Few writers have been as negative about sport as Lewisohn was.

In the best of his many novels, *The Old Bunch* (1937), Meyer Levin tells the story of a group of second-generation Chicago Jews whose determined drive for Americanization makes of them doctors, lawyers, teachers, union organizers, businessmen, criminals, artists. There is no rabbi among them, but one of the bunch becomes a passionate bicycle racer. Why Levin did not choose a more typically representative sport, baseball or boxing, is puzzling, but Sol Meisel's races are dramatically and positively presented.

When Clifford Odets wrote *Golden Boy* (1937), he had more than simply assimilation in mind. Although several Jewish characters are in the play, Odets chose to make his hero an Italian American— a technique of displacement that he was by no means the last to employ. Odets concentrated not on the abandonment of religious orthodoxy but on the conflict between the concert stage and the boxing arena. Joe Bonaparte plays the violin, which is a stereotyped link to the musical culture of the old country; he is good with his fists as well as with his fingers, which skill draws him toward the new environment. It is not much of a play; the situation is implausible, the characters are flat, the dialogue is stilted, and the conclusion, in which Joe is killed in an automobile crash, is melodramatic. Nonetheless, *Golden Boy* is one of the earliest exploitations of sport as a metaphor for Americanization.

Budd Schulberg, a much better writer than Odets, was drawn, as Odets was, to sport as well as to the workers' struggle for unionization. (Schulberg's screenplay *On the Waterfront* can be compared with Odets's *Waiting for Lefty.*) *The Harder They Fall* (1947) is a landmark in the literary use of sport. The story of Argentine heavyweight boxer El Toro Molino is of far more than historical importance. One can still read it for insight into the penumbra of subterfuge, deceit, and criminality that surrounded the ring. It is not, in the words of one of Schulberg's characters, about "violinists with brittle hands" (8). No more than Odets, however, did Schulberg focus upon the Jewish boxers who were then vastly overrepresented in the profession. He chose to model El Toro Molino on the Italian heavyweight Primo Carnera, whose career certainly had its comic and its tragic moments. Schulberg concentrates on the tragic. Boxing is "a genuinely manly art, dragged down through the sewers of human greed" (281). The writer-narrator is asked, "Mr. Lewis, what is it that turned a fine sport into a dirty business?" "Money," he replies (7). In this case the money is made by a cabal of crooks who build the untalented giant's reputation with a series of fixed fights and then, when he is battered and hospitalized in the aftermath of his one genuine bout, cheat him of his earnings and abandon him. His owner's heartless comment? "Did you ever see a worse bum?" (334).

A Stone for Danny Fisher (1951) is not in the same aesthetic class with *The Harder They Fall*, but Harold Robbins deserves mention as one of the very few authors to have created a Jewish boxer. Driven by poverty, Danny Fisher ignores his father's vehement, horrified, religiously motivated opposition and begins to make a name for himself as a fighter. Unlike Schulberg's innocent, victimized Argentine, Robbins's hero double-crosses his gangster owner and wins a fight he had been paid to lose. He compounds his sins by winning the love of the owner's girlfriend and repeatedly mauling the hitmen who attempt—over the next several years—to mete out gangland justice. In the end, inevitably, the mob gets its revenge and the moral is plain. There are better roads to success than the crooked street of the fight business. (In subsequent best-sellers, Robbins seems to have explored most of them.)

The year after Robbins's *A Stone for Danny Fisher* appeared, Bernard Malamud published his first novel, *The Natural* (1952). Although the novel's glory has faded somewhat, it too has historical importance. Not yet aware that his true vocation as a writer was to create a mythical ghetto peopled with cobblers, bakers, tailors, marriage brokers, and storekeepers who might just as well have lived in Warsaw or Vilna as in New York, Malamud attempted a fantasy of sport and religious myth. Malamud's real interest lies less in baseball than in the vegetation myths of divine death and rebirth that are a main theme of Sir James Frazier's *The Golden Bough* and form the central structure of T. S. Eliot's poem, *The Waste Land*. Roy Hobbs is a version of the grail knight questing after the cup from which Jesus drank at the Last Supper, and Roy's manager, Pop Fisher, is a version of the mysteriously wounded Fisher King, whose impotence has made the wasteland, in this case the baseball field, arid and infertile. In many ways the book is an erudite literary spoof.

Malamud's hero comes from the Far West rather than from the slums of Baltimore or the sidewalks of New York. When he arrives in the city, the grass of the outfield turns green and he "romped in it like a happy calf in its pasture" (66). The pastoral elements are heightened to myth. Roy's magic bat, Wonderboy, is also his "foolproof lance" (9), with which he terrorizes luckless pitchers. The ancient goddesses—Ishtar, Isis, Aphrodite—appear in the guise of the mysterious Harriet Bird, referred to as "a snappy goddess" (25). The first part of the novel ends when Roy is shot by Harriet Bird in his Chicago hotel room. The scene mingles memories of the dead gods—Tammuz, Osiris, Adonis, Jesus—with less mythical resemblances to the sad fate of Eddie Waitkus.

The stage is set for the second part of the novel, in which Malamud introduces his version of Eliot's mythic poem. The wounded Fisher King, who rules over the sterile land, appears as Pop Fisher, manager of the New York Knights, a man afflicted with itchy hands. He waits vainly for the life-giving rain: "It's been a blasted dry season. No rains at all. The grass is worn scabby in the outfield and the infield is cracking. My heart feels as dry as dirt for the little I have to show for all my years in the game" (34–35). Hobbs brings rain to the parched land and an end to the team's slump. The first time he comes to bat, a tremendous noise cracks the sky and "a few drops of rain spattered to the ground" (63). Moments later comes the deluge, which turns the grass green at last. Pop Fisher's hands heal. Unfortunately, Roy demonstrates a selfish pride that finally makes him unfit for the task of the grail knight. His obstinate love of wicked Memo Paris, rather than earth motherly Iris Lemon, dooms him. His recognition comes too late. The novel concludes not with the resurrection of the fertility god but with recollections of the Black Sox. Roy changes his mind about throwing the play-off game, but his beloved Wonderboy splits in two, he strikes out impotently, and the newspapers expose his past and present misdeeds. "Say it ain't true, Roy," begs the newsboy, and Roy cannot (190). Malamud has exploited the possibilities of baseball as a rite of spring to moralize about ambition and ingratitude. The baseball buff might enjoy the allusions to Eddie Waitkus or "Shoeless" Joe Jackson, but no American is liable to confuse Malamud's wacky descriptions with anything that happens on a baseball diamond. The point is, finally, that Malamud realized that baseball was a perfect vehicle for an *American* version of a universal myth.

Bernard Malamud and Philip Roth arrived almost simultaneously on the literary scene and have long been recognized as leading literary exponents of peoplehood (Malamud) and assimilation (Roth). In his first collection of stories, *Goodbye, Columbus* (1959), Roth, despite his enthusiasm for sport, beautifully expressed in an essay entitled "My Baseball Years," satirized its worship by assimilated American Jews. The title story opens with the brilliant evocation of two worlds.

The first time I saw Brenda she asked me to hold her glasses. Then she stepped out to the edge of the diving board and looked foggily into the pool; it could have been drained, myopic Brenda would never have known it. She dove beautifully, and a moment later she was swimming back to the side of the pool, her head of short-clipped auburn hair held up, straight ahead of her, as though it were a rose on a long stem. She glided to the edge and then was beside me. "Thank you," she said, her eyes watery though not from the water. She extended a hand for her glasses but did not put them on until she turned and headed away. I watched her move off. Her hands suddenly appeared behind her. She caught the bottom of her suit between thumb and index finger and flicked what flesh had been showing back where it belonged. My blood jumped.

That night before dinner, I called her.

"Who are you calling?" my Aunt Gladys asked.

"Some girl I met today."

"Doris introduced you?"

"Doris wouldn't introduce me to the guy who drains the pool, Aunt Gladys."

"Don't criticize all the time. A cousin's a cousin. How did you meet her?"

"I didn't really meet her. I saw her."

"Who is she?"

"Her last name is Patimkin."

"Patimkin I don't know."

Neil Klugman wants desperately, too desperately it turns out in the end, to move from the working-class ghetto of Newark to the airy expanse of suburban Short Hills. Brenda can make it possible. He meets Brenda at the pool. He sees her again in the middle of a tennis match. When he visits Short Hills, he enters a ludic fantasy:

Outside, through the wide picture window, I could see the back lawn with its twin oak trees. I say oaks, though fancifully, one might call them sporting-goods trees. Beneath their branches, like fruit dropped from their limbs, were two irons, a golf ball, a tennis can, a baseball bat, basketball, a first-baseman's glove, and what was apparently a riding crop. (21–22)

When Brenda suggests he begin running, he goes to the track and runs, "and always at the end there was the little click of the watch and Brenda's arms" (73). He plays table tennis and basketball with her younger sister (who must always be allowed to win). He attempts conversation with sport-obsessed Ron Patimkin, his prospective brother-in-law, whose mind (what there is of it) remains forever caught somewhere back on the basketball courts of Ohio State University. If there is a single criticism to be made of Roth's use of sport as a symbol of Americanization, it is that the symbolism is probably too obvious.

It was probably inevitable that Roth write a novel about baseball. Unlike Malamud, whose relationship to baseball seems wholly literary, Roth was a passionate baseball fan before he was a writer. Of this passion for the game, Eric Solomon writes (1984), "For Melville, whaling, for Twain, the river, for Hemingway, war, for Roth, baseball" (65). His baseball fiction, *The Great American Novel* (1973), is no more realistic than *The Natural*, but its combination of literary parody ("Call me Smitty" is the Melvillean first sentence), baseball allusion, and mythic high jinks has turned out to be more durable. The book traces the comic adventures of the Ruppert Mundys, a team in the mythical Patriot League. Their story is told sympathetically by the loquacious baseball writer Word Smith. With characters such as Gil Gamesh (identified, in case anyone missed the reference, as a Babylonian), Roth seems to have a wonderful time. Certainly most readers do, if they have a taste for rollicking satire and hyperbolic burlesque. Throughout, Roth makes the most of ethnic humor. Frenchy Astarte, for instance, has played for Latin American and Japanese teams and now fears sale to India, where he would be "playing ball next with a bunch of guys talking it up in Hindi and running around the bases in bedsheets" (Roth 1973, 98). Jews figure in the novel as owners rather than as players. They are proud of their role, which they see as the final certification of their Americanization. "Only in America . . . could a Jew rise to such heights! Only in America could a Jew ever hope to become the owner of a major league baseball team!" (272). True enough. Where else can Jews own baseball teams?[1]

---

1. Max Apple's novel *Zip* (1978) is a variant of the theme of Jewish sports ownership. Ira Goldstein inherits a junkyard and becomes the backer of a Hispanic fighter whose adventures include a fight in Havana arranged by Fidel Castro and Lyndon Johnson, reported by Howard Cosell, and witnessed by J. Edgar Hoover, suspended over the ring in a basket.

There is little in Roth's novel that one can point to as a sign of the author's Jewishness. There is even less in the baseball stories of Mark Harris. Indeed, it is a question whether *The Southpaw* (1953) and *Bang the Drum Slowly* (1956) are in any significant way *Jewish*. Harris himself has rather heatedly insisted that they are, but it is doubtful that readers unfamiliar with Harris's autobiography have been aware that he is a Jew. His protagonist, Henry Wiggen, is a twentieth-century version of Mark Twain's vernacular heroes. He is a modern Huck Finn, telling his own story in his wonderfully vivid, and wonderfully ungrammatical, language. Henry Wiggen is Everyman on the mound, the ordinary person with a special talent, pitching. The best part of the novel is not the plot, which is minimal, but the characterization, which is a delight.

The Southpaw is a good novel; *Bang the Drum Slowly* is a great one, the only baseball novel to rival Robert Coover's brilliant *The Universal Baseball Association*. In this second novel, Henry Wiggen has comic difficulties with the Bureau of Internal Revenue, but the book is not about *his* problems at all. The book is about Bruce Pearson, of Bainbridge, Georgia, a country boy who functions as a symbol of rural simplicity and an emblem of man in nature. He learned to play baseball in a pre–Jimmy Carter field of peanut hay: he was astonished to learn that the New York Mammoths intended to pay him money to continue at the game. The big leagues are a mixture of urban and rural types, but Henry's advice to Bruce, who lacks confidence in his own abilities, is suggestive: "Half the pitchers you face are only country boys like yourself, and the other half are only country boys from the city" (Harris 1956, 73).

The plot of the novel is a pastoral version of the Lou Gehrig story. Bruce calls Henry from the Mayo Clinic in Minnesota and tells him that he has been given only a few months to live. His speech is comical: "It means I am doomded" (12), but the novel is a strange combination of comedy and tragedy. Henry and Bruce spend the time just before spring training in Bainbridge, Georgia, where Bruce's family welcomes the two to sit on the front porch, to talk of crops and hogs, to comment on the sultry weather, to reminisce in a slow country way. The countryside is full of memories for Bruce, who overcomes his taciturnity enough to tell a few stories and give Henry a sense of the place.

The baseball season is a contrast, partly comic, partly grim. There is rough-and-tumble competition, the grate of personalities against one another as men travel and live together under tension; there is hostility and meanness as well as prankish camaraderie. Henry finds himself changed by the knowledge of Bruce's illness—"When your roomie is libel to die any day on you you do not think about bonus clauses, and that is the truth whether anybody happens to think so or not" (139). When the rest of the team learns about Bruce's fate, there is an extraordinary moment of harmony and reconciliation that begins when one of the players sings Bruce's favorite song.

> O bang the drum slowly and play the fife lowly
> Play the dead march as they carry me on,
> Put bunches of roses all over my coffin,
> Roses to deaden the clods as they fall. (212)

"It made me feel very sad," writes Henry. "Yet I knew that some of the boys felt the same, and knowing it made me feel better" (212). He goes on to express love in the awkward, touching way appropriate to the situation: you felt warm towards them, and you looked at them, and them at you, and you were both alive, and you might as well said, 'Ain't it something? Being alive, I mean! Ain't it really quite a great thing at that.' and if they would of been a girl you would of kissed them, though you never said such a thing out loud but only went on about your business" (212). Alas, when Bruce dies, Henry is the only member of the club at the burial. Pastoral harmony is never more than momentary. Harris has written sequels to these first two Henry Wiggen novels, but he has not yet matched the greatness of *Bang the Drum Slowly.*

What Malamud, Roth, and Harris leave fairly implicit in their novels about baseball, none of which has a Jewish protagonist, Irwin Shaw has made quite explicit. In *Voices of a Summer Day* (1965), baseball has become a traditional way to claim an American identity. Israel Federov "was made into an American catching behind the plate bare-handed in the years between 1895 and 1910" (142). His son Benjamin, the novel's protagonist, played baseball in his youth. Taking *his* son Michael to a game, Benjamin thinks of the Jews as an "uprooted people" who have abandoned their "tribal paraphernalia." He goes with Michael to the Polo Grounds, because "when *he* was six *his* father had taken him to the Polo Grounds" (152–53). Watching Michael play, years later, Benjamin realizes even more deeply what the game means to him.

> The sounds were the same through the years—the American sounds of summer, the tap of bat against ball, the cries of the infielders, the wooden plump of the ball into catchers' mitts, the umpires calling "Strike three and you're out." The generations circled the bases, the dust rose for forty years as runners slid in from third, dead boys hit doubles, famous men made errors at shortstop, forgotten friends tapped the clay from their spikes with their bats as they stepped up to the batter's box, coaches' voices warned, across the decades, "Tag up, tag up!" on fly balls. The distant, mortal innings of boyhood and youth. (12)

Besides having made the symbolic nature of sport wholly and vividly explicit, Shaw is also the only Jewish writer (to my knowledge) to have explored the world of the risk-intoxicated downhill skier and sport parachutist. Michael Storrs, the neurotic protagonist of *The Top of the Hill* (1979), is a WASP banker when he is not seeking to break his bones. He finally overcomes his suicidal impulses, which suggests perhaps that Shaw had begun to feel his age.

Malamud, Roth, Harris, and Shaw are established writers with international reputations. They are by no means the only Jewish writers to have written baseball fiction. Charles Einstein's *The Only Game in Town* is a youthful effort and best forgotten, but Eliot Asinof's *Man on Spikes* (1955) is a fine account of a young player (possibly but probably not Jewish) who spends years in the minor leagues and then, given one last chance to make the majors, fails. On the other hand, the protagonist of Roger Kahn's *The Seventh Game* (1982) is successful enough professionally to pitch in the World Series, but he has lost his way morally. His punishment is to lose the seventh game, but Kahn grants him insight and a second chance to recoup the moral failure. Don Kowet's novel, also called *The Seventh Game* (1977), is a thriller (the pitcher's daughter is kidnapped and the blackmailers want him to lose the game for them) of some literary substance. Jerome Charyn's *The Seventh Babe* (1979) is a grotesque fantasy in the tradition of *The Natural* and *The Great American Novel.* The younger writers seem to have moved beyond the point where baseball functions symbolically as a meta-phor of Americanization. They take it for granted that they are Americans and that baseball is, of course, their national game.

One reason for lessened symbolic emphasis is that baseball can no longer claim to be the undisputed national game. If it has not lost that cherished position to football, it must, at the very least, share the limelight (and the television screen) with football and basketball. Jews have been comparatively hesitant about football as a metaphor. Most of the many football novels that have appeared in the past decade have been written by Gentiles (or by Jews who have changed their names and escaped identification as Jews). Because Jews have not neglected boxing as a subject for fiction, it is difficult to imagine that football's violence is the reason for the relative lack of interest.

The neglect is not total. Dorian Fliegel and Sam Koperwas are among the Jews who have dramatized football. Fliegel's *The Fix* (1978) belongs in the tradition of Ernest Hemingway and Sherwood Anderson. In "I Want to Know Why" and "My Old Man" Hemingway and Anderson told of the disillusionment of boys who realized that their fathers were dishonest sportsmen. In *The Fix,* Fliegel's narrator, Jack Rose, learns to his dismay that the coach whom many have idealized worked hand in glove with assorted mobsters to fix a whole series of games. Fliegel explores the dishon-esty of commercialized sport, but, although indicating a sharp eye for the ethnic relationships in modern sport, he has no point to make about ethnicity. Koperwas, however, revels in ethnicity and creates a Jewish running back who loves the violent aspects of the game and fights like an animal for a place on a semipro team dominated by black athletes.

Jake, the hero of Koperwas's *Westchester Bull* (1976), prays to the God of the Chosen People to choose him. "Ace of Aces, Make me fast. In the end zone I will sing your praises. I swear it." If chosen, he promises to be "your little Jewboy forever" (223). His mother sits *shivah* because she considers Jake ritually dead, but his brother offers him tasteless encouragement: "Score touchdowns for the Six Million. Gain yardage for the religion that's been around" (9). It is just as well that Ludwig Lewisohn did not live long enough to discover this debased form of assimilation through sport.

For reasons that escape detection, Jewish writers have begun to publish novels about basketball now that black players have replaced the Jews who were among the great names of the 1940s and 1950s. Indeed, Jay Neugeboren's *Big Man,* which explores a point-fixing scandal and its consequences, has a black protagonist. Neugeboren's empathy is remarkable, and the book deserved the enthusiastic reviews it received. Jeremy Larner's *Drive, He Said* (1964) concerns the erotic and athletic adventures of one Hector Bloom. The novel, a somewhat surrealistic rendering of college life, was awarded the first Delta Prize by Walter van Tilburg Clark, Leslie Fiedler, and Mary McCarthy. The hero of Charles Rosen's *Have Jump Shot Will Travel* (1975) is probably not a Jew, but Robert Greenfield's *Haymon's Crowd* (1978) and Bob Levin's *The Best Ride to New York* (1978) are novels about Jewish basketball players. All three of these more recent novels depict a world of fast talk and hard knocks. They dramatize racial tension, which is scarcely surprising in a sport where black players have ousted whites from stardom, and in Greenfield's novel the tension erupts into violence. In this way too, sadly, sport is a useful metaphor.

One can well end with Jenifer Levin's fine novel, *Water Dancer* (1982). It is nearly unique on two counts: it is a work of serious sports fiction written by a woman; it is about a female athlete. That the swimmer Dorey Thomas is indeed the central character is not entirely certain because much of the novel concerns David "Sarge" Olsen and his wife Lana, both of whom withdrew from the world and from each other after their son, trained by Sarge for the feat, froze to death attempting to swim the San Antonio Strait. Dorey Thomas persuades Sarge to train her for the same hazardous swim. The two grow to love each other. He becomes totally absorbed in her effort: " 'You'll be'—he fished for her wrist and held it, rubbed the sponge along her arm—'the strongest lady on earth. Tear things down a little, they grow back stronger' " (145). The reference is clearly to his psychic wound as well as to her muscles. Levin forgoes the conventionally expected adultery. The book, psychologically as well as physiologically subtle, concludes with the heroic accomplishment of the impossible task. The exhausting physical feat, carried out in defiance of the bitterly cold water, heals the psychic wounds and ends the coldness between Sarge and his wife. No doubt it is a romantic novel, but some kinds of romanticism are more effective than others.

Generalizations about three generations of writers, some major, some minor, are not easy, but it is reasonable to repeat that Jewish writers have been unusually frequent among those who have turned to sports. Originally, one motive was clearly the writers' realization that sport was a central institution and, in its high ideals and its sometimes low practices, a perfect symbol for Americanization. In the passage of nearly a century, however, sport has tended gradually to become a metaphor not for an *American* but for a *human* identity. When the contemporary writer is pessimistic about the human condition, as many are, dramatization of the violent side of sport suggests a larger disillusionment. When, on the other hand, the writer clings to the notion that life is a game that can be won as well as lost, self-realization becomes the theme. Whether one thinks of the gloom of Greenfield's *Haymon's Crowd* or the glory of Levin's *Water Dancer,* sport seems as good a metaphor as it ever was.

10

Eric Rolfe Greenberg's *The Celebrant*
The Greatest (Jewish) American Baseball Novel

Eric Solomon

Eric Greenberg's *The Celebrant* (1983) stands in the history of base-ball fiction from the early efforts of Charles Van Loan and Ring Lardner through the golden age of Bernard Malamud and Philip Roth to the metafictional works of Robert Coover and W. P. Kinsella as the finest achievement in the fictional re-creation of the great game of baseball. In his novel that both in concrete detail and lyric evocation captures a young Jewish man's love of and despair with baseball as well as his identification with the superb New York Giants pitcher Christy Mathewson, Greenberg focuses mainly on the game's combination of myth and fact. Just as William Faulkner insists that the best aspect of hunting is the talk, so an important aspect of baseball is what used to be termed "the hot stove league," oldsters' winter memories of anecdotes and talk about the summer game. *The Celebrant*, following baseball's rhythms and the form of any traditional fictional discourse, moves from moments of intense concentration on the playing of the game to relaxed musing in the interior stadium of the observer's mind. And baseball, like the novel, sustains its moral code as to what is and is not done.

As I have pointed out elsewhere (1984, 43–66), the history of baseball fiction by Jewish American writers is remarkably rich, stretching from the early realistic novels of Eliot Asinof, Charles Einstein, Mark Harris, Irwin Shaw, and Gerald Green through a high point of mythic and comic fiction by Bernard Malamud, Philip Roth, Jay Neugeboren, Jerome Charyn, and Sylvia Tennenbaum to immediately contemporary baseball novels by Roger Kahn, Louis Rubin, Harry Stein, and Gary Morgenstern. Baseball references resonate in Jewish American fiction from Nelson Algren to Chaim Potok, from Paul Goodman to E. L. Doctorow, from Delmore Schwartz to Max Apple. As I have also tried to document, the reasons for the Jewish American novelist's fascination with baseball are straightforward: assimilation, acculturation, and instant historical referent, a talmudic fascination with statistics, an urban-rural common ground—in short, a substitute for *shul* and *shtetl*. And as generations change, so do the themes and forms of baseball novels. What makes Eric Rolfe Greenberg's work special, I think, is the consideration that his novel is as good as, if not better than, the classic work of Lardner, Coover, and Kinsella. Jewish acculturation as well as Christian religious concepts make *The Celebrant* not only the finest Jewish American baseball novel but, arguably, the best of all novels in the baseball genre.

● ● ●

What Greenberg accomplishes is a complex yoking of many forces of baseball narrative. He joins the historical sense of Roger Angell (badly forced in Damon Rice's *Seasons Past* or strained in Daryl Brock's *If I Never Get Back*) to the superb game descriptions of John Tunis, the ethnicity themes of Irwin Shaw or Roger Kahn, and the essentially Christian and pagan mythology of Bernard Malamud's *The Natural*. Greenberg catches the hard-boiled dialogue and colorful characterizations that reporters from Ring Lardner to Red Smith have reconstituted. The novel reflects oral history sources, such as Lawrence Ritter's *The Glory of Their Times,* and historical research like that in Eliot Asinof's *Eight Men Out,* with sure accuracy. Additionally, Greenberg enriches his sports text with the countertext of ethnic American business fiction—Abraham Cahan's *The Rise of David Levinsky* and Jerome Weidman's *I Can Get It for You Wholesale* lurk behind *The Celebrant*'s subplot of corruption. And, yes, the author puts a theoretical spin on his fiction; we must consider reader response and cultural discourse approaches as this novel's form encounters baseball's own. Finally, and most crucially, Greenberg evokes the special role that the observer, the nonparticipant, the fan, plays in the game—as W. P. Kinsella imagines in *Shoeless Joe* or Frederick Exley, regarding football, personalizes in *A Fan's Notes*. The boy-to-adult and corruption-of-heroes baseball themes in the early years of the twentieth century are versions of perhaps the oldest American tragedy: the loss of Eden, the rise of the city, the fall from innocence. As in a well-played ball game, all these strands, like an appropriate use of a team's bench or a perfectly performed play at the plate, coexist and intertwine.

The surface story of *The Celebrant* is simple. A naive immigrant jeweler, Jackie Kapp—né Yakov Kapinski—sustains for most of the novel two identities: he is an artist and a loyal Jewish family man; but he is also an American baseball fan who (over) worships Christy Mathewson. Jackie might have been a pitcher himself, but a sore arm and commitment to his family's needs and their sense that Jews do not play games for a living force him to play the role of knowledgeable celebrant of baseball's ideal form rather than that of participant. While Jackie's brother, Eli, is drawn into the darker aspects of gambling on the game, Jackie himself sticks to his imagined double, the pure figure of the college-educated, gentile, supremely skilled, hero-martyr, Christy Mathewson. And the novel moves from an account of both men's youthful hopes and achievements to their despair and ultimate loss of faith in baseball, in sport, in play. The novel culminates in the black betrayal of the 1919 World Series.

Jackie's skill in designing jewelry allows him to create magnificent rings to present to Mathewson, and later to the entire Giants team, as a celebration of baseball success. Greenberg's book is a larger version, in prose narrative, of this art of recapturing, of turning into art, a game and its players. Eli's failure is also linked to baseball and the making of these rings; both become commercial enterprises, corrupting the players, the game, and Eli himself. The novel ends in loss of belief. An aged great pitcher, Amos Rusie, becomes a ticket taker; a disappointed Mathewson commits symbolic suicide and fades away from his World War I gas wounds; Eli kills himself; and Jackie, like Ishmael and his whaling, alone remains to tell his baseball tale.

How do I love this novel? Let me count the ways. First, some brief theoretical considerations. Certainly, there are late-Marxist elements here. Greenberg is talking about kinds of labor, the economic labor of Jackie the jeweler and the originally joyous, nonalienated labor (play, actually) of Christy the pitcher. Both these work ethics, foregrounded early in the fiction, shift as gambling and ownership—McGraw, the Giants' manager, has a master-slave relationship with Mathewson and, later, with the outfielder Ross Youngs—allow the business society to take hegemonic control over the game and its players. Yet Jackie's art is primarily linguistic, and he preserves the rhetorical ethos of the game's descriptiveness. There is a mutual intercoding between the pitcher's and the jeweler's creativity.

The novel also sustains a psychoanalytic reading. Jackie's overidentification with Mathewson, despite Greenberg's insistence on both men's heterosexuality, has romantic undertones. The brother relationship ends in a final return of the repressed. Predictably, a dark figure such as Hal Chase, the enormously gifted but crooked first baseman, seems given over to destroying what he loves.

Baseball, though an end in itself, only seems simplistic; the object—to win games, pennants, World Series—is also an aesthetic form. Because most players are selfish individuals and part of a social function, the ritual of the game, always the same, always something new, takes on a ceremonial significance without ever ceasing to function in a world of money, where the cash nexus obtains: fans pay, players earn, owners take financial advantage. Thus, on a social and personal level Greenberg decenters the structural determinants. The spectacle, by 1919, becomes an illusion; there is a contradiction between winning and losing when players throw the game—and the artistry, the lyric beauty of baseball, is co-opted and submerged.

There are other possibilities in this richly textured novel: anthropological (the rings presented to World Series winners are surely fetishes) and linguistic (poetry and vernacular encode the game's sentimental and naturalistic aspects). What Greenberg's *The Celebrant* ultimately reifies is a double vision: Jackie/Christy, Jewish/Christian, a sympathetic knowledge of baseball/a professional distancing from the game. Baseball, then, in Greenberg's pages becomes at once lovely spectacle and structurally overdetermined. Yet the novel incorporates these considerations easily, both hailing and attacking baseball as a referent to the quality of American social discourse.

Like many baseball novels, *The Celebrant* follows the ingrained structural rhythm of the game itself—fundamentally that of rise and fall, springs full of hope to autumns of reality, an at-bat full of potential until the third strike crosses the plate. Because such structures are natural to fiction, Greenberg readily integrates his protagonists' fates at first with the game's youth and follows to the disintegrations of age. The novel describes first Jackie's youthful fascination with and love for the game, culminating in his worship of Matty in *his* heights of innocence and achievement as he starts in the 1905 series. The first half of the book resembles baseball juveniles—Frank Merriwell or Baseball Joe come to mind—in its joyful success and enthusiasm ("It's great to be young and to be a Giant," says infielder Larry Doyle). Interestingly, *The Celebrant*'s movement from a narrative of hope and victory to one of fear and defeat parallels the history of baseball fiction itself: the early juveniles concern ways of winning; the later serious novels cast gloomy eyes on measures of loss. But nothing in the pages of Coover or Malamud matches Greenberg's grim views in the novel's second half: errors (Merkel), cheating (Chase), war (Mathewson's wounding), aging (the Giants, baseball itself, the sad fates of the fictional characters), betrayal (the Black Sox), and death (McGraw, Mathewson, Eli, Youngs).

In Greenberg's analysis, defeat always lurks behind victory. After each moment of ecstasy, such as the joy when the Giants beat the Cubs, is the awful truth that Fred Merkle missed second base. At that moment of reversal, Greenberg introduces his ironist, a finely rendered Hugh Fullerton, the sportswriter who teaches the dreamer Jackie Kapp, and Chicago newspaper readers, about the ugly corrupting influence of gamblers. If the gloriously gifted Mathewson—with his skill, intelligence, education, beauty, and idealism—dominates the first half of the novel's celebration of baseball, the sinister, nearly allegorical figure of Hal Chase—gambler, solipsist, pragmatist—shadows the second half. Matty is the essence of team loyalty; Chase cares only for self: "I'm better off getting out of this crazy coop altogether. They pay well in the California leagues, and there's plenty of action on the side" (144). Mathewson, portrayed as a spiritual philosopher as well as a great pitcher, accepts with considerable grace changes in his career, his rise and fall paralleling the novel's form. "The old order is passing, Jack. If Marquard [the

Giants' new ace] isn't the league's best pitcher, he soon will be" (178). For Jackie, even the 1912 series resembles a game of ghosts as he matures, and business and family become more important than baseball.

The entire Black Sox scandal becomes a lengthy epilogue, covering about one-fifth of the text and bringing together motifs of family (Eli's gambling), baseball history (the thrown series), and Mathewson's final disillusionment (he and Fullerton watch from the press box). The brother, the game, postwar America, and the business ethic that condones betrayals are all sad indicators of a dying fall. Baseball history, which the text examines in a leisurely fashion in the early parts of the novel, speeds up. Christy Mathewson dies in 1925, Ross Youngs in 1927, John McGraw in 1933—a death foreshadowed in the 1933 All-Star Game when McGraw, the wily proponent of the inside game of sacrifices and squeeze plays, loses as manager to Babe Ruth's home run. The novel, which started with the two brothers gloriously ascending the hill to watch the young Giants win, ends with Jackie mourning his dead brother who has driven his car off that same hill, Coogan's Bluff.

The Celebrant mainly celebrates baseball history. The events and players of the century's early years present an instant past for a country that (unhappily, Brecht would add) needs heroes. "Remember Keeler, with his hands way up here . . . Remember Brothers? . . . Jennings, Reitz, Kelly, Joe McGinnity, Roger Breshnahan?" (43ff.). Jackie's father-in-law recalls Alexander Cartwright, which is about as far as baseball memories can go. The great names of baseball thicken the novel's texture: Plank, Schreckengost, Bender, Devlin, Donlin, Tenney, Seymour, Doyle, Herzog, Merkle, Snodgrass, Evers, Tinker, Kling, Pfeister, Brown. Greenberg's loving re-creation of baseball's past includes games "watched" in taverns or in Madison Square Garden where play is represented on a huge wooden painted diamond, and players are moved, after telegraphic communication, as on a board game (an equivalent to the novelist's technique?).

Just as baseball serves as a focal point, the city reflects the game's place in the social nexus. In 1908, "I felt that all New York had become Coogan's Bluff overlooking the Polo Grounds and reverberating with its echoes. Shows would succeed or flop, stocks would rise or fall, juries would acquit or convict in the temper of victory or defeat" (116). But when business power, owners' greed, and gamblers' interferences mar the dreamlike game, Jackie, like Nick in *The Great Gatsby* (where the Jewish gambler Arnold Rothstein appears as Meyer Wolfsheim) muses on the changing urban landscape. "There was an ugliness emerging from the city's heart . . . I saw it first on the train to the Polo Grounds: two youths were scrawling obscenities about the Cubs on the walls of the car" (160). Unlike Fitzgerald's Nick Carraway, who can still believe in past dreams (despite his horrified reaction to the man who fixed the World Series) and try to erase the obscenities from Gatsby's drive, Greenberg's Jackie Kapp sees the present destroy the value of memories. Now pickpockets roam the stands, the mob gathers, a man falls from the stands and dies. Yet Jackie's nephew loves the game as much as his uncle had as a youth and keeps meticulous records of players such as Schalk, Weaver, Jackson, Hooper, Speaker, Lewis, and Groh. The United States, said John Dos Passos, is the speech of the people; baseball, Greenberg recalls, is names: Dummy Taylor and Chief Myers, Bugs Raymond and Smokey Joe Wood (Nathan 1989, 100).

Baseball history is games played as well as the players, and Greenberg matches the finest game descriptions created by such novelists as Mark Harris. Paralleling the novel's structure, the author describes in detail seven games: a no-hit game in St. Louis (July 15, 1901), McGraw's first game as manager (April 1902), McGinnity's opening-day victory in 1905, and Mathewson's World Series win over New York (October 14, 1905)—all Giants victories. Then come Merkle's failure (September 23, 1908), a tie leading to a loss. The most detailed game portrayal concerns the Giants' October 16, 1912, loss to the Boston Red Sox, caused by Snodgrass's muffed fly ball. The game reportage culminates in the October 14, 1919, Chicago White Sox loss—an evil betrayal of winning and losing—to the Cincinnati Reds. Yet Greenberg includes one last World Series game to indicate that life goes on, baseball survives, and even old heroes can be reborn: a resurrected Walter Johnson finally gains his sole career series victory on October 7, 1925, Washington over Pittsburgh. But Matty dies on the eve of that World Series.

If there is one weakness in Greenberg's novel, it is the language. Even though the author realizes the importance of the poetry and of the slang of baseball, he catches these aspects only fleetingly. At times the prose is overblown, as when he forces iambic pentameter on one passage and imitates an Anglo-Saxon bardic form in another ("see the men who chart and chronicle the event" [250]). Greenberg handles the vernacular better, as in a finely rendered passage of badinage that leads to momentary male bonding among Irish and Jewish fans on Coogan's Bluff. But the prose sometimes succumbs to the sentimental, a temptation few baseball novelists resist. "The pale light of the afternoon played over the dusty diamond, rutted by a season's play, and the autumn wind described spontaneous patterns in the bending grass of the outfield. The fielders, white against the sateen ebony of their uniforms, fidgeted with excitement" (90). Poetic lyricism on the one hand, vernacular explosiveness on the other, Greenberg's language does manage to sustain the reader's double response to a game and a novel that is at once sweetly nostalgic and bitterly critical even though this language is sometimes forced. Here is a brief dialogue between manager John McGraw and umpire Hank O'Day after O'Day has called Merkle out. "'I'll get you for this, you bog-crawling Mick! Nobody fucks with John McGraw!' The door opened. 'Especially Mrs. McGraw, you randy, rat-faced turd,' said the umpire" (141).

Greenberg brilliantly joins two American themes, the love of sheer play (Matty's superb pitching) and the ever-darkening business ethic. One brother, Jackie, discovers on his first day as a boy newly arrived in New York "clay diamonds," the novel's controlling, double-edged image. Diamonds are later the substance of Jackie's art as a jewelry designer, and they provide his family's business; clay refers to baseball's infield dirt and players' (and all of our) mortality. Throughout the novel Eli, the other brother, is the anticelebrant, the one who loves the game largely for its cash value. As a gambler he represents early on the corruption that will later dominate the game and turn into public shame in 1919. Although his brother's refusal to help cover bets hastens Eli's death, he has himself used, rather, worshiped, his connections with the Giants for crass financial gain: betting, softening up buyers, advertising. As he destroys himself and brings harm to the national game, another brother, Arthur, the arch-pragmatist—for Eli is, in his way, a romantic risk taker, closer to Jackie in a sense of baseball as play—cynically defines the Jewish-American business involvement with baseball: "by appointment to the Polo Grounds, jewelers to his royal bigness, John McGraw" (112), the Giants' Irish American manager. And the jewelry business loses its early simplicity, growing in size and complexity (and dishonorable practices) just as baseball moves from its rural beginnings as the town game to its urban financial success as the city's business. Although Jackie idolizes Christy Mathewson as hero and friend, the business exploits him for advertising and thus prostitutes both Jackie's baseball art (the rings) and Mathewson's pitching artistry. Further, as we shall see, economic considerations undercut the novel's religious motif. Arthur remarks of Mathewson to Jackie, "You think he's a kind of God, and I suspect that he shares your belief" and "business is not an abbey and you are not a monk illuminating pages for the greater glory of God" (120). Arthur's business views are pharisaic; to Jackie's dismay at Mathewson's appearance at the opening of the new Boston branch of the jewelry store before the World Series, Arthur ironically responds, "Why not? . . . Christ walked among publicans and sinners" (179). Ultimately, Eli's Willy Loman-like role as salesman makes him a martyr to the road. Unlike an artist or a ballplayer, when the salesman comes off the road, says an old uncle," what's he got? Orders, big orders. We start a little shop, now we got a factory bigger than the whole *shtetl* I was born in" (189). Growth of a business threatens early family solidarity and a pure art; growth of baseball leads to the corruption of White Sox players exploited by their profit-driven employer, Charles Comiskey.

•   •   •

Other baseball novels have achieved the effects delineated here. But *The Celebrant* moves beyond the previous works in the genre because of its spiritual and symbolic thrust, which Malamud approaches through Arthurian reference or Roth handles by historical parody. For Greenberg, the relationship between fan and player provides the game's essence and the novel's larger vision.

In a small way, a familiar Jewish American fictional theme, the relationship between brothers and between fathers and sons, underscores the novel's fundamental linkage of family and baseball, of generations and baseball history. Eli uses the game as object of his gambling; for Jackie, "the game was all" (15), a prime subject, all spirit and the best America can offer. While Eli bets, often intentionally losing to seduce business customers, Jackie sees "the inner game, the fierce battle between pitcher and batter where power and control [also a defining aspect of the jewelry designer's art] sought mastery over instinct and guess" [a fair definition of crude business practice] (16).

"Fathers and Sons" the poet and baseball lyricist Donald Hall entitles his baseball essays, and Irwin Shaw, Gerald Green, Mark Lapin, Sylvia Tennenbaum, Alan Lelchuck, and other Jewish-American novelists weave these family connections into the warp and woof of their fictions. When his son is three, Jackie states, "For my son's initiation, only the Polo Grounds would do" (168), an early bar mitzvah. When the Giants seem about to defeat the Red Sox, Eli and Jackie indulge in some brotherly bonding, and another generation of baseball fans joins in. "'I love you,' I said. 'Don't be silly,' he said. 'World's champs . . .' the children cried" (206).

Baseball is both test and escape. Greenberg refers briefly to Mathewson's son, an average athlete compared with his immensely gifted father. The boy must face "unfair expectations whenever he picks up a glove" (219). And Jackie Kapp, finally maturing, realizes that the game is just a game and understands it as an escape for children. He wonders about another generation ("Does it attract him as it did us when we were young?") and recalls, as does Irwin Shaw in *Voices of a Summer Day*, the first game Papa took him to: "He'll remember that when the day comes that he takes his own grandchild" (259). When he was a child, Greenberg says elsewhere, his grandfather took him to see only terrible teams, like the Browns, Senators, or Athletics (Nathan 1989, 11). Thus, in *The Celebrant* a baseball game can establish a code for family relationships just as the history of baseball can reflect that of the larger society.

More crucially in the American grain, *The Celebrant* deals with that theme basic to most of our novelists, the loss of innocence, in the book's progression from Jackie's youthful initial total immersion in the beauty and heroism of baseball to his final harsh suspicions of the commodification of the game and its increasing corruption. Greenberg himself does not consider his novel primarily about this theme, but he grants that Jackie is "opting for innocence" when he turns Mathewson into a kind of god and that the Black Sox represented the "end of American innocence" (see Henry May's classic study of early twentieth-century social history in the United States) as much as did World War I—and certainly innocence ended for one of the greatest practitioners of baseball fiction, the man who molded the form, Ring Lardner (Nathan 1989, 12, 16)

That baseball is not as innocent as it seems is established early in the novel, but Jackie Kapp remains a slow learner. On the child's first day playing in the park, a man going after a fly ball runs into Jackie and says, "Well, *shit*'—the first words ever spoken to me on a ballfield" (11). The last words of the novel are "*Eli, Eli*," as Jackie mourns the departed innocence of Christy Mathewson, the final act of suicide of his defeated brother, and Jackie's own growth to experience.

The seeds of doubt are planted early in the novel when the boy starts to grasp the distinction between a good player and a good man as well as the place of money in sport. Jackie receives a silver cup at a sports banquet from a grizzled Giants player, Jack Warner, who has just delivered an eloquent speech about the beauties of baseball achievement. "Practice, dedication, clean living, and fair play" are the qualities he extols before "he turned to the organizer of the event and asked for his fee" (13)—and Warner will subsequently turn out to be an anti-Semite.

Still, Jackie clings to his dream of baseball heroism for as long as possible, largely because he has a fine objective correlative for his hero worship—the New York Giants—"In the matter of rooting, a boy's first team is his team forever" (17)—and in the team's central figure. When the boy first glimpses Mathewson, the pitcher is surrounded by hard-faced veterans in the clubhouse, but "at the center stood Mathewson, young as an April morning in that sweltering July, and I, small in the crowd" (20). Yet Matty is the quintessential youth, the innocent, for he is still playing a boy's game, while Jackie is more attuned to the real world because he has given up playing baseball. "My youth had ended on a ragged lot by the Hudson when the curve ball had beaten my arm and my spirit" (26), and he reports to work at his Uncle Sid's jewelry shop.

Even early in the novel the game itself is losing its innocence. "Many of our clients were frankly disgusted with big-league ball, the pastoral game where local heroes bore the honor of the city against the invading foe had transformed into a disquieting brawl among mercenaries" (40–41). Thus, Jack Warner's money-grubbing was prophetic, and ideas of pastoral and knightly tournaments have given way to a crude urban professionalism. Christy Mathewson clings to a belief that baseball is different from, better than, life in the real world, more ideal, more straightforward. "Baseball is all clean lines and clear decisions . . . Oh, for a life like that, where every day produces a clear winner and an equally clear loser" (86). The novel, and baseball history, go on to disprove the pitcher's naïveté: Merkle's bonehead play becomes baseball's most disputed decision, the Black Sox its greatest disparity between genuine winners and losers. Indeed, Greenberg focuses on the youthful spirit of the outfielder Fred Merkle: "There is nothing that can so delight the heart as being a boy again, and there is no greater transport to that happy past than a victory in a boy's game" (135). But the moment is now 1908, no longer that innocent time when Jackie and Eli could celebrate a clear Giants victory by joyously singing "Take Me Out to the Ball Game" with interpolated Yiddish lines. Merkle's youthful sparkle leads only to wearied sadness when he forgets to touch second base; the clear victory becomes a disputed tie and eventually a loss. Life is not as Mathewson sees it, even baseball life. Past Jack Warner's speech and Fred Merkle's pillorying by the press, Jackie becomes a baseball realist, and the game is not a tourney, not a religious ceremony, but a real-life event: "I'd always held that over the course of a season, with all its errors and accidents, the better team prevailed and the better players defeated the odds, that the game, at bottom, was just. Now I knew that the field of play was not exempt from life's injustices—a lesson nowhere heard in after-dinner speeches" (150). Farewell Frank Merriwell, hello, Roy Hobbs. Jackie's Uncle Sid, wise in the ways of the world and very, very Jewish, reminds the young man that baseball is "not life, Yakov" (157). And Jackie leaves that last Black Sox series game early, a real fan's transgression, foreshadowing loss, season's end, and death of innocence. Reluctantly, the maturing celebrant must relinquish his commitment to baseball, America's national game, as it and the country alike become more sophisticated in dirty tricks. "I sought out the attractions of the city that I'd always ignored in favor of a ballgame" (175). Music, restaurants, art, family, business become the stuff of an adult life when the dream of baseball fades.

One of the fundamental tenets of most Jewish American fiction is the importance of the mind; indeed, many sports novels attest to the mind-body struggle between parents who hate their sons' athletic fascinations and the boys who finally choose the life of the mind—or professions—but elegiacally create fictions about baseball. *The Celebrant* contains the theme of the family business versus the son's love of baseball, but only marginally. Part of the reason for the Jewish acceptance of baseball in *The Celebrant* stems from the game's intellectual force. According to Greenberg, Christy Mathewson "had the intellectual capacity to place himself realistically and properly in this context" (Nathan 1989, 13) as a craftsman with the ability to transform the crowd by his art. The older generation of Jewish businessmen is stymied by Mathewson's choice of professions: "He could be a doctor or lawyer or stockbroker, but there he is pitching for the Giants" (37). Jackie as fan is especially drawn to the pitcher as the subtle artist, the "college man, reading books as he does," as opposed to Iron Man Joe McGinnity, "a good Irish hardballer," but "an ignoramus" (39).

Because both Mathewson's and Jackie's parents oppose baseball, ethnicity combines with class feelings. "It wasn't a fit career for a gentleman, after all . . . the major leagues! It just wasn't done" (89). Class and ethnic lines merge, however, during a conversation in a gentleman's club between Sonnheim, a highly cultured Jewish businessman, and Mathewson. After playing chess, they discuss the mathematics of baseball. "Nothing in the game is easy, yet nothing is impossible. It's a game of intricate simplicity" (84). The oxymoron recalls catcher-professor Red Traphagen's definition of the laughter and tears of a death in baseball in Mark Harris's *Bang the Drum Slowly*. The conversation moves to the parallel between baseball and an Afghan tribal game in which the teams struggle for the head of a decapitated goat, often involving the death of a horseman (a reference to a passage in Philip Roth's *The Great American Novel*). Mathewson comprehends, as a baseball player must, the idea of sacrifice, but this knowledge compounds the novel's fundamental irony that his understanding of the game's corruption will lead to his self-sacrificial death. Like a Jewish Roger Angell, Sonnheim waxes lyrical about baseball as civilized, subtle, refined, artificial, "creating its own time, existing within its own space. There is nothing real about it." Although he is a surrogate for the authorial voice here, Mathewson has a grasp of the game's underlying personal aspect, an important concept for the baseball novelist. To

Sonnheim's "There is nothing real about it," Matty responds, "except the men who play it" (84–85). Here, then, is the novel's central point, understood by player and observer: baseball is above all those who play it; not mathematical, not abstract, but *human*, the game is the stuff of fiction. Mathewson's sacrifice, Kapp's hero-worshiping celebration are personal, powerful, extreme gestures, responses to the human condition in a tough, quotidian world that is at once primitive and physical, "throwing and clubbing" (86), while at the same time engaging the intellect. Apes (McGinnity) and angels (Mathewson) dance alike on diamonds made of clay and jewels.

One of the concomitants of postmodern fiction is a reflexive attitude by the author (proving his existence?), who throughout comments on the fictional strategies that create the work. For Greenberg, the trope of Jackie as artist employing placement of jewels in a ring to commemorate a no-hit game works as a parallel to the novelist's attempt to use words to re-create action. Creating a diamond in jewels and engraving words in gold is Jackie's equivalent of Greenberg's creation of a baseball novel. The ring is like a fiction. "Imagine it with the etching and the engraving, think of the small chips here, here, and here—diamonds, yes, but small and integrated into the design without overwhelming it. . . . It signifies a team" (70). These signifiers create a bond between pitcher and artist, for each considers the other's achievement extraordinary.

Throughout, Jackie's comments reflect Greenberg's fictional approach. "A line score is a very stark statement. . . . The numbers tell the essential story. All the rest is mere detail" (87); true for the reader of the sports page who knows that these figures represent a deconstructed view of a game's narrative, true for this novel, replete as it is with line scores. Jackie's commemorative rings make moments of past games real again, as does Greenberg's prose. The description of fans watching a series game re-created on a board informs how readers must respond to *The Celebrant*'s re-creations of baseball games through printed words on a page. "All could envision the blond master hitching his belt, flexing his right arm, and bending in to face the foe" (94). Most crucially, the former pitcher and present jeweler Kapp, the self-conscious star pitcher Mathewson, and the author Greenberg—on all three of whom, as Henry James insisted, nothing is lost—share the ability to make disparate units cohere as a team, as an artistic production, as a discourse. "The game was the process that welded them into a meaningful form, and the pitcher was the gemstone" (130).

Like the novel's readers, fans need suspense, the drama and tension that emanate from the uncertainty of whether Mathewson and the Giants will win. Like us, people at the turn of the century lived "in cities that had never seen these men save on cigarette cards and etched woodcuts" (130).

Although Jackie's cynical brother, Arthur, mocks Jackie's worship of Mathewson as a Christ figure (179), thus undercutting possible narrative sentimentality, the sportswriter Hugh Fullerton speaks directly for Greenberg—and for all creative narrators, whether their subject be baseball or economic theory, whether their expressive form be history or fiction. "My immortality lies in his. No one will ever dig my columns out of the morgue for the sake of my literary genius. It will be to read about Christy Mathewson or Smokey Joe Wood or Tris Speaker, or any of those demigods we create and celebrate" (196). The fundamental theory of baseball writing has to do with "the scribe at his duty" (250), granting, like a godlike creator, a writer, immortality, a place in a Valhalla, a plaque in the Hall of Fame.

The most interesting aspect of *The Celebrant*, as the title indicates, is Greenberg's assumption of the fan's viewpoint throughout, employing first-person narration of an observer, a technique often used in journalism—Arnold Hano's *A Day in the Bleachers* or Barry Gifford's *The Neighborhood of Baseball* come to mind—but rarely throughout a baseball novel. According to the author, who considered writing from Hugh Fullerton's or Ross Youngs's angle of vision, the fan's view was appropriate. "You're not a ballplayer and thus you can't write convincingly as a ballplayer. You're not a sportswriter. . . . You are in the crowd. You are a fan. . . . But it had to be a fan who was somehow involved with Mathewson, so I imagined my grandfather as a young sports fan in love with this perfect pitcher" (Nathan 1989, 10). Greenberg chose the title *The Celebrant* rather than *Matty* so that the novel's focus would be on the Jewish observer rather than on the Christian actor. (Nathan 1989, 15).

Jackie Kapp, then, *witnesses* Mathewson's great exploits and his artistic perfection—"His rhythm and motion were balletic" (23)—

understands the inner game of baseball, and *identifies* with the hero—
"This was Mathewson's place and moment; my whole being was
with him" (26). The pitcher, a youthful athlete playing a game,
keeps the Jewish intellectual (he is a writer, after all, of this text)
young: "I watched Mathewson, and he became my youth." The
overidentification becomes manifest when Greenberg shifts Jackie
Kapp's viewpoint into Christy Mathewson's mind and body, as
imaginative fans, especially youthful ones, are wont to play baseball
of the mind. "I waste a pitch high, ball one. . . . I turn, I bend. I
look for Warner's sign." (Or, as Walt Whitman chants, "I was the
man, I suffered, I was there.") Unlike Robert Coover's J. Henry
Waugh, however, Greenberg's narrator only momentarily loses touch
with reality. When the game ends, the fan is effaced, and "the team
leaps to touch and embrace" Mathewson (27), not me.

The young Jackie realizes that part of his admiration for the
professional pitcher stems from the role as observer, as failed athlete. "He was everything I was not. . . . I had nothing to offer him"
(29). But in his role as artist Kapp solves his problem two ways,
within the text by creating commemorative rings for baseball heroics and without by narrating, creating, the text itself. Therefore,
Jackie Kapp's narrative voice is particularly privileged. Even after
four years have passed, he can reenter his hero, his quasidouble.
"Once more my focus narrowed until I seemed to live within him,
to bend and sway and drive with him and to finish with my hands
at the ready to field the ball" (94). Not merely the narrator but all
fans—and readers—respond to the baseball celebrations as participants. As Matty wins a series game, after the final out, the first
baseman throws the "ball high in the air. It caught the sun, dropped
toward a thousand reaching hands, and disappeared. . . . Wave upon
wave of celebrants danced over the field." But the hero vanishes (see
John Updike on Ted Williams's refusal to tip his hat after hitting
a home run in his final at-bat: gods do not answer letters).
Mathewson, in Greenberg's discourse, seems both god and artist;
we are both fans and readers. "I thought that if he could he would
order time to stand still, leaving him suspended for eternity in this
pose, at this breath, but only gods and artists can stop time.
Mathewson had to pitch" (99). Jackie weeps when he watches his
triumphant idol, for Mathewson is no god, and he will surely die,
as the greatness of the Giants will pass away.

Jackie, for his part, postpones adulthood and its rejection of dreams as long as possible, using baseball as an anodyne, a relief from the mundane aspects of the outer world of telegrams and anger, as E. M. Forster would put it, of business and family, thus allowing in a counter-Wordsworthian sense the child to *remain* father to the man. "I fooled Wildfire Schulte with a fadeaway. I . . . walked Frank Chance. . . . I was ahead and cruising in the seventh, and Mathewson was warming up in the bullpen in case I needed late-inning help." When Jackie works at his art, as the novelist must have worked on his text, and seeks to create a design that will symbolize baseball, he inflates this game, and its players, to near-religious status.

> To be a pitcher! I thought. A pitcher standing at the axis of events, or a catcher with the God-view of the play all before him; to be a shortstop, lord of the infield, or a center fielder with unchallenged claim to all the territory one's speed and skill could command; to perform the spontaneous acrobatics of the third baseman or the practiced ballet of the man at second, or to run and throw with the absolute commitment of the outfielder. And to live in a world without grays, where all decisions are final: ball or strike, safe or out, the game won or lost beyond question or appeals. (128)

In this passage, all the novel's themes are valorized: loss of innocence, Jewish mysticism, reflexivity, baseball history and theory. The narrator is naive and wrong, and the burden of Greenberg's text is to prove that neither baseball nor life is simple, and ambiguities prevail. The author uses the character of the darker-spirited brother, Eli, the baseball cynic and gambler who needs a scapegoat (Fred Merkle) when bets are lost to contrast with the idealistic Jackie, who seeks a godlike hero to worship.

This theme of fandom is most clearly set forth by the veteran observer, the sportswriter Hugh Fullerton, who understands fully what Jackie only partly grasps about his relationship to Christy Mathewson—"He certainly has a hold on my imagination" (195). Fullerton terms Kapp the "high-priest, the celebrant-in-chief" (196), even one who hopes for failure in order to be relieved of the fan's burden. Incisively, Fullerton, who has learned from Mathewson that his greatest fan was once a pitcher himself, avers, "I suspect that your work is infused with the wish that you were he. You're not alone. Inside every sportswriter there's a frustrated athlete. . . . The same thing is inside every fan, or anyone who ever picked up a bat and ball" (197). But it is easier to be a fan, who can evade suffering even when "called to witness" (230).

The novel closes on notes of dying fandom. Jack Kapp ages along with the game and the country, and he attends fewer games: "I prefer the memory. . . . Everything was simpler then" (230). If true fans are worshipers in the temple of baseball, the 1919 Chicago White Sox indicated the possibility of false gods. "They moved as champions, who shared a sacred mystery denied to those of us who stared at them from our high remove" and, Judas-like, betrayed innocent fans who "would witness the event; they would shape it to their will" (222). Interestingly, the darkest moment in Boston Red Sox history, the betrayal some fans claim prohibits Boston from ever again winning a World Series, takes place just before the 1919 series: Babe Ruth is sold to the Yankees. Greenberg draws his fans's notes to a close as this series takes place. The reporters also are fans: "See them set apart from the great host, these makers of heroes and legends: see Lardner, Runyon, Rice . . . Spink . . . Pegler . . .Fullerton." Mathewson, transmuted for the nonce into a reporter, is hailed one last time by his fan, now a fan betrayed by the corrupt Black Sox eight. "Know that he alone among those jurists has performed on the field below, to win such glory and to suffer such devastating disappointment. See Christy Mathewson on high" (250). The ceremony bespoiled, the games fixed, Kapp and Mathewson, the true fans, both break one of fandom's cardinal rules and leave before the end: baseball is no longer worth celebrating.

•   •   •

The Celebrant reaches after a particular dignity as a genuinely ethnic-religious baseball novel, one that combines Jewish and Christian strains. The book is partly autobiographical—Greenberg's grandfather, "like Jackie . . . was also an immigrant who came off the boat with nothing and who learned how to be an American on the ball field"—and the novel evokes traditional religious concepts as, for example, when Mathewson worships false idols—his "tragedy, as I wrote it, is that he came to believe too much in his own image" (Nathan 1989, 11, 12). *The Celebrant* strengthens and questions parallels between baseball and religion.

The connection of ethnicity and the game in the novel comes through at the very start. The first paragraph takes place in 1889, describing the Atlantic crossing; the second focuses on baseball. "Our family came to New York in the winter of '89, and in the spring I saw my first game of baseball" (11). As is typical in nearly all Jewish American baseball novels, baseball equals acculturation. "First by imitation, then by practice, we learned the game and the ways of the boys who played it. . . . Our accents disappeared, our studies became quick and confident." The shift from Jewish immigrant to American ballplayer resonates in his name change. Having become a left-handed submarine-ball pitcher, he is no longer a Jewish outsider but a New York insider. "'Get those knuckles dirty, Jackie,' my infielders would shout—Jackie not Yakov" (12). The novel reflects similar accounts from Jewish American writers such as Irwin Shaw or Roger Kahn in that family traditions clash with American baseball ambitions. Jackie becomes a pretty fair curveball pitcher and wants to accept a contract to play ball for Altoona, but "my parents wouldn't hear of it." To them, ballplayers were "suspect, disreputable. . . . An underclass supported them. Ballpark crowds are mean and roistering." Crucially, the Jewish strain defeats the American: "all the pressures of a family's traditions, hopes and plans pressed down upon me" to enter the business of a family "who had not crossed the ocean to find disgraceful employment." So Jackie gives in to his father's threat to consider his son dead and to say *kaddish* for his sole, entering the family jewelry business rather than playing an American professional sport (13–14). As Philip Roth, among others, has written autobiographically, denied the right to play baseball, Jewish Americans often sustained their fascination with the game by other means, becoming celebrants and, by implication here, baseball novelists.

Greenberg includes much Jewish social history in his novel. Just as Abraham Cahan opposed Russian Jews learning about baseball and was reluctant to print directions to the Giants' park in the *Jewish Daily Forward*, so Greenberg shows an earlier generation of German Jews scandalized by the idea of going to the Polo Grounds. With the name change from Kapinski to Kapp, however, Jackie's brother Eli draws the Jewish business close to the American national game when he sells himself to clients as quintessentially American by taking them to a baseball game, "an afternoon at the ballpark, so refreshing, so American" (17).

Despite some early resentment by a few anti-Semitic Giants players, the Kapps become part of the Giants entourage. Like Mathewson, Jackie has other options; although his arm has failed, he can turn to his art, business, and family. But baseball, in what might seem a sacrilegious way, replaces Judaism. In a scene that summarizes both Jackie's move away from and baseball's substitution for religion, Greenberg emphasizes the religio-cultural transformation that privileges American baseball over Jewish ritual. After starting out for temple on the Jewish New Year, Jackie (unlike Sandy Koufax, who refused to pitch on Yom Kippur) decides to worship baseball: "Instead I handed my tallith and yarmulke to Edith and boarded a northbound trolley. The stars and stripes waved from a hundred flagpoles above the Polo Grounds, that secular house of worship" (95). Point taken. Yosef Hayim Yerushalmi has described the psychological Jew as one who is alienated from traditional Jewish texts but insists on Jewish traits such as intellectuality, freedom of mind, high ethical and moral standards, and belief in social justice. Surely, Greenberg and the cohort of Jewish American novelists who treat baseball with the seriousness that defines Jewish identity fit these definitions of secularization (Stern 1922, 43).

On the other hand, after baseball—like other American institutions such as business, family values, the times themselves—seems to be sinking into corruption, Greenberg's protagonist turns again to his Jewish religious roots rather than sticks to the convoluted, mock-Christian adoration of Mathewson in which Jackie has been indulging. The narrative reverses the earlier Polo Grounds scene. "On Saturday the pull to Fenway Park was unendurable. I searched out the oldest and most thoroughly orthodox synagogue in the city and buried myself there until the sabbath ended at sundown" (186). The Giants lose. The Jewish connection strengthens while the family pulls together to cover Eli's peculations. Speaking mostly in Yiddish, Uncle Sid defends the salesman, for the sake of retaining solidarity, the genuine Jewish commitment to the family team rather than an American involvement with the fortunes of a baseball squad. "He don't remember a *shtetl* with a well, you get one bucket because everyone needs. He's in America where the faucets run forever" (189), a line connected to Dreiser's view of late-nineteenth-century urban America, seen in Hurstwood's explanation to Carrie that there are no lawns in New York.

Finally—as the novel drifts to an ending indeterminate for baseball, Jackie's family, and America—Jewish roots continue to deepen in value. In World War I, "it seemed rank to ally with the Russian tsar and the French of the Dreyfus affair against the Germans whose Jews were the freest in Europe" (214). Historical ironies aside, one grasps at this stage in the novel the importance of Jewish ethnicity after various family deaths and understands the ephemeral qualities of American baseball. *The Celebrant*'s last word on Jewish matters is ironic, mocking solidarity. According to Eli Kapp, Arnold Rothstein's greatest betrayal was not of the grand old American game of baseball but of his Jewish compatriots whom he failed to inform that the fix was in. "I could see it if it were some Mick gambler, but to think that Rothstein would do this and not get the word to *mishpocha*!" (242).

Perhaps more important to the intertextuality of *The Celebrant* than the Jewish elements are the Christian and pagan religious overtones that reflect the influence of another Jewish American baseball novelist, Bernard Malamud, who made great use of Christian-Arthurian-Hellenic elements in *The Natural* (note the similarity of titles, and the difference). Greenberg was quite conscious of this religious overlay; he sought to establish Mathewson, the author says, as one who sits in judgment over baseball and thinks that he is Christ, and Jackie takes the pitcher as a new god at the expense of the old. "He decides he will take Mathewson for his savior and sin no more." The author argues that the Christian aspects simply became appropriate during the composition of the novel. "I didn't know when I named the character Eli that I was going to finish the book with 'Eli, Eli,' Christ on the cross. That's 'My God, my God, why hast thou forsaken me,' " and having already identified Mathewson as a Christ figure, this last scene emphasizes the religio-baseball motif.

Allen Hye has pointed out that there are dozens of religious images and allusions in *The Celebrant* and that John McGraw, the Giants manager, is something of a deity too, worshiped by the crowd, having an advent. But he is a false god to Jackie, no Messiah—perhaps closest to John the Baptist. "The last quarter of the novel depicts Mathewson neither as a Greek god nor as a deified folk hero, but as a suffering, atoning, and ultimately punishing Christ" (Hye 1989, 46). Just as William Faulkner partly creates a Christ image in "The Bear," with Sam Fathers as high priest, so, Hye points out, Fullerton calls Jackie Kapp Mathewson's high priest, his chief celebrant who can sympathize with the Gethsemane of the pitcher's suffering. The celebration of the mass may be echoed in the title, and the culminating defamation of baseball by gamblers, whom Mathewson abhors, may refer to the game's fall and money changers in the temple. Matty also reflects a pagan god; Greenberg recalls admiring Greek statuary in the Brooklyn Museum: "I especially admired the athletes, gods in marble" (Nathan 1989, 39).

Still, the essential use of the Christian symbolism connects with the familiar acculturation concept, seemingly omnipresent in baseball novels by Jewish American writers. Jackie argues that his worship of Christ-y Mathewson is not a denial of Jewish heritage. When Eli calls his brother "a worshipper from afar," Jackie insists that his approach remains Jewish: "Isn't that the proper distance for worship? You don't crawl into the ark to worship *torah*" (42). And he denies the heresy of worshiping false idols, conflating Christianity with Americanism, thus allowing for the Jewish assimilating hyphen between Jewish and American. Jackie informs Eli that no heretical worship of Mathewson in the religious sense is taking place, then clarifies. "A very American heresy, Mister Kapp" (not Kapinski; they have already denied a Jewish name and accepted an American one) and goes on to parody Christian American baseball. "And now the batteries: pitching, Jackie the Jew; catching, Eli the Hebe . . . *yenkee duddle*" (42).

Although trying to avoid any intimacy with his godlike hero, Jackie nevertheless continues to salute Mathewson and offers him the private homage of a fan. Yet as Hye points out, Mathewson is a god compared to McGraw, whom Greenberg draws as an antigod or, in my reading, a pagan devil: "the wiry body, the thin arms, the triangular face and the jug ears that stuck out from under his cap, foolish and duncelike" (45) and full of "arrogance and self-serving puffery" (63). At the very least, he resembles a dwarf, a familiar of the forces of evil. Mathewson's opponents are often desanctified. The great Cubs pitcher Mordecai Brown is "a deformed, three-fingered devil of a pitcher" (161). But McGraw is special, in Pope's words "a being darkly wise and rudely great" who knows the game perfectly and turns players into marionettes (90).

The Celebrant is a mélange of religions. As Greenberg has noted, the Greeks also contribute to the novel's religious underpinning. McGraw ponders Matty's naked body and says (as the manager will later repeat in reference to Ross Youngs), "Give me a body like that . . . and I'd have been twice the player I was" (71), but Jackie has looked upon such a body in the statue of a Greek god: "Not of flesh, I thought . . . in marble" (71).

The great Pirate shortstop Honus Wagner is a different kind of pagan god who "matched Mathewson for size, and in the infield he stood like a gnarled oak with bowed roots" (80). Mathewson creates much of his own Christian imagery, especially in the latter part of the novel. At one point he describes McGraw as a savior and baseball as pentecostal: "You've got to go through the fire!" (91). And Jackie weeps for Matty at the hero's ascendancy as a winner, knowing, as Jackie does, that life sacrifices heroes: "the penny prints assigned to him the purity of Galahad. . . . Capless, his blond hair shining in the sun, his smile dazzling [after] the perfection of his performance. There on the hill, a foot above the rest, he was the golden idol of the land" (108). Mathewson is America's best, a Scott Fitzgerald golden youth, "an icon on self-display" (111). Fans commune with him. In a moment of epiphany, Jackie sees Mathewson arrive early on the field where he is "the solitary uniformed player. . . . His spikes left a clean straight track . . . bear the weight of a city's hopes . . . lonely . . . exposed (129). But gods, games, nations grow older. After Fred Merkle's mistake, "the rookie's crucifixion had begun" (150) in this "very devil of a game" (137), and Mathewson himself changes. "Four years had added breadth to his shoulders and chest, and the color of his skin was slightly more pale" (136). Advertising agencies create life-size cardboard cutouts of Mathewson, which demean him. "To decorate Mathewson entirely, as if he were a knight errant, and then to offer his shield and blazon for sale so that every man might be a Mathewson" (167) makes a mockery of the hero, like the selling of cheap religious images.

The text resonates with religious references increasingly as the novel moves toward its close. The Polo Grounds is "resurrected" (169); Matty acts as his brother's keeper in getting the ancient pitcher Amos Rusie a job as ticket taker (170). Mathewson's ghosted autobiography falsely sentimentalizes his Christianity; the sportswriter responsible avers that "no writer since the author of the Gospels had borne a greater responsibility" (175). The end of a baseball hero is equivalent to the death of a god. Although Hugh Fullerton, the wise scribe, sees Mathewson's suffering before a crucial game as Christ-like, the novel emphasizes that such suffering fulfills the ceremonial role of the baseball hero. "The world makes you a god and hates you for being human, and if you plead for understanding it hates you all the more. Heroes are never forgiven their success, still less their failure" (196). Fiction must be free to re-create a historical figure such as Mathewson, as E. L. Doctorow would argue, for when Greenberg has a boy remark at seeing the Red Sox outfielder Harry Hooper smile, he acts "just like a real person" (204).

The 1912 World Series loss to the Red Sox marks the Giants' and Mathewson's last hurrah. Even baseball gods must succumb to the powers of fate. Mathewson, after seven lean years, a "famine of luck" since his 1905 victory, is within an inning of glory once more; again Jackie identifies. With three outs, Mathewson could "resurrect the glory of his youth and the joy of my own" (207). But whatever the magical number three could contribute to Christ's resurrection, Matty, the Giants, and Jackie's family all collapse under a betrayal, an error—not by Fred Merkle this time but the muff of an outfield fly by Fred Snodgrass. Like Jesus, "Mathewson wept," and Eli, the bettor, like Judas demands from his young nephew two bits, a handful of silver (210).

Other betrayals await Christy Mathewson, and Greenberg hastily sums them up. As manager of the Reds, the retired pitcher is "either the most credulous man in America or the greatest model of Christian forgiveness" (219) in his dealings with Hal Chase, who gambles on—and throws—games. After Chase's dereliction, the narrative indirectly accounts for Mathewson's fall. He enters the army, mysteriously becomes involved in a gas attack (a suicide attempt?), and recovers after hospitalization. But he is no longer an important figure to the press, which ignores his illness, whereas earlier "the *World* would publish an extra to announce that Mathewson had risen from his sickbed" (224). Now all that remains is the long day's dying from tuberculosis that will end in a

Saranac sanitorium. As Jackie's involvement with baseball and Mathewson wanes, and Jackie becomes family and business oriented, he rediscovers his self-image and eschews the Christian image making that distinguishes the novel's middle passages. The Reds' new manager, Pat Moran, is "but a Joshua to Mathewson's Moses" (229). Ross Youngs, the Giants' brilliant outfielder, becomes the team's new god—but only in the Greek aspect as a yearling fawn (who also dies early). McGraw conflates his role as mentor-seducer, even repeating the "if I had his body" passage applied earlier to the pitcher. The game has changed, as has America, and both the country and the game now worship gods of power, that is, Babe Ruth and the home run. In a *memento mori* section, Jackie muses on the deaths of many ballplayers, even minor deities after their "fragile celebrity passes," and they become "shadows, walking ghosts, figures to trigger a memory of days past. . . . They ended as statistics . . . mere measurements against today and tomorrow, gravestones" (234).

Toward the end, the situation becomes more realistic, with a mature Jackie observing the coming Black Sox debacle, but the language becomes richer and verges on religio-sentimentalism. Ballplayers become knights once more, not ironically as in *The Natural*, and the discourse seems to be veering out of control. "See the knights who bear the city's emblem on their breasts: they are all in white, their lances are burnished wood, their gauntlets calf-brown leather" (250).

Mathewson, the former manager, gives up his insistence that his club had been clean and refuses the job that Fullerton claims could "turn St. Francis of Assisi into a butcher" (255). Having rejected the game he once loved, Mathewson can articulate the role of the fan, and his homage to Jackie is expressed in increasing religious metaphors. "I called him a celebrant. He was a voice of communication many years ago, and the time will come for another encounter. He'll not deny me" (256). Casting himself as a man imitating Christ, Mathewson makes Jackie a better St. Peter.

The final meeting between the great pitcher and the great fan recapitulates the novel's Jewish American *and* Christian American themes in the discussion of life and values between the men. The dying Mathewson has reverted to youth and emphasizes his self-as-Christ image; Jackie meets Mathewson dressed in his college varsity sweater and holding a Gideon Bible. First, Jackie confesses about his Jewish ethnicity as a barrier to full participation in American baseball. He did not become a major league player, as all except some 150 Jewish American boys who loved baseball have not. "The truth of the matter was that my parents wouldn't allow me to sign a contract. I [a Jew] couldn't—I couldn't go against their command. I hadn't your courage." Mathewson, on the other hand, was not held back by cultural or religious fiat, so he disobeyed his Christian father. The pitcher responds, "Nor my willful disobedience. And here I be" (260). Almost wallowing in his religiosity, Mathewson saves Jackie from breaking faith with baseball (by laying off Eli's bets on the White Sox). Much like a Dreiser character muttering about popular science, Mathewson calls his series rings "this damned trinity," refers to Merkle as "a mere pawn to be sacrificed," and accuses himself of error in blaming Snodgrass in the "trial that I failed" (261).

In *The Celebrant* baseball appears not so much as a game, or even a cultural entity, certainly not a business, but as a moral event that demands justice—a traditional theme of Jewish writing. Accelerating the Christian motifs, Mathewson casts McGraw once again as a haranguing devil who, like Dorian Gray, has eternal youth: "as young as his youngest player, [he] repurchased his youth by renewing his roster" (262). Conversely, Christy Mathewson now views himself as not just a muscular Christian hero—celebrated by Jackie Kapp—but as *the* Christ, whose disciple Jackie should be. Mathewson gained perfection as a pitcher before "doubt, confusion, and finally betrayal." In a passage presaging madness, he alludes to his war experiences: "then followed my death, for it was death, in the explosion and the pain. And then I rose from that death, I walked among the people as of old, and finally, finally, I came to sit in judgment of those I'd walked among, to root out their sin and damn them for it" (262). The reader must have accepted the seriousness of baseball, which serves as a narrative force for the author Greenberg and his narrator Kapp, or else Mathewson's fulmination approaches melodramatic claptrap. Somehow the rhetoric works, if one understands the world the novelist has made, where to the fan baseball is a religion, parallel to both Judaism and Christianity. Mathewson, as Greenberg conceives him, goes far as a characterization, perhaps as far as Robert Coover's Henry Waugh, who also imagines himself to be a god and baseball a religious ritual. Christy

Mathewson condemns all the players who betrayed baseball in 1919. "I do damn them, I damn Cicotte. I damn Jackson. I damn Risberg and Gandil and Williams. . . . I will root them out and damn them for eternity" (262). If religion is overdone here, still we must trust the narrator, particularly his Jewish skepticism that allows him the privilege of distancing Mathewson's crazed brand of Christianity. Clearly verging on insanity, he nevertheless saves his celebrant, his witness, and justifies Jackie's life and Greenberg's text. "You were there from the first, you knew even then how high I stood among other men" (263); and Mathewson demands in his name that Jackie choose once more between the dictates of baseball and his family, between American acculturation and Jewish brotherly feeling, between a pure game and corrupt gambling—between God and Eli. Mathewson's Christ obsession does not mask the issue. Like Jackson and Chase, Eli is one who "diced for His robe while He suffered on the cross. Will you do that while I lay dying? no, you will not" (263). This time Jackie weeps for Matty, the dying god, and scrawls a note to Eli. Greenberg reflects in a brilliant linguistic coup one of baseball's fine attributes, the language that moves easily from lyrical to gritty; this baseball language undercuts the previous religious pomp: "All bets off" (263).

Eli buys a fancy car with the gambler's money and dies as one who betrayed baseball and his symbols; he dies as a suicidal Judas whose car "jumped the roadway onto Coogan's Bluff . . . sailed high into the air over the cliff . . . hit the jagged cliffside and tumbled over and over again until it came to rest, shattered and burning against the blank walls of the Polo Grounds" (264).

If baseball is life, it is also death: third strikes, third outs, game losses, pennant losses, career endings. In this temple of baseball, then, exists an American religious spirit at once much less and perhaps a bit more than the latter-day Judeo-Christian forms. In the American context of baseball, Greenberg's narrator can weep when he learns that his World Series rings have been buried with Christy Mathewson, but in a fine baseball *ubi sunt*, Jackie Kapp weeps for all dead players: "Where is King Kelly? Dead these thirty years. Where is Big Ed Delahanty? Did they ever find the body, when they dragged the river below Niagara Falls? Where is Cap Anson? Where's Monte Ward? Charlie Gangel, Buck Ewing, Big Dan McGann? All gone: the flesh is mortal" (268). Greenberg has been celebrating baseball's religious aspects, but he has done so with skill and humor, verging toward the end of *The Celebrant* with overimmersion in his religious concerns, but while employing the ethnic trope to retain judgment along with sympathy. Baseball's legends abide, and the Hall of Fame and the records books provide immortality even for "one Edward Sylvester Nolan, who played with Indianapolis in 1878 and was the first player of that name and thus earned a nickname 'The Only Nolan'" (269). Although he had only five undistinguished seasons, he once threw a shutout, and, true to the way baseball history really works, "a boy watched him pitch that game and was inspired by it" (268). The boy became an old man with whom Jackie Kapp talks baseball, nothing more, Nolan and Mathewson, Amos Rusie and Sandy Koufax, all connect as baseball gods, just as all writers do in a manner Herman Melville, the Christy Mathewson of American fiction, well understood: "For genius, all over the world stands hand in hand, and one shock of recognition runs the whole circle round."

Greenberg's thesis is that baseball moves properly beyond scores, statistics, and records; we each celebrate our own heroes, a Nolan or a Mathewson. For Jackie Kapp it happened to be Mathewson. "The greatest I ever saw was Christy Mathewson, on a terribly hot day in St. Louis, young as an April morning in that sweltering July, the perfect pitcher" (269). We all as fans and readers are formed in youth. But we all become adults too, and novelists like Eric Rolfe Greenberg remind us of our humanity by projecting a world, here one that joins baseball history with individual and family lives and deaths, with Jewish and Christian motifs in a creation that in *The Celebrant* recalls the perfect diamond of Jackie's art and of the field of baseball dreams. "It was my happiness to celebrate that perfection, in his age and suffering he would accept that vision of my youth, entwine it with his own hard faith, and end in madness" (269). Jackie ends sane, and his last words mingle Christian celebration, baseball lyric, but mostly Jewish brotherhood. "Eli, Eli." This is as good as baseball fiction gets.

Works Cited

Index

Works Cited

Manuscript Files, Papers, and Scrapbooks

Allen, Lee. Files. BBHFL.
Baseball Files. AJA.
Bloom, Morrie. Scrapbooks. Copy at Chicago Jewish Historical Society. Spertus College. Chicago.
Boxing Scrapbooks. 24 vols. Chicago Historical Society. Chicago.
Greenberg, Hank. File. Newspaper clippings. BBHFL.
Harris, Harry. Scrapbooks. 3 vols. (microfilm) New York Public Library. (Original at AJA).
Jewish Athletics. Scrapbook. AJA.
Miller, Davey. Scrapbook. Chicago Jewish Historical Society. Spertus College Library. Chicago.
Vertical Files. BBHFL.
Vladeck, Baruch Charney. Papers and Scrapbooks. BV.

Letters

Brundage, Avery. Letter to Albert D. Lasker. Mar. 30, 1936. AB, Box 234.
————. Letter to Edward James Smythe. Jan. 6, 1936. AB, Box 153.
Lasker, Albert D. Letter to Avery Brundage. Apr. 14, 1936. AB, Box 234.
Rickey, Branch. Letter to Roscoe Hobbs, Nov. 29, 1944. Branch Rickey Papers. National Archives. Washington, D.C.
Smith, Wendell. Letter to Lester Harrison. RRS 1946–47 Season. Sept. 11–Nov. 26, 1946. BHF.

Archival Sources

Bers, Janice Smith. "Report of the Directress of Camp Council for Summer 1939," 1–7. Camp Council Records, PJAC.

"Calling All Girls!" 1936. *Center News*, 3, Nov. 19: 2. Miscellaneous YMHA and JCC Files, 92d St. YM-YWHA.

Camp Council, Inc. "A Brief History of 50 Years, 1925–75." Camp Council Records, PJAC.

Copy of Player Contract of William P. Gates. Sept. 26, 1946. NBL.

Educational Alliance. 1898. House Committee Meeting. Nov. 18. File 13. YIVO Archives (YIVO).

———. 1900. *Printed Program of Activities, 1899–1900*, File 54. YIVO.

———. 1902. Minutes of the Board of Directors Meeting. Mar. 10. Microfilm Reel 2. YIVO.

———. 1905. "Report of the Special Committee on Reorganization." Apr. 7. File 25, YIVO.

———. 1910. "Report of the Head of Women's Work." Nov. 14. Reel 2, YIVO.

———. 1911. "Report of the Committee on Education." Jan. 1. Reel 2, YIVO.

———. 1912. "Report of the Head of Women's Work." Feb. 19. Reel 2, YIVO.

———. 1916. "Report of the Director of Girls' Clubs." Dec. 7. Reel 4, YIVO.

———. 1917. "Report of the Director of Girls' Clubs." Apr. 30, Reel 4, YIVO.

———. 1919. Minutes of the Committee on Education Meeting. Jan. 31. Reel 4, YIVO.

Feldman, Rose. 1928. "Report of Athletic Counsellor—Tennis, Basketball, Baseball," Sept. 4, 1–2, Ray Hill Camp. 92d St. YM-YWHA Archives.

Freeman, Minnie E. 1928. "Report of the Executive Director for the Season of 1928," Sept. 18, 1–3, Ray Hill Camp. 92d St. YM-YWHA Archives.

Friedman, Joel E. 1942. "'Expert's' Advice Is Proffered to Female Gym Enthusiasts." *The Y.M.H.A. Bulletin* 44, Nov. 13: 1. 92d St. YM-YWHA Archives.

"Hows and Whys of Big Burg's Y's. 110th Street Y.W.H.A. Has Most Comprehensive Physical Education System of Type in Entire Country." 1935. *New York Post*. Jan. 17. YWHA Records. 92d St. YM-YWHA Archives.

Jewish Training School. *Second Annual Report of the Jewish Training School of Chicago of 1890–1891*. Spertus Institute/Chicago Jewish Archives. Chicago.

————. *Ninth Annual Report of the Jewish Training School of Chicago for 1889–1899*. Spertus Institute/Chicago Jewish Archives. Chicago.

Jewish Welfare Board. 1937. Report of the Study of the Jewish Peoples' Institute, Chicago, Illinois. New York: Jewish Welfare Board. Municipal Welfare Council Papers, Chicago Historical Society. Chicago.

Kahn, Frances. 1915. "Live a Little Longer." *Kol Alamoth* 1. June: 10. YWHA Records, 92d St. YM-YWHA Archives.

"Les Harrison on Fence Regarding Shift of Royals to BAA," RRS, 1946–47, BHF.

Lewis, Helen. 1928. "Report of Counsellor in Charge of Archery, Sewing, and Picnic Lunches." Sept. 4, 1–2. Ray Hill Camp. 92d St. YM-YWHA Archives.

Minutes of First Meeting of Glendale Country Club. 1924. Jan. 28. Schwabacher Family Papers. Seattle Jewish Archives Project. Univ. of Washington Library, Seattle.

Minutes of the Ray Hill Camp Committee. May 1926 and 1927. 92d St. YM-YWHA Archives.

NBA. *Bulletin*.
    No. 2, Aug. 9, 1949.
    No. 41, Nov. 14, 1949.
    No. 47, Dec. 1, 1949.
    No. 63, Jan. 27, 1950.
    No. 138, May 14, 1951.
    No. 187B, June 19, 1951.
    No. 242, Dec. 6, 1951.
    No. 308A, Aug. 19, 1952.

"Physical Department Increases Its Facilities." 1952.

Ray Hill Camp Brochures. 92d St. YM-YWHA Archives.

"Rise of Les Harrison, Royal Owner an Alger Saga." RRS 1946–47. BHF.

Rochester Royals 1946–47 Official Program. BHF.

"Rochester Royals Probably Best Team in Country." 1946. *We*, Apr. 15. RRS, 1945–46. BHF.

Rochester Royals Scrapbook, 1946–47 Season. BHF.

Rochester Royals Souvenir Program. RRS. 1946–47. BHF.

Rochester Royals Souvenir Program of Testimonial Dinner Honoring Al Cervi, RRS. 1945–46. BHF.

Seligs, Isadore. "A Study of the Basement Clubs of Lawndale District." Ernst Burgess Papers. Box 142, Folder 3. Special Collections, Univ. of Chicago Library.

Weinberg, S. Kirson. "Jewish Youth in the Lawndale Community." Ernest W. Burgess Papers. Box 139, Folder 3, 26. Special Collections, Univ. of Chicago Library.

Women's Swimming Association. 1920. "Program of the National Championship Meet. Women's Swimming Association of New York at the Young Women's Hebrew Association, March 13, 1920." WSA Archives.

————. 1921. "A Word of Thanks." *W.S.A. News,* Mar. WSA Archives.

Y Bulletin. May 1907. In Atlas Athletic Club Scrapbooks. 92d St. YM-YWHA Archives. New York.

"Y" Journal, The. Silver Jubilee, 1927–1952. YMHA-YWHA. St. Louis. May 16: 10–11. PJAC.

"YMHA Yearbook and 31st Annual Report of the Physical Division" (1905). 92d St. YM & YWHA Archives. New York.

Young Women's Hebrew Association. *Bulletin of Classes, 1916–1917, 1920–29.* 92 St. YM-YWHA Archives.

————. "Class Report." 1911. Jan. 1–Feb, 1. YWHA Records. 92d St. YM-YWHA Archives.

————. *Printed Materials of Class Activities, February 1934.* 92d St. YM-YWHA Archives.

————. *Program of Activities, 1938.* YWHA Records. 92d St. YM-YWHA Archives.

————. Scrapbooks 1920s and 1930s. YWHA Records. 92d St.YM-YWHA Archives.

————. 1924. *The Story of Six Years' Work of the Young Women's Hebrew Association 1919 Through 1924.* Feb. 92d St. YM-YWHA Archives.

————. *Thirteenth Annual Report, February 1916.* YWHA Records. 92d St. YM-YWHA Archives.

————. *Twentieth Anniversary Luncheon and Annual Meeting Young Women's Hebrew Association February 28, 1922.* 92d St. YM-YWHA Archives.

————. *Twenty-fifth Anniversary, 1902–1927, Young Women's Hebrew Association, New York City.* 92d St. YM-YWHA Archives.

————. *Twenty-fourth Annual Report, January 1927.* 92d St. YM-YWHA Archives.

Young Women's Union of Philadelphia. *Annual Report, 1916–1917.* Neighborhood Centre Records. PJAC.

————. *Director's Report, April 1917 to April 1918.* Neighborhood Centre Records. PJAC.

————. "History." Neighborhood Centre Records. PJAC.

————. 1941. "Report of the Committee on Clubs and Athletics, 1940–1941." Neighborhood Centre Records. PJAC.

————. *Twenty-fifth Anniversary Report, 1885–1910.* Neighborhood Centre Records, PJAC.

————. *Twenty-seventh Annual Report.* 1912. Neighborhood Centre Records. PJAC.

Newspapers

Abramson, Jesse P. 1933. "De Bruyn Wins Marathon to Port Chester." *NYHT,* Oct. 13, 23.

————. 1935a. "Olympics Ban Tabled in Strife by Met AAU." *NHYT,* Oct. 9, 26.

————. 1935b. "AAU Defers Fight over Olympic Issue After Five-Hour Debate." *NYHT,* Dec. 9, 3: 1.

————. 1935c. "AAU Approves Olympics Entry; Mahoney Resigns." *NYHT,* Dec. 9, 1, 20.

————. 1935d. "AAU Elects Brundage Head, No Rival Slate." *NYHT,* Dec. 9, 20.

————. 1936. "Metropolitan Association Drops Kiviat, Silver, Veteran Officials." *NYHT,* Feb. 29, 18.

Bell, Stuart. 1934a. "Flag Race Still Hot." *Cleveland Press.* Sept. 14, 36.

————. 1934b. "Greenberg Slams Pair." *Cleveland Press.* Sept. 11, 18.

Bingay, Malcolm W. 1934. "Will Break Down Vicious Prejudices." *Detroit Jewish Chronicle.* Sept. 21, 1.

B'nai B'rith Messenger (Los Angeles). 1936. Aug. 14.

Booker, James. 1951. "Joe Yancey All American Coach." *New York Amsterdam News,* Mar. 3, 7.

Boston Evening Transcript.
    1904. Apr. 20, 8.
    1905. Apr. 20, 4.
    1932. Apr. 19, 1.

Boston Globe.
    1904. Apr. 19, 1.
    1934. Sept. 12, 20.

Boston *Herald.* Sept. 11, 20.

Boston Post. 1934. Sept. 11, 17.

Brooklyn Eagle. 1909. Feb. 12, 1.

Burr, Harold. 1934. "First Year World Series Hoodoo Needn't Worry Hank Greenberg." *New York Evening Post.* Sept. 19, 20.

Carlisle, John. 1934. "2 Homers on Rosh Hashanah Prick Hank's Conscience." *Detroit News.* Sept. 11, 1.

Carveth, Jack. 1934. "Henry Prayed and Swung His Way to Baseball Glory." *DFP.* Sept. 11, 19.

Chicago Daily News. 1907. Aug. 27, 1.

Chicago Herald-American.
    1940. Mar. 13, 23.
    1948. May 9, 33; May 10, 20; May 11, 22.

Chicago Jewish Chronicle. 1934. Sept. 14, 10.

Chicago Tribune.
    1920. Dec. 19, sec. 2, 2.
    1934. Sept. 9, 2: Sept. 11, 21; Sept. 12, 24; Sept. 21, 27.
    1950. Oct. 6, 22.

Cincinnati Enquirer.
    1903. Nov. 17.
    1934. Sept. 11, 13.

Cleveland Plain Dealer. 1934. Sept. 8, 17; Sept. 20, 14; Sept. 23, sports
    sec., 2.

Cohen, Haskell. 1934. "The Year 5694 in the Sporting World." *The
    Jewish Advocate.* Sept. 7, sports sec., 1; features, 2.

Columbia Daily Spectator. 1935. Dec. 3, 1, 4.

Cunningham, Bill. 1934. Snags Hit New York Scrap." *Boston Post.* Sept.
    11, 19.

(Chicago) *Daily Jewish Courier* (CFLPS).
    1910. May 10.
    1912. Aug. 23.
    1914. Apr. 26.
    1927. July 21; Aug. 13.

Daley, Arthur J. 1932. "Steiner Victor in Metropolitan Title Marathon,
    de Bruyn Second, Far Behind." *NYT,* May 9, 22.

Dearborn Independent. 1934. Sept. 21, 1.

Detroit Free Press. 1934. Sept. 5, 1; Sept. 8, 12; Sept. 11, 1, 19; Sept. 21,
    20; Sept. 28, 1, 5.

Detroit Jewish Chronicle. 1934. Sept. 7, 7; Sept. 14, 10; Sept. 21, 1; Sept.
    28, 6.

Detroit News.
    1934. September 11, 1–2, 18; Sept. 18, 20.
    1945. Nov. 1, 6.
    1970. Apr. 25, 4.

Detroit Times. 1934. Sept. 10, sports sec., 1.

Effrat, Louis. 1934. "Marathon Crown Kept by Steiner." *NYT,* Mar. 26, 25.

Flynn, William J. 1955. "Costes Clips Record in Taking National AAU
    Marathon Championship." *NYT.* May 23, 32.

Frank, Stanley B. 1935. "German-American AC Heils Athletes but Not
    Hitler: Jewish Members Play a Big Part." *New York Post.* Jan. 3, 20.

Guest, Edgar. 1934. "Speaking of Greenberg." *DFP.* Oct 4, 6.

Hunt, Marshall. 1934. "Rowe Blanks Yankees, 12-0." *New York Daily
    News.* Sept. 19, 39.

Iffy the Dopester. 1934a. "Hank's Homers Strictly Kosher." *DFP.* Sept.
    11, 19.

————. 1934b. "Promising Young Man." *DFP*. Sept. 19, 16. Isaminger, James. 1934. "Tips from the Sport Ticker." *Philadelphia Inquirer.* Sept. 9, 6.

Jewish Daily Bulletin.
　1925. Mar. 25.
　1934. Sept. 9, 8; Sept. 14, 6.

Jewish Daily Forward (CFLPS)
　1923. July 16.
　1926. May 9.
　1928. May 5.

Lewis, Franklin. 1934. "Tiger Park Still Hard on Slugger." *Cleveland Press,* Sept. 22, 7.

Meany, Tom. 1934. "Yanks-Tigers." *New York World-Telegram.* Sept. 20, 29.

Milwaukee Sentinel. 1911. Feb. 12.

Murphy, Sam. 1934. "Tigers Needed Heavy Hitting of Greenberg." *New York Sun.* Sept. 19, 33.

New York American. 1936. Aug. 14, 23; Aug. 15, 19; Aug. 16, S3.
New York Daily News. 1934. Sept. 11, 54.
New York Evening Journal. 1934. Sept. 19, 25.
New York Herald Tribune. 1934. Sept. 11, 20.

New York Post.
　1934. Sept. 19, 20.

New York Times.
　1912. Jan. 19, 9; Jan. 23, 9; Jan. 25, 9; Jan. 26, 9; Feb. 23, 12.
　1914. Apr. 26, 7; Apr. 27, 13.
　1915. Feb. 23, 12; May 3, 9.
　1921. Apr. 20, 14.
　1925. Oct. 13, 29.
　1932. Aug. 21, 2.
　1933. June 5, 1.
　1934. Sept. 19, 18.
　1935. Oct 24, 8; Oct. 30, 16.
　1936. Jan. 4, 18; May 31, 4; Aug. 5, 23; Aug. 17, 12.
　1938. May 31, 24.
　1940. Apr. 20, 12.
　1946. Feb. 19, 28; Apr. 21, V: 1, 4; Apr. 26, 24; Oct. 24, 38.
　1948. Feb. 10, 29; Apr. 8, 33; May 9, S7; May 11, 34.
　1949. Aug. 4, 29; Oct. 16, V: 10.
　1951. Mar. 5, 26.
　1954. Mar. 15, 30, 33; May 17, 29; June 20, V: 4.
　1955. Apr. 29, 15.

1956. May 1, 39.
1957. Feb. 15, 27; Apr. 4, 45.
1958. Mar. 27, 46; Apr. 8, 39.
1959. Feb. 8, V: 1; Feb. 23, 29; June 26, 36; July 26, 36, V: 2.
1964. July 8, 35.
1967. Jan. 19, 31.
1970. Feb. 7, 29; Feb. 8, V: 1.
1972. June 26, 36.
1976. Mar. 8, 28.
1983. July 10, III: 8.
New York Tribune. 1920. Apr. 20, 15.
New York World. 1916. Jan. 2.
New York World-Telegram. 1934. Sept. 11, 32.
Otis, Sam. 1934. "Hank Seeks Advice and Rises Fast." *Cleveland Plain Dealer.* Sept. 22, 9.
Philadelphia Inquirer. 1934. Sept. 1, 17; Sept. 9, 6; Sept. 19, 29.
Pittsburgh Courier. 1946. Nov. 2, 16; Nov. 30, 16.
Port Chester Daily Item.
1926. Oct. 13, 1.
1931. Oct. 10, 1.
1937. Oct. 13, 5.
1938. Oct. 13, 1.
Reel, William. 1970. "The Yates Major in Commitment." *New York Daily News.* Apr. 25, 4.
Reform Advocate (Chicago). (CFLPS)
1891. May 22.
1912. Jan. 13, 817.
1926. Mar. 20, 907.
Rochester Democrat and Chronicle.
1940. Mar. 18, 9.
1945. Nov. 9, 27.
1946. Oct. 16, 21
1947. Apr. 2, 26; Apr. 12, 8.
1950. Nov. 2, 40.
1951. Apr. 23, 10.
1957. Mar. 28, 27; Apr. 3, 1; Apr. 4, 43; Apr. 7, 24.
1958. Mar. 19, 1–2; Mar. 27, 43; Mar. 29; Apr. 1, 20; Apr. 3, 36; Apr. 5, 19; Apr. 8, 1.
1984. Feb. 7, 4D, 10A; May 13, 1E, 1: 4E.
1986. Feb. 1, 2B.
Rochester Times-Union.
1941. Mar. 17, 11A.
1946. Oct. 16, 15A.

1951. Apr. 23, 26.

1953. Feb. 27, 46.

1956. July 3, 1.

1957. Apr. 23, 14.

1958. Apr. 8, 26.

1988. Mar. 30, 5D.

Rud, Rennie. 1934. "Tigers' Flair Fan Sentiment." *NYHT.* Sept. 21, 27.

St. Louis Post-Dispatch. 1934. Sept. 9, 1f.

Salsinger, Harry G. 1934a. "About Mr. Greenberg." *Detroit News.* Sept. 11, 21.

———. 1934b. "Playing for Community." *Detroit News.* Sept. 11, 21.

———. 1934c. "Greatest Jewish Player in Baseball." *Detroit Jewish Chronicle.* Sept. 21, 1.

Segar, Charles. 1934. "Yanks Win, 5-2." *New York Daily Mirror.* Sept. 20, 31.

Shaver, Bud. 1934. "Foxx Helps Tutor Hank." *Detroit Times.* Sept. 18.

Smith, Wilfrid. 1934. "Rain Again Defers Ross, McLarnin Bout." *Chicago Tribune.* Sept. 9, 2:1.

Spirit of the Times.

1896. 132, Sept. 26, 334.

1898. 136, Nov. 12, 419.

1900. 139, June 9, 444

Sport Call.

1937. 6, Oct. 16, 2, 3, 11; Nov. 27, 2, 3.

1938. 7, Mar. 19, 4; Apr. 23, 2; May 28, 4.

The Sporting News.

1896. Oct. 17, 7.

1897. June 13.

1934. Sept. 20, 32; Oct. 4, 3; Oct. 11, 3.

1937. Mar. 25, 1.

1941. May 15, 4; Dec. 25, 4.

1942. Mar. 19, 5.

1945. June 21, 1; Nov. 1, 6.

1946. Feb. 28, 7.

Stark, George. 1934. "She Learns About Homers First Time at Ball Game." *Detroit News.* Sept. 18, 20.

Sunday Jewish Courier (Chicago) (CFLPS). 1922. April 2, 1927. Sept. 25.

Vaughn, Irving. 1934. "Back in Stride." *DFP,* Oct. 7, 6.

Ward, Charles. 1934a. "Greenberg's Two Home Runs Give Tigers 2 to 1 Victory." *DFP.* Sept. 11: 19, 25.

———. 1934b. "Bengals Fatten Bat Averages." *DFP.* Sept. 27, 13.

———. 1934c. "Cochrane Changes Lineup." *DFP.* Oct. 6, 1–2.

Washington Post. 1934. September 19, 17.

Weiner, Morris. 1934a. "Slants on Sports." *Jewish Daily Bulletin*. Sept. 14, 7.
————. 1934b. "The Year in Jewish Sports." *Detroit Jewish Chronicle*. Sept. 14, 10.
————. 1934c. "Greatest Jewish Baseball Player." *Detroit Jewish Chronicle*. Sept. 21, 1.
Weintraub, Phil. 1934. "Why So Few Jews in Baseball." *The Jewish Advocate*. September 7, 11.
Worner, Ted. 1938. "Pat Dengis of Baltimore Repeats in Yonkers Marathon Championship." (Yonkers) *Herald Statesman*. Nov. 7, 17.
Veyoveh, Yaaleh. 1934. "Hank's Rosh Hashanah." *Detroit Jewish Chronicle*. Sept. 14, 1, 4.

Interviews, Correspondence, and Conversations

Abrams, Calvin, and May Abrams. Interview. AJC.
Arcel, Ray. Interview. AJC.
————. Telephone interview with Steven A. Riess. Apr. 17, 1984.
Beahon, George. Telephone conversation with Donald Fisher. June 1, 1992.
Bentley, Ben. Interview with Steven Riess. Apr. 7, 1984.
Blum, Howard. Interview with Steven Riess. Jan. 3, 1984.
Cervi, Alfred Cervi. Interview with Donald Fisher. Jan. 9, 1992.
Cohen, Andy. Interview. AJC.
Gehringer, Charles. Interview with William Simons. Jan. 9, 1979.
Glickman, Marty. Interview. AJC.
Greenberg, Hank. Correspondence with William Simons. Feb. 8, 1979.
————. Questionnaire from William Simons. Feb. 8, 1979.
Harrison, Lester. Interview with Donald Fisher. Nov. 8, 1991.
————. Telephone conversation with Donald Fisher. May 14, 1992.
Lapchick, Richard. Interview with Ted Koppel. "Nightline." ABC-TV. Jan. 24, 1989.
Leane, Andrew. Correspondence with Donald Fisher. Mar. 10, 1992.
Levine, Al. Interview with Steven Riess. Mar. 7, 1984.
Levy, Ed. Interview with Pamela Cooper. Jan. 15, 1992.
Lieb, Frederick. Interview with William Simons. Nov. 15, 1978.
Marovitz, Judge Abraham Lincoln. Interview with Jerry Gems. Dec. 10, 1990.
Massino, Alfred. Interview with Donald Fisher. Apr. 16, 1992.
Melnick. Murray. Correspondence with Pamela Cooper. Aug. 10. 1994.
Morgan, William. Conversation with William Simons. Summer 1979.
Ocorr, David. Correspondence with Donald Fisher. Mar. 23, 1992.
Regan, Richard. Telephone conversation with Donald Fisher. June 18, 1992.

Soule, Aileen Riggin. Telephone conversation with Linda Borish. June 1995.

Wanzer, Robert. Interview with Donald Fisher. Aug. 21, 1991.

Books and Periodicals

Abramson, Jesse. 1945. "Democratic Ideal: The Pioneer Club." *Amateur Athlete,* Sept. 11: 15.

Addams, Jane. 1960. *Twenty Years at Hull House.* 1910; Reprint New York: New American Library.

————. 1923. *Spirit of Youth and the City Street.* New York: MacMillan.

Adelman, Melvin L. 1980. "The Development of Modern Athletics: Sport in New York City, 1820–1870." Ph.D. diss., Univ. of Illinois.

————. 1986. *A Sporting Time: New York City and the Rise of Sports, 1820–70.* Urbana, Ill.: Univ. of Illinois Press.

Akers, Dwight. 1947. *Drivers Up! The Story of American Harness Racing.* 2d ed. New York: Putnam.

Albertanti, Francis. 1926. "Maxie Rosenbloom, Greatest Light Heavyweight Hebrew Prospect since Days of Battling Levinsky." *Ring* 5, Sept.: 16–17.

————. 1936. "Mike Jacobs, Successor to Tex Rickard." *Ring* 15, July: 6–7.

————. 1948. "When the 'Swells' Put Glamour into Boxing." *Ring,* 27, Sept.: 22.

Alexander, Charles C. 1995. *Rogers Hornsby: A Biography.* New York: Henry Holt.

Alouf, Jehosua. 1973. "Physical Culture in the Period of the Talmud (Abstract)." *Physical Education and Sports in the Jewish History and Culture. Proceedings of an International Seminar.* Edited by Uriel Simri. 39. Natanya, Israel: Wingate Institute for Physical Education and Sport.

Amateur Athletic Federation. 1930 *Handbook, 1929–1930.* New York: Amateur Athletic Foundation.

Amateur Athletic Union of the United States. 1928, 1932, 1936. *Minutes of the Annual Meeting of the Amateur Athletic Union of the United States.* New York: Amateur Athletic Union.

American Hebrew.
    1917. July 13.
    1919. May 16, 711; June 6, 96; Dec. 5, 98.
    1920. July 2.
    1923. May 4.
    1925. June 5, 151; Sept. 4, 489; Oct. 16, 760; Nov. 6, 828, 857.
    1926. June 4, 125.

1929. May 3, 958, 970.

1930. July 4, 125.

"American Jews as Sportsmen." 1920. *American Hebrew* 106, Apr. 2: 596, 598, 687.

"Among the Country Clubs." 1924. *American Hebrew* 111, June 6, 123: 135–36, 138–39.

————. 1926. *American Hebrew* 115, June 4: 123.

Anderson, Arthur. 1938. "The Bronx Bomber." *Baseball Magazine.* Sept.: 451.

Anderson, Dave. 1991. *In This Corner: Great Boxing Trainers Talk About Their Art.* New York: Morrow.

Andre, Sam, and Nat Fleischer. 1981. *A Pictorial History of Boxing.* New York: Bonanza.

Angevine, Elbert. 1951. *Basketball in Rochester.* Rochester, N.Y.: Harold P. Bittner.

Appel, Martin, and Burt Goldblatt. 1974. *Baseball's Best: The Hall of Fame Gallery.* New York: McGraw Hill.

Applin, Albert. 1982. "From Muscular Christianity to the Marketplace: The History of Men's and Boy's Basketball in the United States, 1891–1957." Ph.D. diss. Univ. of Massachusetts.

Ashe, Arthur R. Jr. 1988. *A Hard Road to Glory: A History of the African-American Athlete since 1946.* New York: Warner Books.

Asinof, Eliot. 1963. *Eight Men Out: The Black Sox and the 1919 World Series.* New York: Holt, Reinhart and Winston.

Auerbach, Red, with Ken Dooley. 1991. *MBA Management by Auerbach.* New York: Macmillan.

Auerbach, Red, and Joe Fitzgerald. 1977. *Auerbach: An Autobiography.* New York: Putnam's Sons.

Baldwin, P. M. 1980. "Liberalism, Nationalism, and Degeneration: The Case of Max Nordau." *Central European History* 13: 99–120.

Baltzell, E. Digby. 1959. *Philadelphia Gentlemen: The Making of a National Upper Class.* New York: Free Press.

Barney, Robert K. 1982. "Knights of Cause and Exercise: German Forty-Eighters and Turnvereine in the United State During the Antebellum Period." *Canadian Journal of History of Sport* 13, n. 2: 62–89.

Barth, Gunther. 1980. *City People: The Rise of Modern City Culture in Nineteenth Century America.* New York: Oxford Univ. Press.

Barzell, David. N.d. "Benny Leonard and Nathan Straus." Article in Scrapbooks Containing Newspaper and Magazine Clippings Concerning Jewish Athletics. AJA.

The Baseball Encyclopedia. 1969. 1st ed. New York: Macmillan.

The Basketball Encyclopedia. 1996. 10th ed. New York: Macmillan.

"Basket Ball." 1923. *I.K.S. Neighbors* 1, Dec. 1: 5.

Baskhi, Meir. 1973. "Physical Culture in the Writings of Maimonides (Abstract)." *Physical Education and Sports in the Jewish History and Culture. Proceedings of an International Seminar.* Edited by Uriel Simri. 50. Netanya, Israel: Wingate Institute for Physical Education and Sport.

Baum, Charlotte, Paul Hyman, and Sonya Michel. 1976. *The Jewish Woman in America.* New York: Dial.

Bayor, Ronald H. 1978. *Neighbors in Conflict: The Irish, Germans, Jews, and Italians of New York City, 1929–1941.* Baltimore: Johns Hopkins Univ. Press.

Bell, Daniel. 1960. *The End of Ideology: On the Exhaustion of Political Ideas in the 1950s.* Glencoe, Ill.: Free Press.

Bellow, Adam. 1990. *The Educational Alliance: A Centennial Celebration.* New York: The Educational Alliance, Inc.

Berenson, Senda, ed. 1901. *Spalding's Athletic Library Basket Ball for Women.* New York: American Sports Publishing Co.

Berkow, Ira. 1977. *Maxwell Street: Survival in a Bazaar.* Garden City, N.Y.: Doubleday.

Bernett, Hajo. 1973. "The Role of Jewish Sportsmen During the Olympic Games in 1936." In *Physical Education and Sports in the Jewish History and Culture. Proceedings of an International Seminar.* Edited by Uriel Simri. 88–113. Netanya, Israel: Wingate Institute for Physical Education.

———. 1978. *Der judische Sport im nationalsozialistichen Deutschland, 1933–1938.* Schorndorf, Germany: Hofmann.

Bernheimer, Charles S. 1905. *The Russian Jew in the United States.* Philadelphia: J. S. Winston.

Bernstein, Elizabeth. 1993. "Jewish Chicago Story: A Nostalgic Look Back at Some Kosher-Style Capones." *JUF News,* June: 60–69.

Biles, Roger. 1984. *Big City Boss in Depression and War: Mayor Edward J. Kelly of Chicago.* DeKalb, Ill.: Northern Illinois Univ. Press.

Birmingham, Stephen. 1967. *Our Crowd: The Great Jewish Families of New York.* New York: Pocket Books.

Bjarkman, Peter C. 1990. "Six-Pointed Diamonds and the Ultimate Shiksa: Baseball and the American-Jewish Immigrant Experience." In *Cooperstown Symposium on Baseball and the American Culture.* Edited by Alvin L. Hall, 306–47. Westport, Conn.: Meckler.

Black, David. 1977. *The Fortunes of August Belmont: The King of Fifth Avenue.* New York: Dial.

Blady, Ken. 1988. *The Jewish Boxers Hall of Fame.* New York: Sapolsky.

Blitzer, Grace Rosenberg. 1924. "Junior Jottings—and—Golf and Tennis." *American Hebrew* 115, Nov. 7: 853.

Bloodgood, Clifford. 1934. "A Star Rookie of 1933: Believe It or Not a Hebrew Tiger and a Good One." *Baseball Magazine.* Feb.: 407.

————. 1945. "The Tigers—In Seven Games." *Baseball Magazine.* Dec.: 223.

Borish, Linda J. 1994. "Review of *Ellis Island to Ebbets Field: Sport and the American Jewish Experience* by Peter Levine." *American Jewish History* 82: 410–11.

————. Forthcoming. "Charlotte Epstein." In *Jewish Women in America: A Historical Encyclopedia.* Edited by Paula E. Hyman and Deborah Dash Moore. New York: Carlson Publishing.

Brandes, Stuart. 1976. *American Welfare Capitalism.* Chicago: Univ. of Chicago Press.

Breines, Paul. 1990. *Tough Jews: Political Fantasies and the Moral Dilemma of American Jewry.* New York: Basic Books.

Brenman-Gibson, Margaret. 1981. *Clifford Odets: American Playwright.* New York: Atheneum.

Brenner, Teddy, and Barney Nagler. 1981. *Only the Ring Was Square.* Englewood Cliffs, N.J.: Prentice-Hall.

Broeg, Bob. 1970. "Greenberg—Hammered Way into Hall of Fame." *TSN.* Oct. 3, 18.

————. 1971. *Superstars of Baseball.* St. Louis, Mo.: *Sporting News.*

Brooks, Thomas R. 1974. *Walls Come Tumbling Down: A History of the Civil Rights Movement, 1940–1970.* Englewood Cliffs, N.J.: Prentice-Hall.

Bryson, Bill. 1938. "League of Nations." *Baseball Magazine.* July: 365–66.

Burko, Faina. "The American Yiddish Theater and Its Audience Before World War II." In *The Legacy of Jewish Migration: 1881 and Its Impact.* Edited by David Berger. New York: Brooklyn College Press.

Burns, George. 1980. *The Third Time Around.* New York: Putnam.

Cahan, Abraham. 1896. *Yekl.* New York: Appleton.

————. 1914. "The New Writers of the Ghetto." *Bookman* 39, Aug.: 633.

————. 1917. *The Rise of David Levinsky.* New York: Grosset and Dunlap.

Cantor, Eddie. 1928. *My Life Is in Your Hands.* New York: Harper & Bros.

Capeci, Dominic J. Jr. 1977. *The Harlem Riot of 1943.* Philadelphia: Temple Univ. Press.

Carroll, Ted. 1936. "Playboy of the Ring." *Ring* 15, Dec.: 29, 45.

————. 1942. "Army Gets East Side Jewel." *Ring* 20, Aug.: 22.

————. 1947a. "The Merry Madcaps." *Ring* 15, May: 28, 36.

————. 1947b. "A Champion to Remember." *Ring* 26, July: 9–10.

Carson, Mina. 1990. *Settlement Folk: Social Thought and the American Settlement Movement, 1885–1930.* Chicago: Univ. of Chicago Press.

Carvalho, S. N. 1880. "Cor. Sec. Y.M.H.A. of Harlem, N.Y." *American Hebrew* 3, July 30: 129.

Chalk, Ocania. 1975. *Pioneers of Black Sport.* New York: Dodd, Mead.

Chicago Hebrew Institute. 1909. *Lincoln Week Program.* 1909. Feb. 10–13.

"The City Athletic Club." 1908. *American Hebrew* 84, Nov. 20: 74.

City Athletic Club. 1912. "Constitution, By-Laws, and House Rules." New York: N.p.

"City Athletic Club to Build." 1920. *American Hebrew* 106, Apr. 2: 622.

Cohane, Tim, and Harry Grayson. 1954. "The Slugging of Ray Arcel." *Look.* Jan. 26: 42–44.

Cohen, Morris R. 1919. "Baseball." *Dial* 67, July 26: 57–58.

———. 1949. *A Dreamer's Journey: The Autobiography of Morris R. Cohen.* Boston: Beacon Press.

Cohen, Naomi. 1984. *Encounter with Emancipation: The German Jews in the United States 1830–1914.* Philadelphia: Jewish Publication Society.

Cohen, Sarah Blacher, ed. 1983. *From Hester Street to Hollywood: The Jewish-American Stage and Screen.* Bloomington: Indiana Univ. Press.

Cohen, Stanley. 1978. *The Game They Played.* New York: Farrar, Straus, & Giroux.

Cole, William T. 1910. *Motives and Results of the Social Settlement Movement.* Publications of the Department of Social Sciences in Harvard Univ., No. 2. Cambridge, Mass.: Harvard Univ. Press.

Collier, Malcolm. 1975–76. "Jens Jensen and Columbus Park." *Chicago History* 4, no. 4: 225–43.

Committee on Fair Play in Sports. 1935. *Preserve the Olympic Ideal: A Statement of the Case Against American Participation in the Olympic Games at Berlin.* New York: Fair Play Committee in Sports.

Considine, Bob, and Fred G. Jarvis. 1969. *The First Hundred Years: A Portrait of the NYAC.* Toronto: Macmillan.

Conzen, Kathleen Neils, and David A. Gerber, Ewa Morawska, George E. Pozzetta, and Rudolph H. Vecoli. 1992. "The Invention of Ethnicity: A Perspective from the U.S.A." *Journal of American Ethnic History* 12, fall: 3–41.

Cooper, Pamela L. 1992. "The 'Visible Hand" on the Footrace: Fred Lebow and the Marketing of the Marathon." *Journal of Sport History* 19: 244–56.

Coughlan, Robert. 1955. "How the IBC Runs Boxing." *Sports Illustrated* 1, Jan. 17: 17.

Counter, Cross. 1945. "The Pride of the Ghetto." *Ring* 24, May: 18.

"Cruising on Summer Seas." 1925. *American Hebrew* 117, June 5, 154–55.

Cutler, Irving. 1995. "The Jews of Chicago: From Shtetl to Suburbs." In *Ethnic Chicago.* Edited by Peter d'A. Jones and Melvin Holli. 40–79. Grand Rapids: Wm. B. Eerdmans.

Daley, Arthur. 1962. *Kings of the Home Run.* New York: Putnam.

"Dancing! Gymnasium! Swimming!" 1923. *I.K.S. Neighbors* 1, Oct. 25, 4.

Daniel, Daniel M. 1944. "Leonard's Kayo of Welsh Dramatic." *Ring* 22, Aug.: 14–16.

————. 1945. "Attell and Moran in Classic Draw." *Ring* 23, Mar.: 14–15, 42.

————. 1946. "Driscoll v. Attell, Battle of Ghosts." *Ring* 24, Jan.: 24–26, 40.

————. 1950. *The Mike Jacobs Story*. New York: Ring Book Shop.

————. 1959. "Tendler Reveals How Leonard Suckered Him." *Ring* 38, Sept.: 17–18.

Davis, Allen F. 1967. *Spearheads for Reform: The Social Settlements and the Progressive Movement, 1890–1914*. New York: Oxford Univ. Press.

————. 1973. *American Heroine: The Life and Legend of Jane Addams*. New York: Oxford Univ. Press.

Davis, Michael M. 1911. *The Exploitation of Pleasure: A Study of Commercial Recreation in New York City*. New York: Dept. of Child Hygiene of the Russell Sage Foundation.

Derderian, Tom. 1993. *Boston Marathon: The History of the World's Premier Running Event*. Champaign, Ill.: Human Kinetics.

Desser, David, and Lester D. Friedman, eds. 1993. *American-Jewish Filmmakers: Traditions and Trends*. Urbana, Ill.: Univ. of Illinois Press.

Devereux, Edward C. Jr. 1980. *Gambling and the Social Structure: A Sociological Study of Lotteries and Horse Racing in Contemporary America*. New York: Arno.

Dickey, Glenn. 1991. *Just Win, Baby: Al Davis and His Raiders*. New York: Harcourt, Brace, Jovanovich.

Diner, Hasia R. 1995. *A Time for Gathering: The Second Migration, 1820–1880*. Vol. II. *The Jewish People in America*. Edited by Henry L. Feingold. Baltimore: Johns Hopkins Univ. Press.

Dinnerstein, Leonard. 1994. *Antisemitism in America*. New York: Oxford Univ. Press.

Dinnerstein, Leonard, and David Reimers. 1975. *Ethnic Americans: A History of Immigration and Assimilation*. New York: Harper & Row.

Dizikes, John. 1981. *Sportsmen and Gamesmen*. Boston: Houghton Mifflin.

Drees, Jack, and James C. Mullen. 1973. *Where Is He Now? Sports Heroes of Yesterday*. Rev. 2d ed. Middle Village, N.Y.: Jonathan David.

"Dr. Eliot on Jewish Physique." 1909. *The American Hebrew*. Dec. 27: 207.

Duis, Perry. 1983. *The Saloon: Public Drinking in Chicago and Boston, 1880–1920*. Urbana, Ill.: Univ. of Illinois Press.

Ebner, Michael. 1988. *Creating Chicago's North Shore: A Suburban History*. Chicago: Univ. of Chicago Press.

Ebony. 1955. July: 103–6.

Edelstein, Tilden G. 1983. "Cohen at the Bat." *Commentary* 76, Nov.: 53–56.

Edmonds, Anthony O. 1973. *Joe Louis*. Grand Rapids, Mich.: Eerdmans.

Educational Alliance. 1895. *Souvenir Book of the Fair of the Educational Alliance and Hebrew Technical Institute, 1895*. New York: Frederick Spiegelberg.

Educational Alliance. *Fifth Annual Report (1897)*.

————. *Thirteenth Annual Report (1905)*.

"1895-GREETINGS-1925; A Brief History of the Irene Kaufmann Settlement." 1925. *Irene Kaufmann Settlement Neighbors* 3. Jan. 15: 1–3.

Eisen, George. 1979. "The Maccabiah Games: A History of the Jewish Olympics." Ph.D. diss., Univ. of Maryland.

————. 1984. "The Voices of Sanity: American Diplomatic Reports from the 1936 Berlin Olympics." *Journal of Sport History* 11, winter: 56–77.

————. 1991. "Sport, Recreation, and Gender: Jewish Immigrant Women in Turn-of-the-Century America (1880–1920)." *Journal of Sport History* 18, spring: 103–20.

Eisen, George, and David K. Wiggins, eds. 1994. *Ethnicity and Sport in North American History and Culture*. Westport, Conn.: Greenwood Press.

"Emma Farm Camp News." 1924. *I.K.S. Neighbors* 2, July 1: 6.

Endelman, Todd M. 1979. *The Jews of Georgian England, 1714–1830: Tradition and Change in a Liberal Society*. Philadelphia: Jewish Publication Society of America.

Erens, Patricia. 1984. *The Jew in American Cinema*. Bloomington: Indiana Univ. Press.

Ewen, Elizabeth. 1985. *Immigrant Women in the Land of Dollars: Life and Culture on the Lower East Side, 1890–1925*. New York: Monthly Review Press.

Falls, Joe. 1975. *The Detroit Tigers*. New York: Macmillan.

Farrington, Dick. 1934. "Greenberg, Young Tiger Star." *TSN*. Oct. 4, 3.

Fass, Paula S. 1989. *Outside In: Minorities and the Transformation of American Education*. New York: Oxford Univ. Press.

Feingold, Henry L. 1992. *A Time for Searching: Entering the Mainstream, 1920–1945*. Vol. IV. *The Jewish People in America*. Edited by Henry L. Feingold. Baltimore: Johns Hopkins Univ. Press.

Feldman, Chick. 1937. "Arnovich Started Out to be Shortstop." *TSN*. July 1, 3.

Figone, Albert J. 1989. "Gambling and College Basketball: The Scandal of 1951." *Journal of Sport History* 16: 44–61.

Fischer, Donald M. 1990. "The Rochester Royals and the Transformation of Professional Basketball, 1945–57." *International Journal of the History of Sport* 10, Apr.: 20–48.

Fleischer, Nat. 1928. "Leach Cross Reminiscences." *Ring* 7, June: 10–11.

————. 1932. "The Fighter Who Doesn't Care." *Ring* 11, June: 6.

————. 1942. *Max Baer, Glamour Boy of the Ring.* New York: Press of C. J. O'Brien.

————. 1943. *Terrible Terry McGovern.* New York: N.p.

————. 1946. "Nat Fleischer Says." *Ring* 25, Dec.: 19.

————. 1947a. *Leonard the Magnificent.* New York: N.p.

————. 1947b. "Alias Leach Cross." *Ring* 26, Dec. 1947: 12–14.

————. 1951. "Waxman Key Figure in Dempsey's Success." *Ring* 30, Mar.: 26.

————. 1958. *50 Years at Ringside.* New York: Fleet.

Flinn, John J. 1891. *The Standard Guide to Chicago for the Year 1891.* Chicago: Flinn and Sheppard.

Frank, Morris J. 1908. "Activity of the Jews in Athletics." *American Hebrew* 83, Sept. 18: 477.

Frank, Stanley. 1936. *The Jew in Sport.* New York: Miles.

————. 1941. "Hank Made Greenberg." *Saturday Evening Post.* 213, Mar. 15: 37.

Franks, Joel S. 1991. "Rube Levy: A San Francisco Shoe Cutter and the Origin of Professional Baseball in California." *California History* 70: 174–91, 234–36.

Fried, Albert. 1980. *The Rise and Fall of the Jewish Gangster in America.* New York: Holt, Reinhart and Winston.

Fried, Marc. 1991. *Corner Men: The Great Boxing Trainers.* New York: 4 Walls, 8 Windows.

"From Marbles to Polo." 1924. *American Hebrew.* 115, June 6: 121.

Gabler, Neal. 1988. *An Empire of Their Own: How the Jews Invented Hollywood.* New York: Crown.

Gallico, Paul. 1938. *Farewell to Sport.* New York: Knopf.

Gems, Gerald R. 1994. "Sport and the Americanization of Ethnic Women in Chicago." In *Ethnicity and Sport in North American History and Culture.* Edited by George Eisen and David K. Wiggins. 177–200. Westport, Conn.: Greenwood Press.

————. 1995. "Sport and the Forging of a Jewish-American Culture: The Chicago Hebrew Institute." *American Jewish History* 83, Mar.: 15–26.

Gerstein, Joseph. 1952. "Anti-Semitism in Baseball." *Jewish Life* 6, July: 21–22.

Gilman, Sander. 1991. *The Jew's Body.* New York: Routledge.

"Girls Play Volley Ball." 1926. *I.K.S. Neighbors* 4, May 15: 53.

"Girls, Use the Shower Baths and Swimming Pool!" 1925. *I.K.S. Neighbors* 3, Feb. 15: 23.

Glanz, Rudolf. 1976. *The Jewish Woman in America: Two Female Immigrant Generations, 1820–1929.* Vol. I. *The Eastern European Jewish Woman.* Vol. II. *The German Jewish Woman.* N.p.: KTAV Publishing House and National Council of Jewish Women.

Glenn, Susan. 1990. *Daughters of the Shtetl: Life and Labor in the Immigrant Generation.* Ithaca, N.Y.: Cornell Univ. Press.

Glickman, Marty, with Stan Isaacs. 1996. *The Fastest Kid on the Block: The Marty Glickman Story.* Syracuse, N.Y.: Syracuse University Press.

Golden, Harry. 1969. *The Right Time: An Autobiography.* New York:

Goldman, Jonah. 1932. "The Jew in Baseball." Article in Scrapbooks Containing Newspaper and Magazine Clippings Concerning Jewish Athletics. AJA.

Goldstein, Ruby, and Frank Graham. 1959. *Third Man in the Ring.* New York: Funk and Wagnalls.

Golenbock, Peter. 1984. *Bums: An Oral History of the Brooklyn Dodgers.* New York: Putnam's Sons.

Goodman, Cary. 1979a. *Choosing Sides: Playground and Street Life on the Lower East Side.* New York: Schocken Books.

————.1979b. "(Re)Creating Americans at the Educational Alliance." *The Journal of Ethnic Studies* 8, winter: 1–28.

Gordon, Franklin. 1925. "A Long Drive down the Fairway." *American Hebrew* 117, June 5: 138, 151, 158–59, 162.

Gordon, George. 1926. "Yachting as a Sport." *American Hebrew* 119, June 4: 104, 141, 151.

Gordon, John Steele. 1990. "The Country Club." *American Heritage* Sept.-Oct.: 75–84.

Gorn, Elliott. 1986. *The Manly Art: Bare-Knuckle Prize Fighting in America.* Ithaca, N.Y.: Cornell Univ. Press.

Gottlieb, Moshe. 1972. "American Controversy over the Olympic Games." *American Jewish History* 61: 181–213.

Graffis, Joe. 1925. "Seven Chicago Golf Clubs." *American Hebrew* 117, June 5: 137, 163, 166–67, 174.

Graham, Frank. Jr. 1969. *Great Hitters of the Major Leagues.* New York: Random House.

Green, Constance McLaughlin. 1957. *American Cities in the Growth of the Nation.* New York: J. De Graff.

Greenberg, Cheryl Lynn. 1991. *Or Does It Explode? Black Harlem in the Great Depression.* New York: Oxford Univ. Press.

————. 1992. "The Politics of Disorder: Reexamining Harlem's Riots of 1935 and 1943." *Journal of Urban History* 18: 395–441.

Greenburg, Eric Rolfe. 1983. *The Celebrant: A Novel.* New York: Everest House.

"Greenberg, Hank." 1948. *Current Biography 1947.* New York: H. W. Wilson.

Greenberg, Hank. 1989. *Hank Greenberg: The Story of My Life.* Edited by Ira Berkow. New York: Times Books.

Greene, Sam. 1945. "Greenberg Gives New Flag Punch to Tigers." *TSN.*

June 21, 1.

Greene, Sam. 1934a. "Greenberg's Holiday Ends Infield Streak." *Detroit News.* Sept. 19, 20.

————. 1934b. "Greenberg's Punch Gains Clean-up Job." *TSN.* Sept. 20, 1.

Greifer, Julian L. 1948. "Neighborhood Centre—A Study of the Adjustment of a Culture Group in America." Ph.D. diss. New York Univ.

Grombach, John V. 1977. *The Saga of the Fist.* South Brunswick, N.J.: A. S. Barnes.

Gropman, Donald. 1992. *"Say It Ain't So, Joe!": The True Story of Shoeless Joe Jackson.* 2d. ed. New York: Carol.

Gumpert, Bertram Jay. 1928. "A Rising Star, Clara Greenspan, Winner of Many Championships." *American Hebrew* 123, Aug. 3: 389.

Gunther, John. 1960. *Taken at the Flood: The Story of Albert D. Lasker.* Harper & Bros.

Gurock, Jeffrey. 1979. *When Harlem Was Jewish: 1870–1930.* New York: Columbia Univ. Press.

Guttmann, Allen. 1971. *The Jewish Writer in America: Assimilation and the Crisis of Identity.* New York: Oxford Univ. Press.

————. 1978. *From Ritual to Record.* New York: Columbia Univ. Press.

————. 1984. *The Games Must Go On: Avery Brundage and the Olympic Movement.* New York: Columbia Univ. Press.

————. 1985. "Out of the Ghetto and on to the Field: Jewish Writers and the Theme of Sport." *American Jewish History* 74, Mar: 274–86.

————. 1991. *Women's Sport. A History.* New York: Columbia Univ. Press.

"Gym and a Swim for Vigor and Vim." 1925. *I.K.S. Neighbors* 3. Oct. 15: 96.

"Gym Work for Girls." 1923. *I.K.S. Neighbors* 1, Apr. 1: 4.

Halberstam, David. 1981. *The Breaks of the Game.* New York: Knopf.

Haller, Mark. 1971–72. "Organized Crime in Urban Society: Chicago in the Twentieth Century." *Journal of Social History* 5: 210–34.

————. 1976. "Bootleggers and American Gambling, 1920–1950." In U.S. Commission on the Review of the National Policy Towards Gambling. *Gambling in America: Final Report of the Commission on the Review of the National Policy Toward Gambling.* Washington, D.C.: Government Printing Office, 102–43.

————. 1979. "The Changing Structure of American Gambling in the Twentieth Century." *Journal of Social Issues* 35, no. 3: 98–108.

Handler, Andrew. 1985. *From the Ghetto to the Games: Jewish Athletes in Hungary.* Boulder, Colo.: East European Monographs.

Handlin, Oscar. 1973. *The Uprooted.* 2d ed., enl. Boston: Little, Brown.

Hansen, Marcus Lee. 1940. *The Immigrant in American History.* Cambridge, Mass.: Harvard Univ. Press.

Hardy, Stephen. 1982. *How Boston Played: Sport, Recreation, and Community, 1865–1915.* Boston: Northeastern Univ. Press.

———. 1986. "Entrepreneurs, Organizations, and the Sport Marketplace: Subjects in Search of Historians." *Journal of Sport History* 13: 14–33.

Hare, Nathan. 1971. "A Study of the Black Fighter." *Black Scholar* 3, Nov.: 6–8.

Harris, Mark. 1956. *Bang the Drum Slowly.* New York: Knopf.

———. 1988. "Horatio at the Bat, or Why Such a Lengthy Embryonic Period for the Serious Baseball Novel." *Journal of Sport Literature* 5 spring: 1–11.

Harrison, Walter Lee. 1981. "Six-Pointed Diamond: Baseball and American Jews." *Journal of Popular Culture* 15, Sept.: 112–18.

Hart, Gordon. 1925. "New Golf Courses Lure to the Links." 117, June 5: 134, 164–65, 168–69, 172.

Heinze, Andrew. 1990. *Adapting to Abundance: Jewish Immigration, Mass Consumption, and the Search for American Identity.* New York: Columbia Univ. Press.

Heller, Peter. 1973. *"In This Corner. . .!" Forty World Champions Tell Their Story.* New York: Simon and Schuster.

Henry, Harley. 1992. "'Them Dodgers Is My Gallant Knights': Fiction as History in *The Natural* (1952)." *Journal of Sport History* 19: 110–29.

Herberg, Will. 1960. *Protestant-Catholic-Jew: An Essay in American Religious Sociology.* Rev. 2d ed. Garden City, N.Y.: Doubleday.

Hertz, John, and Evan Shipman. 1954. *The Racing Memoirs of John Hertz.* Chicago: N.p.

Hertzberg, Steven. 1978. *Strangers Within the Gate City: The Jews of Atlanta, 1845–1915.* Philadelphia: Jewish Publication Society of America.

Higham, John. 1963. *Strangers in the Land: Patterns of American Nativism, 1860–1925.* Boston: Atheneum.

"Highlights on Links and Polo Fields." 1928. *American Hebrew* 123, June 1: 94–95, 104, 106, 108.

Hill, Art. 1978. *"Don't Let Baseball Die:" I Came to Watch.* AuTrain, Mich.: N.p.

Hirschberg, Al, and Sammy Aaronson. 1957. *As High as My Heart: The Sammy Aaronson Story.* New York: Coward McCann.

Hoberman, John M. 1989. "Sport and the Myth of the 'Jewish Body.'" Paper presented at the annual meeting of the North American Society for Sport History. Clemson, S.C., 1989.

Hollander, Zander, and Larry Fox. 1966. *The Home Run Story.* New York: Norton.

Hollandersky, Abraham. 1943. *The Life Story of Abe the Newsboy: Hero of a Thousand Fights.* Los Angeles: Abe the Newsboy Publishing Co.

Holzman, Red, with Leonard Lewin. 1971. *The Knicks.* New York: Dodd, Mead.

—————. 1987. *Red on Red.* New York: Bantam Books.

Holzman, Red, and Harvey Frommer. 1991. *Holzman on Hoops.* Dallas: Taylor Publishing

Horowitz, David. 1977. "Hakoah in New York (1926–1932): A New Dimension for American Jewry." *Judaism* 25, summer: 375–82.

Howe, Irving L. 1976. *World of Our Fathers.* New York: Harcourt, Brace, Jovanovich.

Howe, Irving L., and Kenneth Libo. 1979. *How We Lived, 1880–1930.* New York: R. Marek.

Hurwitz, Maximillian. 1936. *The Workman's Circle, Its History, Ideals, Organizations, and Institutions.* New York: Workmen's Circle.

Hye, Allen E. 1989. "The Baseball Messiah: Christy Mathewson and *The Celebrant.*" *Aethlon* 7, fall: 41-49.

Hyman, Paula E. 1991. "Gender and the Immigrant Jewish Experience in the United States." In *Jewish Women in Historical Perspective.* Edited by Judith R. Baskin. 222–42. Detroit: Wayne State Univ. Press.

—————. 1995. *Gender and Assimilation in Modern Jewish History: The Roles and Representations of Women.* Seattle: Univ. of Washington Press.

"Improving Your Husband's Game." 1924. *American Hebrew* 112, June 6: 145.

"Irony." 1919. *American Hebrew* 105, June 6: 96.

"It's Not the Same Game in Japan." 1941. Editorial. *TSN* 18, Dec.: 4.

Jable, J. Thomas. 1984. "The Public Schools Athletic League of New York City: Organized Athletics for City School Children, 1903–1914." In *The American Sporting Experience: A Historical Anthology of Sport in America.* Edited by Steven A. Riess. 219–38. West Point, N.Y.: Leisure Press.

Jackson, Kenneth T. 1985. *Crabgrass Frontier: The Suburbanization of the United States.* New York: Oxford Univ. Press.

Jacobson, Louis. 1990. "Herman Goldberg: Baseball Olympian and Jewish-American." *Baseball History* 3. Edited by Peter Levine. 71–89. Westport, Conn.: Meckler.

Janis, Ralph. 1978. "Flirtation and Flight: Alternatives to Ethnic Confrontation in White Protestant Detroit, 1880–1940." *The Journal of Ethnic Studies* 6, no. 2: 1–17.

Jenkins, Burris. 1941. "Out for Another Fly" (cartoon). *TSN.* May 15, 4.

Jenkins, Thomas J. 1955. "Changes in Ethnic and Racial Representation among Professional Boxers: A Study in Ethnic Succession." M.A. thesis, Univ. of Chicago.

"The Jewish Athlete." 1908a. *The American Hebrew.* 83, Oct. 2: 544.

"The Jewish Athlete." 1908b. *The American Hebrew.* 84, Dec. 11: 171.

"The Jewish Athlete." 1909. *American Hebrew* 86, Oct. 2: 544.

"Jewish Influences in American Life." 1921. *The International Jew.: The World's Foremost Problem.* Detroit: Dearborn Publishing 3: 38ff.

"Jewish Physique." 1909. *The American Hebrew* 86, Dec. 27: 200.

Jones, Jersey. 1948. "Busy Beets." *Ring* 27, Nov.: 22–23.

Joselit, Jenna W. 1983. *Our Gang: Jewish Crime and the New York Jewish Community, 1900–1940.* Bloomington: Indiana Univ. Press.

———. 1994. "The Jewish Way of Play," in *A Worthy Use of Summer: Jewish Summer Camping in America.* Edited by Jenna Weissman Joselit. 15–28. Philadelphia: National Museum of American Jewish History.

Justice.

1934. July 1, 15.

1935. Jan. 2, 10; Jan. 15, 5, 9, 11; Feb. 1, 9, 11; May 1, 4; June 15, 12; July 15, 12.

Kahn, Roger. 1972. *The Boys of Summer.* New York: Harper and Row.

Kallick, Maureen, et al. 1976. "Survey of American Gambling Attitudes and Behavior." In U.S. Commission on the Review of the National Policy Toward Gambling. *Gambling in America: Final Report of the Commission on the Review of the National Policy Toward Gambling.* Washington, D.C.: Government Printing Office. Appendix 1.

Kanfer, Stephen. 1989. *A Summer World.* New York: Farrar, Straus, and Giroux.

Katcher, Leo. 1959. *The Big Bankroll: The Life and Times of Arnold Rothstein.* New York: Harper.

Kazin, Alfred. 1951. *A Walker in the City.* New York: Harcourt, Brace.

Kearns, Jack "Doc," with Oscar Fraley. 1963. *The Million Dollar Gate.* New York: Macmillan.

Kefauver, Estes. 1951. *Crime in America.* Edited by Sidney Shalett. Garden City, N.Y.: Doubleday.

Kessner, Thomas. 1977. *The Golden Door: Italian and Jewish Immigrant Mobility in New York City, 1880–1915.* New York: Oxford Univ. Press.

Kidd, Bruce. 1978. "Canadian Opposition to the 1936 Olympics in Germany." *Canadian Journal of the History of Sport and Physical Education* 9, Dec.: 20–40.

———. 1980. "The Popular Front and the 1936 Olympics." *Canadian Journal of the History of Sport and Physical Education* 11, May: 1–18.

Kirksey, George. 1940. "The Trading Mart." *Baseball Magazine,* Aug.: 408.

Klein, Gene, and David Fisher. 1987. *First Down and a Billion: The Funny Business of Pro Football.* New York: Morrow.

Koperwas, Sam. 1976. *Westchester Bull.* New York: Simon and Schuster.

Kopkind, Andrew. 1979. "Bess Bets." *The Village Voice.* Nov. 12: 19.

Koppett, Leonard. 1968. *24 Seconds to Shoot.* New York: Macmillan.

Kraft, Louis. 1967. "A Century of the Jewish Center Movement—1854–1953." In *The Development of the Jewish Community Center: Purposes, Principles, and Practice.* 1–30. New York: National Association of Jewish Center Workers.

Kraft, Louis, ed. 1954. *Aspects of the Jewish Community Center.* New York: National Jewish Welfare Board.

Kramer, William M., and Norton B. Stern. 1974. "San Francisco's Fighting Jew." *California History* 53: 333–46.

———. 1984. "The Turnverein: A German Experience for Western Jewry." *Western States Jewish Historical Quarterly* 16 Apr.: 227–29.

Kraus, Bea. 1994. "South Haven's Jewish Resort Era: Its Pioneers, Builders & Vacationers." *Michigan Jewish History* 35, winter: 20–25.

Kruger, Arnd. 1976. "The 1936 Olympics—Berlin." In *The Modern Olympics.* Edited by Peter J.Graham and Horst Ueberhorst. 173–86. West Point, N.Y.: Leisure Press.

———. 1978. "'Fair Play for American Athletes': A Study in Anti-Semitism." *Canadian Journal of the History of Sport and Physical Education* 9, May: 42–57.

Landesco, John. 1929. *Organized Crime in Chicago.* Part 3 of the *Illinois Crime Commission Survey, 1929.* Reprint. 1968. Chicago: Univ. of Chicago Press.

Landesman, Alter F. 1969. *Brownsville.* New York: Bloch.

Lane, Frederick C. 1926. "Why Not More Jewish Ball Players?" *Baseball Magazine* 36, Jan.: 341

———. 1935. "Baseball's New Sensation, Hank Greenberg." *Baseball Magazine* 54, Oct.: 483.

Langfeld, William. 1928. *The Young Men's Hebrew Association of Philadelphia: A 50 Year Chronicle.* Philadelphia: YM & YWHA of Philadelphia.

Lay, Tracy Hollingsworth. 1925. *The Foreign Service of the United States.* New York: Prentice Hall.

Leitner, Irving. 1972. *Baseball: Diamond in the Rough.* New York: Abelard-Schuman.

Leonard, Fred Eugene, and George B. Affleck. 1947. *A Guide to the History of Physical Education.* Philadelphia: Lea & Febiger.

Leseman, Charles. 1947a. "The Kid Who Dropped Leonard." *Ring* 26, May: 32.

———. 1947b. "Boxed Seven Champs but Never Held a Crown." *Ring* 26, Oct.: 22–23.

———. 1947c. "The Man in the Iron Hat." *Ring* 26, Nov.: 15, 41.

Levin, Jenifer. 1982. *Water Dancer.* New York: Poseidon Press.

Levine, Peter. 1989a. "'My Father and I, We Didn't Get Our Medals': Marty Glickman's American Jewish Odyssey." *American Jewish History* 79: 399–424.

————. 1989b. *American Sport: A Documentary History.* Englewood Cliffs, N.J.: Prentice-Hall.

————. 1992. *Ellis Island to Ebbets Field: Sport and the American Jewish Experience.* New York: Oxford Univ. Press.

————. 1995. "The *American Hebrew* Looks at 'Our Crowd': The Jewish Country Club in the 1920s." *American Jewish History* 83, Mar.: 27–49.

Lewisohn, Ludwig. 1928. *The Island Within.* New York: Harper and Bros.

Liben, Meyer. 1967. "Athletic Jews." *Commentary* 43, Feb.: 80.

Lieb, Frederick G. 1935. "Oi, Oi, Oh Boy! Hail That Long-Sought Hebrew Star." *TSN.* Sept. 12.

Liebling, A. J. 1990. "The University of Eighth Avenue." In *A Neutral Corner: Boxing Essays.* Edited by Fred Warner and James Barbour. 16–44. New York: Simon and Schuster.

Lipson, David. 1965. *The Yiddish Theater in America.* New York: T. Yoseloff.

Lissak, Rivka Shpak. 1989. *Pluralism and Progressives: Hull House and the New Immigrants, 1890–1918.* Chicago: Univ. of Chicago Press.

Litsky, Frank. 1975. *Superstars.* Secaucus, N.J.: Derbibooks.

Littleton, Martin W. 1957. *My Partner-in-Law: The Life of George Morton Levy.* New York: Farrar, Straus, and Cudahy.

Littlewood, Thomas B. 1969. *Horner of Illinois.* Evanston, Ill: Northwestern Univ. Press.

Livingston, Bernard. 1973. *Their Turf: America's Horsey Set and Its Princely Dynasties.* New York: Arbor House.

Lloyd, Frank S. 1931. "The Place of Physical Education in the Jewish Center Program." *The Jewish Center* 9, Dec., 6–10.

Long Distance Log: A Publication for Runners by Runners. 1959. Mar., 22.

Lynn, Erwin. 1987. *The Jewish Baseball Hall of Fame: A Who's Who of Baseball Stars.* New York: Shapolsky.

McAuley, Ed. 1940. "Boudreau and Mack, 'Mike and Ike' of Indian Infield." *TSN.* May 30, 3.

McKelvey, Blake. 1961. *Rochester: An Emerging Metropolis, 1925–1961.* Rochester: Christopher Press.

Malamud, Bernard. 1952. *The Natural.* New York: Harcourt, Brace.

Malin, Irving. 1965. *Jews and Americans.* Carbondale, IL: Southern Ill.: Univ. Press.

Mandell, Richard. 1971. *The Nazi Olympics.* New York: Macmillan.

Manners, Ande. 1972. *Poor Cousins.* New York: Coward, McCann and Geoghegan.

Marazzi, Rich. 1986. "Al Schacht, 'the Clown Prince of Baseball.'" *Baseball History* 1, winter: 34–45.

Martin, David E., and Roger W. H. Gynn. 1979. *The Marathon Footrace: Performers and Performances.* Springfield, Ill.: Charles C. Thomas.

Marvin, Carolyn. 1982. "Avery Brundage and American Participation in the 1936 Olympics." *Journal of American Studies* 16, Apr.: 81–106.

Mayer, Paul Y. 1980. "Equality—Egality. Jews and Sport in Germany." *Leo Baeck Institute Year Book.* 221–41. London: Secker and Warburg.

Mazur, Edward. 1977. "Chicago: From Diversity to Community." In *The Ethnic Frontier.* Edited by G. Holli and Peter d'A. Jones. Grand Rapids Mich.: Wm. B. Eerdmans.

————. 1990. *Minyans for a Prairie City: The Politics of Chicago Jewry, 1850–1940.* New York: Garland.

Mead, William. 1978. *Even the Browns: The Zany, True Story of Baseball in the Early Forties.* Chicago: Contemporary.

Meites, Hyman L. 1924. *History of the Jews of Chicago.* Chicago: Jewish Historical Society of Illinois.

Merin, Samuel. 1934. "An Italian Baseball Guide." *Baseball Magazine.* Mar.: 464.

Messick, Hank. 1978. *The Politics of Prosecution: James Thompson, Richard Nixon, Marge Everett, and the Trial of Otto Kerner.* Ottawa, Ill.: Carolina House Books.

Metzner, Henry. 1924. *A Brief History of the American Turnerbund.* Pittsburgh: National Executive Committee of the American Turnerbund.

Miller, Bill. 1932. "The Jew in Boxing." *Ring* 10, Dec.: 8–9.

Miller, James E. 1990. *The Baseball Business: Pursuing Pennants and Profits in Baltimore.* Chapel Hill: Univ. of North Carolina Press.

Miller, Kerby. 1985. *Emigrants and Exiles: Ireland and the Irish Exodus to North America.* New York: Oxford Univ. Press.

Moore, William H. 1974. *The Kefauver Committee and the Politics of Crime.* Columbia: Univ. of Missouri Press.

Mormino, Gary Ross. 1982. "The Playing Fields of St. Louis: Italian Immigrants and Sports, 1925–1941." *Journal of Sport History* 9, summer: 5–19.

Morrow, Donald and Mary Keyes. 1989. *A Concise History of Sport in Canada.* Toronto: Oxford Univ. Press.

Mrozek, Donald, 1983. *Sport and American Mentality, 1880–1910.* Knoxville: Univ. of Tennessee Press.

Nagler, Barney. 1964. *James Norris and the Decline of Boxing.* Indianapolis: Bobbs-Merrill.

Naison, Mark. 1985. *Communists in Harlem During the Depression.* Urbana: Univ. of Illinois Press.

Nasaw, David. 1985. *Children of the City: At Work and At Play.* Garden City, N.Y.: Anchor Press/Doubleday.

Nash, Roderick. 1970. *The Nervous Generation: American Thought, 1917–1930.* Chicago: Rand McNally.

Nathan, Daniel A. 1989. "Touching the Bases: A Conversation with Eric Rolfe Greenberg," *Aethlon* 7, fall: 9–19.

———. 1995. "Anti-Semitism and the Black Sox Scandal." *Nine* 4, Dec.: 94–100.

National Police Gazette.
    1903. Aug. 22, 3; Sept. 30, 10.
    1920. Oct. 9, 6.

Neft, David S., and Richard M. Cohen. 1990. *The Sports Encyclopedia: Pro Basketball.* 3d ed. New York: St. Martin's.

"The New Art of Recreation." 1923. *American Hebrew:* 112, May 4, 779.

Observer (Chicago Hebrew Institute).
    1912. Nov.–Dec.
    1913. Feb.–Dec.
    1914. Jan.; Apr.; Oct.; Nov.
    1915. June 7; Sept.; Nov.

O'Connor, Gerry. 1986. "Bernard Malamud's *The Natural:* 'The Worst There Ever Was in the Game.'" *Arete* 3: 37–42.

Oren, Daniel. 1985. *Joining the Club: A History of Jews at Yale.* New Haven, Conn.: Yale Univ. Press.

Peiss, Kathy. 1986. *Cheap Amusements: Working Women and Leisure in Turn-of-the-Century New York.* Philadelphia: Temple Univ. Press.

"Personalities in Sports." 1924. *American Hebrew* 115. June 6: 126.

Peterson, Robert W. 1990. *Cage to Jump Shots: Pro Basketball's Early Years.* New York: Oxford Univ. Press.

Polacheck, Hilda Satt. 1989. *I Came a Stranger: The Story of a Hull-House Girl.* Edited by Dena J. Polacheck Epstein. Urbana: Univ. of Illinois Press.

Poliakoff, Michael. 1984. "Michael, Job, and Other Wrestlers: Reception of Greek Sport by Jews and Christians in Antiquity." *Journal of Sport History* 11, summer: 48–65.

Porter, David L., ed. 1989. *Biographical Dictionary of American Sports: Basketball and Other Indoor Sports.* Westport, Conn.: Greenwood Press.

Postal, Bernard, Jess Silver, and Roy Silver. 1965. *Encycopedia of Jews in Sports.* New York: Bloch.

Poznanski, Ira. 1935. "The Luckiest Men in Baseball." *Baseball Magazine* 54, Oct.: 509.

Provizer, Stephen. 1993. "Playing a Different Tune: Changing Jewish Roles in American Popular Music." *JUF News.* May: 9.

Quirk, James, and Rodney D. Fort. 1992. *Pay Dirt: The Business of Professional Team Sports.* Princeton, N.J.: Princeton Univ. Press.

Rabinowitz, Benjamin. 1948. *The Young Men's Hebrew Association (1854–1913).* New York: Jewish Welfare Board.

Rader, Benjamin G. 1977. "The Quest for Subcommunities and the Rise of American Sport." *American Quarterly* 29: 355–69.

———. 1983. *American Sports: From the Age of Folk Games to the Age of Spectators.* Englewood Cliffs, N.J.: Prentice-Hall.

———. 1984. *In Its Own Image: How Television Has Transformed Sports.* New York: Free Press.

———. 1991. "The Quest for Self-Sufficiency and the New Strenuosity." *Journal of Sport History* 18: 255–67.

———. 1995. *American Sports: From the Age of Folk Games to the Age of Spectators.* Rev. 3d ed. Englewood Cliffs, N.J.: Prentice-Hall.

Raphael, Marc Lee. 1979. *Jews and Judaism in a Midwestern Community: Columbus, Ohio, 1840–1875.* Columbus: Ohio Historical Society.

Rawidowicz, Simon, ed. 1952. *The Chicago Pinkas.* Chicago: College of Jewish Studies.

Ribalow, Harold. 1948. *The Jew in American Sports.* New York: Bloch.

Ribowsky, Mike. 1991. *Slick: The Silver and Black Life of Al Davis.* New York: Macmillan.

Riess, Steven A. 1980. *Touching Base: Professional Baseball and America in the Progressive Era.* Westport, Conn.: Greenwood Press.

———. 1985a. "A Fighting Chance: The Jewish-American Boxing Experience, 1890–1940." *American Jewish History* 74, Mar: 223–54.

____. 1985b. "In the Ring and Out: Professional Boxing in New York, 1896–1920." In *Sport in America.* Edited by Donald Spivey. 95–128. Westport, Conn., Greenwood Press.

———. 1989. *City Games: The Evolution of American Urban Society and the Rise of Sports.* Urbana: Univ. of Illinois Press.

———. 1990. "Professional Sports as an Avenue of Social Mobility in America: Some Myths and Realities." In *Essays on Sport and Mythology.* Edited by Donald G. Kyle and Gary D. Stark. 83–117. College Station: Texas A&M Univ. Press.

———. 1991. "A Social Profile of the Professional Football Player, 1920–1980." In *American Professional Sports: Social, Historical, Economic, and Legal Aspects.* Edited by Paul Staudohar and J. A. Mangan. 222–460. Urbana: Univ. of Illinois Press.

———. 1995. "Sport and the American Jew: A Second Look." *American Jewish History* 83, Mar.: 1–14.

Rischin, Moses. 1962. *The Promised City: New York City's Jews, 1870–1914.* Cambridge, Mass.: Harvard Univ. Press.

———. 1991. "The Jewish Experience in America: A View from the West." In *Jews of the American West.* Edited by Moses Rischin and John Livingston. 10–31. Detroit: Wayne State Univ. Press.

Road Runners Club New York Association Newsletter.
  1965. Summer, 1.
  1966. Winter, 1.
  1967. Fall, 2–3.
  1968. Winter, 1.
  1970. Spring, 1.
Roberts, Frederic M. 1995. "Dem Bums Become the Boys of Summer: From Comic Caricatures to Sacred Icons of the National Pastime." *American Jewish History* 83, Mar: 52–63.
Roberts, Randy. 1979. *Jack Dempsey: The Manassa Mauler.* Baton Rouge: Louisiana State Univ. Press.
Roberts, Randy, and James Olson. 1989. *Winning Is the Only Thing: Sports in America since 1945.* Baltimore: Johns Hopkins Univ. Press.
Robertson, Louis J. 1926. "The Golf Club as an All-Year-'Round Club." *American Hebrew* 119, June 4: 120, 130.
Rochester Basketball Classic Program, 1991.
Roeder, Bill. 1948. "Bob Davies—Royal Playmaker." *Sport.* Feb.: 50–53, 87.
Rose, Charley. 1952. "The Fighting Dentist." *Ring* 30, Jan.: 34, 43.
Rosen, Charles. 1978. *Scandals of '51: How the Gamblers Almost Killed College Basketball.* New York: Holt Reinhart, and Winston.
Rosenberg, D., D. Morrow, and A. J. Young. "A Quiet Contribution: Louis Rubenstein." *Canadian Journal of History of Sport.* 13, No. 1: 1–18.
Rosenberger, Ruth. 1929. "Personalities in the World of Golf and Tennis." *American Hebrew* 124, May 3: 966, 974.
Rosenzweig, Roy. 1983. *Eight Hours for What We Will: Workers and Leisure in an Industrial City, 1870–1920.* Cambridge, England: Cambridge Univ. Press.
Ross, Barney, and Martin Abrahamson. 1957. *No Man Stands Alone: The True Story of Barney Ross.* Philadelphia: Lippincott.
Ross, Edward A. 1914. *The Old World in the New: The Significance of Past and Present Immigration to the American People.* New York: Century.
Ross, H. Browning. 1957. Editorial. *Long Distance Log: A Publication for Runners by Runners* 2, Aug.: 2.
Roth, Philip. 1959. *Goodbye, Columbus.* Boston: Houghton Mifflin.
———. 1973. *The Great American Novel.* New York: Holt, Reinhart, and Winston.
———. 1975. "My Baseball Years." In *Reading Myself and Others.* New York: Farrar, Strauss, and Giroux.
Roth, Walter. 1991. "Scrapbook Provides Glimpses of An Unusual Chicago Jewish Life." *Chicago Jewish History* 14, winter: 1, 7–9.

————. 1993. "The Kingfish Knew How to Give, and Take, a Solid Hit." *Chicago Jewish History* 16, fall: 9–11.

"Runyon on Davey Miller." 1991. *Chicago Jewish History* 14, winter: 9.

Russell, John D. 1986. *Honey Russell: Between Games, Between Halves.* San Francisco: Dryad.

Sachar, Howard M. 1992. *A History of Jews in America.* New York: Knopf.

Salzberg, Charles. 1987. *From Set Shot to Slam.* New York: Dell.

Sammons, Jeffrey. 1988. *Beyond the Ring: The Role of Boxing in American Society.* Urbana: Univ. of Illinois Press.

Sanders, Charles J. 1985. "In Search of the Great American Baseball Dream." *Baseball Digest* 44, Feb.: 36–45.

Sarazen, Gene. 1925. "The Common Ground of Golf." *American Hebrew* 117, June 5: 135.

Scandurra, Aldo. 1981. "History of Long Distance and Road Racing." *Long Island Running News* 1, May: 9–18.

Schacht, Al. 1941. *Clowning Through Baseball.* New York: A. S. Barnes.

————. 1955. *My Own Personal Screwball.* Garden City, N.Y.: Doubleday.

Schmertz, Fred. N.d. *The Wanamaker Millrose Story: History of the Millrose Athletic Association, 1908–1967.* Yonkers, N.Y.: Millrose Athletic Association, c/o John Wanamaker Westchester.

Schreier, Barbara A. 1994. *Becoming American Women: Clothing and the Jewish Immigrant Experience, 1880–1920.* Chicago: Chicago Historical Society.

Schulberg, Budd. 1947. *The Harder They Fall.* New York: Random House.

Schwartz, Barbara, ed. 1961. *History of Chicago Jewry, 1911–1961.* Chicago: Sentinel.

Seymour, Harold. 1971. *Baseball.* Vol. II. *The Golden Age.* New York: Oxford Univ. Press.

Shapiro, Edward. 1985. "The World Labor Athletic Carnival of 1936: An American Anti-Nazi Protest." *American Jewish History* 74: 255–73.

Shapiro, Judith J. 1970. *The Friendly Society: A History of the Workmen's Circle.* New York: Media Judaica.

Shaw, Irwin. 1965. *Voices of a Summer Day.* New York: Delacorte Press.

Simons, William M. 1982. "The Athlete as Jewish Standard Bearer: Media Images of Hank Greenberg." *Jewish Social Studies* 44, spring: 95–112.

————. 1985. "Adolph Schayes Interview." *American Jewish History* 74: 287–307.

————. 1986. "Abel Kiviat: Interview." *Journal of Sport History* 13: 235–66.

————. 1995. "Brandeis: Athletics at a Jewish Sponsored University." *American Jewish History* 83, Mar: 65–81.

Simri, Uriel. "The Place of Jewish Athletes in the Modern Olympic Games." In *Physical Education and Sports in the Jewish History and Culture.*

Proceedings of an International Seminar. Edited by Uriel Simri. 81–87. Netanya, Israel: Wingate Institute for Physical Education.

Slater, Robert, ed. 1992. *Great Jews in Sport.* Rev. ed. Middle Village, N.Y.: Jonathan David Publishers.

Smith, William C. 1939. *Americans in the Making.* Reprint. 1970. New York: Arno.

Sollors, Warner, ed. 1989. *The Invention of Ethnicity.* New York: Oxford.

Solomon, Eric. 1984. "Jews, Baseball and the American Novel." *Arete* 1, spring: 43–66.

———. 1985. "Bullpen of Her Mind: Women's Baseball Fiction and Sylvia Tennenbaum's *Rachel, the Rabbi's Wife.*" *Journal of Sport Literature* 3, Jan.: 19–31.

———. 1987a. "The Boy of Summer Grows Older: Roger Kahn and the Baseball Memoir." *Baseball History* 2, summer: 27–47.

———. 1987b. "Counter-Ethnicity and the Jewish-Black Baseball Novel: The Cases of Jerome Charyn and Jay Neugeboren." *Modern Fiction Studies* 33, spring: 49–64.

———. 1988. "Varieties of American Work and Play Experience: The Example of a Popular Jewish Baseball Novelist." In *Corebos Triumphs: Readings in Sport Literature.* Edited by Susan Bandy. 106–27. San Diego: San Diego State Univ. Press.

———. 1994. "Jews and Baseball: A Cultural Love Story." In *Ethnicity and Sport in North American History and Culture.* Edited by George Eisen and David K. Wiggins. 75–102. Westport, Conn.: Greenwood Press.

Somers, Dale A. 1972. *The Rise of Sports in New Orleans, 1850–1900.* Baton Rouge: Louisiana State Univ. Press.

Sorin, Gerald. 1990. *Nurturing Neighborhood: The Brownsville Boys' Club: A Jewish Community Institution in Urban America.* New York: New York Univ. Press.

———. 1992. *A Time for Building: The Third Migration, 1880–1920.* Vol. 3. *The Jewish People in America.* Edited by Henry L. Feingold. Baltimore: Johns Hopkins Univ. Press.

Sorrell, Richard. 1972. "Sports and Franco-Americans in Woonsocket, 1870–1930." *Rhode Island History* 31: 117–26.

Spaner, David. 1997. "Greenberg to Green: Jewish Ball players." In *Total Baseball,* edited by John Thorn, et al. 171–80. New York: King Penguin.

Spears, Betty. 1991. "Senda Berenson Abbott: New Woman, New Sport." In *A Century of Women's Basketball: From Frailty to Final Four.* Edited by Joan S. Hult and Marianna Trekell. 19–36. Reston, Va.: National Association for Girls and Women in Sport, Education, Recreation and Dance.

Spink, John G. 1934. "'Three and One'." *TSN.* Oct. 4, 4.
———. 1940a. "That's My Pop." *TSN.* Nov. 7, 4.
———. 1940b. "'Three and One'." *TSN.* Nov. 7, 4.
The Sporting News Official Baseball Register. 1996. St. Louis: The Sporting News.
Sports Almanac, 1927. 1927. Chicago: *Chicago Tribune.*
The Sportsman. 1944. "Shadows of the Past." *Ring* 23, Mar.: 17, 44.
———. 1947. "50 Years Later." *Ring* 26, Sept.: 10–11.
Starr, Mark. 1937. "Bread and Circuses." *Sport Call* 6, Dec. 25: 2.
Steinberg, Stephen. 1989. *The Ethnic Myth: Race, Ethnicity, and Class in America.* Boston: Beacon Press.
Steiner, Desiree. 1973. "My Father, the Boxer." *The Jewish Digest* 18, July: 63–64, 65–66.
Stern, Richard. 1926. Polo—The Royal Sport." *American Hebrew* 119, June 4: 114, 151.
Sugar, Bert R., ed. 1981. *The Ring 1981 Record Book and Boxing Encyclopedia.* New York: Atheneum.
"Summer Sports Attire." 1924. *American Hebrew* 115, June 6: 117.
"A Survey of Country Clubs Throughout the United States." 1926. *American Hebrew.* 119, June 4: 126, 134.
Suttles, Gerald. 1968. *The Social Order of the Slum: Ethnicity and Territory in the Inner City.* Chicago: Univ. of Chicago Press.
Swichkow, Louis J., and Lloyd P. Gartner. 1963. *The History of the Jews of Milwaukee.* Philadelphia: Jewish Publication Society of America.
Swope, Tom. 1937. "Alex Kampouris, Majors' Only Greek." *TSN.* Aug. 26, 3.
Thernstrom, Stephan. 1973. *The Other Bostonians: Poverty and Progress in the American Metropolis, 1880–1970.* Cambridge, Mass.: Harvard Univ. Press.
Thrasher, Frederick. 1963. *The Gang: A Study of 1,313 Gangs in Chicago.* Abridged ed. Chicago: Univ. of Chicago Press.
"Thrice Western Women's Golf Champion." 1925. *American Hebrew* 117, Nov. 6: 828.
"Thumb Nail Sketches." 1939. *Ring* 18, July: 15.
Toll, William. 1984. *The Making of an Ethnic Middle Class, Portland Jewry over Four Generations.* Albany: SUNY Press.
Torry, Jack. 1995. *Endless Summers: The Fall and Rise of the Cleveland Indians.* South Bend, Ind.: Diamond Communications.
Tuchman, Barbara W. 1966. *The Proud Tower: A Portrait of the World Before the War: 1890–1914.* New York: MacMillan.
Turner, Victor W. 1969. *The Ritual Process: Structure and Anti-Structure.* Chicago: Aldine.

Tygiel, Jules. 1983. *Baseball's Great Experiment.* New York: Oxford Univ. Press.

Ueberhorst, Horst. 1978. *Turner Unterm Sternenbanner: Der Kampf der Deutsche-Amerikanischen fur Einheit, Freiheit, und Sociale Gerecktigkeit, 1848 bis 1918.* Munich: Moos.

U.S. Cong. House Committee on the Judiciary, Organized Professional Team Sports. 1958. *Hearings Before the Antitrust Subcommittee of the Committee on the Judiciary.* 85th Cong., 1st Sess. Washington, D.C.: Government Printing Office.

U.S. Cong. Senate Committee on the Judiciary. 1958. *Organized Professional Team Sports. Hearings Before the Subcommittee on Antitrust and Monopoly of the Committee on the Judiciary.* 85th Cong., 2d sess. Washington, D.C.: Government Printing Office.

———. 1961. *Professional Boxing: Hearings Before Subcommittee on Antitrust and Monopoly.* 86th Cong., 2d. sess., Pursuant to S. Res. 238. Dec. 5–14, 1960. Washington, D.C.: Government Printing Office.

U.S. Dept. of Commerce. Bureau of the Census. 1952. *Census of Population. 1950; a Report of the Seventeenth Decennial Census of the United States.* Washington, D.C.: Government Printing Office.

———. 1961. *Population: 1960; the Eighteenth Decennial Census of the United States.* Washington, D.C.: Government Printing Office.

University Settlement Society. 1893. *Report and Plans for the Winter's Work of the University Settlement Society.* New York: Concord.

Veeck, Bill. 1965. *The Hustler's Handbook.* New York: G. P. Putnam's Sons.

Vertinsky, Patricia. 1995. "The 'Racial' Body and the Anatomy of Difference: Anti-Semitism, Physical Culture, and the Jew's Foot." *Exercise and Sports Sciences Review* 4, no. 1: 38–59.

———. 1997. "Body Matters from Goethe to Weininger: Race, Gender, and Perceptions of Physical Ability." In *The Invention of Identity* and the Practice of Intolerance: Nationalism, *Racism, and Xenophobia in Germany and the United States.* Edited by Dietmar Schiemer and Norbert Finzsch. Cambridge: Cambridge Univ. Press.

Vincent, Ted. 1991. *The Rise & Fall of American Sport: Mudville's Revenge.* Lincoln: Univ. of Nebraska Press.

Voigt, David Q. 1966. *American Baseball.* Vol. 1. *From Gentleman's Sport to the Commissioner System.* Norman: Univ. of Oklahoma Press.

Vorspan, Max, and Lloyd P. Gartner. 1970. *History of the Jews of Los Angeles.* Philadelphia: JPSA.

Wagenknecht, Edward. 1964. *Chicago.* Norman: Univ. of Oklahoma Press.

Wagner, Ralf. 1988. "Turner Societies and the Socialist Tradition." In *German Workers' Culture in the United States, 1850 to 1920.* Edited by Hartmut Keil. 221–40. Washington, D.C.: Smithsonian Institution Press.

Wald, Lillian. 1915. *House on Henry Street.* New York: H. Holt.

Walker, Mickey, with Joe Reichler. 1961. *Mickey Walker: The Toy Bulldog and His Times.* New York: Random House.

Wallman, Shel. 1993. "151 Jews Have Played in the NFL." *National Jewish Post & Opinion* 59, Feb. 10: 16.

Ward, John J. 1945. "Urbanski of the Braves." *Baseball Magazine.* June: 368.

Wasserman, Earl R. 1986. *"The Natural:* Malamud's World Ceres," in *Bernard Malamud: Modern Critical Views.* Edited by Harold Bloom. 47–64. New York: Chelsea House.

"The Water Is Fine on Mondays." 1927. *I.K.S. Neighbors* 5, Mar. 13: 34.

Weales, Gerald. 1985. *Odets the Playwright.* London: Metheun.

Weinberg, S. Kirson, and Henry Arond. 1952. "The Occupational Culture of the Boxer." *American Journal of Sociology* 57, Mar.: 460–69.

Weisbord, R., and N. Hedderich. 1993. "Max Schmeling: Righteous Heroism?" *History Today* 43, Jan.: 36–41.

Weissbach, Lee Shai. 1995. "Kentucky's Jewish History in National Perspective: The Era of Mass Migration." *The Filson Club History Quarterly* 69: 255–74.

Wenn, Stephen R. 1989. "A Tale of Two Diplomats: George S. Messersmith and Charles Sherrill on Proposed American Participation in the 1936 Olympics." *Journal of Sport History* 16: 27–43.

———. 1991. "A Suitable Policy of Neutrality? FDR and the Question of American Participation in the 1936 Olympics." *International Journal of the History of Sport* 8: 319–35.

Wettan, Richard. 1977. "Charlotte Epstein—Women's Emancipation and the Emergence of Competitive Athletics for Women in the United States." In *Physical Education and Sport in the Jewish History and Culture. Proceedings of the Second International Seminar July 1977.* Edited by Uriel Simri. 98–111. Natanya, Israel: Wingate Institute for Physical Education and Sport.

White, G. Edward. 1996. *Creating the National Pastime: Baseball Transforms Itself, 1903–1953.* Princeton: Princeton Univ. Press.

Wiggins, David. 1983a. "The 1936 Olympic Games in Berlin: The Response of America's Black Press." *Research Quarterly for Exercise and Sport* 54: 278–92.

———. 1983b. "Wendell Smith, the Pittsburgh *Courier-Journal,* and the Campaign to Include Blacks in Organized Baseball, 1933–1945." *Journal of Sport History* 10, summer: 5–29.

Williams, Gar, and Jeff Darman. 1978. "History of the Road Runners Club of America." In *The Road Runners Club of America Handbook: A*

Guide to Club and Race Administration. Edited by Gar Williams. New York: Road Runners Club of America.

Willis, Joe D., and Richard G. Wettan. 1975. "L. E. Meyers, 'World's Greatest Runner.'" *Journal of Sport History* 2, fall: 93–111.

Wirth, Louis. 1928. *The Ghetto.* Chicago: Univ. of Chicago Press.

Wittke, Carl. 1939. *We Who Built America: The Saga of the Immigrant.* New York: Prentice-Hall.

————. 1952. *Refugees of Revolution: The German 48ers in America.* Philadelphia: Univ. of Pennsylvania Press.

Wohlgelernter, Elli. 1995. "Interview with Calvin R. and May Abrams." *American Jewish History* 83: 109–22.

Wolf, Dave. 1972. *Foul! The Connie Hawkins Story.* New York: Warner Books.

Wood, Charles. 1941. "Hammering Hank." *Baseball Magazine.* Mar.: 437.

Zborowski, Mark, and Elizabeth Herzog. 1952. *Life Is with People: The Jewish Little-town of Eastern Europe.* New York: International Univ. Press.

Index